OCT 3 8 2013

W9-BRS-935

THE
NHL

D'ARCY JENISH

THE

NHL

100 YEARS OF ON-ICE ACTION AND BOARDROOM BATTLES

DOUBLEDAY CANADA

Library and Archives Canada Cataloguing in Publication

Jenish, D'Arcy, 1952-, author
    The NHL : 100 years of on-ice action and boardroom battles / D'Arcy Jenish.

Includes bibliographical references and index.
Issued in print and electronic formats.
ISBN 978-0-385-67146-0

    1. National Hockey League--History. I. Title.

GV847.8.N3J44 2013   796.962'64   C2013-902640-1

Cover and text design: Andrew Roberts
Cover image: Focus on Sport / Getty Images
Printed and bound in the USA

Published in Canada by Doubleday Canada,
a division of Random House of Canada Limited

www.randomhouse.ca

10 9 8 7 6 5 4 3 2 1

To Hélène

CONTENTS

PART IV
THE BETTMAN ERA (1993–)

INTRODUCTION

TO SURVIVE AND TO GROW

A HISTORY OF THE NATIONAL HOCKEY LEAGUE could be written as an account of games and seasons, wins and losses, triumphs and defeats. The writer could cast his or her gaze upon the coaches and general managers or the extraordinary athletes who blazed through opponents, lifted their teammates and won championships and seared on our psyches vivid memories of their sublime talents. We—reader and writer—could focus on those great teams that extended their domination to three or more seasons and have come to be known as dynasties, and we would include in any such work the Ottawa Senators of the 1920s, the Leafs of the late forties and early sixties, the Red Wings of the early fifties, the Canadiens of the late fifties, late sixties and late seventies, and the Islanders and Oilers of the eighties. Histories devoted to any or all of these matters might be accurate, lively, even compelling, but they would be deficient.

Any work that purports to be a history of a league must recognize and take account of the two fundamental challenges of forming and operating such an entity. The first is to survive. The second is to grow. A thumbnail sketch of NHL history will suffice to demonstrate the truth of this observation. The league formed in the latter stages of World War I was a flimsy and fragile organization that struggled to find firm footing in turbulent, uncertain times.

This infant enterprise enjoyed a growth spurt in the Roaring Twenties, when American promoters from Boston, New York, Pittsburgh, Chicago and Detroit came north brandishing fistfuls of dollars and demanding entry, and it then endured a decade and a half of hard times and diminished fortunes during the Great Depression and World War II. It will come as a surprise to many that survival was very much an issue for much of the postwar Original Six era, which is often—but incorrectly—seen as a period of glorious competition, packed arenas and balance sheets engorged by record profits.

The year 1967 was the fulcrum on which the history of the league turned. It was the start of the second wave of expansion—the first was in the latter half of the twenties—and this second wave lasted till the year 2000. During those three-plus decades, the NHL grew from six to thirty teams, though there were countless crises, numerous failures and more than a few flops along the way. In short, some of the newly awarded franchises never found an audience. They cost their owners huge sums of money and they either moved or folded.

The NHL has awarded no new franchises in the first years of the twenty-first century, but it has never ceased to be preoccupied with growth: growing the league's footprint in the U.S., especially the sunbelt states of the southern U.S.; growing live attendance and television audiences; growing sponsorships, advertising, merchandise sales and revenues.

These two central challenges—survival and growth—are the business of league executives and the owners, the latter being a confederacy of competitors who form the board of governors. The student of the sport who sets out to write about their endeavours will inevitably encounter three major impediments. First, the principals from bygone eras are long since deceased. Second, those who are still with us are very often reluctant to talk. Finally, the NHL has in its possession a vast archival record, but stubbornly refuses to grant even the most limited access to outside researchers and writers.

Despite these impediments, many volumes have appeared in recent years that purported to tell us about the business of the NHL. Most have been speculative in nature—based more on rumour and anecdote than documents and verifiable fact—and most have been variations of the same doleful but compelling narrative. We have been told that the league has generally been comfortably profitable, and sometimes fabulously so. We have been told that—prior to the big-money era of the 1990s and 2000s—the players were badly paid and ruthlessly exploited. We have been told these things so often that they have acquired the weight and heft of conventional wisdom, which few will examine and even fewer question.

This work tells a different story. It challenges conventional wisdom. It is based on both firsthand accounts of participants and more NHL archival documents than any previous writer has ever used. Three chapters are built on unpublished verbatim transcripts of annual and semi-annual meetings of the board of governors between the years 1941 and 1957. These transcripts—hitherto unseen—are held in the archives of the Hockey Hall of Fame and give us the first accurate picture of the challenges and difficulties the league faced during the Original Six era.

These transcripts will give the reader a fly-on-the-wall perspective on the debates that took place within the inner sanctum of the NHL. We can hear Clarence Campbell, Conn Smythe, Frank Selke, Lester Patrick, Art Ross, James Norris and others speaking candidly and openly about the most difficult challenges they faced.

The transcripts will reveal—for the first time—that the NHL considered expanding immediately after World War II and heard from delegations representing Los Angeles, San Francisco and Philadelphia. They reveal the gravity of the crisis facing the six-team league in the early- to mid-1950s when two of its franchises—Chicago and Boston—were in danger of folding. They depict owners and general managers attempting unsuccessfully to improve the competitive balance between the Canadiens, Wings and Leafs and the three weak clubs—the Rangers, Bruins and Hawks.

Readers will find here leaguewide regular-season and playoff gate receipts—year by year—from 1946 to 1966. These figures are contained in confidential reports of Clarence Campbell to the board of governors, and the reports are stored in the Molson Fonds at the National Archives of Canada in Ottawa. These figures have never been published, though they should have been.

It would appear that other researchers—specifically David Cruise and Alison Griffiths, authors of the highly influential 1991 work *Net Worth: Exploding the Myths of Pro Hockey*—had access to the figures. They tell us in the endnotes to their book that they examined the Molson Fonds. Yet the gate receipts contained in the Campbell reports do not appear in *Net Worth*. Nor is there any reference to them—perhaps because they undermined the authors' thesis that the league was fabulously profitable and the players cruelly exploited.

Readers will also find Montreal Canadiens financial statements from this era that demonstrate conclusively that this organization paid its players fairly while making reasonable profits. The chapter on the 1967 expansion draws on a memo to the board from David Molson, chairman of the expansion committee, and explains how the governors set the fee for the six new franchises at $2 million apiece.

Later chapters are based on both contemporary sportswriting and the author's own interviews with dozens of participants, representing all interests and points of views. Among those who contributed were Mike Ilitch, the late Harley Hotchkiss, Gary Bettman, Alan Eagleson, Bill Torrey, Jim Devellano, Mike Gartner, Mike Liut and the agents Ron Salcer, Ritch Winter and Rick Curran.

The author conducted some fifteen hours of interviews with former president John Ziegler. These interviews are the most candid and comprehensive that Ziegler has granted since he resigned as president in June 1992, and he has provided fresh perspectives and valuable insights on the expansion era, the catastrophic war with the WHA, the league's return to health and profitability in the eighties and the events leading up to the players' strike of April 1992.

Readers may be surprised by the conversational exchanges and snatches of dialogue that appear frequently in the following pages. If surprise should turn to skepticism, and skepticism to the suspicion that some of it has been invented, let me assure you that I have fabricated nothing. Every bit of conversation and dialogue comes from the transcripts, from those I interviewed or from previously published accounts of events.

The distinguished British biographer Antonia Fraser once wrote that history is rarely simple and never straightforward. This is true whether the subject is the kings and queens of England or the triumphs and setbacks of the NHL. The writer's duty is to look as clearly and deeply into things as possible, to unravel the complexities, to resolve the contradictions and to get it right.

I have endeavoured to the utmost to do all these things and believe that the story herein is fresh, revealing and full of surprises. It will demonstrate: that owning a franchise has, more often than not, been a licence to lose money rather than to print it; that the NHL has been a financially precarious enterprise for most of its ninety-six seasons; and that, with its centennial just around the corner, the survival and growth of this league is something well worth celebrating.

PART I

THROUGH THICK AND THIN WITH FRANK CALDER

(1917–1943)

1

THE WAR WITH EDDIE LIVINGSTONE
(1916-1924)

THE EIGHTH AND FINAL SEASON of the National Hockey Association began with a burst of optimism and excitement on a Wednesday evening, two days after Christmas, 1916. The front pages of the country's newspapers were filled with accounts of the bloody European war then raging unabated, with no end in sight, but on the sports pages all that mattered was Canada's great winter pastime. "Pros Are Ready," proclaimed a headline in the *Toronto Daily News*, and the columnist Charlie Good announced, "The salaried hockey gentry begin operations tonight and the indications are that the N.H.A. will have a good season, despite the fact that several erstwhile stars are in khaki."

The Blueshirts of Toronto had caught a train to Montreal to take on the defending league and Stanley Cup champion Canadiens. The Montreal Wanderers had travelled down to Quebec City to meet the Bulldogs, and the Ottawa Senators had ventured west to Toronto to tangle with the NHA's sixth and newest club, the 228th Infantry Battalion. The soldiers' team, as it quickly became known, was stacked with some of the best pros in the land, all of them recently enlisted.

The commanding officers of the 228th, also known as the Northern Fusiliers, had made a point of recruiting hockey players. By the fall of 1916, they had sixty-three among their ranks—enough to enter one team in the Ontario Hockey Association senior league, one in the OHA junior circuit, three in the Toronto Beaches League and one in the NHA. "We are in the hockey business," explained Lieutenant Colonel Archie Earchman, "because we believe that a little sport and recreation helps the men and gives [them] something to cheer for. We also think it will attract recruits to our battalion."

The 228th applied for an NHA franchise on September 30, and the league's frequently fractious directors readily assented. A soldiers' team would draw crowds and lend an aura of respectability to the sometimes-questionable business of professional hockey. The men of the 228th were equally enthusiastic and began training in mid-November, six weeks before the puck dropped.

On opening night, they sprinted onto the ice at the Mutual Street Arena in downtown Toronto in musty green uniforms bearing the insignia of the Northern Fusiliers. They were in peak condition and cruised to an easy win over the Senators, who had only managed to complete their player signings moments before boarding a Toronto-bound train.

The Blueshirts, having worked out for six weeks as well, dispatched the self-assured but out-of-shape Canadiens with similar ease even though their goaltender, Claude Wilson, had missed the train without explanation and the team had used a thirty-seven-year-old retired pro named Billy Nicholson, who lived in Montreal. The Wanderers and Bulldogs were expected to be the weak links in the league, and the Wanderers were the lesser of the two that night and were soundly beaten.

All six teams were back in action three nights later, and so it went through the month of January. There was a full slate of games each Wednesday evening and another on Saturdays. By the end of the month, the clubs had played ten games apiece and completed the first half of a split season. Under this unusual arrangement, the winners of the first and second halves would advance to a postseason playoff and the winner would meet the champions of the Pacific Coast Hockey Association in a Stanley Cup series.

The Canadiens and Senators tied for the first-half lead, the soldiers were a close second and the Blueshirts right behind them, while the Wanderers and Bulldogs were buried in fifth and sixth. The tight race for top spot had piqued the interest of the public and the press. Attendance was solid and the league was enjoying its best season since the start of the war. But the addition of the soldiers' team had not yielded the anticipated publicity bonanza. The officers in charge, Lieutenant Colonel Earchman and Captain Leon Reade, had had several highly publicized spats with Blueshirts owner Eddie Livingstone—a slight, bespectacled man who had the gentle demeanour of a pastor but the fastidious personality of a tax collector or a customs inspector. He was invariably certain of the correctness of his position and would fight to his last breath to defend it.

Livingstone and the military officers had first tangled during their preseason training camps over the rights to Gordon Keats, a star forward. He had enlisted in the 228th, but Earchman had conceded his rights to Toronto in exchange for the veteran goaltender Percy LeSueur. LeSueur refused to report. The lieutenant colonel wanted Keats back and threatened to pull the Fusiliers out of the league if he didn't get him. Livingstone refused, and NHA president Frank Robinson had to arbitrate.

Another confrontation occurred on the evening of January 20 after a chippy, hard-hitting game. The Fusiliers had won, but Earchman was irate and warned Livingstone that his Blueshirts had better clean up their act or Keats would be prohibited from playing. Livingstone had no intention of surrendering him, and the military man backed down.

Earchman and Livingstone clashed prior to a Blueshirt-Battalion game on February 7. Earchman threatened to make Keats sit it out. Livingstone threatened to pull the Blueshirts and Robinson had to intervene again. He sent a telegram to Livingstone insisting the game must be played. The latest round of bickering was the last straw for one senior officer. Afterward, he told *Daily News* columnist Good: "You can make this as emphatic as you like. We are thoroughly disgusted with the notoriety we have been subjected to in connection with hockey. . . . I am of the opinion that it would have been better for everybody if the 228th had not engaged in sports at all."

As it happened, the next day, the Fusiliers received their orders to leave for overseas, which sent shock waves through the small, battered business of professional hockey. Or, as the *Ottawa Citizen* informed its readers, "The National Hockey Association is verging on a state of chaos."

Robinson called a directors' meeting for February 11, a Sunday, at the Windsor Hotel in Montreal. It was, by all accounts, a stormy session. The teams were already three games into the second half of the split season and the directors debated long and hard whether to include those results as part of a revised second half or whether they should simply start over. The other contentious issue was whether they would continue with five teams or drop down to four.

Livingstone did not attend because, as he later explained, "I had a very painful boil on my neck." He did send a telegram arguing for a five-team league. But Livingstone had made enemies in his three seasons as an owner. He had nearly exchanged blows more than once with Sam Lichtenhein, proprietor of the Wanderers, and had had vehement disagreements with George Kennedy, the short, tough managing director of the Canadiens.

Lichtenhein and Kennedy wanted to rid themselves of their cantankerous partner and persuaded Mike Quinn of the Bulldogs and Martin Rosenthal of the Senators. That day, the four of them voted to suspend the Toronto franchise for the season and they distributed the players amongst themselves. For good measure, they included "instructions to President Livingstone to dispose of the said franchise on or before June 1, 1917."

These drastic measures generated vigorous debate. "This season ought to have been a hummer at Toronto," Tommy Gorman, *Citizen* sports editor, wrote, "but Eddie Livingstone and Capt. Reade declared war on one another before the season and their inability to deal with their problems in a sportsman-like way led to so much scrapping that the welfare of the league has been seriously impaired."

The Toronto sportswriters were understandably miffed. "The pro league has always been run on the cheap by cheap people and their latest move is only evidence of that," Charlie Good wrote. "It may be that the members of the National Hockey Association hold the opinion that they can play fast and loose with the Toronto public. If they are counting upon returning to this territory . . . they are making a mighty mistake. The fans in this neighbourhood are totally disgusted with the NHA and all who are connected with that organization."

Initially, Livingstone raised no objections. On the contrary, he claimed to be "tickled to death." He had enjoyed a good season financially. His Blueshirts had only two home dates left and three road games and were out of the race. But he wasn't content for long. He sent Robinson a letter on February 27 demanding reinstatement. Then he learned that Lichtenhein had been trying to find off-season jobs for Ken Randall and Alf Skinner, two of the Blueshirt players the Wanderers had claimed in the dispersal draft. He suspected the rival owner was trying to keep them in Montreal so they could play for his club again the following winter. This was tampering, according to Livingstone, and he fired off an accusatory letter to Robinson.

"I charge unhesitatingly that the Wanderer Club is and has been attempting to secure players illegally and unconstitutionally from the Toronto Club," he wrote. "The penalty I hereby demand is the expulsion of the offender from the National Hockey Association of Canada Ltd., and the forfeiture of the franchise of the Wanderer Hockey Club Ltd. I name players Randall and Skinner. Conclusive evidence is in my possession and is at the disposal of the league."

Lichtenhein was furious. "I will give Mr. Livingstone just ten days from today, that is March 19, to prove his charges in writing or retract his charges," he said in a statement issued to the newspapers. "If he fails to do this, I will have him charged with criminal libel if possible, and if not, civil libel, the first time he comes into the province of Quebec and will also try to have it done in the province of Ontario if the law permits me. This man has been bluffing long enough. He says he has a lot of evidence and other foolish rot, now let him produce it."

Meantime, Livingstone had filed a lawsuit against the NHA and its four remaining clubs. He sought a court order rescinding the suspension of his franchise. He also wanted: an injunction preventing his competitors from employing players under contract to him; compensation for losses incurred through the cancellation of his team's two remaining home games; and unspecified damages for what he deemed other "unlawful, unconstitutional and illegal acts."

On Saturday, March 10, Livingstone boarded a train for Ottawa, writs in hand. The Senators were home that night to the Canadiens in the second half of a two-game, total-goal series to determine the league champion. "Ted Dey's rink was taxed to the utmost capacity, which meant that close to seven thousand people were crowded into the enclosure," one newspaper reported. "Fabulous prices are reported to have been paid by visitors from outside who failed to provide themselves with ducats before arriving in town."

Livingstone attended, not to savour the excitement of the moment, but to serve his writs. He handed a copy to George Kennedy, who stuffed it into his pocket and walked away. Sam Lichtenhein refused his and informed Livingstone he could deliver it at his office—in Montreal. Martin Rosenthal tossed the writ into a locker in the Senators dressing room and forgot about it until advised several days later that he ought to examine it.

The Senators won the game, but the Canadiens claimed the series by a single goal and with it the right to meet the Pacific Coast champions for the Stanley Cup. Two days later, the Canadiens left Windsor Station in downtown Montreal, waving and lifting their hats to salute the two hundred cheering supporters who had come to see them off. They travelled some three thousand miles west, played a best-of-five series against the Seattle Metropolitans and lost.

For the first time, a U.S.-based team had claimed Lord Stanley's celebrated silver cup. To many in the East, though, that seemed a curious footnote to a brief, conflicted campaign. It had been an "undignified fiasco," lamented the *Ottawa Journal*. "The season for professional hockey in Eastern Canada this winter has ended in such as a way as to ridicule arguments which have been used to justify continuance of the sport during the war. Professional sport in Canada . . . has received this winter a blow from which it may not recover for years."

THAT CERTAINLY APPEARED TO BE the case when the National Hockey Association held its annual meeting on September 29, 1917. Frank Robinson was absent, but sent a letter saying he did not wish to continue as president. Eddie Livingstone did not attend, though his lawsuit was still before the courts and slated to go to trial in February 1918. The Senators had announced they were suspending operations for the year—and perhaps the duration of the war—and did not send a representative. And so the dispirited directors of the Canadiens, Wanderers and Bulldogs adjourned the meeting till late October.

By then, a number of things had changed. The Senators had decided they would play after all, but the Bulldogs were short of quality players due to the war and were wavering. And there was more confusion out of Toronto. Livingstone attempted to form a new league comprising the Blueshirts, Senators and two Montreal senior teams—the Shamrocks and Nationals—but no one took his efforts seriously. There were rumours he would sell his interest in the team and rumours he had refused to withdraw.

The owners of the Toronto Arena Company—a syndicate of investors, most of them Montrealers—intervened next. They wanted a pro team playing out of the big rink on Mutual Street to ensure that it turned a profit that winter. They offered to buy Livingstone's franchise and he, at last, seemed ready to sell, but the deal was left hanging by other developments.

The Bulldogs still had not declared themselves. They repeatedly requested more time to get their affairs in order, and some newspapers reported that they were holding out for better terms from the Quebec Arena. The Senators finally forced the issue. In mid-November, they made it known that they favoured leaving the Bulldogs out and accepting a Toronto team, even one managed by Livingstone. They called for a special meeting and the *Citizen* reported, "Never before was professional hockey in such a muddle."

On November 22, representatives of the Canadiens, Wanderers, Senators and Bulldogs met at the Windsor Hotel—the imposing eight-storey brick-and-stone landmark located two blocks north of Windsor Station and a short walk south of St. Catherine Street. They began shortly after lunch, and late that afternoon they were still talking.

Frank Calder, secretary-treasurer of the NHA, was the first to leave the room. He strode briskly along the corridor to the elevator that would take him down to the lobby and out to Peel Street and into the pale, tepid end of afternoon sunlight. He neither checked his stride nor tipped his hat as he walked past his old friend and former colleague Elmer Ferguson, sports editor of the *Montreal Herald*.

"Hey Frank," Ferguson asked. "What happened?"

"Nothing much, Fergie," replied Calder, who was anxious to make it home in time for dinner with his wife and children.

George Kennedy emerged next, a smile on his face, a sparkle in his eyes and his impeccably tailored suit smartly accented with matching diamonds, one embedded in his tie clip, the other mounted in his thick gold ring. Ferguson put the same question to him, and the affable Kennedy put his hand on the shoulder of the big reporter, gestured toward the elevator and said, "Well, let us go down to the bar and I'll tell you what happened."

They ordered their drinks, and then Kennedy explained. "We formed a new hockey league," he said. "It's called the National League and it's just about the same as the NHA, with one exception."

"You haven't invited Eddie Livingstone into the new group," Ferguson speculated.

"No, we haven't," Kennedy replied. "I guess we forgot. Anyway, he is still a member of the National Association and he has a franchise in that fine body. Of course, he may have a little difficulty getting a place to play or any teams to play against because the rest of us just resigned and formed this new league. Eddie still has his team and association franchise. Good luck to him."

"It's strictly legal," added Sam Lichtenhein, who had accompanied them. "We didn't throw Eddie Livingstone out. Perish the thought. That would have been illegal and unfair. It wouldn't have been sporting."

"Great day for hockey," bellowed Tommy Gorman, *Citizen* sports editor and part owner of the Senators, who joined them before catching the evening train back to the capital. "Livingstone was always arguing. No place for arguing in hockey. Let's make money instead."

And so it went, according to Ferguson, who recounted from memory the events of that November day in a feature article written several years later. It had been a great day indeed. Immediate problems had been solved, crises averted and the pro game in eastern Canada saved for the time being—something very much in doubt for most of that topsy-turvy autumn. But there was still much to be done before the puck dropped, and four days later, on Monday, November 26, 1917, the same men and a few others met again at the Windsor and gave shape and form to this new entity that would be known as the National Hockey League.

THERE WOULD BE FOUR TEAMS: the Canadiens, Wanderers, Senators and the Toronto Hockey Club under the ownership of the Toronto Arena Company. Each would play twenty-four games. Opening night was set for December 19, and the final matches would be played March 9. The schedule would be split. The winners of the first and second halves would play off for the league championship and the right to represent the East in a best-of-five Stanley Cup series against the champs of the Pacific Coast Hockey Association.

Frank Calder had been named president and secretary at a salary of $800 a year. Calder was solidly built with slightly sloped shoulders, a full, round face and reddish hair. When he looked at someone, he fixed them with a hard, direct gaze and he spoke with a distinct accent that reflected his origins.

Calder was born in Bristol, England, on November 17, 1877, to Scottish parents, and upon completing his education he became a teacher. But he had an itch to travel and settled on two preferred locations: Canada or the British colony of Newfoundland. A toss of a coin settled the matter, and in 1900 he set out for Canada. He landed a teaching position at a private English-language institution in Montreal and soon fell for a fellow teacher, Amelia Cope, whom he married. Their union produced a daughter and three sons.

The ambitious young immigrant, an enthusiastic cricketer and soccer player, quit teaching in 1905 to become sports editor of the *Montreal Witness*. Two years later, he assumed the same position at the larger, more influential *Montreal Herald*, where he hired Elmer Ferguson, a youthful sportswriter recently arrived from Moncton, New Brunswick. Calder quickly earned a reputation for honesty and integrity. He would not turn a blind eye when promoters fixed horse races or rigged prizefights, and he could not be bought off with gifts or bribes.

But Calder was not content to be a mere sideline observer. He founded the Montreal School Rugby League. He served as secretary of the Montreal District Football League, which was actually a soccer circuit, and he was also treasurer of the Quebec Football Association. On November 15, 1914, the directors of the NHA appointed Calder secretary-treasurer, and he served in that capacity for the league's final three seasons.

Calder performed his first public duty as head of the National Hockey League when he announced the decisions taken at the meeting of November 26, 1917. He would serve the NHL loyally and diligently for the next twenty-six years—through periods of growth and prosperity, through years of retreat and adversity, through the Roaring Twenties and the Great Depression and into World War II and the advent of the Original Six era.

Calder was the NHL's sole employee for a number of years. He handled the smallest piece of league business himself and at his desk he kept a portable type-writer, which he used to produce a voluminous stream of letters and other correspondence. The owners eventually insisted that he hire a secretary and a receptionist, and he complied, reluctantly.

Calder saw as many games as he could, largely to watch the work of his officials, and in later years flew from one NHL city to another. By the end of the 1939–40 season he had become one of the first people to log more than 100,000 miles with American Airlines, and on August 24, 1940, the president of the company, C.R. Smith, sent Calder a signed certificate proclaiming him an Admiral of the Flagship Fleet in recognition of his contribution to "increased public use of air travel."

The punishing workload wore him out and contributed to his demise on February 4, 1943, at age sixty-six while recuperating from a major heart attack. Doctors ordered complete rest, but Calder ignored them. As his old friend Ferguson wrote, "He was in his hospital bed, the league books spread around him . . . when death tapped him on the shoulder."

Somewhere along the way, perhaps in his years as a teacher or a newspaperman, or in those years when he kept the minutes and managed the finances of the NHA, Calder learned how to handle hard-headed, egotistical men, how to keep the peace among them and how to resolve the crises that inevitably arose, and the first test of his abilities occurred before the start of the National Hockey League's inaugural season.

THE NEW LEAGUE, LIKE ITS PREDECESSOR, was national in name only. Its four teams were located in three cities, none of them more than a five-hour train trip apart. It was a small organization and in danger of becoming smaller just as the club managers began assembling their lineups. Trouble arose in the Wanderers camp, and it had sportswriters and fans asking: Would the Wanderers be able to put a team on the ice this winter? And, had it really come to this for the once mighty Montrealers?

For a few brief, scintillating seasons, the Wanderers had been the most famous team in hockey. This was back in those happy-go-lucky days at the dawn of the new century and the advent of professionalism, before young men in every corner of the country and every walk of life had set down books or tools or skates and sticks and donned the khaki, marched off to war and died by the thousands in the muddy, desolate, shell-pocked battlefields of France.

The Wanderers wore off-white woollen sweaters adorned with a red collar and waistband, one broad, chest-level band and a bold red *W* stitched to an off-white shield. They became known as the Redbands, and they were champions.

Four times in five seasons, they had won the Stanley Cup. They had beaten a medley of tough opponents—the Silver Seven, the Thistles, the Victorias, the Maple Leafs of both Toronto and Winnipeg and the Eskimos—before surrendering the Cup to the Senators and then snatching it back a year later.

They had last won the prized trophy in 1910. Sam Lichtenhein had acquired the Wanderers the following season, and his teams had usually been competitive but never champions. Nonetheless, they occupied an important place in the sporting landscape of the country. The Wanderers were Canada's first full-fledged professional hockey team, and they were the standard-bearers of English Montreal just as the Canadiens represented the French side of that linguistically divided city.

Things had started to go wrong for the Wanderers the very day the new league was announced. Sprague Cleghorn slipped on an icy sidewalk on St. Catherine Street. He went down hard, his right leg "snapped like a pipe stem," as one newspaper put it, and he was out for the season. Next, the Wanderers lost Cleghorn's younger brother Odie, who had been exempted from military service on the condition that he not play pro hockey. The loss of the Cleghorns punched two large, unfillable holes in the team's eight-man roster.

The Westmount-born brothers had joined the Redbands in 1912. Odie, twenty-six, was a goal scorer and had finished with the third-highest total in the NHA the previous season. Sprague was twenty-seven. He was big—six foot two and 185 pounds. He was tough, he could carry the puck and a newspaper report at the time of his injury described him as "the most brilliant defence player in professional hockey."

The Wanderers had acquired the rights to four members of the Quebec Bulldogs in a dispersal draft held after the Bulldogs decided to sit out the season. But manager Art Ross was unable to sign them, and he told Elmer Ferguson: "Unless the other clubs hand us over players at once the Wanderers will not think of operating this season. We have lots of amateur material out with us, but this will not make us strong enough to cope with the other teams."

A few days later, Lichtenhein turned up the heat. "You may say this for me," he told the *Quebec Chronicle*, "and make it as emphatic as you can, that unless the Wanderers get some players from some of the other teams in the National Hockey League the Redbands will not have a team this season."

The normally taciturn Calder was dismayed and said so publicly. "I am greatly surprised at hearing Sam Lichtenhein use the word quit," he told Ferguson. "In all the years I have been associated with him in sport I have never before heard him talk quit."

Calder consulted the other owners, but in some quarters there was precious little sympathy. "Let the Wanderers get out," the Canadiens' George Kennedy declared. "Who cares? The time to complain about scarcity of players was before the schedule was made up, not now."

Fortunately, there was one cool head in the crowd. It belonged to Calder. He met with Ross on December 10 and gave him and Lichtenhein twenty-four hours to decide whether they were in or out. He also suggested two players they could acquire from the Canadiens and a trade with Toronto that would bolster their lineup. In any event, Lichtenhein and Ross dropped their complaints and went back to work, and a Wanderers squad was ready to go on opening night of the National Hockey League's inaugural season.

All four teams were in action that evening. The Canadiens took an after-noon train to Ottawa to meet the Senators, and a big crowd packed Dey's Arena for a highly anticipated contest between those staunch rivals. The game was delayed fifteen minutes by a contract dispute between the Senators and six of their veterans, and two of them refused to dress.

The Canadiens prevailed, and so did the Wanderers, who opened at home against Toronto. Wanderer defenceman Dave Ritchie scored one minute into the game—that goal is generally considered the first in NHL history—and he and his teammates put ten more pucks past Sammy Hebert in the Toronto net, but gave up nine themselves. A paltry crowd of seven hundred attended—the poorest turnout in memory for a Montreal home opener—and one press box observer noted, "The game was a demonstration of the scarcity of players as men who would not have been used as substitutes a year ago were on the benches of both teams last night."

The Wanderers lost their second, third and fourth games and were sched-uled to meet the Canadiens on the evening of January 2. That contest was never played. Shortly before noon that day, a fire broke out at the Westmount Arena—home of both Montreal professional teams. The Arena had stood since 1898 on the corner of St. Catherine St. and Wood Avenue, one block west of where the

Montreal Forum would one day be built. It was the first rink designed exclusively for hockey, and it had a four-foot-high fence around the ice surface—an innovation that changed the way the game was played. This barrier permitted more body contact and allowed the players to advance the puck by chipping it off the boards. The building could reasonably accommodate about seven thousand spectators in its nine rows of seats, but as many as ten thousand had packed it for big games.

The fire started in the dressing rooms. The flames quickly sliced through the dusty, cobwebbed undersides of the old wooden stands, ignited the worn and polished paint of the benches and raced from one end of the building to the other. Flame and smoke filled the cavernous interior. One wall collapsed shortly after the Westmount Fire Department arrived. The boilers exploded. The roof came crashing down and the heat drove the firefighters back and shattered windows in the homes across the street. The Montreal Fire Department was called in. The two forces pumped thousands of gallons of water, but by 4 p.m. Montreal's premier hockey venue was nothing more than a soggy, smouldering ruin and the sticks, uniforms and equipment of two of the NHL's four teams had been incinerated. Only a few pairs of battered, well-worn skates, sent out for sharpening in preparation for that night's game, had survived.

Calder summoned the directors to an emergency meeting two days later. He had scarcely called the meeting to order when Lichtenhein announced that the Wanderers were finished. His losses in the fire amounted to $1,000. This was on top of all the other money he'd lost in professional hockey since 1914—no less than $30,000, he figured—and he was bound to lose more if the Wanderers continued. They were a weak team, a poor attraction, and the war had left the other clubs so bereft of talent that they had no spares or reserves to loan him.

His fellow directors pleaded with him to reconsider. They reminded him that he had posted a $3,000 bond at the start of the season, as they had all done, and that they would make a claim for that money if he pulled out. But Lichtenhein would not be persuaded.

Had George Kennedy folded the Canadiens, the NHL would have been finished then and there. But Kennedy was no quitter. Sport was in his blood. He had started in the wrestling business—fighting as an amateur, organizing bouts, bringing in wrestlers from the United States, Europe and as far away as Turkey and drawing his audiences from the densely populated, blue-collar districts in Montreal's French-speaking east end.

Kennedy had founded the Club Athlétique Canadien to promote physical fitness among French-Canadian residents of the city and to train boxers and wrestlers. Hockey had caught his attention, and in the fall of 1910 he had acquired the Canadiens from Ambrose O'Brien, the wealthy young man from Renfrew, Ontario, whose father, M.J. O'Brien, had made millions building railways and developing a silver mine and had bankrolled the Canadiens in their inaugural season.

Kennedy was, in the eyes of many of his contemporaries, the founder of the Canadiens. He had designed and redesigned the uniform until settling on the *bleu, blanc, et rouge* that has endured to this day. He had incorporated the Club de Hockey Canadien and chosen the CHC crest that would become the team's famous standard, and he had turned a talented group of players into champions who had won the Stanley Cup in 1916. His working-class wrestling fans had become staunch and loyal supporters and piled into the Westmount Arena season after season to support the Canadiens.

Kennedy was not about to throw away what he had so assiduously built. He would carry on, and the small, feeble National Hockey League would survive as well. The Canadiens would play their home games at the Jubilee Rink. It was located at the east end of St. Catherine Street, deep in the French-speaking district, and it could accommodate about four thousand people—seated and standing. Three nights after the disastrous Westmount Arena fire, Kennedy put his Canadiens on the ice at the Jubilee, in sweaters and equipment borrowed from a neighbourhood men's league team. The Canadiens beat the Senators that evening in the twenty-seventh minute of overtime. They finished atop the standings in the first half of a split schedule. The Toronto Arenas prevailed in the second half and beat the Canadiens in a rough, penalty-filled, two-game, total-goal playoff to become the NHL's first champions.

There was one more piece of business to be dealt with before the new league's inaugural season was complete: a best-of-five playoff for the Stanley Cup. The Arenas hosted the Vancouver Millionaires, champions of the Pacific Coast Hockey Association, the rival league founded in December 1911 by those transplanted Montrealers, Frank and Lester Patrick.

The Patrick brothers and their Pacific Coast Association had been a thorn in the side of the eastern professional teams from the outset. They had poached some of the best players, driven up salaries and convinced the Cup trustees that their league was good enough to contend for the big prize.

The 1918 final was the sixth showdown between east and west, and the east had won three of the previous five. This time around, the westerners fought gallantly and pushed the series to the brink. But the Arenas emerged triumphant, allowing the men behind the NHL to claim that their compact, three-team, three-city league was the best pro hockey circuit in existence.

THE NHL BEGAN ITS SECOND SEASON with the same three teams—and virtually the same three rosters—as the previous winter. The bloody and debilitating war in western Europe had ended, but the league's war with Eddie Livingstone had resumed with fresh ferocity. Livingstone attended board meetings, made demands, provoked shouting matches, schemed and plotted, issued writs and generally made a nuisance of himself.

But the man did have a legitimate grievance. He had been stripped of his franchise and his players and had never been compensated. Furthermore, the Toronto Arena Company, which had taken over Livingstone's franchise, had profited nicely from the use of his athletes. Five of them—centre Reg Noble, right winger Alf Skinner, defenceman Harry Cameron and the subs Corbett Denneny and Ken Randall—had been members of the Cup-winning Arenas. And the spring 1918 final had been a big success, producing a gate in excess of $20,000.

Afterward, the company had offered Livingstone nearly $6,000 to settle their differences. He turned them down. They went to $7,000. He countered by suing for $20,400.50. Despite all this, Livingstone still hoped to get back into the business, and in the fall of 1918 he attempted to revive the National Hockey Association. When that failed, he tried to form a competing league called the Canadian Hockey Association. He didn't get very far, but nevertheless sent contracts to Noble, Skinner, Cameron and several others and ordered them not to train with the Arenas.

Arenas manager Charlie Querrie convinced them otherwise and most began working out in early December. Livingstone then threatened to get a court injunction to prevent the players from appearing in the Arenas' home opener December 23 against the Canadiens. Nonsense, Querrie replied, and he told a Toronto newspaper: "The hockey public can take it from me that there will be no interference from E.J. Livingstone or those associated with him. . . . He may annoy us, but he cannot stop us from playing."

The Arenas lost the game before a small crowd of 2,500. They kept on losing, and the fans drifted away. They won only three of ten games in the first half of a split twenty-game schedule. They fell so far behind in the second half that they pulled out with two weeks to go in the season. The league cancelled the remaining games and replaced them with a best-of-seven championship series between its two remaining teams, the Senators and Canadiens.

The NHL had hit a low point, but in the fall of 1919, the league's fortunes took a turn for the better. Mike Quinn resurrected the Quebec Bulldogs. Two other groups, one from Toronto and a second from Montreal, applied for franchises, but they were turned down partly due to uncertainty over ice time in both cities. The Toronto Arena Company sold its franchise to a group that included Querrie and two brothers, Fred and Percy Hambly, and they renamed it the St. Patricks. The Canadiens were building a new rink, the 6,500-seat Mount Royal Arena, and expected to open the season there on December 27 against the Ottawa Senators.

And the fans were back. Record crowds attended games in Ottawa, Montreal and Toronto. Nearly 7,500 people packed Dey's Arena in Ottawa for a January 7 game between the Senators and Canadiens. "The seats were sold an hour after the plan was opened in the forenoon," the *Ottawa Citizen* reported. "Hundreds, as on the occasions of previous games, had to be satisfied with standing room, so great was the crush."

The Mount Royal Arena opened two weeks behind schedule on the evening of January 10, a Saturday. The Canadiens played the St. Pats. Both teams were fighting for second place, trailing the league-leading Senators. Six thousand witnessed the contest, and hundreds were turned away when the arena management cut off ticket sales. One week later, the Canadiens and Senators drew an even bigger crowd. Every seat was sold by the noon hour on Friday, except for a section reserved for Ottawa fans who came down by train late Saturday afternoon. Half an hour before game time, the Mount

Royal Arena was surrounded by men clamouring for standing-room tickets. Police cut off sales, leaving hundreds standing outside on a fiercely cold night and prompting the next day's *Citizen* to declare, "Montreal, like Ottawa and Toronto, is hockey mad."

A crowd of 8,500—an NHL record—watched a close, hard-hitting game between the Senators and the St. Pats in Toronto on February 21. The hometown fans "thundered encouragement" throughout, according to the *Citizen*. A small section of Ottawa supporters cheered themselves hoarse and bet heavily on the outcome, which was in doubt until late in the third. The Senators went ahead by two, and their followers leapt from their seats.

"They tossed hats, caps, coats and furs into the air," according to a report in the *Citizen*. ". . . For many minutes after play had ended, with Toronto people filing out of the rink, thunderstruck by the downfall of their idolized Saints, Ottawa supporters were cheering and acclaiming their happiness."

There were few such joyous outbursts at the 4,500-seat Quebec Arena that winter. The Bulldogs won just four of twenty-four contests and only one in the second half—a dismal performance for an organization with a long and distinguished past. Members of the city's English community had formed the Quebec Hockey Club, as the Bulldogs were formally known, in 1880—a mere five years after the first rudimentary indoor game at Montreal's Victoria Rink in March 1875, and twelve years before Governor General Frederick Arthur Stanley donated the trophy that would bear his name. The Bulldogs won that prize in consecutive seasons—1912 and 1913.

Their captain in those championship years and beyond was Joe Malone, known alternately as Gentleman Joe or Phantom Joe, the former because he played hard but clean and the latter because he could dash the length of the ice so quickly and dart around defenders so deftly that he sometimes seemed more ghost than man.

Malone was one of the most prolific scorers of his day. Three times he registered forty goals or more in a season. In 1917–18, when the Bulldogs let their franchise lapse, he scored forty-four in twenty games for the Canadiens, a record that would stand until Maurice Richard's fifty in 1944–45. Malone still had his touch when he returned to the Bulldogs for the 1919–20 season. He beat opposition netminders thirty-nine times and won the scoring championship. It was a remarkable achievement and the highlight of an otherwise dreary season that proved to be the end of the road for the Bulldogs.

FRANK CALDER HAD TWO BIG PROBLEMS on his plate in the fall of 1920: Quebec was finished as an NHL venue and Eddie Livingstone was back with a vengeance. The busybody from Toronto was promoting his Canadian Hockey Association—for the second time—and he had acquired a key ally. His friend Percy Quinn was managing the Mutual Street Arena, and the pair planned to put two franchises in the building. A third would be based south of the border, possibly in Cleveland, and a fourth in Hamilton.

The steel-producing centre at the west end of Lake Ontario was an attractive market. It was Canada's fifth-largest city and had a thriving amateur hockey scene. The senior Tigers had won the Allan Cup in 1919 and Hamilton had a brand new arena that seated 4,500 and had standing room for 3,000. The building had an artificial ice plant, five dressing rooms, a press box, a ladies washroom and a men's-only smoking room.

The *Hamilton Herald* announced on August 26 that Livingstone's league was coming to the city. The directors of the Abso-Pure Ice Company had agreed to purchase a franchise, and arena manager Percy Thompson would run the team. "The new league is a certainty," the *Herald* declared optimistically. "Those connected with the Toronto clubs have control of the Toronto arena and . . . feel that the NHL is none too popular and that a general house-cleaning is in order."

But the NHL was not prepared to yield anything to Livingstone. The league needed a home for its Quebec franchise, and Hamilton was the most promising option. In late September a delegation visited the city, met with Thompson and toured the arena. Neither side made any official announcements, but the *Herald* reported that Hamilton had been offered the Bulldog franchise and added: "The NHL refuses to die without a fight. The Ottawa and Montreal clubs have moved so quickly to stave off defeat that they stand a mighty fine chance of . . . putting the Livingstone league out for the count."

The jousting over Hamilton was just one front in the battle between Livingstone and the NHL. The main event was the fight for control of the

Mutual Street Arena. "Getting ice in Toronto or not getting it means the death of one league or the other," Livingstone told a reporter in late November. "This has been admitted by both and is beyond controversy. That we have right on our side is incontrovertible in light of the sweeping judgment of Chief Justice Falconbridge as confirmed by the Court of Appeal."

He was referring to a decision by Sir William Glenholme Falconbridge in January 1920. The judge had ruled against the Toronto Arena Company— owner of the Mutual Street facility—and awarded Livingstone damages of $20,093.54 for the loss of his franchise and players. The company appealed, but lost, and that pushed the whole enterprise over the edge. The business could not generate sufficient revenues to cover both its existing liabilities and the judgment.

The company declared bankruptcy, and Livingstone countered with another court action. This time, he wanted an order giving him control of the arena. The case was heard December 9. The presiding judge, a Justice Francis Latchford, disliked hockey and made that clear during the proceedings.

"I saw a hockey slaughter at Ottawa once and such brutal conduct was tolerated by the crowd that I haven't been near a game since," the judge stated.

"Something like the old Roman amphitheatre?" said Livingstone's lawyer, W.R. Smythe.

"Worse," Latchford snapped.

The hockey season was just around the corner, and both sides impressed upon the judge the urgency of a quick decision. Latchford may have detested the sport, but his ruling—issued the next day—shaped the pro hockey landscape of eastern Canada. He decided against Livingstone, who was just another creditor, nothing more. The receiver in the bankruptcy, Charles Robin, would retain control of the Mutual Street Arena.

Livingstone had reached an agreement with his friend Percy Quinn for ice time. Calder had negotiated a deal with Robin. That was a wise move. The NHL would have a home in Toronto. The CHA was dead. That left Hamilton open, and so the Quebec Bulldogs disappeared and resurfaced as the Hamilton Tigers.

THE TIGERS MADE THEIR NHL DEBUT at home against the Montreal Canadiens on December 22, 1920. The Canadiens arrived on game day, and managing director George Kennedy was not in his usual buoyant mood. He had bought his players new skates and sweaters, but they hadn't been able to use either. The weather had been unusually warm and the Mount Royal Arena was not equipped with an ice-making plant. The Canadiens had had to forgo training camp. They were out of shape and no match for the Tigers on opening night.

Hamilton skated to an easy five-nothing win, but Kennedy professed his satisfaction with one thing. "This is a fine arena," he said afterward. "The lighting is excellent, the seating fine and the ice surface is the largest in the NHL. I am surely surprised."

Two things about pro hockey had impressed Hamiltonians. The players wielded their sticks with greater force and to greater effect than the amateurs, and they received less protection from the referees. And the refs used whistles to signal stoppages in play as opposed to the hand-held bells that were then the norm in amateur hockey in Ontario. "Here's one thing in connection with NHL hockey that Hamiltonians will not stand for," the *Herald* observed. "It's the whistle."

The Tigers compiled a record of six wins against eighteen losses and finished last in both halves of the split schedule. They wound up in the same position in each of the next three seasons. Hamilton was the soft spot in the four-team NHL of the early 1920s.

The Ottawa Senators were the league's powerhouse. They finished first six times and won four Stanley Cups between 1919 and 1927. Dominant teams—or dynasties, as they came to be known—have come and gone throughout the history of the NHL, but the Senators differed from the others in one essential way: their championship clubs were made up largely of local talent. During those eight illustrious seasons, thirty players wore the red, white and black of the Senators. Twenty-two of them had learned the game in Ottawa's highly competitive amateur leagues or had been recruited from nearby communities.

But top-notch prospects occasionally slipped away. In the fall of 1921, right winger Billy Boucher signed with the Canadiens rather than join older brothers Frank and George, who both played for the Senators. One year later, Montreal sent its aging star Newsy Lalonde to the Saskatoon Sheiks of the Western Canada Hockey League in exchange for left winger Aurèle Joliat, another Ottawa product and a fierce and talented competitor despite his diminutive dimensions. (He was five feet, seven inches tall, weighed 136 pounds and was known as the Mighty Mite.)

In 1923–24, the Canadiens inserted a tough, hard-shooting, lightning-quick centre—Howie Morenz of Stratford, Ontario—between Boucher and Joliat, and Montreal had the best forward line in the NHL. The Senators still finished first by six points. But the Canadiens triumphed in a two-game playoff that set both cities ablaze with excitement. The series opened in Montreal. Hundreds of fans ignored wind and sleet and lined up all afternoon outside the Mount Royal Arena for rush seats. Some of the overflow crowd watched from the girders forty feet above the ice.

The Canadiens prevailed by a margin of one-nothing. Three days later, nearly a thousand Montrealers clambered aboard twelve railway cars and travelled to Ottawa for the second game. A crowd of twelve thousand watched the younger, quicker Canadiens skate to another impressive victory, to the delight of their supporters.

"The King is dead, extremely, completely, entirely dead," declared Elmer Ferguson in the next day's *Montreal Herald*. "Advancing years and a general breakup of the system have claimed hockey's once robust monarch. King Ottawa." The Canadiens then defeated the Vancouver Millionaires of the Pacific Coast Hockey Association and the Calgary Tigers of the Western Canada Hockey League to win their second Stanley Cup.

The 1923–24 season marked the end of an era for the NHL. The league had survived its turbulent birth. The troublesome Eddie Livingstone had been subdued. Four solid franchises were firmly planted in eastern Canadian cities, and each enjoyed a healthy fan base. The annual Stanley Cup showdowns had established the superiority of the NHL over the Pacific Coast Hockey Association and the Western Canada Hockey League, the two pro circuits in the West.

Survival was no longer the objective. The men who ran the league had grander ambitions. They wanted to grow. They got started that fall, and within three years had transformed their little four-team, four-city, interprovincial league into a robust, ten-team, international enterprise with franchises based in some of the biggest cities in America.

2

HERE COME THE AMERICANS
(1924–1930)

ONE DAY, EARLY IN MARCH 1924, Charles Adams and a journalist, A. Linde Fowler, boarded a train in Boston and settled into a snug, private, well-appointed compartment and made themselves comfortable for a long trip north. They were bound for Montreal and the opening game of the NHL championship series between the Canadiens and Ottawa Senators, and they witnessed a stirring spectacle. The Mount Royal Arena was packed and the crowd boisterous, but the sportswriter Elmer Ferguson spotted the visitors from south of the border and informed his readers, "Mr. Adams has been negotiating with the NHL for several months with a view to establishing professional hockey in Boston next season."

Adams was the wealthy owner of the largest chain of grocery stores in New England. He was forty-eight and a fan of hockey, horse racing and baseball, though his youth in rough-and-tumble northern Vermont had allowed little time for sport of any kind. He had been pulled from school early and put to work to help support the family, first as an errand boy in a corner grocery and then visiting logging camps, where he haggled and bargained for lumber to supply his father's sawmill. He left the hard life and limited opportunities of his native state as a young man and settled in Brookline, a suburb of Boston, landing a position with a maple syrup company and later a banking and brokerage firm before turning to the grocery business.

Adams wasn't the only affluent American interested in bringing big-time pro hockey to the United States. The New York boxing promoter Tex Rickard announced during the Canadiens-Senators series that he had reached a deal with the league to acquire a franchise for Madison Square Garden in 1924–25, provided he could have an ice-making plant installed to start the season. A textile manufacturer from Providence, Rhode Island, Hubert C. Milot, showed up in Montreal to sound out the possibilities of acquiring a franchise, though that city did not have a rink of any kind. "There are tremendous possibilities there," Milot told several journalists. "Providence is in the centre of a thickly populated district of fine sporting proclivities and hockey is now extremely popular. Thousands are out skating at every opportunity." Then a small group of wealthy Montrealers announced plans to build a big new arena on St. Catherine Street, west of downtown, on the site of an open-air roller-skating rink known as the Forum, and they too wanted an NHL franchise. These were the first tremors in an upheaval that was about to transform the league.

Rumours and speculation were rampant through that spring and into the summer, and they created so much uncertainty that Frank Calder summoned the NHL governors to Montreal for a special meeting July 6. Calder had received two more applications for franchises, one from the Ravina Rink Company of Toronto and another from Philadelphia. He had had further discussions with Rickard, and the governors authorized him to visit New York and to interview the promoter and his partner, Colonel John S. Hammond. There was always the danger that some of these parties might try to launch a competing league, and so Calder asked the governors to sign a document he had prepared that would bind them to the NHL for ten years.

By the latter half of August, things had changed again. New York was out because Rickard planned to build a new and larger Madison Square Garden. Meantime, negotiations with Adams had begun in earnest. By October 1 he had agreed to acquire a franchise for $15,000 and had hired Art Ross as manager and coach. "Ross represents all that is high class in hockey," Adams told the *Boston Daily Globe*. "He's a thorough sportsman, a gentleman, a prosperous Montreal merchant and is grounded in all aspects of hockey. Boston fans will like Art Ross."

Ross was thirty-eight. He stood six feet tall and weighed 190 pounds—and had been a prominent figure in Canadian sporting circles for two decades, though he was far from universally popular. He was prickly and combative and had tangled with a good number of the men who ran pro hockey. But he was a superb athlete. Ross was an ambidextrous pitcher who would switch from his right arm to his left if he carried a solid lead into the late innings. He was a prodigious kicker in football and could loft the ball downfield equally well with either foot. He was one of the leading trap shooters in Quebec. He raced motorcycles and had once slipped on boxing gloves and gone several rounds with a professional fighter. This was in a dressing room in the rink in Brandon, Manitoba, and it was all over a small wager with teammates, which he won by knocking out the boxer.

Ross had played fifteen seasons of senior and professional hockey, mostly with the Wanderers, but also with an assortment of other teams, including the Senators, the Haileybury Comets, Kenora Thistles and Brandon Wheat Kings. Along the way, he appeared in six Stanley Cup series and won twice. After retiring in 1918, he refereed NHL games and ran his business, Art Ross & Company Sporting Goods.

Ross's first challenge was to find players, and he immediately embarked on a recruiting expedition that took him as far afield as Sault Ste. Marie, Ontario, and Duluth, Minnesota. He didn't come up with much though. The talent pool was not very broad or deep, and besides, Ross had competition.

The Canadian Arena Company, which was building the new rink on St. Catherine Street, had formed the Montreal Professional Hockey Club and hired Cecil Hart, a prominent coach and sports promoter, to manage its team. Hart was aggressively recruiting players even though the NHL had not awarded the company a franchise and the negotiations with the league were not going well.

The investors in this enterprise included the president of the Canadian Pacific Railway, two members of the Molson family, the presidents of both the Bank of Montreal and the Royal Bank, as well as a number of stockbrokers and other chief executives. They wanted in without paying for a franchise. They argued that they were contributing a magnificent new rink—sure to be the finest in Canada—and reviving interest in pro hockey among English Montrealers, which had waned after their team, the Wanderers, had folded in January 1918.

The governors of the existing clubs insisted on a $15,000 franchise fee. The Canadian Arena Company threatened to form a new international league, and a spokesman declared: "We already have five cities, including Montreal, ready to play. Unless there is immediate and definitive action, you can look for fireworks and the biggest hockey battle ever staged in Canada."

But just as quickly as this storm had gathered, it blew over. The league held a special meeting October 12 at the Windsor Hotel and resolved the dispute behind closed doors. The arena company agreed to pay $15,000 for the privilege of joining the NHL, and at the annual meeting on November 1 the league formally awarded franchises to the Boston Professional Hockey Association and the Montreal Professional Hockey Club. The governors also approved the schedule for the 1924–25 season. Each team would play thirty games, up from twenty-four the previous season, a move that would lead to the NHL's first labour dispute and cost one city its franchise.

THE NHL'S TWO NEW TEAMS made their debut on December 1 at the Boston Arena. Charles Adams's squad wore brown uniforms trimmed with gold stripes—colours that were no surprise to those acquainted with him. "The pro magnate's four thoroughbreds are brown," the *Boston Daily Globe* noted. "His fifty stores are brown, his Guernsey cows are the same color, brown is the dominant color of the Durco pigs on his Framingham estate and the Rhode Islands are brown . . ."

Adams and Ross nicknamed their team the Bruins, apparently at the suggestion of Bessie Moss, a former Montrealer who served as Ross's assistant. The men behind the Montreal Professional Hockey Club decided they would do without a nickname. Their players wore maroon sweaters with white bands around the collar, wrists and waist and MONTREAL emblazoned across the chest. Sportswriters initially referred to the team as the Montreal pros, or professionals, but soon began calling them the Maroons, and the name stuck.

The Bruins won that inaugural game, and the local journalists in attendance witnessed a faster, rougher version of the sport than the amateurs played. "The professional game brought out a great deal of good hockey," the *Boston Herald*'s writer noted, "the most rugged body checking that Boston fans have ever seen and a couple of very promising fights, yet only a scattered and rather chilly gathering [of fans]."

Attendance was sparse at most of the Bruins' fifteen home games that season. The team played Monday nights, the only evening when the 5,000-seat Boston Arena was available. The rest of the week was reserved for amateurs, and they often drew better than the pros. Apart from that, the Bruins were a poor team. After their opening-night victory, they lost eleven straight. They finished last with a record of six wins and twenty-four losses, and as the schedule wound down their future looked grim.

"According to reports from Boston it is by no means certain that the Bean city will be represented in the National Hockey League next season," the *Montreal Herald* noted in late February 1925. "Amateur hockey has been very popular in the Hub for years and it is said that the Arena netted $180,000 from amateur games last winter. The pro team pays a rental fee of $20,000 for the season and attendance has not been as expected."

The Maroons were blessed with loyal followers from the start. English Montrealers embraced the team as their own, just as they had supported the Wanderers, and before them the Shamrocks, Victorias and Winged Wheelers of the Montreal Amateur Athletic Association. Five thousand attended the Maroons' home opener at the Forum against the Hamilton Tigers. On December 27, 1924, eleven thousand fans—a record for eastern Canada—packed the building for a high-spirited contest between them and the Canadiens. But for all their success at the box office, the Maroons weren't much better than the Bruins: they landed in fifth.

The Hamilton Tigers surprised everyone by finishing first after four straight seasons in last place. Manager Percy Thompson had resurrected the team with some shrewd recruiting. He had signed two brothers from Sudbury, Redvers and Wilfred Green, popularly known as Red and Shorty, and put between them his best centre, the American-born Billy Burch. Thompson also brought in a new coach: Jimmy Gardner of Montreal, who had enjoyed a long, distinguished amateur and professional career during the pre-war era.

With Gardner behind the bench and Burch and the Greens leading the attack, the Tigers opened the 1924–25 season with four straight wins. They lost for the first time in mid-December to the Canadiens, and then played the Canadiens again on New Year's Day in Hamilton. "Every seat in the Arena has been sold for the struggle," the *Hamilton Herald* reported before the game. "If there were several thousand more available they'd be gobbled up too. The city is hockey mad."

The Tigers prevailed that day. They hung on to first place, tenuously at times, through January and February and finished with thirty-nine points, one up on Toronto and three better than the Canadiens. They played their final game March 9 in Montreal, and afterward returned to Hamilton by train to await the outcome of a playoff between the Canadiens and St. Pats. Then they were to meet the winner in the league championship series.

Their fans were jubilant, but the players were not. They had played thirty games that season, six more than the previous year, without a corresponding adjustment to their salaries. They had also been required to report to training camp early and at their own expense. The players kept their discontent to themselves until that train trip back to Hamilton. Shorty Green visited Percy Thompson in his compartment and delivered an ultimatum. He and his teammates wanted two hundred dollars each or they would not participate in the championship series.

Club and league officials tried over the next forty-eight hours to defuse the crisis, but to no avail. Thompson was adamant: the team would not meet the demands for extra money. Frank Calder told the press that the standard NHL contract bound the players from December 1 till the end of March rather than for a specific number of games, and added: "The Hamilton players can suit themselves. If they don't care to play against either the St. Pats or the Canadiens they don't have to. We will easily overcome the trouble."

Green conferred with Calder in Toronto prior to the second game of the St. Pats–Canadiens series and wouldn't budge. The Canadiens eliminated Toronto that night, and Calder awarded them the league championship.

"That ends it," Thompson told the *Hamilton Herald*. "We will abide by the league's action. I am very sorry that our first prosperous season has ended so poorly." Later, he added: "The present players will not be with us next year. We will sell 'em all."

The players were equally unyielding. "We would be more than pleased to represent Hamilton again in the NHL for the benefit of the fans who have so generously patronized our games," they said in a prepared statement. "But this is final: We do not ever intend to ever play again for the present management."

THE DUST FROM THAT FRACAS had barely settled when a fresh problem arose: Eddie Livingstone was back. He was promoting a new international league. Press reports in late March 1925 maintained that he had solid backers for franchises in Toronto, Montreal, Pittsburgh and Philadelphia. That wasn't the end of the story, though. Livingstone wanted a team in New York and had approached Tex Rickard and his partner, Colonel John S. Hammond, who were building a colossal, new, eighteen-thousand-seat Madison Square Garden in midtown Manhattan. This was supposed to be NHL territory.

Colonel Hammond had granted a Montreal promoter named Thomas Duggan the right to put an NHL team in the building for the 1925–26 season. Now, according to the *Montreal Star*, Livingstone and his backers were trying to persuade Rickard to abandon the NHL in favour of their league.

Calder responded swiftly. He called a board meeting for April 12, a Sunday. It was held in Montreal, and representatives of the six existing NHL clubs attended. They officially awarded a franchise to the recently formed New York Hockey Club, which had sent a four-member delegation comprising Duggan, Hammond, Eugene L. Carey and Tommy Gorman, who had been hired to coach and manage the new entry.

"You have made the finest possible choice," Calder told them. "The task of getting you a winning team is a great one, but if it is humanly possible to gather one Tommy Gorman will do so. He has accomplished wonders at the head of the Ottawa team and we all know he will not fail in New York."

Gorman promptly began recruiting. After the meeting, he approached Maroons president James Strachan and manager Eddie Gerard about purchasing goaltender Clint Benedict. They turned him down. He also went after Joe Simpson, described in an *Ottawa Citizen* report as the "dynamic right defensive player of the Edmonton Eskimos." And there were persistent rumours that he was trying to acquire the suspended Tigers players who were adamant about not returning to Hamilton.

In fact, Gorman and Duggan—the two Tommies, as the sportswriters called them—negotiated quietly over the summer with Hamilton manager Percy Thompson. Gorman made six trips to the Steel City and was still talking to Thompson in mid-September when a Toronto newspaper reported that the Tigers were going to sell their players for $75,000. Thompson assured

Hamiltonians that their team was staying put, and director William H. Yates declared in a prepared statement: "The Hamilton NHL club will operate this season as usual. No sale has been made, nor will one be made now."

Despite these assurances, the talks continued, and on September 25 the *Hamilton Spectator* reported, "At the meeting of the NHL in New York tomorrow night the local franchise, with every signed player last year included, will be turned over to the New York interests for the sum of $75,000, payable as follows: $7,000 down, $18,000 on November 1, $25,000 on January 2, 1926, and the balance on January 2, 1927."

Tigers fans felt betrayed and said so in letters to the editor. "Our own Canadian national game has been, in a degree, prostituted for the monetary consideration of $75,000," J.M. McGill wrote in the *Spectator*. "I personally (and a thousand others) have supported this Hamilton team through thick and thin. There was game after game, season after season, that we knew they had no chance for the Cup. Still we supported them and I personally never cashed a booked ticket in five years. Yet what did we get last year when we had a winning team? First, no chance of any old fans increasing their booking; second, scalpers galore selling tickets refused to regular customers and, as a climax, the players got in the same game and they cheated, I repeat, cheated the fans out of a playoff series. Now, today, we are informed that our own, good Hamilton team has been sold, bag and baggage, to New York."

THE NEW YORK MEETING WAS held on September 26, a Saturday. It was the first gathering of the NHL board outside Canada, and the league's New York hosts chose a location that was certain to impress: the Biltmore Hotel, one of four large, luxurious establishments built around Grand Central Terminal. Sportswriters attended from Montreal, Ottawa, Toronto, Boston and elsewhere, and each club sent a larger delegation than usual. There were two significant pieces of business on the agenda.

The governors ratified the sale of the Hamilton players to the New York club, now nicknamed the Americans. They welcomed the three representatives of the Americans: Colonel John Hammond, president; Tom Duggan, managing director; and Tommy Gorman, manager. The club's new owner was not present, however. The press still referred to the Americans as "Tex Rickard's team," but Rickard had sold a controlling interest to William Dwyer, a man who avoided the spotlight, and for good reason: he was a prominent figure in New York's criminal underworld.

Dwyer, known as Big Bill, was in his early forties. He was a large man with a round face, a warm smile and straight, slicked back hair. He had been a stevedore for two decades, but with the advent of Prohibition had quit that tough trade for the more lucrative business of bootlegging. Within five years, he had made a fortune.

Dwyer controlled the movement of alcohol on the New York waterfront. He relied on a fleet of eighteen ocean-going ships to sail the high seas and acquire liquor from distributors in Canada, Europe and the Caribbean. He then used speedboats, which were powered by aircraft engines and capable of outrunning the fastest U.S. Coast Guard patrols, to take delivery of the goods from vessels anchored a few miles offshore, just outside U.S. territorial waters. His crews were handling up to twenty thousand cases a week, most of which were distributed to speakeasies in the city or across the river in New Jersey. There was also a Manhattan brewery that produced 800,000 half-barrels of beer annually. These enterprises generated enormous profits, which Dwyer invested in legitimate businesses, first a racetrack and then an NHL franchise.

The other big item on the agenda that day was an application for a Pittsburgh franchise. Hockey was a well-established winter pastime in the Pennsylvania steel-making centre. The city had a nine-thousand-seat arena: Duquesne Gardens, a former streetcar barn that had been converted to a rink with an artificial ice-making plant—one of the first on the continent. In 1902, a Canadian team had played a series of exhibition matches at the arena and, upon returning, the manager told a Toronto newspaper: "Pittsburgh is hockey crazy. Over ten thousand turned out for our three games there."

Two years later, Pittsburgh was one of five cities to enter a team in the International Professional League, hockey's first pro circuit, which operated until 1907. The Pittsburgh Yellow Jackets, founded in 1915, were a powerhouse in the United States Amateur Hockey Association and won the league championship in 1924 and 1925 with a roster that included goaltender Roy Worters, defenceman Lionel Conacher and forwards Harold Cotton and Harold

Darragh, all of whom were Canadian. The newly formed Pittsburgh Hockey Club planned to use these players as the core of its NHL team, but the proposal aroused considerable skepticism. The governors questioned whether such largely unknown amateurs would be competitive and whether they could withstand the rigours of NHL play. Nevertheless, they awarded the franchise, although the Senators delegation argued that the league was expanding too quickly and objected.

After the day's business was concluded, there was a reception and a sumptuous meal in the Biltmore's grand and spacious ballroom. "William Dwyer gave a banquet to the delegates, friends, associates and sportswriters, which will live long in the memory of every one of the three hundred or more who were privileged to attend," the *Ottawa Citizen*'s Ed Baker wrote. "The banquet was a gorgeous affair in every respect. Nothing was overlooked."

New York's deputy mayor sat at the head table and dozens of other prominent New Yorkers were sprinkled throughout the crowd. Once the plates had been cleared and coffee served, there were speeches. Stanley Cup trustee William Foran gave his blessing to the NHL's move south and stated, "It is a step in the right direction and augurs well for further international goodwill." And Tex Rickard, the man most responsible for bringing the NHL to New York, predicted that hockey, "harboured by the Canadians for so long would be recognized as the world's greatest sport."

HENRY J. TOWNSEND, PRESIDENT of the Pittsburgh Hockey Club, controller of Duquesne Gardens and one of the wealthiest men in Pennsylvania, led his city's delegation to the New York meeting. He made the trip by rail in his own comfortable Pullman car and he travelled with Lionel Conacher and a business associate. He had sent his chauffeur ahead in the biggest and stateliest of his cars, a sleek, shiny Pierce-Arrow; the driver was there at the station when they arrived and he drove them to the Cadillac—Townsend's New York City hotel.

Townsend was sick in bed with a bad cold when the governors gathered at the Biltmore, but he was on his feet Monday morning and miffed at the suggestion that his city might not have much of a team. "Too weak for the National

Hockey League," he growled at an enterprising reporter on his way into the Claridge Hotel for a meeting with Big Bill Dwyer, Tom Duggan and Tommy Gorman. "We'll show them."

Townsend declared that he was willing to spend a million dollars to produce a winning team, and he promptly demonstrated that he meant business. He offered $25,000 for Joe Simpson, who was about to sign with New York, and $30,000 for Red and Shorty Green. Then he asked Dwyer how much he wanted to part with Gorman.

"Our price for Gorman is five hundred thousand," Dwyer replied, and that ended the conversation.

Townsend left New York empty-handed, but his bold foray into pro hockey was front page news in Canada the next day. "Pittsburgh Magnate Makes Huge Offers," the *Ottawa Citizen* announced in a banner headline. And in smaller type: "Makes Offers That Stagger The Market."

The NHL's hasty expansion, aimed largely at shutting out Eddie Livingstone or any other aspiring interlopers, unleashed a mad scramble for talent and drove up salaries accordingly. On October 2, Gorman arrived in Ottawa with a certified cheque for $10,000, hoping to purchase the Senators' captain and star defenceman George Boucher. "It's a lot of money," he conceded in an interview, "but I feel that George Boucher is worth it. He is a brilliant stickhandler and would make a great impression in New York."

Senators owner Frank Ahearn said no thanks and Gorman returned to New York, cheque in hand. But over the next month, one player after another signed for money that would have been unthinkable just a few years previous. Sprague Cleghorn left the Canadiens and joined the Bruins for $5,000 per season. Joe Simpson got $6,000 from the Americans and former Tiger Billy Burch $6,500. Conacher signed a three-year deal with Pittsburgh at $7,500 per season, and rumour had it that the Maroons had offered the Canadiens $20,000 for Howie Morenz.

The market became so overheated that there was talk that the league would have to impose limits on salaries, as well as rumblings that the American clubs were ruining the sport, a charge that was hotly denied. "We have not bought one player without the consent of the Canadian clubs and the National Hockey League," Duggan told the Canadian Press in late

October. "Stories in the Canadian papers about the alleged Americanization of hockey are absurd."

TEX RICKARD SCRAMBLED UP A final set of stairs to the last row of seats in the upper balcony of his new Madison Square Garden as a sportswriter from the *New York World* scrambled to keep up. When they had reached the top, the two men paused, then gazed intently, silently and, for a few moments, breathlessly at the magnificent building before them with its three vast, elliptical tiers of seats, one on top of another, each capable of seating some six thousand spectators and not a pillar or a post to ruin anyone's view. Way down below, on the floor of the arena, hundreds of workers scurried here and there as if heeding the beat of some distant and mysterious drum.

Rickard broke the silence. "Well, here it is," he said to the writer, Hype Igoe, "my life's work, my dream come true. They'll have to like it. I've given them something Rome never had. Caesar would have turned pink with envy if only he had seen this place, eh? What a place to throw 'em to the lions, eh, Igoe?"

Igoe was thunderstruck. "I call it New York's GRAND CANYON," he wrote in the November 22 edition of the *World*, "because standing high up among the unfinished seats of the top balcony with Rickard at my side, I could think of nothing that more adequately describes this monster temple of play and promotion. It IS a GRAND CANYON. It IS beyond description. It IS Tex Rickard's monument, whether he lives another day or another century."

Rickard's Madison Square Garden—the third building of four to be so named—was a testament in bricks and mortar and steel to the extraordinary drive and ambition and energy that had propelled this scarcely educated, inarticulate man from the fringes to the heights of American society. Rickard was born in January 1871 in Clay County, Missouri, christened George Lewis and grew up in the frontier town of Sherman, Texas. He had made and lost several fortunes and had worn many hats in his pre–New York days. As one biographer wrote, "Tex had been, successively, a cowboy, a town marshal in Texas, a prospector in the Yukon, a gambling-saloon owner in the Klondike and Nevada gold rushes, a soldier of fortune in South Africa and a cattle baron in Paraguay."

He had become famous as a fight promoter, and the new Madison Square Garden would play host to prizefights, as well as rodeos, horse shows, circuses, six-day bicycle races, basketball games, Sunday night dances and NHL hockey. It was the new home of Big Bill Dwyer's New York Americans, though their first date was not till December 15. In the meantime, there was training camp and four road games.

Tommy Gorman ordered his players to report to Niagara Falls, Ontario, to prepare for the upcoming season, and Rickard and Colonel Hammond put in an appearance as well—sportswriters and photographers in tow—donning goaltender's equipment and the dazzling, star-spangled, red, white and blue uniforms of the Americans. They posed for the cameras, like opposing centremen, with Gorman between them to drop the puck, and that earned the team a big photo spread in the *World*.

The Americans launched their season December 2 at Duquesne Gardens against the newly formed Pittsburgh Pirates, who had made one significant addition to their roster of former Yellow Jackets: they had acquired Odie Cleghorn from the Canadiens to serve as player-coach. Cleghorn had his charges well prepared for their debut. A crowd of eight thousand witnessed a tightly played game that was tied one-one after sixty minutes and decided in New York's favour three minutes and ten seconds into overtime. The victorious Americans then went on to Toronto, where they lost; Montreal, where they won; and Ottawa, where they lost again, before heading to New York and their home opener.

Rickard wisely declared it a benefit for the Neurological Institute. The newspapers had provided plenty of advance publicity and the game was a sellout. Men and women in formal evening attire filed the boxes in the lower tier of the arena; most would be attending a dinner and dance at the Biltmore afterward. Two marching bands—the Governor General's Foot Guard and the West Point Cadet Band—welcomed the teams with stirring tunes and then performed their respective national anthems. New York mayor John F. Hylan presided over a ceremonial faceoff and, moments later, the game was underway.

Shorty Green scored an early goal for New York, but the Canadiens thoroughly outplayed the home side en route to a three-one victory. For many observers, though, the pomp of the evening overshadowed the game. "It was the night of nights," the *New York Sun* gushed. "Never has a more glittering spectacle surrounded a sporting event in this city. Flags of Canada and the States vied with each other from the boxes and tiers. Society, both from this city and from Canada, was out in force and the gorgeous gowns of the women created a picture at which even an artist would marvel."

ACCORDING TO ONE PRE-GAME REPORT, Tommy Gorman had scoured the remotest corners of the Dominion of Canada for players. "He went out a time back to the wide open spaces," the *New York World* reported, "where every boy wears a pair of skates almost constantly from November to April and sleeps with his favorite hockey stick by his side and, under instructions to get the best for New York, has put together what probably will be the best hockey combination this city has ever seen."

The truth was more prosaic. The New York Americans of 1925–26 were, for the most part, the Hamilton Tigers of 1924–25. The Tigers finished first, the Americans fifth. New York's robust nightlife, with its speakeasies and night-clubs—said to number some thirty-two thousand—contributed to their slide. The longer road trips may also have been a factor. And the new Madison Square Garden played a role. Tex Rickard kept the place heated to sixty degrees Fahrenheit for the comfort of the patrons. Gorman pleaded with him to turn down the heat and eventually had to seek a court injunction ordering Rickard to maintain the temperature at forty degrees Fahrenheit during hockey games. Gorman submitted an affidavit stating that female spectators could "sit in light evening clothes without a wrap thrown over their shoulders." Shorty Green contended that his teammates became "dry and parched to such an extent that they cannot even keep saliva in their mouths." The judge who heard the case issued a temporary order in favour of the team—this was in December 1926—and set the matter over until mid-January 1927 for a full hearing. But by then, Rickard had relented.

In any event, the Americans of 1925–26 failed to meet expectations. So did the Toronto St. Pats. They finished sixth. The Canadiens slipped to the bottom of the heap, but for good reason. Their great goaltender, Georges Vézina, had contracted tuberculosis. He left the team one game into the season and died in a hospital bed in his hometown of Chicoutimi in March 1926.

Art Ross guided his Boston Bruins to a fourth-place finish. Odie Cleghorn led the Pirates to third and a playoff spot. Eddie Gerard's Montreal Maroons finished second, and the powerful Ottawa Senators were league champs for the sixth time in nine NHL seasons. The Maroons knocked off the Pirates, eliminated the Senators and then beat Lester Patrick's Victoria Cougars in the Stanley Cup final.

The four-game series attracted record attendance of 43,200. The Cougars received $659.68 each for their efforts and the Maroons $839.52, plus $1,000 apiece from the directors of the Montreal Professional Hockey Club. One element of the annual Stanley Cup series was missing that year: the trophy itself. It was back in Victoria and arrived by train on April 25, about three weeks after the series ended. A delegation of Maroon players and officials was waiting at Windsor Station to receive it. But they discovered that there was no room left to engrave their names. and the first of many silver bands was added to the base to honour the Maroons and subsequent champions.

SUDDENLY, THERE WAS A RUSH to get into the National Hockey League. One application after another landed on Frank Calder's desk in late March and early April 1926. There were a dozen all told, from individuals and from groups, all apparently willing to pay the price of admission: $50,000 per franchise. They came from New York, Jersey City, Hamilton, Cleveland, Windsor, Detroit and Chicago. The governors rendered quick decisions on most of them at a meeting on April 17 at the Windsor Hotel.

Tex Rickard had let it be known during the season that he wanted in. The Americans had been a bigger box-office attraction than expected, and putting another team in Madison Square Garden would create a natural rivalry. Rickard even had a nickname for his club (the Rangers) and a coach (Conn Smythe of Toronto) waiting in the wings, and the board granted him a franchise.

Delegations from the other cities made presentations, but the board turned most of them down. The exceptions were Detroit and Chicago. There were five applicants from the former, two from the latter. Neither city had an adequate arena. But there were plans in Detroit to erect a fifteen-thousand-seat stadium and one of the Chicago applicants—Paddy Harmon—was trying to raise financing for a building that would be bigger and grander than Rickard's Madison Square Garden.

Frank Ahearn, owner of the Ottawa Senators, objected to any further expansion, but others reasoned that the NHL risked losing Detroit and Chicago to the Central Hockey Association, a pro circuit being organized by former members of the United States Amateur Hockey Association. In fact, some of the Detroit applicants were making noises about joining that league, if necessary, and Paddy Harmon was explicit about his intentions.

"I will be in hockey," Harmon told a group of reporters. "I have a franchise already in the Central league. I prefer to operate in the National Hockey League and if I don't get in I will be forced to fight. . . . I would rather have peace, but if there must be war we will show the National Hockey League that we mean business."

The NHL could not ignore such a threat. But the governors needed time and more information before making a decision on the competing bids from Detroit and Chicago. So they appointed a three-member committee of Calder, the Canadiens' Leo Dandurand and the Maroons' James Strachan and instructed them to visit those cities, examine the finances of the applicants and assess the prospects of having new buildings finished and open in time for the 1926–27 season. They adjourned their proceedings and agreed to meet again on May 1, a Saturday, to revisit the issue of expansion.

WITHIN FORTY-EIGHT HOURS OF RECEIVING their assignment, Calder, Strachan and Dandurand had packed their bags, purchased their tickets and left Montreal aboard a westbound train. However, they had not, apparently, been asked to address one crucial question: Where would any new owners acquire enough talent to assemble NHL-calibre teams? The solution to that problem arrived, unsolicited, from an unlikely source: Frank Patrick, president of the Vancouver Maroons of the Western Hockey League.

Patrick had come east for the Stanley Cup final with older brother Lester and his Victoria Cougars and had stayed afterward. He turned up at the Windsor Hotel on April 17, mingled with the prospective franchisees and held private discussions with some of them. Patrick had a plan in mind, one based on his astute observations of the emerging economics of pro hockey.

The western owners could not compete with NHL salaries. Their rinks—Vancouver's ten-thousand-seater excepted—were much smaller and their pockets nowhere near as deep as those of Charles Adams, Big Bill Dwyer or the millionaire backers of the Montreal Maroons. Furthermore, the U.S. clubs were starved for talent, and their Canadian partners weren't willing to bust up their teams to help them out.

The NHL and WHL had a territorial agreement that gave the latter exclusive rights to all players west of Chicago and Port Arthur, Ontario (contemporary Thunder Bay). Nevertheless, Patrick recognized that the NHL's American partners would eventually come calling, chequebooks in hand, to lure away players like George Hainsworth, the short, pudgy, moon-faced squirt of a goalie with the Saskatoon Sheiks, who was fast, fearless and nearly unbeatable most nights. Or Herb Gardiner and Eddie Shore, the one a defenceman with the Calgary Tigers, the other with the Edmonton Eskimos, both of whom were hard-hitting, fearsome competitors and good with the puck. Or Dick Irvin, the goal-a-game forward with the Portland Rosebuds. Frank Fredrickson, the Victoria Cougars' tall, strong centre and two-time western scoring champion. Or Patrick's own star centre and peerless playmaker Frank Boucher.

The western league might survive such losses, but only as a minor-pro circuit—subservient to the NHL and incapable of challenging for the Stanley Cup. Patrick had presented this scenario to his fellow owners in Portland and the Prairie cities before joining the Cougars for the trip east. He had proposed an alternative, and all but Saskatoon bought in.

"I got five of six clubs in the western league to entrust their players to me to do with them whatever seemed best," Patrick wrote several years later in an article commissioned by the *Boston Globe*. "These clubs were Vancouver, Victoria, Edmonton, Portland and Calgary. . . . The plan was to amalgamate the five clubs with which I had been entrusted into three strong teams and sell each of those three, en bloc, for $100,000."

Patrick quietly began looking for buyers during the Stanley Cup final. He approached his boyhood friend Art Ross and showed him a list of the players. Ross checked off three names—Fredrickson, Shore and Shore's Edmonton teammate Gordon (Duke) Keats. He would take them for his Bruins and he would help his old chum find buyers for the rest.

After the series, he and Patrick went to New York and met with Colonel Hammond and Conn Smythe of the Rangers. Patrick produced his list and told them they could have a dozen players for $100,000. But Hammond and Smythe turned down the offer. They were confident they could find enough good talent on their own.

At that, Ross and Patrick tried Bruins owner Charles Adams. To their great surprise, he was prepared to buy the entire league, Saskatoon excepted. He would pay $250,000, not $300,000. He would keep a few key players to strengthen the Bruins, sell the new owners in Detroit and Chicago twelve good players each to ensure that they started with capable and competitive teams, and offer the rest to the established clubs. Adams gave Patrick a $50,000 cash deposit, and then all three—Adams, Ross and Patrick—left for Montreal and the May 1 meeting.

IT TURNED INTO ONE OF THE stormiest gatherings in the league's short history. The governors were in accord over the Detroit franchise. They awarded it to Wesley Seybourn and John Townsend, who were representing a syndicate of seventy-three investors formed by Charles Hughes, a sports promoter and founder of the Detroit Athletic Club. The syndicate included Edsel Ford, S.S. Kresge of the five-and-dime retail chain and William E. Scripps, a newspaper publisher.

But the debate over Chicago split the board and nearly destroyed the league. The trouble began with friction between the New York franchises. Tex Rickard hoped to build a big new arena in Chicago. He favoured a group led by Huntington R. Hardwick, who went by the nickname Tack. Hardwick had been an extraordinary, all-around athlete at Harvard and star quarterback of the varsity football team. He had settled in Boston after graduating, accepted a position with a brokerage firm, and had come before the board with seemingly good intentions.

"I think hockey is the greatest game in the world," he told the governors. "I'd like to see hockey planted in Chicago so I could see the game played by the best teams. I'd like to put a good team in Tex Rickard's rink out there and show the western city the real game of hockey. I know it would go over big."

But Tommy Gorman and Tom Duggan of the Americans suspected that Rickard had recruited him to apply for the Chicago franchise so that he—

Rickard—would have a hockey team for the arena he intended to build in that city. Gorman and Duggan had had a number of disputes with Rickard during their one season at Madison Square Garden and feared that he was trying to extend his influence in an expanded league.

Rickard dismissed their suspicions, saying he had only met Hardwick once and scarcely knew him. A heated and protracted debate only drove the New York delegations further apart. The league constitution required unanimity before a new franchise could be granted, hence there was no point in putting the matter to a vote. Rickard walked out in frustration. Charles Adams and Art Ross followed and the Pirate and Maroon representatives joined them.

They huddled in the corridors to plot their next move. Some suggested they quit the NHL and form their own league, and the idea was discussed at length, apparently within earshot of curious reporters. Rickard pulled one of them aside to tell him what he thought of the situation. "Hockey is a game with great and wonderful possibilities," he said. "Within five years it will be drawing more spectators than boxing. But some of your owners are nervous and small. They talk like children. They are against every suggestion to widen the game, particularly as concerns the United States."

At that moment, James Strachan had an idea: amend the constitution so that franchises could be awarded by a simple majority vote. Such an amendment could be effected with the approval of two-thirds of the board. Gorman and Duggan may have disagreed, but the rest of the governors saw it as an acceptable compromise. The crisis was averted and the governors resumed their meeting. They agreed that Hardwick would get the Chicago franchise, though a formal vote on the matter would wait until yet another meeting, on May 15.

The peace among the governors lasted all of several minutes. Adams and Ross announced their deal with Patrick, and it hit the room like a bomb. Some were livid. Some cried foul. But they were united in their resolve to overturn the transaction. Adams was furious and walked out, with Ross right behind him. They immediately sat down with a lawyer—a number of the delegations had brought legal counsel with them—and began preparing a lawsuit against the NHL.

But the common front against Adams quickly crumbled. The governors and their entourages were all staying at the Windsor Hotel, and that evening a number of them visited Adams's suite. Colonel Hammond was the first to drop by.

"How about selling me Frankie Boucher?" the colonel suggested.

"How can I sell you a player the league has taken away from me?" Adams replied.

The two men skirted the problem easily enough. Adams agreed to sell Boucher for $20,000, and Hammond pledged his support for the Boston governor's plan to distribute the players equitably among the weaker teams.

Henry J. Townsend of the Pittsburgh Pirates visited Adams next and inquired about certain players, and the two men made a similar deal. Hardwick and the Detroit representatives had their own meetings, and each agreed to buy entire teams for the asking price of $100,000. When the board resumed its deliberations in the morning, the tide had turned. Most of the governors had seen the wisdom in what Adams was doing. Patrick was called into the room and the biggest auction of talent in the history of the game—up to that point—was underway.

The Detroit syndicate agreed to purchase the Victoria Cougars, and Hardwick's group took the Portland Rosebuds. The Bruins laid claim to Eddie Shore, Duke Keats and two others: Harry Oliver and Percy Galbraith. The Rangers grabbed Boucher. And so it went. By the end of the day, the NHL clubs had acquired some sixty players. The auction had generated $267,000, which Patrick would distribute among the western owners.

Two weeks later, on May 15, the governors reconvened at the Windsor and formally awarded the Chicago and Detroit franchises. There were conditions attached, though. The new owners had to provide assurances by September 1 that they had assembled NHL-calibre teams. They were also expected to have new arenas completed by November 10.

Before adjourning, the governors gave Frank Calder a hefty raise. Rickard described him as a "big man and the brightest man I have met in hockey." He proposed that they double his salary to $15,000, but the board settled on $12,500 and instructed Calder to devote his full attention to hockey.

A DECADE AFTER IT WAS CREATED, the NHL stood as the best league in the sport. It had survived the demise of the Wanderers, Bulldogs and Tigers, the litigation of Eddie Livingstone and all the other early setbacks and challenges. It had outflanked and subdued rival organizations that threatened to occupy major eastern cities and compete for supremacy. And the NHL had erased professional hockey from the sporting landscape of the West.

The pro game had taken root and flourished in that region due largely to the daring, determination and enterprise of Lester and Frank Patrick. The Patricks had acquired their passion for hockey as boys growing up in the Montreal suburb of Westmount and as young men playing on senior and professional teams in eastern Canada. They left the sport behind in the summer of 1907, moving west with their father, Joseph Patrick, to start a lumber business in Nelson, British Columbia. But in the spring of 1911, amid a worldwide shortage, the Patricks sold their timber leases and mills to a British businessman for $440,000.

With their newfound wealth, Lester, then twenty-seven, and Frank, twenty-five, decided to introduce hockey to the West Coast. They built rinks in Vancouver and Victoria—the first in Canada equipped with ice-making plants. They raided the rosters of the eastern pro teams and in the fall of 1911 launched the Pacific Coast Hockey Association with three teams, the third being New Westminster, which played its home games in Vancouver.

The Patricks kept their league operating, some years with three clubs, some years with four, until the fall of 1924, when they merged with the Western Canada Hockey League to create a six-team circuit comprising Vancouver, Victoria, Edmonton, Calgary, Regina and Saskatoon. Regina dropped out prior to the 1925–26 season. That franchise shifted to Portland, Oregon, and was christened the Rosebuds.

The Patrick brothers greatly expanded hockey's horizons, and they changed the way the game was played. They allowed their goalies to flop, sprawl or do whatever it took to make a save, whereas eastern rules stipulated that netminders had to remain on their feet at all times. They allowed forward passing, began awarding assists and put numbers on players' sweaters. They painted blue lines across the ice to create two defensive zones with a neutral zone between them.

The brothers convinced their eastern counterparts to participate in an annual east-west postseason playoff that would be called the World Series and would determine the Stanley Cup champion. The first was held in the spring of 1914 and the last twelve years later. The East won most of these showdowns, but the West produced three champions: the Vancouver Millionaires in 1914, the Seattle Metropolitans in 1917 and the Victoria Cougars in 1925.

Had it not been for the ambitions of the NHL, the West may well have continued to support top-notch, pro hockey, and many westerners lamented the demise of their league. Vancouver had established itself as "one of the best hockey cities on the North American continent," an editorial in the *Sun* newspaper declared. "It is an unfortunate thing that hockey, Canada's favorite and the world's best sport, should have followed the commercial course of baseball. It is unfortunate that almost the sole remaining professional game in Canada should have fallen into the clutches of big business."

A sportswriter in Victoria wrote of his city's loss in more personal terms: "For the thousands of fans who have stuck loyally to the Cougars through fair weather and foul it means the breaking of sentimental and thrilling cords. Those whose practice since 1911–12 has been to write down certain dates each week for hockey thrills must look elsewhere or to amateurs."

THERE WERE TEN TEAMS IN the NHL of 1926–27. The league was split into two divisions: Canadian and American. Each team played forty-four games, up from thirty-six the previous year, and the season opened earlier than ever—November 17, a Tuesday. The Canadiens were in Boston, the Americans were in Pittsburgh, and the defending Stanley Cup champion Maroons were in New York for the debut of the Rangers.

Madison Square Garden was packed. The 126-piece West Point Cadet Band led the Rangers onto the ice and around the rink and screen star Lois Moran performed a ceremonial faceoff by dropping a puck between the sticks of the opposing centres, New York's Frank Boucher and Montreal's Nels Stewart.

The Garden ice was soft and sticky, but the teams put on a fine show anyway. There was plenty of hitting, one fight and just a single goal. Rangers right winger Bill Cook scored late in the second after a clever series of passes among himself, his brother Bun on left wing and their linemate, Boucher. "The battle was such a dog-eat-dog affair that it made a very fashionable crowd act quite human and yell its head off," one New York paper reported.

Chicago's new team debuted the following evening at home against the Toronto St. Pats, but not in the big new rink that was supposed to be ready for opening night. Home, for the time being, was the Coliseum, an amphitheatre with an arched roof and a chateau-style façade, complete with stone turrets and towers. The Coliseum was erected in 1898. It had been used for large events of all sorts, most notably political gatherings, and could seat about eight thousand.

An enthusiastic but untutored crowd turned out for opening night, though there was no mention of Tack Hardwick in the next day's papers. In fact, the Chicago franchise had already changed hands. On June 1, Hardwick had informed Frank Calder by letter that "a Chicago man will shortly be elected President, and the Board of Directors will be composed largely of Chicago men."

The following day, Major Frederic McLaughlin incorporated the Chicago National Hockey Team, Inc. He became the club's president and its governor on the NHL board. McLaughlin was forty-nine and a prominent figure in Chicago. He and an older brother owned McLaughlin's Manor House Coffee, a family firm they had inherited from their father, and he was married to the glamorous Irene Castle, who was thirty-three and had achieved international acclaim in her twenties as a ballroom dancer, Broadway performer and screen star.

McLaughlin was a striking figure. "His face was lean, with a long, narrow nose and haughty eyes," journalist Trent Frayne once wrote, adding that he was "a brisk erect man of military background and bearing who wore a bow tie, a clipped moustache and kept his thin hair combed smoothly back."

McLaughlin had commanded a machine gun battalion in the U.S. Army's 86th, or Black Hawk, Division during the First World War, and the division supplied the name for Chicago's NHL franchise. The team would be the Black Hawks. McLaughlin would later buy out his partners and become the club's sole owner. He would run the team for the next eighteen years, until his death on December 17, 1944, and he would hire and fire thirteen coaches during his first ten years as boss, earning a well-deserved reputation for eccentric behaviour.

But on opening night in 1926, he was merely the proud and beaming president of the victorious Chicago Black Hawks. "They defeated the St. Patrick's sextet from Toronto, Ont., 4 to 1, on the Coliseum's new rink," Frank Schreiber of the *Chicago Tribune* reported. "The sport was accorded a great reception. More than 7,000 pushed their way into the building and there were cheers from the time the game started until the final whistle."

Detroit's home opener against the Boston Bruins was a plain and unadorned affair—no marching bands, no ladies in evening dresses, no men in tuxes. The owners had taken the Victoria Cougars, practically intact, and put them in new red-on-white uniforms with an Old English D—for Detroit—on the chest, but kept the nickname. They, like McLaughlin and his partners in Chicago, had been unable to get a rink built for November 10, as per their commitment to the league. The Cougars started the season across the river at the Border Cities Arena in Windsor, Ontario, and Detroit residents had to take a ferry to get there.

Tickets went on sale in both cities four days ahead of the game, and most were sold by the time the doors opened. A full house wasn't enough to carry the Cougars to victory, though. They lost two-nothing, and opening night was a sign of things to come. The Cougars played all twenty-two home games at the Windsor rink, and the losses piled up as the season went on. Detroit won a mere twelve games, earned just twenty-eight points and finished last overall.

But the injection of western talent had a major impact elsewhere. McLaughlin's Hawks placed third in the American Division and sixth of ten teams. They made the playoffs, and ex-Rosebud Dick Irvin was second in scoring. The Bruins, bolstered by Eddie Shore and his former Edmonton Eskimo teammates, had their best season to date. The Rangers claimed top spot in their division. Bill Cook won the scoring race and brother Bun landed in seventh. The Canadiens rebounded from a miserable season in 1925–26, when they wound up last. They compiled the second-best record in the league, with just two significant roster changes. They had acquired defenceman Herb Gardiner from Calgary and goaltender George Hainsworth from Saskatoon, and Hainsworth shut out the opposition fourteen times in forty-four starts.

The Ottawa Senators were once again the league's best team. They eliminated their old rival, the Canadiens, in the divisional final and advanced to the championship series against Boston. Games one and two were played in Boston before noisy, sellout crowds, and the team could have sold thirty thousand tickets, according to one newspaper, had there been seats available. The first ended in a scoreless draw and the second in an Ottawa victory.

Demand outstripped supply in the Canadian capital as well. Fans were lined up outside the ticket windows at the Ottawa Auditorium by 4 a.m. on the day of game three. That contest was tied zero-zero after twenty minutes of overtime when the officials judged the ice unfit to continue.

Two nights later, the Auditorium was jammed again for game four. The Senators clinched their ninth Stanley Cup with a three-one victory, but the evening ended badly. There were several fights in the third period and a ruckus under the stands afterward. Bruins owner Charles Adams and manager Art Ross followed referee Jerry Laflamme to his dressing room, berating him all the way. The players got involved and defenceman Billy Couture knocked Laflamme to the floor.

"It was a disgraceful ending," the *Ottawa Citizen* declared, and Frank Calder, who had witnessed it all, agreed. He suspended Couture for life, banished a member of the Senators for the first month of the 1926–27 season and levied fines against several others.

THE SENATORS WERE ONE OF THE top attractions in the expanded NHL. They drew big crowds, often full houses, when they visited New York, Boston and the other American venues. They were good, of course, but there was more to it than that. The Senators had been formed nearly half a century earlier, in 1883, when hockey was strictly an amateur pastime, when there were seven men to a side, when the game was played mostly outdoors and the seasons were short.

Other teams, even entire leagues, had come and gone in those formative years, but the Senators had endured, wearing the same red, white and black colours from the earliest days, always competitive and frequently champions. Now this venerable organization was losing money and Redmond Quain, a lawyer and club director, disclosed the bad news during the NHL's 1927 annual meeting, held September 24 at the Congress Hotel in Chicago.

Attendance at home games had dwindled to just under 3,700 fans per game, on average, while operating costs, particularly travel, had risen dramatically with expansion. Quain proposed a change to the league's revenue-sharing agreement. Visiting teams then received 3.5 per cent of the gate. He suggested that the Senators receive an increased share sufficient to cover up to 15 per cent of operating expenses, but the rest of the board rejected the idea and the Senators' difficulties slowly and quietly mounted.

A second Canadian franchise, the Toronto St. Pats, had also drifted into troubled waters. Toronto had slipped to the bottom end of the standings since winning the Stanley Cup in 1922. Fan support dwindled. Some members of the ownership group wanted out, and in November 1926 a potential buyer appeared: the Philadelphia sports promoter C.C. Pyle—popularly known as Cash and Carry. He told the shareholders to name their price. They wanted $200,000. The newspapers got wind of the negotiations and alerted their readers. "What is most important about the deal—if it goes through—is that Mr. Pyle will transfer the club intact to Philadelphia," the *Telegram* reported.

That caught the attention of the ambitious and energetic young businessman and hockey executive Conn Smythe. He had been hired in the spring of 1926 to coach the Rangers and then been fired in the fall in favour of Lester Patrick. Smythe went back to running his aggregates business, C. Smythe for Sand, and formed a senior team called the Varsity Grads, comprised largely of former players with the University of Toronto Blues.

Smythe told anyone who would listen, including the newspapers, that Toronto would be out of the NHL for a long time if the St. Pats left town. Finally, he went to see Jack Bickell, a Bay Street mining executive and one of the franchise's principle shareholders. They made a deal: Bickell would keep his money in—about $40,000—provided Smythe could find investors willing to put up $160,000 and buy out the rest of the group. The final point was that Smythe would run the team.

He was jubilant. He slapped down $10,000 on the spot and went to work. By the end of January 1927 he had the investors and the money. The deal closed in mid-February, and a headline in the Toronto *Globe* signalled a new era of professional hockey in the city:

GOODBYE, ST. PAT'S!
HOWDY, MAPLE LEAFS

Smythe scrapped a name designed to appeal to Toronto's Irish and adopted one that he believed would resonate more broadly and deeply. Canada's fighting men had worn the maple leaf on their badges and insignia during the Great War of 1914 to 1918 and Canadian hockey players had worn the same symbol on their sweaters when they won Olympic gold at Chamonix, France, in 1924.

Smythe's rebranding took effect immediately, and a team that had begun the 1926–27 season sporting the green and white of the St. Pats finished it wearing the blue and white of the Maple Leafs. The other clubs did not object, and the board approved the changes when it met at the Congress Hotel in September 1927.

THE BIRTH OF THE MAPLE LEAFS coincided with the start of a brief period of stability in the NHL. No new franchises were granted. None of the existing ones folded. Nor did any relocate. And there were a number of positive developments. New arenas opened in each of the next three seasons.

Olympia Stadium in Detroit hosted its first hockey game on the evening of November 22, 1927. The University of Michigan marching band delivered a rousing musical welcome for the Cougars and their opponents, the defending Stanley Cup champion Ottawa Senators. Mayor John Smith presented the home team's new coach, Jack Adams, with bunches of brilliant yellow chrysanthemums. Radio station WGHP broadcast the game and hired Foster Hewitt to call it play by play. Figure skaters entertained between periods, and ten thousand spectators filled every seat in the sparkling new building designed by the celebrated architect C. Howard Crane, who made his reputation creating extravagant but gorgeous movie theatres. The evening didn't end well for the Cougars, though. They lost two-one to the reigning champs.

Boston Garden opened in the fall of 1928. The building was nothing less than magnificent, according to the newspapers, and the Bruins began the season there against the Canadiens on November 20, a Tuesday. The crowds outside were so thick ninety minutes before game time that the players could barely get in and the attendance that night surged well above the official capacity of fifteen thousand.

As one press report put it: "Thousands of wild hockey fans, unable to buy either seats or standing room, stormed the doors, swept aside police lines and flowed into the building, filling every lick of standing space and almost bulging on to the ice. Windows were smashed and doors broken in the wild assault on the building."

The opening faceoff was delayed twenty-five minutes, and even then, half the seats were empty because those who had bought tickets were still fighting their way through the throngs packed into the aisles and corridors. "It was the maddest crowd that ever saw an athletic event in Boston," the Montreal *Gazette* reported, "intensely partisan and therefore desolate to the last degree when Sylvio Mantha, tall defenceman of the Habitants, stormed into the picture and scored the only goal of the game."

Chicago Stadium was the biggest and grandest of the new buildings. "In its entirety it will shame New York's palatial Madison Square Garden," the *Chicago Tribune* declared shortly before it was completed in early March 1929. *Scientific American* and *Popular Mechanics* magazines both ran feature stories on the Stadium, the latter calling it "The World's Greatest Sports Arena."

It would hold 30,000 for prize fights, 20,000 for hockey and 18,000 for bicycle races, and, at 300 feet in length, it was as long as a football field. Several million bricks had been used to build the exterior walls. Polished marble panels lined the walls of the lobby and thirty-six 1,000-watt lights hung from the rafters, ready to illuminate the floor below. The *pièce de résistance* was the pipe organ—the largest instrument of its kind in the world. It had cost $150,000, and a single organist seated at the semicircular, upright keyboard could pump out as much sound as a 2,500-piece brass band.

The sports promoter Paddy Harmon, one of the applicants for Chicago's NHL franchise, raised $7 million largely from the city's wealthy elite to build the multipurpose Stadium, and the Black Hawks became a tenant in mid-December 1929. The move from the cramped, rundown Coliseum saved the franchise. The Hawks had lost money in each of their first three seasons. They played six home games at the Coliseum in the fall of 1929, and the gates averaged just under $6,300. At the Stadium, the team took in $14,000 per night.

By the spring of 1930, after four full seasons as a ten-team league, certain things were becoming clear about the NHL's rapid and far-flung thrust into the United States. Detroit and Chicago had not achieved the on-ice success necessary to create solid fan bases, but committed ownership would ensure their survival for the time being. The NHL had flourished in New York and Boston. The Rangers and Americans had both developed large, loyal followings and the Rangers had won the Stanley Cup in 1928—their second season.

The Bruins took hold in Boston thanks to Art Ross's genius as a manager, coach and salesman of the game. He was a popular after-dinner speaker, and in the early years he accepted every invitation. He entertained his listeners with tales about two imaginary French-Canadian habitants—Jules Levesque and Joe Laporte—and spoke with an impeccable French-Canadian accent. It may have been corny, but it was effective. As one admiring Boston journalist later wrote: "People who had never seen a hockey game decided they must see what Ross did for a living. Hockey must be good if Ross was in it."

Ross's Bruins won the Stanley Cup in 1929 and completely dominated the 1929–30 regular-season schedule. With Cecil Thompson in goal, Eddie Shore and Lionel Hitchman on defence and Ralph Weiland, Dit Clapper and Norm Gainor up front, they won thirty-eight of forty-four games and scored a record 179 goals. The Canadiens upset them in the final, however, and one of hockey's most enduring rivalries was born.

The NHL did not take in Pittsburgh. Mediocre teams and a lousy building—the old Duquesne Gardens—had a deadening effect and the Pirates rarely sold out. In October 1928, a group led by retired lightweight boxing champion Benny Leonard acquired the franchise, though the largest investor was said to be Big Bill Dwyer, the bootlegger. Leonard was the front man and the manager, but under his watch the Pirates went from weak to woeful. Toward the end of the 1929–30 season, a writer with the *Pittsburgh Press* declared, "Pittsburgh's hopes for a National Hockey League berth next season have grown as cold as a mother-in-law's kiss."

He was right. The future of the franchise was high on the agenda when the league held its 1930 annual meeting on Saturday, May 10, at the King Edward Hotel in Toronto. The board decided to move the Pirates, possibly to Atlantic City, and they left the matter with Frank Calder and the owners of the franchise, confident that the Pittsburgh problem would be more a hiccup than a hurricane.

In fact, an economic cataclysm that would come to be known as the Great Depression was already causing havoc. The big burst of expansion of the latter half of the 1920s would soon be a distant afterthought. Survival would be the sole objective for the NHL and most of its ten teams.

3

FROM TEN TO SIX (1930-1943)

A FEW DAYS AFTER THANKSGIVING 1930, a heavy snowfall hit parts of southern Ontario, and out west, an equally unseasonable blizzard buried bountiful Prairie crops. Storm or no storm, the few hundred young men who played pro hockey—or aspired to—were on the move. Bidding farewell to tearful, well-wishing wives and children, or parents and siblings. Leaving behind summer jobs and pastimes. Boarding trains in distant, forlorn whistle stops sprinkled across the vast Dominion of Canada and travelling to training camps where, if they were veterans, they would tune up for the 1930–31 NHL season, or, if they were hopefuls, they would try to catch on with the Leafs or Canadiens, Senators or Maroons or one of the six U.S.-based clubs.

Training camp was a time of hope and optimism—rare commodities in the fall of 1930. The talk in boardrooms and committee rooms, among friends, neighbours and strangers, was about the gathering economic gloom and measures hastily devised to lift it. The federal government was raising tariffs and adopting stiff anti-dumping rules to shelter domestic growers, producers and manufacturers. Ottawa, the provinces, municipalities and railways were pumping close to $100 million into capital works and relief programs to create jobs and alleviate unemployment. Hopeful editorialists assured readers that these steps were already generating "a new sense of confidence," and furthermore "there is every indication that much unemployment will be relieved." Two of the country's leading bankers added their voices to this chorus of premature optimism after a conference held in Victoria, British Columbia. "We have reached the bottom and are at the turn," said Royal Bank president Sir Herbert Holt. His Bank of Montreal counterpart, Sir Charles Gordon, added: "The revival is coming. But it will be gradual."

All of this was background noise for Frank Calder and the board of governors of the NHL. They were wrestling with problems of their own, which had more to do with the rapid expansion of the late 1920s than current economic conditions. The board met three times that fall, once in late September, twice in October.

The future of the Pittsburgh franchise remained unresolved. The Atlantic City deal had unravelled and there was no going back to Pittsburgh, so the Pirates were transferred to Philadelphia, where they became the Quakers. Home ice would be a ten-year-old arena that seated six thousand, and they would have a new coach. Cooper Smeaton, the league's referee-in-chief, had resigned to try his hand behind the bench, and he sounded an optimistic note in a preseason interview. "I know there are better teams than the Quakers in the league," Smeaton said. "But we are going to have a fighting combination."

Ottawa was the NHL's other big problem. In the three seasons since the 1927 Stanley Cup championship, management had tried gimmicks and desperate measures to keep the franchise afloat. They had sold Hooley Smith, star forward of that Cup-winning team, to the Montreal Maroons, and they had peddled Ed Gorman to Toronto. They had lowered ticket prices. They had installed wider, more comfortable bench seats. They had transferred home games to Detroit, New York and elsewhere. They had appealed unsuccessfully to the NHL board for a more generous cut of the gate when they played on the road.

But there was no stopping the slow, grim decline. In January 1929, owner Frank Ahearn announced that this illustrious civic institution would be sold or moved. This did nothing to enhance the team's morale or its performance. Nor did it bring forth a rush of potential buyers. In the end, there was only one: the Auditorium Company of Ottawa, which faced the dismal prospect of losing its major tenant.

Ahearn's price was $125,000, but the Auditorium Company did not have the cash required and borrowing it was out of the question. Instead, the Auditorium issued $125,000 worth of preferred shares paying a seven per cent dividend annually and intended to sell them locally. The deal was concluded over the summer, and in August 1929, Ahearn relinquished control.

Two months later, stock markets around the world crashed. The international economy went into a tailspin. The Senators lost $25,000 on the 1929–30 season even though attendance and revenues had risen. Given the circumstances, selling securities proved a Sisyphean undertaking. By mid-1930, the Auditorium Company had moved only $50,000 worth of its preferred shares. The team was broke and needed an injection of cash.

The roster included two established stars capable of stepping into any lineup in the league. The first was goaltender Alex Connell. The second was Frank (King) Clancy, the captain and anchor of the defence. Clancy had joined the Senators in the fall of 1921. He was then eighteen, still a student at Ottawa Collegiate Institute, and had never skated on artificial ice. He had to obtain his father's permission before signing a contract. His mother purchased an overnight bag and packed it prior to his first road trip. Years later, recalling that westbound train ride, he would say, "I was tickled pink to be among the famous Ottawa Senators."

By the fall of 1930, Clancy was admired around the league. The Rangers reportedly made a rich offer for him. Detroit was apparently interested. Another published report said the Maroons were prepared to pay $35,000 and part with winger Jimmy Ward. Conn Smythe coveted Clancy as well, and in early October made a pitch for him. Before leaving for Ottawa, Smythe announced his intentions in the Toronto newspapers and readers swamped the papers with letters to the editor. "If I had $50,000 I would buy the player myself and give him to you," one admirer wrote. "Oh Clancy, Clancy, you are the man I fancy," said another. "See Smythe for sand," added a third, "get Clancy for forty grand."

On October 10, Smythe and the Senators announced a deal. Clancy was sold to the Leafs for $35,000 and two prospects. The club had put up $25,000 and Smythe covered the balance with money he had won at Woodbine Racetrack by wagering on a long shot named Rare Jewel.

The Senators made one more preseason deal. They sold three young players—Syd Howe, Allan Shields and Wally Kilrea—to Philadelphia for $35,000 and, in so doing, more or less gave up on the future. In Philadelphia, meanwhile, manager Benny Leonard was singing a different tune. "This is only the first move to bring a winner here," he said. "We must make a good start and I will spare no expense to give the fans what they want. We have other deals in mind if the men we have now fail to deliver."

The Quakers played their home opener on November 11, 1930, against the Rangers. They wore new orange and black uniforms. The ushers wore tuxes. Flags hung from the roof of the arena. A solid crowd of four to five thousand turned out. The Quakers lost three-nothing. They did not score a goal until their third game and did not register a win until their sixth. The Quakers then lost a league-record fifteen in a row. In the second half of the season, the minor-pro Philadelphia Arrows of the Canadian-American Hockey League were drawing better crowds.

The Quakers finished with a paltry four wins against thirty-six losses and four ties. The Senators were only marginally better. They won ten, lost thirty and tied four. The league held its annual meeting on May 9, 1931, at the Lincoln Hotel in New York. The governors deferred until the fall decisions about the two troubled franchises. They were merely playing for time, hoping that some miraculous solutions might materialize over the summer.

But there were no buyers and nowhere to move either team. On September 26, the board met in Montreal and agreed to requests from both clubs to suspend operations for one year. The demise of the Quakers was scarcely noticed in Philadelphia or elsewhere, but many lamented the end of the Senators. "Ottawa has nothing in her hockey record of which she cannot be proud," a *Citizen* writer declared. "No longer able to stand the heavy financial strain, she retires from the major league with her record, her memories and her famous sons to keep her name alive."

WITH THE ACQUISITION OF KING CLANCY, Conn Smythe was confident he had a team capable of winning the Stanley Cup. Lorne Chabot was the goaltender. Clancy, Hap Day and Red Horner made for a formidable defence. Joe Primeau, Busher Jackson and Charlie Conacher formed the Kid Line, and the Leafs had two other very good forwards in Ace Bailey and Baldy Cotton.

There was one problem, though. The Leafs played in the aging and outdated Mutual Street Arena, built just before World War I. It seated eight thousand and there was standing room for another thousand. Gate receipts in 1929–30 totalled $186,251, barely enough to cover salaries and operating expenses and well below the revenues earned by teams with big, up-to-date facilities.

Smythe was convinced the Leafs needed a new arena, and in the fall of 1930 he began promoting the idea. He met with business leaders, newspapermen and anyone else who would listen. Most of them promptly replied, "It can't be done." Few believed he could find the money required—about $1.5 million—in a small city like Toronto, which had a population of about 600,000. Besides, those who had money weren't likely to risk it when the world economy was slipping into an ever-deeper depression.

Nevertheless, Smythe persisted, and backers slowly emerged. Sun Life, a major Montreal-based insurance company, agreed to put up $500,000. Sir John Aird, president of the Bank of Commerce, offered the bank's support. With two big institutional investors behind him, Smythe lined up a board of directors that read like a who's who of the Toronto business community. He incorporated Maple Leaf Gardens, Ltd. on February 24, 1931, and then decided on a public stock offering to raise the balance of the money. The new company would sell 70,000 preferred shares at $10 apiece and issue 35,000 common shares with no set par value. Smythe knocked on doors while his assistant, Frank Selke, and his star player Ace Bailey phoned season-ticket holders and other potential investors.

The entire project nearly went down the drain when Sun Life tried to pull out. Smythe appealed to Sir Edward Beatty, president of the Canadian Pacific Railway and a Sun Life director, and Beatty used his muscle to keep the insurer onside. A second crisis arose in late May. All the shares had been sold and Smythe had tapped out every conceivable source of financing. Aird called a meeting in his office to open the bids for construction of the new arena. The lowest was several hundred thousand dollars above the amount they had raised. The consensus in the room was: wait till better times returned.

Smythe suggested they take a break. He left to consult Selke, who was seated in the corridor. At the moment when all seemed lost, they conceived a solution. Perhaps the men who would build the arena—some 1,300 construction workers—could be convinced to give up twenty per cent of their salaries in exchange for Gardens common shares. Selke offered to approach the unions, and he was just the person to make the pitch. He was a certified electrician, a member of the International Brotherhood of Electrical Workers and the honorary business manager of the Toronto local.

As Smythe later told the story, the Allied Building Trades Council of Toronto was meeting that day. Selke ran all the way to the Labour Temple and interrupted the gathering. The union leaders heard him out and Selke made two convincing arguments. He had mortgaged his home to buy $4,500 worth of Gardens stock. And the project would provide five to six months' work for a lot of men who might otherwise be unemployed for the summer. The council approved the stock-for-pay proposal in principle. The various locals ratified it and the project was saved.

Contracts were awarded on May 31 and at midnight June 1 demolition crews began clearing the site on the northwest corner of Church and Carlton Streets. Three huge steam shovels and a fleet of trucks worked around the clock excavating the foundation—in the process removing some thirty thousand cubic yards of dirt. The first concrete was poured on June 26, and from then on the building rose with remarkable speed, although, as the Toronto *Mail and Empire* noted, "at no time since the work commenced . . . has there been much Sunday labor, just that which was absolutely necessary."

The *Mail*'s C.W. MacQueen got a glimpse of the interior on November 11—the day before the Leafs were scheduled to play their home opener against the Chicago Black Hawks. He was struck by the loftiness of the structure. "Immediately one thinks of a cathedral," MacQueen wrote. "The distance from the ice to the top of the domed roof is sufficient for the erection of a 13-storey building."

Crowds began converging at Church and Carlton by six o'clock on opening night, two and a half hours before game time. "At 7:30 streets for blocks around were teeming with motor cars, pedestrians and streetcars," the *Mail and Empire* reported. "Outside the arena, the streets were packed with slowly moving throngs of hockey fans. The brightly lighted walls of the huge building reflected a glow which made Carlton Street like day."

The Gardens sat 12,473, and every seat was occupied. Another thousand fans had purchased standing-room tickets. The workers who had built the Gardens were there that night. The ice-level boxes were filled with women in evening gowns and white gloves, men in suits, tuxes and, according to the *Mail*, "enough silk high-hats to do all the weddings from now until the end of next June."

As the opening ceremonies began, the players stood side by side along their respective blue lines. The marching bands of the 48th Highlanders and the Royal Grenadiers assembled on the ice and played "Happy Days Are Here Again." A group of dignitaries, including Frank Calder, Ontario premier George S. Henry and Mayor W.J. Stewart, assembled before a microphone.

Gardens president Jack Bickell delivered what one reporter described as "an after-dinner speech." Restless fans heckled and jeered, and when Bickell paused momentarily, a lone spectator bellowed: "Play hockey. Quit talking." The premier got the message and kept his remarks to a bare minimum, and the mayor earned a hearty ovation when he said: "You came to see a hockey game, not to hear speeches. Let's go!"

One thing spoiled Toronto's party that evening: the game itself. It was, according to MacQueen's report, "nothing beyond an opening fixture and the showing of the locals was a great disappointment." They lost two-one.

THAT FALL, DICK IRVIN WAS sitting at home in Regina and trying to sort out his future. He had coached the Black Hawks the previous winter and they had advanced to the Stanley Cup final against long odds and then surprised everyone by pushing the powerful and superior Montreal Canadiens to a fifth and deciding game. They may well have won except that several of Irvin's best players succumbed to the temptations of Montreal's racy nightlife and awoke on the morning of the crucial contest with excruciating hangovers.

It proved to be a costly misstep, not for the wayward athletes but for Irvin, a teetotaller and non-smoker. He was packing his bags early in November 1931, preparing to leave for training camp, when a delivery boy arrived at his door bearing a telegram. It was from Major Frederic McLaughlin, the owner and, up until that moment, his employer. The message was short and curt. His services were no longer required.

Irvin was thirty-nine. His hockey career had spanned ten pro seasons as a player with the Regina Capitals, Portland Rosebuds and the Hawks and a single season behind the Chicago bench, and now—he was certain—it was over. He would likely go back to the meat business—not as a butcher, like his father James, but as a salesman travelling from one dreary Prairie town to another along dusty and rutted gravel roads. Then, on November 25, Conn Smythe called and got right to the point.

"Do you want to coach the Toronto Maple Leafs?" he asked.

"What's wrong with the Leafs?" Irvin inquired.

"There's nothing wrong with the Maple Leafs," Smythe barked. "They need a new coach."

The Leafs were winless in five starts and languishing at the bottom of the Canadian Division. Art Duncan was the architect of this dismal record, and Smythe had fired him moments before calling Irvin.

Irvin asked for a day to consider the offer since his wife, Bertha, was expecting their first child in the spring.

"I'll call you back in twenty minutes," the Leafs boss replied, and he did.

Irvin accepted and the next day boarded a train bound for Toronto. He took his place back of the Leaf bench for the first time on November 30. The New York Americans were visiting, and the game ended in a three-three tie. Irvin quickly surmised that the team was young, fast and enthusiastic, but out of shape. He corrected that problem in a hurry, and the Leafs began to climb in the standings. They finished a close second to the Canadiens in their division and third overall. They eliminated the Hawks and Maroons and lined up against the Rangers in the final. Game one was played at Madison Square Garden before sixteen thousand fans, who maintained "a steady uproar," according to a newspaper account. The game itself was "a rugged, rough, sensational hockey battle" and the Leafs won six-four.

The circus bumped the Rangers out of their building, and they chose to play their second home game in Boston. The Leafs prevailed again and the teams headed north for game three. By then, Irvin's acumen was widely admired, as a *Globe* sportswriter observed: "The Leafs under his careful, calculating eye, his shrewd system of training and his cheerful banter, have developed into the outstanding team in the NHL."

Irvin's youthful charges could taste victory, and so could the citizens of Toronto. Thousands lined up outside the Gardens box office, hoping to buy tickets for game three, and the *Globe* captured the mood of the city and Leafs supporters elsewhere in a front-page headline:

FOURTEEN THOUSAND INSIDE
MAPLE LEAF GARDENS
AND MILLIONS OUTSIDE
READY TO WHOOP FOR JOY
IF LEAFS DOWN RANGERS TONIGHT

The Leafs grabbed a quick lead and never surrendered it. The Rangers scored three times late in the third, but the Leafs cruised to a six-four win and the city's first Stanley Cup championship in ten years. The entire crowd—14,366 frenzied fans—stood and cheered as time wound down. The final buzzer sounded and they unleashed a deluge of programs and other paper projectiles.

Inexplicably, the Stanley Cup was sitting in the league offices in Montreal. Gardens officials hastily set up a microphone near the penalty box and connected it to the public address and radio transmission systems. Irvin, Smythe and captain Hap Day spoke briefly, but the crowd wanted King Clancy. He happily obliged, and the fans roared when he said hello to his mother back in Ottawa.

THE LEAFS' STANLEY CUP TRIUMPH was a rousing and happy occasion for a city and a country worn down by a winter of tough times and discouraging news. Wall Street stocks had sunk to their lowest levels since the fall of 1929. Wheat was selling for ten cents a bushel. Drought and low prices had obliterated farm incomes. Premier John Brownlee of Alberta was proposing work camps for the hordes of jobless, single men.

And in Toronto: "Distress has been acute in thousands of homes this winter," the *Globe* noted on Monday, April 11, 1932, the same edition that celebrated the Leaf championship. Fourteen thousand families were receiving relief from the House of Industry, a century-old charity funded jointly by churches and the city. The House was serving 1,500 meals a day and providing beds for 250 desperate souls and 150 impoverished old people.

The NHL was hurting in a big way as well. The league held its 1932 annual meeting in New York on May 10 and, as usual, Frank Calder presented the governors with a report on attendance. The total for all eight teams, excluding playoffs, was 1,672,702, down 105,615 from 1930–31, and nobody expected an improvement in the short term. The only alternative was to cut costs.

Rosters were trimmed to fourteen players from sixteen, team payrolls were capped at $70,000 and individual salaries were limited to $7,500, whereas some of the top players had been making as much as $11,000. As well, the governors instructed Calder to negotiate the best possible rates with the hotels where the visiting teams stayed.

Meantime, another problem was lurking in the background. The Detroit franchise had been pushed into receivership, which came as no surprise. Detroit had been one of the weaker U.S. expansion teams. In six seasons (1926–27 through 1931–32), the club had achieved one winning record and made the playoffs twice, losing in the first round both times. During those difficult years, the organization had had two coaches. The first, Art Duncan, lasted a season and quit to resume his playing career. The second was Jack Adams.

Adams had arrived in the fall of 1927. Until then, he had been a hockey nomad—moving from team to team for the next opportunity or contract. A native of Fort William, Ontario, Adams played senior for the hometown Maple Leafs in 1914–15. He signed on with senior teams in Calumet, Michigan, Peterborough, Ontario, and Sarnia, Ontario, before turning pro with the Toronto Arenas midway through the NHL's inaugural season of 1917–18. He made eight hundred dollars that winter and helped the Arenas to a Stanley Cup victory.

A sportswriter once described the youthful Adams as "a bobcat on skates," and every account of his early playing days includes the tale of the night he wound up in hospital, postgame, his face blood-spattered and badly in need of repairs. He lay on a gurney. A kindly nurse mopped up wounds over one eye, down one cheek and under his chin. Adams was oblivious until the young lady gasped. He looked up. It was his sister Alma. His face was so carved up she hadn't recognized him.

"Jack," she admonished, "hockey will kill you if you don't quit."

Depending on who's telling the story, this happened either during his brief stint with Calumet or when he was with the Arenas. In any event, Adams didn't quit. He played another season in Toronto, three with the Vancouver Millionaires of the Pacific Coast Hockey Association, four with the Toronto St. Pats and finished up with the 1926–27 Cup-winning Ottawa Senators.

Afterward, Adams told Calder he'd like to try coaching, and the president recommended him to Charlie Hughes in Detroit. "He is a very smart, young fellow," Calder said. "He knows the game. He'd like to continue in hockey and I think he'll make a real good coach."

The Cougars improved in each of Adams's first two seasons, but it was an uphill battle. He reported to Hughes, but was employed by a syndicate of investors who were reluctant to spend the money required to produce a winner. Local fans didn't understand the game, so Adams wrote an instructional column called "Following the Puck." It appeared weekly in the *Detroit Times*. The fans who did know hockey lived across the river in Windsor. Unfortunately, they turned out in force when a Canadian team visited the Olympia and vociferously booed the Cougars.

There was worse to come. Automotive production, the backbone of Detroit's economy, plummeted in the first three years of the Depression. Row upon row of empty seats became the norm at Cougar games. A *Times* reporter, Edgar Hayes, later recalled seeing Adams going door to door in downtown Detroit, trying, without success, to peddle tickets to merchants and shoppers.

The city's three daily newspapers decided in the fall of 1930 that a name change might reverse the team's fortunes. They called for suggestions. There were some two thousand responses. The most popular choice—suggested by ninety-two readers—was Falcons. The team bought it, competed as the Falcons and wound up fourth in the division—same as the year before. Attendance was so poor that Adams one night admitted a fan in exchange for five pounds of potatoes.

Under the circumstances, the organization couldn't meet its financial obligations. The investors behind the Olympia and the hockey team had issued $800,000 worth of bonds to acquire the franchise and build the arena. By the summer of 1931, the syndicate had defaulted to the tune of $21,450 on payments to the bondholders. They owed the City of Detroit $47,069.18 in back taxes. And they were in default by $100,000 on another fund.

In July, a bondholders' committee took control of the Olympia and the Falcons. They ran both—on a proverbial shoestring—during the 1931–32 season. "Things are so bad around here that I'm having to put up my own money sometimes to meet payroll," Adams lamented at one point. "We've been riding day coaches all season on the road and eating sandwiches, candy bars and oranges when we can't afford to buy them from the hawkers. I hope we don't break any more sticks because we're at a point where we just can't afford to buy new ones."

Remarkably, the Falcons improved their points total, climbed to third in the American Division and made the playoffs, but lost to the Montreal Maroons. It did nothing for the bottom line. The organization defaulted on a mortgage held by the Union Guardian Trust Company, and on April 28, 1932, Union Guardian foreclosed. Hughes resigned as governor and was replaced by Arthur Pfleiderer, a young banker who represented the creditors.

The talk was that the Falcons would fold, and Adams had a whole summer to fret about the future. However, the creditors didn't pull the plug. Adams was back at his desk in September and was hugely surprised one morning when the young woman who operated the Olympia switchboard had good news for him.

"There's a long-distance call for you from Chicago," she said. "The new owner wants to talk to you."

"New owner?" Adams replied skeptically. "Who?"

"Mr. James Norris, the grain millionaire."

JAMES NORRIS WAS A BIG, Canadian-born, hockey-loving man and a tough, shrewd, ambitious player in the world of trade and commerce. "Norris was everything a Hollywood director would select as a typical tycoon of Big Business," Elmer Ferguson wrote some years later in the *Montreal Herald*. "He was square-built, with a solid chin, a gruff voice, and a strong rugged face, a man of determined ideas and with the personality and wherewithal to enforce these."

He was born in 1879, and was therefore fifty-three when he plucked the Detroit franchise from the shoals of bankruptcy. Norris was a native of Montreal and came from an accomplished family. His grandfather—a ship's captain and businessman—had served as mayor of St. Catharines, Ontario, and represented the city in Parliament. His father, also called James, was a partner in a grain-trading company, Norris and Carruthers.

The young Norris attended Montreal Collegiate Institute, and then enrolled at McGill University. He excelled at tennis, squash and hockey and was good enough at the latter to play three games in the winter of 1898 with the Winged Wheelers, an elite senior team that represented the Montreal Amateur Athletic Association. Their crest was a wheel, flanked by two upright wings, and they had twice won the Stanley Cup, in 1893 and 1894.

Norris may have been an avid amateur athlete, but business was his calling. And he started from scratch. His father's company went broke at some point, leaving behind a pile of debts. Norris paid off the creditors, then departed for Chicago—home to North America's biggest and most important market for agricultural commodities—and went to work as a floor trader.

By the time he acquired the Detroit Falcons, Norris was known around Chicago as Big Jim—a reflection of his physical dimensions, his persona and his standing in the grain trade. He stood six foot two and weighed 225 pounds and had built a mighty business empire. He not only bought and sold grain, he owned terminals where the stuff was stored and a fleet of Great Lakes freighters—said to number forty vessels—that hauled it from place to place. He had acquired several enormous cattle ranches in the American West, and, at different points in his career, served as a director of the First National Bank of Chicago, the Rock Island and Pacific Railroad and the West Indies Sugar Corporation.

But for all that, he never lost his youthful passion for hockey, which he regarded as the king of sports. Each winter, according to the Norris legend, he had a rink built behind the family home in Lake Forest, a suburban community north of Chicago. He would lace up his skates, pick up his stick and play shinny with the chauffeur, the butler, the gardener, the handyman and other members of the household staff, all of whom had to demonstrate to Norris's satisfaction that they knew how to skate and handle a puck in order to be hired.

The occasional game of backyard shinny was not enough to satisfy Norris's towering ambitions. He had backed Paddy Harmon's bid for the franchise that eventually wound up in the hands of Frederic McLaughlin. He put some $600,000 into the construction of Chicago Stadium and tried to land a second

NHL team for the city, but McLaughlin refused to surrender his territorial rights. His path blocked, Norris simply started his own professional team, the Chicago Shamrocks, who joined the American Hockey Association in 1930–31.

The AHA was then challenging the NHL's claim to be hockey's sole major league. The association's upstart board refused to sign an affiliation agreement confirming the NHL's superior status and giving it the right to draft players from AHA clubs. On the contrary, American League teams were poaching talent from the NHL, and the 1931 champion Tulsa Oilers issued a challenge for the Stanley Cup, which the Montreal Canadiens had won.

Cup trustee William Foran of Ottawa turned down Tulsa only because the season was too advanced to hold a playoff. Thus, in December 1931, William Grant of the Duluth Hornets submitted a challenge on behalf of the association. Foran approved it and informed Calder. The NHL president refused to discuss the issue and declared that the league would forfeit the trophy rather than participate in such a series.

Shaky finances ultimately undermined the aspirations of the AHA. The Minneapolis Millers had folded prior to the 1931–32 season. The Buffalo Majors dropped out in January 1932. Others teams were struggling to meet their payrolls, according to newspaper reports. The Stanley Cup challenge series did not take place and Norris, one of the league's major backers, headed for the exit that spring.

He applied to the NHL for a St. Louis franchise. The board said no because of travel costs, but offered him the bankrupt Detroit Falcons on one condition: the Chicago Shamrocks had to cease operations. Norris agreed, and in so doing, dealt a final blow to the AHA's grand ambitions. In August 1932, the association signed an affiliation agreement with the NHL. The trustees of the Falcons eagerly unloaded the money-losing franchise and the Olympia, reportedly for a rock-bottom $100,000, and Norris finally had a foothold in big-time hockey.

THE NEW OWNER QUICKLY PUT his imprint on the organization. There was a name change, which was announced October 5, 1932, at the tail end of a story in the *Detroit Times*. "The Falcons will be garbed in new livery and will not be the Falcons," the paper reported. "They will wear all-red uniforms and will be called Red Wings."

Norris may have borrowed that lyrical name from a minor-league baseball team called the Red Wings, but he reached into his own past for the crest. He took the winged wheel of the Montreal Amateur Athletic Association, adjusted the position of the wings and redesigned the wheel to resemble that of an automobile tire—an appropriate symbol for a team from Motor City, U.S.A.

Norris gave Jack Adams his marching orders in one brief conversation. Adams was told he could coach the Red Wings for the coming season. If the team didn't improve, he'd be gone. The two men concluded the discussion with a smile and a handshake—no contract. But Norris did give Adams some material to work with—namely most of the former Chicago Shamrocks. Training camp opened October 15 and there were twenty-six players on hand to compete for fourteen spots.

As it turned out, Adams survived his probationary season with flying colours. The Red Wings earned a franchise-record fifty-eight points. They tied Boston for first overall. They eliminated the Maroons—the club's first playoff victory—and then met the Rangers in a two-game, total-goal series. The teams squared off first at Madison Square Garden, and then moved to Detroit. A crowd estimated at fifty thousand converged on the Olympia. Those lucky enough to get tickets witnessed a close, hard-fought contest that kept them on the edges of their seats all night.

The Red Wings lost, but they had for the first time captured the hearts of the populace and lifted their Depression-weary spirits. Equally important, Norris and Adams had forged the first bonds of a partnership that would endure until the owner's death two decades later. They had also begun a transformation. The franchise had been a dubious proposition. It would become a powerhouse—a consistent regular-season winner, an occasional Stanley Cup champion and a success at the box office.

THE 1933–34 SEASON OPENED QUIETLY on November 9 and proceeded without unpleasant incidents or nasty surprises until December 12 and game 55 of a 384-game schedule. It was a Tuesday evening, Leafs against Bruins at Boston Garden. The Leafs had dominated the first month. They had won eight, lost three and tied one and had outscored their opponents thirty-eight to fifteen. The Bruins were a middle-of-the-pack team with six wins and five losses.

The Leafs won game fifty-five, though the victory nearly cost one man his life. As the Associated Press reported: "Eddie Shore started the rumpus by tripping Ace Bailey with such force that he [Bailey] was rendered unconscious. Red Horner, Toronto defenceman, then rushed at Shore and knocked him down with a heavy right hook to the jaw. Shore's head struck the ice with such terrific force that he suffered a three-inch gash that required seven stitches."

Teammates carried the unconscious Bailey and a stunned Shore off the ice. The AP went on to report: "Fiery Conn Smythe, manager of the Leafs, became involved with several spectators when he tried to hasten to the side of his injured player. During a scuffle outside the Toronto dressing room, Leonard Kenworthy of Everett, suffered a blow over the eye that shattered his spectacles. Three stitches were needed to close the cut and . . . he told Boston Garden officials that he would apply for a warrant charging Smythe with assault."

The rumpus, as the Associated Press called it, occurred early in the second. The Leafs were two men short. Shore led a rush into the Toronto end. Horner rode him hard into the end boards. Shore went down. Leafs cleared the puck. The Bruins retreated. Shore was the last man back and collided with Bailey near the Leaf blue line.

The first reports out of Boston stated that Bailey's condition was serious but not dangerous and that, an hour after being admitted to Audubon Hospital, he was resting comfortably. The story landed on the front pages of the Toronto newspapers and stayed there for a week, each new twist and development pressed into grim headlines—this one from the December 14 *Mail and Empire*:

BAILEY'S LIFE HANGS IN THE BALANCE

The paper reported that the thirty-one-year-old right winger had suffered a five-inch fracture to the right side of his forehead when he struck the ice. His condition had steadily deteriorated in the first twenty-four hours. Doctors determined that he was hemorrhaging. Pressure was building in his skull. A surgeon punctured Bailey's spine at the base of the skull to drain the fluid and relieve the swelling.

Bailey's wife, Gladys, arrived Thursday morning with their three-year-old daughter, Joanne. Her husband was transferred to City Hospital and she consented to surgery. At 3:30 p.m., he was wheeled into an operating room. A renowned neurosurgeon, Dr. Donald Munro, worked on him for four hours—removing bone fragments and a blood clot said to be the size of a silver dollar. At 1:30 a.m. Friday—December 15—the hospital released a statement that described Bailey's condition as "Fair, but still on the critical list."

That's all the next morning's papers could tell their readers, but the public wanted more. Maple Leaf Gardens switchboard operators fielded two calls per minute, on average, all day from people inquiring about Bailey. The *Mail* received seven hundred phone calls between 7 p.m. and midnight, and Bell Telephone reported that forty Toronto-Boston calls had been placed that day.

Bailey seemed to falter late Friday afternoon. At 6 p.m., Smythe, who had remained at his player's side, phoned Frank Selke and told him it looked like the beginning of the end. But the patient held on and the Saturday *Mail* reported:

BAILEY WAGES
GRIM BATTLE
DURING NIGHT

At noon Sunday, Bailey was back on the operating table. Dr. Munro had diagnosed a serious injury to the left side of the brain. The surgeon worked for two hours to relieve the pressure caused by more hemorrhaging. But Bailey's condition remained precarious for the next forty-eight hours and the Tuesday *Mail* told readers:

"ACE" BAILEY SINKING;
CANNOT LAST LONG, DOCTOR REPORTS

That was the final frightening turn in the drama. By Thursday, December 21, doctors announced that he was out of danger and likely to recover. His hockey career was over, though. Bailey, a native of Bracebridge, Ontario, had broken in with the Toronto St. Pats in the fall of 1926. He was a slight man in a rough-and-tumble sport, standing five foot ten and weighing 160 pounds. But he was a gifted offensive player and had won the scoring title in 1928–29.

The man who caused his devastating injury was one of the most ferocious who ever played the game. Shore was a square-jawed, cold-eyed defenceman who stood five foot eleven and weighed 190 pounds. A native of Fort Qu'Appelle, Saskatchewan, he had honed his skills in the western pro leagues before joining the Bruins in 1926–27. Shore was a reckless, punishing, crash-and-bang player and was wildly popular with Boston's rabid, make-'em-pay fans. He was a big gate attraction in other cities as well.

Given his approach to the game, he may have done more damage to himself than his opponents. In a career that lasted fourteen seasons, he endured an astonishing array of injuries: a broken hip; broken collarbone; and a cracked and displaced vertebra. He fractured his jaw five times, his nose on at least ten occasions and had lost most of his teeth. He took hundreds of stitches and once watched with a hand-held mirror as a doctor reattached his nearly severed ear.

After the Bailey incident, Shore went into seclusion in his Boston apartment. The city's newspapers reported that he was morose and genuinely remorseful, and public opinion shifted from condemnation to sympathy. He insisted he had never deliberately injured anyone and certainly had not intended to hurt Bailey. He told the same story to police interrogators, who let it be known he might face a manslaughter charge if Bailey died.

He said he had been dazed by Horner's crushing check into the end boards. He had fallen to the ice, sprung to his feet and instinctively raced toward his own end. He figured he was travelling twenty-two miles per hour, head down and oblivious, when he crashed into the unsuspecting Bailey. In an interview several days afterward, he told a Boston reporter: "I went to the dressing room to see Bailey. He was conscious. I said: 'Ace, I'm sorry this happened. I hope you're not badly injured. I assure you it was not intentional.' He replied: 'That's alright, Eddie. It's all in the game.'"

Nevertheless, such a deed could not go unpunished. In early January, the league issued a sixteen-game suspension. (Horner got six for that blow to Shore's jaw.) Bruins fans weren't happy with that. The *Boston Transcript* sent several members of the sports department out to canvass public opinion. The paper quoted a stock-and-bond executive who said, "Contrasted with the suspension received by Horner, I believe Shore was not treated in a just manner." A twenty-seven-year-old office worker added, "I believe [the] suspension of Shore has been too severe."

Opinion ran the other way in Toronto. "We think he should have at least got the season," wrote *Mail* sports editor Edwin Allan. ". . . To us the leniency of the suspension can be attributed to dollars and cents. The Bruins are not drawing without Shore, either at home or abroad, and the result is poorer gates than usual."

Smythe wanted more as well. He asked for a special meeting of the board to discuss the issue. It was held January 24. His fellow governors refused to extend Shore's suspension, but would do something to assist Bailey and help cover his medical expenses. Each team would loan the league two or three of its top players for one night. They would form an all-star team and play the Leafs in a Bailey benefit game.

It was held February 14. A crowd of 14,074 attended and produced a gate of $20,910. For most, the pre-game ceremony was the highlight of the evening. Bailey stood at centre ice with Smythe, Foster Hewitt and several other prominent personalities. Hewitt called the players one by one, and Bailey presented windbreakers to the All-Stars and commemorative medals to the Leafs.

Hewitt called Eddie Shore's name and the Boston defenceman came forward. He and Bailey shook hands and people began to stand and applaud. The applause rose to the level of a deafening din and the two players smiled and exchanged words and posed for a battery of newspaper photographers, and then Shore rejoined the All-Stars along their blue line. Only then did the cheering begin to subside. "In that one moment," the *Mail*'s C.W. MacQueen wrote, "Toronto's reputation as being one of the fairest-minded sporting centres in the world was enhanced beyond description. Boston newspaper men who were present were dumbfounded."

BAILEY, WHOSE GIVEN NAME WAS Irvine, was well liked and the Leafs missed him, but they did not allow his absence to affect their performance. They finished first in the Canadian Division. Charlie Conacher won the scoring title and linemate Joe Primeau was second. But the Leafs faltered in the postseason—their perennial problem during the 1930s. They lost to the Red Wings, winners of the American Division. The Black Hawks, who had come a respectable second to Detroit, eliminated the Canadiens and then the Maroons to set up an all-American final.

The series opened in Detroit, where the Hawks hadn't won in four seasons, but they stunned the Wings and their fans. They took both games and were a win away from their first Stanley Cup championship when the series shifted to Chicago. Close to eighteen thousand ready-to-roar fans packed the Stadium, but they spent most of the evening watching tensely, uncertain which way things would go.

Late in the second, the teams were tied at two. There was a scramble around the Wings' net. Goaltender Wilf Cude was struck hard across the face by an errant stick and knocked senseless. He was taken off for repairs, but returned and played the third with his right cheek puffed up and his eye blackened and nearly closed. Yet he held off one furious Chicago attack after another until his teammates broke through the Hawks' smothering defence and scored three times in the final six minutes.

Game four featured brilliant goaltending at both ends. Cude and his Chicago counterpart, Charlie Gardiner, stopped everything fired at them through regulation time and thirty minutes of overtime before right winger Mush Marsh snapped a low, hard shot from the faceoff circle. Cude threw out his foot. He got a piece of the puck, but not enough to stop it. The red light flashed behind him and the Hawks and their fans erupted. As the *Detroit News* reported: "Players who had scarcely been able to skate danced the length of the ice. Louis Napoleon Trudel, the young Frenchman who plays left wing on the Hawks' third line, grabbed the Stanley Cup as soon as it was brought on the ice for the presentation and skated wildly around the rink."

NEWSPAPER ACCOUNTS OF THAT FINAL CONTEST make no mention of James Norris. In all likelihood, he was there and was not pleased with the result. He adored his Wings and hated to see them lose. He would wait two years, until April 1936, before celebrating his first Stanley Cup championship. In the meantime, though, he would enjoy a significant victory of a different sort: he would win control of Chicago Stadium.

The Stadium was the largest indoor amphitheatre in North America. It was conceived amid the reckless euphoria of the Roaring Twenties and completed some six months before the stock market crash of October 1929 and the onset of the Great Depression. It had cost close to $7 million. The promoter Paddy Harmon put up some of his own money, and the company he formed to build the Stadium issued common and preferred shares as well as bonds to cover the balance. Two hundred and twenty wealthy and prominent Chicago business-men, including Frederic McLaughlin, had purchased these securities. Most never saw their money again.

The building had played host to boxing matches, bicycle races and Black Hawk games, among other things. Attendance fell sharply across the board in the early 1930s. The average gate receipts at Hawk games, for example, slipped from $13,800 in 1930–31 to $10,208 the following season and $5,656 in 1932–33. The Stadium corporation was unable to pay its taxes or make the interest pay-ments on the bonds, and finally, on January 20, 1933, an out-of-patience (and out-of-pocket) creditor named Charles E. Perry sued and the World's Greatest Sports Arena—as *Popular Mechanics* magazine had called it—was in receiver-ship. It remained under the control of a receiver for over two years.

On August 22, 1934, a Norris-backed syndicate submitted a rescue plan to the U.S. District Court in Chicago. Norris's partners included his son James Jr. and a business associate named Arthur Wirtz. Wirtz was thirty-three. He was born in Chicago in 1901, the son of a police officer, and he graduated from the University of Michigan in 1922. He began his career as a real estate broker who leased commercial properties. In 1927, he formed his own firm and two years later met Norris when the latter purchased a piece of land through Wirtz's company. Norris was impressed with the young man's knowledge and exper-tise, and the two formed a partnership. With the onset of the Depression, they began buying financially distressed companies at deeply discounted prices.

They acquired the Detroit Olympia and the Red Wings under such circum-stances and for a sum Norris would later describe as "loose change." Likewise, they picked up Chicago Stadium for pennies on the dollar. A bondholders' com-mittee accepted their rescue plan, and in November 1934, District Court Judge

James H. Wilkinson allowed the Norris group to begin managing the building, pending final approval of the offer, which he granted on February 26, 1935.

"Under the plan," the *Chicago Tribune* reported, "Norris and his son and Wirtz must put up $300,000, of which $150,000 will be used to pay off back taxes, $50,000 will be expended for reorganization expenses and the balance will be used as an operating fund."

First-mortgage bonds worth $1.7 million would be converted to second-mortgage bonds of equal value, but those who had purchased shares were left out in the cold. "No provision was made for the owners of the stock," the *Tribune* noted. "About $2,000,000 in common and preferred stock was issued by the old company. . . . The stock now apparently is worthless."

THE 1934–35 SEASON SHOULD HAVE BEEN a celebration for the Montreal Canadiens and their devout, demanding and boisterous fans. "It's the silver jubilee—silver, but built on a golden trail," Elmer Ferguson wrote. "Canadiens are, as everybody knows, the oldest team in the world playing professional hockey. Many teams have sprung up and declined, leagues have tottered, clubs have quit in mid-season, but Canadiens have ALWAYS carried on. Despite fires, wars and flood, they have never missed a game."

They were one of founding franchises of the NHL and had appeared in seven Stanley Cup final series, winning four times, including back-to-back championships in 1930 and 1931. But present difficulties overshadowed past accomplishments. The Canadiens had finished third in their division in each of the three seasons since their last Cup and each time had lost in the first round of the playoffs. Managing director Leo Dandurand decided to rebuild and began with a hard-headed business decision that shocked the players and the fans: he traded Howie Morenz to Chicago.

Morenz had been the heart of the Canadiens for a decade. He was twice a scoring champion and three times the winner of the Hart Trophy. He was the most exciting player in hockey. He was fast. He could hit and take a hit. He forechecked and backchecked. He could rattle a goaltender with his hard, heavy shot. He loved hockey. He loved the city of Montreal and Montrealers loved him.

Morenz could not be replaced, but Dandurand hoped a new leader would emerge from among the players he secured from Chicago and the young recruits he had brought in from elsewhere. It didn't happen. The Canadiens struggled all season. The fans were unhappy. Attendance dwindled. The newspapers were harsh and unforgiving. Stress got the better of coach Newsy Lalonde—a retired player and the team's first great offensive star. He stepped aside in mid-season and Dandurand had to take over.

All the changes produced a familiar outcome—a third-place finish and a first-round loss in the playoffs. To make matters worse, English Montreal's team—the Maroons—won the Stanley Cup. Not long after this unhappy season ended, Dandurand and his partner, Joe Cattarinich, announced that the team was for sale. "We lost $20,000 last year and $40,000 this season," Cattarinich told a reporter. "We like to be loyal, but we can't afford to go on losing at that rate."

Dandurand and Cattarinich negotiated with at least two potential buyers in the summer of 1935. The first was a Cleveland businessman named Al Sutphin. He offered $200,000 for the Canadiens and planned to move the team to Cleveland to play out of a newly built arena there. That prospect caused alarm among French-speaking Montrealers, particularly the blue-collar, working-class men of the city's poorer districts, who were the most ardent fans. Fortunately, three French-speaking Montreal businessmen were equally devoted to the Canadiens. Ernest Savard, Major Maurice Forget and Louis Gélinas made an offer of $150,000. Dandurand and Cattarinich settled for $165,000, and the deal was announced in mid-September.

At that moment, Montreal's two NHL franchises appeared to be solid propositions. However, there were occasional murmurs and utterances to the contrary in the city's newspapers. Skeptical observers noted that the combined attendance of the Canadiens and the Maroons barely matched the crowds supporting one team in Toronto and some of the U.S. venues. Yet each Montreal club had to bear the same operating costs as their opponents. For the time being, though, all doubts were swept aside by the Canadiens' change of ownership, by the Maroons' Stanley Cup championship and by more pressing concerns elsewhere. Big Bill Dwyer was in trouble with various U.S. authorities and the league had to step in and rescue his New York Americans.

PROHIBITION HAD ENDED IN 1933, and Dwyer's problems had begun in earnest in 1934. The Internal Revenue Service charged that he owed the government $4.25 million in back taxes on income earned over a twelve-year period. Dwyer was, understandably, preoccupied with the charges against him, and legal fees were quickly consuming the remains of his once-substantial fortune. Meantime, his Americans were also strapped for money. They had always been the weaker of the NHL's two New York franchises—never as strong as the Rangers, never as big a draw. But Dwyer had been there in times of need to make up any cash shortfalls. That wasn't the case during the 1934–35 season. Several times, the Americans couldn't meet their payroll.

Merv Dutton, one of the players, kept the team afloat. Dutton, known to everyone as Red, was a resourceful young man who had begun his pro career with the Calgary Tigers of the Western Hockey League and had joined the Maroons after the WHL folded. He was traded to the Americans in the fall of 1930 and had been a steady performer on a perennially weak team. During the winter of 1934–35, he was called upon to play the role of team banker as well. He drew upon savings accumulated through the Calgary construction company he and a brother owned and he loaned his teammates about $4,000. By the end of the season, all he had to show for it was a batch of bad cheques from Dwyer.

Over the summer, Dwyer made Dutton playing coach for the 1935–36 season. They agreed to hold training camp in Oshawa, Ontario. But come October, Dwyer was broke and couldn't afford to send the players travel money. Dutton went to Montreal to confer with Marty Shenker, who was managing a Dwyer-owned racetrack in the city. Shenker didn't have the funds, either, but one night summoned Dutton to his hotel room. He'd won a big pot in a crap game. Shenker tossed $4,300 onto the bed. Dutton scooped up $4,000 and dashed to the nearest telegraph office and wired travel money to each of his teammates.

Meantime, Dwyer's troubles continued to mount. During the 1935–36 season, the government won a judgment of $3,715,907 against him. But despite all the turmoil, his Americans enjoyed their best season in several years. Left winger David Schriner, who went by the nickname Sweeney, won the scoring title. The team made the playoffs for the first time since the spring of 1929. They beat the Black Hawks in the opening round, and then lost to the Leafs in the second.

But given the owner's problems, the players had not been paid in full and some had bonuses owing. At the league's annual general meeting on May 7, 1936, the board agreed to pay the players and take over their contracts as security, meaning that they now belonged to the league, not Dwyer.

By the fall, new problems had arisen. Dwyer was behind on his dues to the NHL. There were growing doubts as to whether the Americans would be able to operate for the coming season. Three meetings were held to deal with the crisis. Their patience exhausted, the governors revoked Dwyer's franchise, but agreed to keep the team afloat and leave Dutton in charge. The board incorporated a new company, the American National Hockey Club, Inc., to serve as nominal owner of the club and the player contracts.

Dwyer protested vigorously. He sued, and the NHL dispatched Conn Smythe and Art Ross to negotiate a settlement. They reached a deal that would allow Dwyer back in, provided he met certain obligations by April 15, 1937. Among other things, he could purchase the stock of the American National Hockey Club for $130,000, put up $20,000 against the cost of operating the Americans in 1936–37 and pay off another $20,000 he owed the league. And he must drop all litigation against the NHL.

Meantime, Dutton was trying to recover money he'd loaned Dwyer directly—some $20,000. His lawyer advised him to sue. Before filing suit, Dutton met Dwyer at Madison Square Garden, and he was stunned by what happened. The former king of the bootleggers broke down and cried. "Don't do that, Red," he pleaded. "My hockey club's the only legitimate thing I've had in my life . . . Red, I want my hockey club."

He had no hope of repaying Dutton or meeting the terms of his agreement with the NHL. The April 15 deadline came and went, and the league simply moved on—as owner and operator of the New York Americans.

THE MONTREAL MAROONS WERE the next to go, but unlike Big Bill Dwyer, they exited quickly and quietly after fourteen seasons, eleven playoff appearances and two Stanley Cup championships. They played their final game, at home, on March 17, 1938, and lost, as they had mostly done that winter. Afterward, the players stripped off their gear and a team official made his way around the room, handing out paper bags and issuing instructions: you can keep your sweaters, but leave your equipment. That wasn't quite the end. There were two league meetings to deal with the team's future—one in June, another in August—and the Maroons were history.

Quick and quiet had never been their style. At their best, the Maroons were a punishing physical force—sometimes leading the league in goals and penalty minutes simultaneously. They were known as the Big Red Team, the stalwart, straight-ahead standard-bearers of English Montreal. The Montreal Forum had been built for them. They took possession in the fall of 1924—their inaugural season—and two years later their one great rival, the fleet and flashy Canadiens, vacated the Mount Royal Arena and took up residence at the Forum as well.

By then, games between the city's two professional teams were more like armed combat than routine sporting events. Rowdiness and violence sometimes spread from the ice to the stands. Montrealers of French and English stock packed the Forum to watch their teams go at it. There were usually dozens of extra ushers on hand, as well as uniformed and plainclothes police officers to maintain control.

There were six such meetings per season initially, then eight, and these games came to be known as the Montreal professional hockey series. Each season, commencing in 1927, the winner was awarded the George Kennedy Memorial Cup, named in honour of the second owner of the Canadiens, who had guided the team for eleven years, through its infancy, its first championship and its entry to the NHL, before his untimely death in October 1921 at age thirty-eight.

The Canadiens laid claim to the Kennedy Cup in 1927 by dint of winning five of the season's intracity games. They also won it in 1937–38—the Maroons' final campaign. By then, the rivalry had shed most of its lustre. The Montreal teams were not the powerhouses they had once been. Attendance had been down for several winters. Both were losing money. It was evident that the city could not support two professional hockey clubs, and most of the speculation centred on the Maroons.

The team that was once the pride of English Montreal began its last season with an aging lineup that badly needed an overhaul. The owners were counting their losses and unwilling to spend on fresh talent. General manager Tommy

Gorman, who had coached the team for three seasons, had had enough and hired freshly retired King Clancy to take over behind the bench. It was a big mistake. Clancy had no experience and didn't have a coach's temperament. He was too easygoing and too friendly with the players. They rewarded him by winning six of their first eighteen games. As New Year's approached, the Maroons were in last place. Club president Senator Donat Raymond fired Clancy, and a reluctant Gorman stepped into the breach.

Gorman had always been a motivator rather than a technician, but he could not light a fire under this bunch. The losses mounted. A third-place finish and a playoff berth were out of reach by the end of January. The Maroons concluded the season against the Canadiens. A mere five thousand fans witnessed this final contest, and there were no fireworks on the ice or in the stands.

Off-season speculation had it that the Maroons might relocate to Cleveland or St. Louis, that they were for sale and that the asking price was $150,000. There were no deals in the works when the NHL board met in New York on June 21 and Gorman asked his fellow governors for permission to suspend operations for a year. They said no, and the franchise remained on life support until late August, when Calder scheduled a meeting to deal with the problem.

The Maroons had reached the end of the line and the *Gazette*'s Marc T. McNeil described it as "a drab finish to all the pulsing dramas of their fourteen seasons . . . struggle and sweat; triumph and defeat; achievement and disappointment; feuds and fights and friendships; the frenzied joy of two Stanley Cup conquests; the deep and utter humiliation of cellar occupancy; the memories of the once-flaming Maroon-Canadien rivalry."

AND SO THE NHL CONTRACTED AGAIN, just as the Depression was ending and the economies of Canada and the United States were starting to grow. The league opened the 1938–39 season with seven teams, all playing in the same division, and six would make the playoffs. Early on, the Bruins and Rangers broke from the pack and never looked back. Each of the also-rans had losing records, and they were—in descending order—Toronto, the Americans, Detroit, Montreal and Chicago. Art Ross's mighty Bruins were the class of the league. They won thirty-six games, lost ten, tied two and accumulated seventy-four points, sixteen better than the Rangers. "They were the best team I ever saw," Ross would later say. "That team had no weaknesses at all."

Up front, Boston had three strong, well-balanced lines. They could dominate their opponents even when the top two centres—Bill Cowley and Milt Schmidt—were out with injuries. Rookie Roy Conacher—younger brother of Lionel and Charlie—was the left winger on the third line. He led the league in goals with twenty-six. On defence, they had three veterans—Eddie Shore, Dit Clapper and Flash Hollett—and the rookie Johnny Crawford.

Two Bruin legends were created that season. The first was in goal. Cecil (Tiny) Thompson played five games at the outset. He was a ten-year veteran and had won the Vezina Trophy four times. But one month in, Ross sold Thompson to Detroit for $15,000 and a player and replaced him with an unheralded rookie named Frank Brimsek, a twenty-three-year-old native of Eveleth, Minnesota, then playing for a Bruins farm club.

The move caused an uproar in Boston. "The team took it pretty badly," Schmidt later recalled. "We just couldn't understand Mr. Ross replacing a sure thing with a rookie." Fans dashed off letters to the sports editors. One contended that Ross should have recruited in Canada, while another took a swipe at Brimsek's Slavic ancestry, writing, "Slavs don't have the temperament to be goalies."

Brimsek dispelled all doubts in a little over two weeks commencing December 4. On that evening, he blanked the Black Hawks in Chicago. Two nights later, he shut them out again, this time in Boston. On December 11, the young goalie held the Rangers scoreless at Madison Square Garden. He completed his remarkable streak by shutting out the Canadiens, Wings and Americans. The Rangers' Phil Watson finally put a puck past Brimsek on Christmas night before a raucous crowd of sixteen thousand at Boston Garden. By then, the newspapers had nicknamed him Mr. Zero, and in a postgame interview, Lester Patrick told the writers: "He's quick as a cat. Trying to get him to make the first move is like trying to push over the Washington Monument."

The second Bruin legend was created in the playoffs and was formed of more routine material. His name was Mel Hill. He was the right winger on the third line. Hill was twenty-four, a native of Glenboro, Manitoba, and had tallied ten goals in forty-four games. He added six more in Boston's twelve-game run to the Stanley Cup. Three of them made him famous. He scored the first in New York in game one of the semifinal against the Rangers at 1:10 in the morning and 19:25 of the third overtime period.

Nearly seventeen thousand boisterous fans packed Boston Garden for the second game. Again, sixty minutes of hard-fought hockey failed to settle things. And again, Hill was the hero. That evening, he sent the crowd home a mere 8:24 into overtime. Patrick's Rangers rebounded from those setbacks and pushed the series to seven games. In the seventh, they battled the Bruins to a standstill through three periods of regulation time, through the first overtime, through the second and nearly to the midway mark of the third before Hill tapped in a pass from Cowley. The Boston newspapers crowned their hero Sudden Death Hill, and he wore the name for the rest of his playing days and beyond.

The Bruins capped that glorious season by winning their first Stanley Cup in ten years. They routed the Leafs in five, and delirious fans stood for the dying minutes of the deciding game. They filled the Garden with a jubilant roar. They tossed firecrackers. They blew horns. They rang cowbells and hurled debris onto the ice. At the buzzer, the Bruins poured over the boards, raced to their goal and mobbed Mr. Zero, and then collected themselves and gathered around the table and the microphone that had been placed near the timekeeper's box at centre ice. Frank Calder presented the Stanley Cup to Boston's forty-year-old captain, Cooney Weiland, and uttered a few congratulatory words, but the big crowd drowned him out.

CANADA WENT TO WAR in the autumn of 1939. There was precious little actual fighting that fall—none of it involving Canadians—but the cataclysm long feared and steadfastly avoided had arrived. The loyal Dominion and its small population rushed to the side of the Mother Country, eager to defend freedom, democracy and human decency against the aggression and depredations of Nazi Germany. Newspapers filled their front pages, and many inside pages as well, with stories of every conceivable development. The government began to impose controls on the economic life of the nation. Prime Minister William Lyon Mackenzie King quickly authorized the formation of the First Canadian Division for overseas service—largely to appease the war lust of some members of his own party as well as the fiercely anglophile segments of the citizenry—and the first soldiers left for England in early December.

No individual or organization could remain indifferent or oblivious, though in many quarters it was business as usual. Schools, shops, factories and mills remained open. People still went to the movies. They listened to the World Series on radio. They looked forward to another hockey season, and the NHL would oblige. The board of governors had resolved at a special meeting held September 20, 1939, that the league would carry on. Training camps got underway in mid-October and the season itself on November 2, when the Red Wings visited Chicago.

For the third straight year, the Bruins finished first. They won thirty-one games and racked up sixty-seven points, down slightly from the stratospheric performance of 1938–39, and they owned the best forward line in hockey. Milt Schmidt, Woody Dumart and Bobby Bauer, three young men of German descent, all boyhood pals from Kitchener, Ontario, were known as the Kraut Line. They finished one-two-three in scoring.

But for all that firepower, the Rangers remained right on Boston's heels all winter. Lester Patrick had assembled the best team of his thirty-year career as a hockey executive. Frank Boucher, freshly retired after twelve seasons as the Rangers' top centre and one of the best in hockey, had been appointed coach. Davey Kerr, the goalkeeper, was strong, solidly built, agile, with an extraordinarily quick glove hand, and he outduelled Frank Brimsek for the Vezina Trophy. Art Coulter, the captain, was a tall, lean, tough defenceman from Winnipeg who played with Murray Patrick, Lester's younger son. Muzz, as he was known, was an awkward skater, but got by on natural athletic ability and had once been Canada's best amateur heavyweight.

Boucher had complete confidence in all his forward lines. Neil Colville of Edmonton was the number-one centre, brother Mac was his left wing, and another Winnipegger, Alex Shibicky, played the right side. Phil Watson, a fiery Montrealer of French-Canadian descent, centred the second line. Patrick's older son, Lynn, played left wing, and tough-as-a-bull Bryan Hextall patrolled right wing and led the league in scoring that season. Boucher used a combination of players on the third line—all good enough to add balance and depth. "It didn't matter which of the three I sent out," the coach would later say. "There was always the threat of a goal and they all played their positions, up and down, up and down."

The Rangers demonstrated their prowess early with a record-setting nineteen-game unbeaten streak (fourteen wins, five ties) that began on November 23 and ended in Chicago on January 13. After that defeat, they proceeded to win five in a row. They finished the season on a roll, losing only one of four games in March, and they eliminated the Bruins in the semifinal.

The Leafs advanced to the final for the seventh time since moving into Maple Leaf Gardens. A day before the opener, a cluster of sportswriters gathered round Lester Patrick in the Rangers dressing room. Who was going to take the series? someone asked. Patrick, always ready to play the ham, wrapped a towel around his head, pretended to gaze into a crystal ball and said, "The Rangers will win in six games because they are the better team."

He called it right, though his Rangers had to surmount some big challenges. They took the first two games at home then had to play the last four in Toronto because the circus had moved into Madison Square Garden. Three of their victories came in overtime. Shibicky fractured an ankle in the third game and missed the fourth. He was back in the lineup for the final two games with his injured limb heavily taped and frozen to the knee with injections of painkillers.

The triumphant Rangers returned to New York after the series. A smattering of loyal fans greeted them at Grand Central Terminal. Otherwise, the big city scarcely noticed. The indifference took some of the shine off the moment, but that club would grow in stature with the passage of time. "All in all it was a wonderful team," Boucher told the writer Trent Frayne many years later. "In fact, I'll say it now: it was the best hockey team I ever saw."

THE CANADIENS SAT OUT THE PLAYOFFS that spring. They finished on the road, on a Sunday evening—March 17—and the next morning's edition of *La Patrie* summed up the contest this way: "The Bruins of Boston, champions of the NHL, completed the regular season by beating the Canadiens seven-two. About eight thousand people were there [at Boston Garden] to witness the finale of the Montreal club, which has experienced its most disastrous season ever."

The Canadiens had won ten games, lost thirty-three and tied five. They finished a jaw-dropping forty-two points behind the Bruins. They played fifteen consecutive home games between December 16 and March 7 without a win. They finally snapped that streak on March 9, but there were only four thousand fans on hand, roughly half of them school kids admitted free of charge.

It had taken time for the Canadiens to sink so low. Their troubles had begun in 1934–35—the team's silver jubilee. Over the course of five seasons, there had been a change of ownership. Players and coaches had come and gone. Nothing worked. One manager had traded superstar Howie Morenz. Two years later, another traded to bring him back. Morenz provided a lift, but it was temporary and ended on the night in late January 1937 when he crashed into the end boards at the Forum and fractured his right leg in three places. Six weeks later, he died of a pulmonary embolism—having never left the hospital—and the entire city was shocked and grief-stricken.

Misfortune dogged the organization during that dismal stretch. In June 1939, the Canadiens hired a new coach, Albert (Babe) Siebert, a retired defenceman who had played fourteen seasons, but he never took his place behind the bench. Siebert drowned on August 25, 1939, in Lake Huron while attempting to retrieve a child's toy that had drifted away from shore.

Short of time and bereft of alternatives, manager Jules Dugal turned to Pit Lepine, who had spent his entire thirteen-year career with the Canadiens, mostly as the second centre behind the brilliant Morenz. The Canadiens put together a six-game unbeaten streak under Lepine to start the season. Then they collapsed, but the coach remained blithe and serene as the losses mounted and the team sank. Most nights, the crowds at the Forum were small and listless. Clusters of fans were scattered here and there amid whole rows and entire sections of empty seats.

The team was also a poor draw on the road, and as the disaster of 1939–40 neared its conclusion, the men who ran the NHL began to wonder: Are we going to lose the Canadiens next? Some even floated the idea that the league would be better off without them.

All such thoughts were laid to rest that spring. The Canadian Arena Company, which owned the Forum, purchased the Canadiens. Senator Donat Raymond, president of the company, took on the same role with the team.

Tommy Gorman, who was running the Forum day to day, became the manager. Dick Irvin—released by the Leafs after nine seasons—became the new coach.

Irvin and Gorman immediately launched a rebuild. Veterans would be moved out. Fresh young talent would be brought in. They would build around one player: the left winger Toe Blake. He had been the lone bright spot for the Canadiens during the dreadful years of the late 1930s. Blake was originally a Maroons prospect. He played nine games with them before being traded to the Canadiens. Blake became a regular in 1936–37, and two years later won the scoring championship and the Hart Trophy. He was dogged and relentless and went hard every time he was on the ice and was destined, because of these qualities, to be the next captain.

That summer, the Canadiens recruited three players from the West: defenceman Ken Reardon, centre Elmer Lach and winger Joe Benoit. They brought in John Quilty from Ottawa and acquired Murph Chamberlain from the Leafs and goaltender Bert Gardiner from the Rangers organization. "The NHL at large will be all eyes to see how the Canadiens youth experiment pans out," the *Gazette*'s Marc T. McNeil wrote in a preseason column, "mainly because the pro hockey situation in Montreal has had the league frankly worried for some time past. Practically every rival club is pulling for the Canadiens kids, not for any sentimental reasons, but because the other teams are vitally concerned in the Habitants welfare as an attractive outfit at home and abroad."

The youthful Canadiens started the season with a bang. They fought the still-mighty Bruins to a draw on home ice, and did it before a full house. "You had to be a pretty accomplished pusher to shove your way into the Forum a few minutes before game time last night," McNeil reported. "The SRO signs had been up for hours but those who had tickets and those who didn't . . . were all trying to get in together. And there in that happy, eager, anticipatory crowd you had a plain answer as to how this city feels about pro hockey."

The newly minted Canadiens drew 7,150 fans per night in their first fifteen home dates, up from 5,700 the previous season, and the total gate jumped to $104,841 from $81,068. They were still a long way from being world-beaters—or Stanley Cup champions. They won sixteen games in 1940–41, lost twenty-six and tied six. They finished sixth and made the playoffs, but lost to the Black Hawks. Gorman and Irvin added new faces the following season, all of them

Montrealers: the goaltender Paul Bibeault; the defenceman Emile Bouchard, who would succeed Blake as captain; and the quick, deft, little centre Buddy O'Connor. The Canadiens again finished sixth and lost in the first round. It may not have seemed like progress to some fans, but no one doubted that the crisis had passed and the oldest team in professional hockey would survive.

WHILE THE CANADIENS WERE RECOVERING from their brush with oblivion, the New York Americans were listing and floundering. The league was unable to find a buyer after it took the franchise back in the spring of 1937 and left Merv Dutton in charge. He did an admirable job under trying circumstances. "Every year Red has faced a problem of having to almost completely overhaul his squad," as one New York writer put it. "He's never known just what players would be available at the start of the season."

In 1937–38, Dutton guided the Americans to a winning record and a second-place finish in the Canadian Division. They beat the Rangers in a tight three-game playoff. Over sixteen thousand frenzied fans witnessed the third contest, which was decided forty seconds into the fourth overtime. They advanced to the semifinal round, but lost to Chicago. That was the best the league-owned, Dutton-managed Americans would do.

Attendance dropped. The Americans were chronically short of cash. Dutton had to sell what little talent he had to keep the team afloat, most notably Sweeney Schriner. The former rookie of the year and two-time scoring champion was dispatched to Toronto for $15,000 and four players. Dutton plugged the holes in his lineup with marginal skaters called up from the minors or veterans looking for a place to finish their careers.

Despite all these difficulties, Dutton's Americans broke even, or made a little money, and even whittled away at the club's whopping debts of $185,000, which were largely a legacy of the Dwyer era. The turning point occurred in 1940–41. The Americans won nine games, lost twenty-nine, tied eleven and finished last. The franchise was in critical condition, and the board of governors had to decide what to do with it.

They had a long discussion at a league meeting at the Royal York Hotel in Toronto on June 27, 1941. According to the verbatim minutes, Dutton began by pleading for enough players to put together a competitive team. Art Ross, for one, wasn't interested. "I don't think the American situation will be helped a bit and they will still be the same tail-end team that won't draw in Boston," Ross said. "I think you are making a terrible mistake to carry on with them."

Rangers governor General John R. Kilpatrick was also reluctant. He complained that the Americans had never been able to pay Madison Square Garden the minimum rent of $3,500 per night for midweek games and $5,000 for Saturdays and Sundays. Furthermore, the Garden had to allot half the weekend dates to the Americans. He estimated that the Rangers would have taken in an estimated $80,000 to $90,000 had all the weekends been available to them.

"We netted slightly over $2,000 from the Americans, net, when expenses and everything else was taken out," he said. "We would be unwilling to continue indefinitely on that basis because it is a very undesirable tenant."

Kilpatrick added that the Garden was prepared to give the Americans one more season—to help Dutton and the league. But James Norris worried that losing another team would tarnish the league's image. "I don't like seeing the Americans in the shape they are in, but I don't think it would easy to sell to anybody a franchise . . . under the conditions existing, and seeing the league going down every time with fewer and fewer clubs. It hurts us. I would like to see the league increased, not decreased all the time."

The discussion ended with a motion that Dutton meet with Ross, Conn Smythe, Jack Adams, Lester Patrick and Chicago's William Tobin and that they make an arrangement to get the Americans some adequate players. "If you can get anything out of that group," Smythe wryly noted, "you are a real general manager."

In fact, Dutton didn't get any help, and by the autumn of 1941 a new approach to saving the Americans was under consideration. It originated with General Kilpatrick, and he shared it with the board during a meeting at the Royal York on October 24. Kilpatrick had approached the owners of the Brooklyn Dodgers of the National Football League and suggested they buy the Americans, move them to Brooklyn and rename them the Dodgers. The idea was to build an arena in Brooklyn at some future date. Meantime, the team would continue to play out of Madison Square Garden as the Americans.

"I think it would be a wonderful solution all round for us," Kilpatrick told the board. "They are quite interested. It is still a very vague negotiation."

"I think it is a mighty good idea," Dutton said.

"Are you in favour of it?" Chicago governor William Tobin asked.

"Very much in favour of it," Dutton replied.

"I think any sort of ownership of that sort would be a great thing for the Americans," James Norris added. "This has been their trouble. It has been an orphan."

There was no prospect of selling the franchise to Brooklyn interests in the short term, given that the team was weak, losing money and had substantial debts. But, presumably to advance the idea, the board decided that the club would compete as the Brooklyn Americans for the 1941–42 season, and Dutton told the press that the change was more than mere publicity stunt. "I've always regarded Brooklyn as one of the finest sports centres in the world," he said. "The way the fans support the baseball and football Dodgers convinced me long ago that they would be just as rabid for hockey."

He and some of his players took apartments there. The team practised at an arena in Brooklyn, but played at Madison Square Garden. The rebranding didn't help. The Americans won twice as many games as they had the previous season, but still finished last and missed the playoffs. Moreover, Brooklynites paid no attention.

At the NHL annual meeting on May 15, 1942, the board agreed to cover the team's losses out of a league account, but Patrick and Ross stipulated that their clubs would not subsidize the Americans again. The board also instructed Frank Calder to negotiate a more favourable lease with Madison Square Garden for the coming season. Those talks failed, and that was it for the Americans. On September 25, the governors voted to suspend the franchise for a year and to operate as a six-team league.

ONE MORNING IN MAY 1942, New York Rangers coach Frank Boucher received a call at his farm near Kingston, Ontario. Lester Patrick was on the line, and the news was not good. Patrick feared the league itself would suspend operations for the coming season, and possibly for the duration of the war. "It looks very bleak," Patrick told Boucher. "I would advise you to look for something else."

At the end of August, league officials were still uncertain about the upcoming season. By then, Canada had been at war for three years, the United States for nine months. Seventy-four NHL players had volunteered or been ordered to report for military duty. Stars, future stars and journeymen alike had departed. The Bruins' Kraut Line—Milt Schmidt, Woody Dumart and Bobby Bauer, the best offensive unit in hockey—had played a final game together at Boston Garden in mid-February 1942 and then left to join the Royal Canadian Air Force. Paul Bibeault and Ken Reardon of the Canadiens had enlisted in the army. Rudy (Bingo) Kampman, Wally Stanowski and Frank Eddolls of the Leafs had joined the RCAF, while teammate Bob Goldham had gone to the Canadian Navy.

Every team was affected, and so was the quality of play. That was reason enough, some argued, to suspend. Then there was the moral question: Should a few athletically gifted young men continue to play a child's game—albeit elevated to the level of professional sport—while others put their lives on the line in defence of freedom and democracy? That question loomed very large after the catastrophe at Dieppe on August 19, 1942.

Some 6,100 men, nearly 5,000 of them Canadian, were sent across the English Channel to attempt an amphibious landing near the French port. It was the first assault on Hitler's *Festung Europa*—Fortress Europe. The battle lasted nine hours. On that dreadful day, 907 Canadians died (including 56 officers), 1,946 were taken prisoner and 119 Allied aircraft were shot down. News of this astounding defeat shook the entire Dominion of Canada. Newspapers filled whole pages with photos of the dead, row upon row of individual, thumbnail-sized, head-and-shoulder shots of proud young men in uniform.

At such a moment, Canada's darkest since September 1939, pro sports seemed to some people trivial and irrelevant, mere make-believe struggles in a world of mortal combat. But federal authorities in both Canada and the United States decided otherwise. On the same day in mid-September 1942, government spokesmen in Ottawa and Washington declared that all the leagues should continue to operate for the benefit of public morale.

In Ottawa, Elliott M. Little, director of the National Selective Service, the agency that ran the military draft, issued a one-paragraph statement to the press.

It was directed at the NHL, though the league was not named. "The number of men involved is so small," Little stated, "that it is not considered desirable to destroy the existing media of relaxation through which hundreds of thousands of people—many of them war workers—find enjoyment, which permits them to contribute their maximum to production while they are on the job."

Little's statement was—as Frank Calder put it—a "green light" that allowed the league to move forward. He called a board meeting for September 25. Besides suspending the Americans franchise, the governors extended the season to fifty games from forty-eight and dealt with a number of other matters. Training camps opened in mid-October and the regular season on October 31.

In the first weeks of the campaign, some teams had trouble dressing full rosters of fifteen players, including goalkeepers. In some cases, one side had a complete bench; the other was short. The result was usually a mismatch. The board held a special meeting on November 23 in Boston to deal with the problem, and Bruins governor R.R. Duncan proposed that the league reduce the roster maximum to thirteen players, goalie included. He also suggested eliminating the requirement to dress a minimum number of skaters.

Montreal's Tommy Gorman fully supported the proposal. "We are in terrible shape just now," he said. "On some of the trips we have only been able to take eleven men over the (border). Five of our players are without passports and we may lose one more."

The Bruin proposal passed unanimously after considerable discussion. Every team felt the impact of the war that season, none more so than the Rangers. They fell from first in 1941–42 to last in 1942–43. Their goaltender, Jim Henry, top defence pair of Art Coulter and Muzz Patrick and first line of Alex Shibicky and the Colville brothers had all departed. The Rangers used four goalies in place of Henry. Collectively, they allowed 253 goals, more than five per game. Boucher used thirty-two skaters, fourteen of them for less than ten games. By New Year's, the team was so deeply entrenched in the cellar that they had no hope of making the playoffs.

THE BOARD OF GOVERNORS HELD a special meeting on January 25, 1943, a Monday, at the Royal York Hotel in Toronto and went to work right after breakfast. During the lunch break, Frank Calder announced the playoff format for the six-team league. The first-place club would meet the third, and second would square off against fourth. Both series would be best-of-seven and the winners would advance to the Stanley Cup final, also a best-of-seven. This would be Calder's final pronouncement as president of the NHL.

He was back in his chair for the afternoon session. Five minutes after calling the governors to order, Calder felt a sudden, sharp, overpowering pain in his chest and collapsed. An hour later, he was rushed by ambulance to St. Michael's Hospital. Calder spent nine days there before being deemed fit enough on February 3 to return to Montreal.

Upon arriving, he checked into that city's Western Hospital. His doctors ordered three months of complete rest, but friends and associates expected he would recover since he was, at age sixty-five, trim and fit and played a vigorous one-hour game of handball two to three times a week. On the morning of February 4, Calder ate a light breakfast with his wife and daughter at his bedside. "They had just left the hospital to have something to eat themselves," the *Montreal Star* reported, "when he sank back on the pillow and died."

League executives, active and past, honoured their late president with heart-felt tributes, mingled with dismay. "This is the hardest blow our game has received even in these troubled times," said Tommy Gorman. Art Ross expressed a similar sentiment: "This is the worst news we have had yet. Frank's death is a real shock to me, a shock to our entire organization." Frank Patrick, who had worked in the league office, said, "Frank Calder was so full of life, so vibrant that it's hard to realize that he's left us."

Calder was curt and aloof in public, but his friends outside hockey, especially those who had been handball partners at the Montreal Amateur Athletic Association clubhouse, remembered a warm, generous man. "These noon hour interludes were what 'Mr. Hockey' called his relaxations," Lloyd McGowan recounted in the *Montreal Star*. "Frank loved the meetings at the old club."

They played their games—Calder meticulously recording the scores in a small, loose-leaf journal. Then they would dress and have lunch together. "He would come to the table with his suspenders dangling from the back buttons only," McGowan recalled. "Frank would have a soup, a sandwich, a piece of pie and a cup of coffee. Usually the other members of the Calder crowd would be content to listen as Frank took them back into days that were never dim or distant in his ever-sharp mind. Frank revelled in reminiscing about the old days of Montreal."

Star sports columnist Baz O'Meara offered the most eloquent tribute. "In his death," O'Meara wrote, "Frank Calder has left his friends a lot poorer even if recollections of him endow their memories with riches. . . . We called him the Storm Rider because he survived so many turbulent days, so many troubled nights when controversy raged, tempers seethed and competition flamed in the hot crucible of hockey where, for twenty-five years, his was the steady hand at the helm that usually brought the storm-tossed league to tranquil waters and the soothing peace of summer days."

4

DUTTON'S SHORT SHIFT (1943–1946)

FRANK CALDER WAS NOT UNIVERSALLY LOVED. No man could be who had been compelled—as he so often had been—to arbitrate, mediate and pass judgment. After he was gone, however, even his most ardent and persistent adversaries recognized a hard truth. As one staunch critic—likely Charles Adams or Frederic McLaughlin—put it: "I could never live with Calder at all, but now I don't know how I will get along without him."

For twenty-five years, he had been the indispensible and indestructible leader who solved problems, defused crises, anticipated threats, avoided risks and defended their interests. Now that he was gone, they would have to choose a successor—something they had not discussed or contemplated. They would need someone who was tough, fair and honest, trusted and respected, steadfast and reliable when times were good or bad, but they saw no such candidates, either within their ranks or on the horizon.

In the immediate aftermath of Calder's heart attack, the board asked Merv Dutton, who remained the non-voting governor of the dormant Americans franchise, to run the league office until the status of their president became clear. When they learned in the first days of February that he would be absent for at least three months, the governors improvised again. They formed an executive committee comprising New York's Lester Patrick and Toronto's E.W. Bickle to assume Calder's duties and responsibilities until May 1 and made Dutton managing director to handle routine day-to-day business.

The board held its annual meeting on May 8, 1943, a Friday, at the league headquarters in the Sun Life Building in Montreal. Art Ross implored his counterparts to appoint a successor, even on a short-term basis, to see them through the war. "I believe we have got to elect a man as President . . . even if it is only for a year or two years, but somebody very substantial," Ross argued. "We have to have a man work with him who is also very substantial and here's my thought. Mr. Bickle, right here, should be asked to act as President and Bill McBrien as managing director. Both of these men are connected with Maple Leaf Gardens, but both carry the weight that we need to take [us] over the hard time we are going through."

Bickle and McBrien were directors of the Gardens, and Bickle served as Leaf governor while Conn Smythe was away at war. Ross proposed that the league office be moved to Toronto, along with the minute staff of two—the secretaries Dorothy Pinard and Olga Boyer. "What made me come to this decision and offer this suggestion is that we positively will not operate under present conditions," Ross concluded. "It is just impossible."

Among other things, Ross was troubled by the exodus of talent to the armed forces in both countries and the difficulties in securing adequate replacements and assembling competitive teams. Despite these challenges, Dutton stated in his financial report to the board that "this fourth season under war-time conditions . . . was in respect of both attendance and gate receipts the best in the league's history."

As well, Calder had left the league office and operations in a very healthy financial position. Revenues for the year ended April 30, 1943, had totalled just under $98,500, while costs had been held to $63,500, leaving an operating surplus of $35,000. In addition, there was cash in the bank—$40,272.40 to be precise—and the league held $25,000 in Dominion of Canada bonds. When the outstanding bills had been paid, and money set aside for the injured players' fund, there was a surplus of $53,010.39 to distribute to the six clubs.

Given all that, the rest of the governors did not share Ross's grim view of things. They made Dutton managing director for the coming year and left the president's duties in the hands of Patrick and Bickle. And at their next annual meeting—held May 12, 1944, in Montreal—they convinced Dutton to become president for the duration of the war, a move that generated considerable surprise and skepticism.

"A decision by the F.B.I. to nominate Pretty-Boy Floyd as its chief would have been no more revolutionary than the signing of Mervyn (Red) Dutton as president of the National Hockey League," Trent Frayne wrote in the Toronto-based magazine *Liberty*. "Dutton in his playing days, and later as manager of the New York Americans, had been as tempestuous a character as the NHL had ever seen, a hard-driving, oft-penalized defense man and a roaring, board-thumping manager who loomed as the epitome of what a stately president should not be."

DUTTON DEMONSTRATED HIS FIGHTING SPIRIT early in life. He was born July 23, 1897 in Russell, Manitoba, and was christened Norman Alexander, but had acquired the nickname Mervyn as a youth and kept it. He was one of eight children. His father was a contractor who built branch lines for the Canadian Pacific Railway and roads for the Manitoba and Saskatchewan governments, and he sent young Mervyn to St. John's College, a private school in Winnipeg. That's where he was in the fall of 1914 when war erupted in Europe.

Dutton ditched his books and his favourite sport—he was crazy about hockey—lied about his age, enlisted in the Princess Patricia's Canadian Light Infantry and was promptly sent overseas. He spent almost two years at or near the front lines. His stint as an infantryman ended in northeastern France on April 17, 1917. He and a contingent of his comrades were hauling ammunition to the line. Abruptly, German guns blazed and thundered. A high-explosive shell landed nearby. The blast killed seven men and sprayed Dutton's left side from his belt to his boot tops with hot, jagged fragments of metal—twenty-six in all.

He lay in a trench for three days alongside other casualties, receiving only rudimentary treatment. By the time he was moved to a base hospital, some of his wounds were gangrenous. "The doctors wanted to take the damned leg off," he told an interviewer many years later. "I said: 'No way. I want to play hockey when I get home.'"

Dutton spent eighteen months in hospital. He returned to Canada in February 1919 and went to work for his father's construction company. He wore the heaviest boots he could find and, rather than walk, he ran everywhere to strengthen his leg. "At freeze-up I went back to my folks' place in Winnipeg and skated every day from early morning until late at night. By God, I played hockey in seven different leagues, sometimes two on the same night, playing well past midnight."

In the fall of 1921, Dutton earned a spot on defence with the Calgary Tigers and was a member of the team that won the Western Canada Hockey League championship in 1924 and played in the Stanley Cup final against the Montreal Canadiens. The series was short, just two games, but that's all it took for Dutton to become embroiled in a war with the Canadiens' tough, notoriously mean defenceman Sprague Cleghorn, who speared, butt-ended and elbowed him. Dutton refused to be cowed, and his courage left a lasting impression in the East; several teams coveted him when the western league folded after the 1925–26 season.

Dutton stood his ground during the upheaval that followed the collapse of pro hockey in the West. He was the only western player who refused to allow the Patrick brothers to peddle his rights to one of the NHL's new American-based teams, although Lester Patrick tried hard to get him. He and Lester met in Regina and Patrick made an offer. Dutton put him off. But Patrick wasn't ready to give up, as Dutton later recalled.

"I was working with my brother on one of my father's contracting jobs outside Calgary," Dutton told an interviewer. "Over the grapevine and the barbed wire fences, word came out to the job site that Lester Patrick had arrived in town. Since talking to Lester [in Regina], I had received a wire from Eddie Gerard of the Montreal Maroons asking whether I had signed. Until I heard what the Maroons had to offer, I wasn't going to sign with Lester. But I didn't want to hurt Lester's feelings in case I couldn't come to terms with Gerard.

"The best way seemed to be to duck Lester. So I grabbed a saddle horse and rode up into the hills. I told my brother to stall Lester. If I didn't do business with the Maroons, I could go back to him."

Gerard took a train west and met Dutton in Moose Jaw. The negotiations were brief and went better than Dutton anticipated. The Maroons manager asked about his legs.

"Sound as a bank," Dutton replied. "I'm a hundred and seventy; lean as a rail and hard as a board."

Dutton was hoping for $5,000, considerably more than most of the western players had received. Gerard offered a $5,000 signing bonus, $5,000 annually for three years and additional bonuses if the Maroons made the playoffs, advanced to the Stanley Cup final and won a championship. Dutton was too surprised to speak. Gerard took his momentary bout of speechlessness for a refusal and promptly raised the offer to $6,000.

"Eddie," Dutton sputtered, "you've got a deal."

The robust, high-octane westerner liked nothing better than hammering opponents into the end boards or leaving them sprawled on the ice. He was routinely one of the most heavily penalized players in the league, and at one point, Gerard benched him for three games. That led to a confrontation with the coach. Gerard asked if he could control his temper.

"Temper," Dutton replied incredulously. "There's nothing wrong with my temper. It's my enthusiasm I can't control."

The Maroons traded Dutton to the Americans in the fall of 1930. He was there for twelve seasons as a player and then coach and he was a hit with New Yorkers in both roles. Editorial cartoonists called him "The Red Menace" and delighted in depicting his eruptions, especially when he was behind the bench. Several times a season, Dutton would charge onto the ice to badger referees who, in his opinion, had made bad calls. Or, in his more routine fits of indignation, he merely pounded his trademark pearl-grey fedora against the boards until it was crumpled and useless.

As one New York writer put it: "Red seems more in his element when the breaks are going against him. No one likes a fight better than Dutton, and the tougher the battle, the lustier he piles into things."

DURING HIS FIRST TWO YEARS at the helm of the NHL, initially as managing director and then as president from May 1944 to May 1945, Merv Dutton was one busy fellow. He was running his two Calgary-based businesses—Dutton Brothers and Company and Standard Gravel and Surfacing Company—and they built twenty airports across the West, which were used to groom British, Canadian, Australian and New Zealand air crews under the British Commonwealth Air Training Program.

He flew in small aircraft from site to site to ensure that the projects were being completed on time and to budget and then, as often as not, boarded a big, silver Trans-Canada Air Lines twin-engine turboprop for the long flight east to Montreal or Ottawa to deal with league business.

During those first two years, public perceptions of Dutton shifted remarkably. "The once fiery Dutton, as impulsive a lad on skates as you would find in many a day's march, is now Decorum Incorporated . . . when carrying on official business," Baz O'Meara, sports editor of the *Montreal Star*, wrote. "Around Ottawa, where he had a difficult role keeping the man power people on the side of hockey, they liked him a lot . . . because he didn't hide any cards under the table and told the truth at all times."

Dutton had been equally effective at managing the headstrong, sometimes contrary men who ran the league, according to Trent Frayne. "He is unquestionably the most popular figure in the NHL's upper strata and owns the complete admiration of every club executive in the game," Frayne wrote in *Liberty*. "While there are some who might insist that he is too impulsive, too prone to leap off at bombastic tangents, there are none who question his integrity or fearlessness."

The league's fortunes also rose during the Dutton presidency, so much so that the governors were slightly embarrassed by their gate receipts. At a meeting on December 8, 1944, at the Roosevelt Hotel in New York, Dutton reported that the league's six teams had taken in $605,093.14 in the first thirty-eight games, played up to November 30. That was 16.6 per cent better than the same period a year earlier.

The board gathered again on February 2, 1945, at the league offices in Montreal. Dutton reported on the ninety-nine games completed to January 31. Gate receipts totalled $1,543,769.08, up by $184,132.99, or 13.5 per cent. Those glowing numbers led to the following exchange, taken from the verbatim minutes of the meeting:

> DUTTON: I think it very bad that publicity be given out in regard to the receipts. . . . Money matters should be kept distinctly to the clubs.

> LESTER PATRICK: I move that none of these figures be released to the press except from the office of the President, in his own judgment.

ART ROSS: Second the motion.

FRANK SELKE: You mean the attendance as well as the money?

PATRICK: Leave it all to the President and I suggest further that those owners that might have two or three people that have access to this, be warned about it so that there will be no leak that way.

TOMMY GORMAN: You would not restrict the attendance figures. The newspapers are going to ask you and if you don't give it they draw their own conclusions.

SENATOR DONAT RAYMOND: Let them draw their own conclusions.

DUTTON: If we keep on drawing as in the past we will draw approximately $2,300,000.

SELKE: It is a lot of dough.

DUTTON: It is big business.

The governors held their annual meeting on June 14, 1945, and demonstrated their satisfaction with the status quo by reappointing Dutton for a five-year term.

NAZI GERMANY SURRENDERED IN MAY 1945, and Imperial Japan in August after the United States dropped atomic bombs on Hiroshima and Nagasaki. Peace had arrived at last and people everywhere wondered: What would it bring? Merv Dutton foresaw a bright future for hockey, and he set out his view of things in a statement released in time to be published in the afternoon newspapers of August 25, a Saturday. "I have no doubt that sport is in for a 'golden era' in the near future, an era which will be on a larger scale even than the one following the first Great War.

"... Hockey, baseball, football and other sports will be bigger and better than ever before.... As far as hockey is concerned, I can visualize rinks and stadiums springing up all over the country, on both sides of the international border. I expect hockey to boom in California and in Europe to a status never dreamed of before.

"Air travel will be a boon to the hockey of the future. I hope I live to see the day when each hockey club will own its own airplane. Then, I expect we shall follow much the same policy as they do in baseball, carrying twenty-five or twenty-six men to a team and playing in different cities every night of the week.

"I look for an early expansion in the National Hockey League, and hope that eventually we will be operating a ten-team circuit. Where these teams will come from remains to be seen."

Dutton was right about outside interest in the NHL. Between the fall of 1945 and the spring of 1946, the league received applications for franchises, complete with $10,000 deposits, from five groups: one from Philadelphia, one from San Francisco and three from Los Angeles. Each sent a representative to make a pitch to the board of governors, and one of the parties may well have been raised on the lot of a Hollywood movie studio.

This collection of would-be owners dispatched an emissary named Tony Owen to the annual general meeting at the Commodore Hotel in New York in June 1946. Owen began his presentation by telling the board, "These men are all successes financially and they are all famous in their particular line of work—the motion picture business."

He was speaking for about a dozen investors, and they included Sam Goldwyn and Darryl Zanuck, two major film producers and studio executives, and the actors Randolph Scott, Fred Astaire and Bing Crosby, who would have attended himself, Owen added, had he not been in Lake Louise, Alberta, making a movie. They were planning to put up $4 million to build a twenty-thousand-seat all-purpose arena that would be a Madison Square Garden of the West.

Crosby was prepared to contribute $250,000, Scott $150,000, and Goldwyn would add whatever was required after the others had risked what they could. "It's a stupid remark to make," Owen said, "but you lose the sense of perspective out there as far as money is concerned. These figures don't mean anything."

Furthermore, Crosby and partners were confident that hockey would be a hit in Los Angeles, which then had a population of three million, including some 200,000 Canadians. The populace avidly supported sporting events of all sorts—boxing, horse racing, college football, amateur hockey and skating shows—but there was a thirst for major-league sports. The Cleveland Rams of the National Football League were relocating to Los Angeles, and there was talk that baseball teams would move to the coast as well. "It's a great sports town and it's hungry for big-league hockey," Owen said.

The governors had reservations from the outset. "How is all this going to do us any good in the National Hockey League?" Conn Smythe asked Owen. "They say they are hungry for hockey, but I don't think Toronto is hungry to see a Los Angeles team play in Toronto."

After a presentation by another Los Angeles party, Rangers governor General John Kilpatrick asked his fellow board members: "Is it not rather obvious that we are not ready for major league hockey on the coast? They have not got adequate buildings and the travel cost is high."

Both were valid points. Some of the groups were proposing to build arenas seating 10,000 to 12,000 spectators. The San Francisco applicant was planning to refurbish an existing facility. The Hollywood syndicate wanted a franchise as a condition for going ahead with construction, whereas the board insisted that an acceptable arena be financed and underway before they would award a franchise.

As for travel, Chicago to Los Angeles was a seven-hour flight and New York–Los Angeles fifteen, though that was about to be reduced to ten. It would cost $3,000 to $5,000 per trip to fly a team out there and back, all for one game, or two if there were franchises in both Los Angeles and San Francisco, and each eastern club would have to make three trips per season. The West Coast was just too far away at that moment, and the California groups were all turned down.

The league was prepared to award a franchise to Philadelphia. A Montreal business executive and prominent sportsman named Len Peto was behind the bid. Peto was a past president of the Dominion of Canada Football Association, forerunner of the contemporary Canadian Soccer Association. In 1940, Senator Donat Raymond made Peto a director of the Canadian Arena Company, which owned the Forum and the Canadiens, and he remained on the board until 1944.

When he applied for a franchise, Peto was vice-president and general manager of the Canadian Car and Foundry Company. He put together a group of wealthy individuals from Philadelphia, New York and Washington to back his bid. He had had plans drawn up for a $4.35-million stadium that would seat 19,500 and he had acquired a site. Peto made his pitch to the board at a meeting at the Commodore Hotel in New York on February 15, 1946. He assured the governors that his building would be complete by November 1 and that he would have a team ready to compete in the 1946–47 season.

The board was prepared to transfer the Maroons franchise, which the Canadian Arena Company still owned. A motion to that effect stipulated that Peto and his partners must provide ". . . satisfactory evidence that they have the funds and financial backing sufficient . . . to assure completion of the arena and to permit them to carry on and operate the club."

Peto appeared before the board on three occasions over the next twelve months, but each time failed to convince the governors that he had the financing in place. He was also unable to obtain approval to build from a federal tribunal overseeing the construction industry due to ongoing shortages of materials. Meantime, a major shakeup was underway within the upper echelons of the NHL, and all thoughts of expansion were swept aside for the moment.

MERV DUTTON HAD ALWAYS BEEN a reluctant president. He had businesses to run in Calgary, and besides that, he had his heart set on resurrecting the Americans and operating them out of Brooklyn. With that in mind, he resigned as league president in the summer of 1946 and turned over his responsibilities to a young man recently hired as his assistant and understudy: Lieutenant Colonel Clarence Campbell, OBE (Officer of the Order of the British Empire). Dutton chaired his last board meeting on September 4 that year. The governors approved Campbell's appointment as president and Dutton apprised them of his work on the Brooklyn franchise.

He had assembled a group of investors. He had hired an architect to draw up plans for an arena, but had not been able to acquire a site. As well, he doubted whether the U.S. government would allow construction of a sports and entertainment facility due to an ongoing shortage of construction materials.

Therefore, he was putting his application for a franchise on hold. He did intend to be back, though.

"I am very desirous of being a member of the NHL at some future date," he told the board. ". . . I want it and want it very badly."

There was one thing he was seeking from the board: an assurance that there would not be a second franchise in Madison Square Garden. They were not prepared to grant that. "Nobody knows [what will happen] in ten years' time," said Chicago governor William Tobin. ". . . In ten years' time it might be advantageous to have a second team in New York."

General John Kilpatrick of the Rangers added, "I could not say that we would—through a sense of obligation to you personally—agree that we never would hope for another franchise in New York, which might be greatly to the benefit of the league and to my stockholders."

"Then, gentlemen," Dutton replied, "you can disregard my application."

Dutton returned to Calgary. He enjoyed a very successful career in business. He became wealthy and was occasionally described in newspaper stories as one of the wealthiest men in Canada. He was elected to the Hockey Hall of Fame in 1958. But he always felt the board had reneged on a promise to grant him a franchise after the war and he never set foot in an NHL arena until he was asked, many years later, to perform the ceremonial opening faceoff at a game in Calgary.

PART II

THE LONG REIGN OF CLARENCE CAMPBELL

(1946–1977)

5

A LOPSIDED LEAGUE (1946-1955)

CLARENCE CAMPBELL PRESIDED OVER HIS first annual general meeting of the National Hockey League board of governors on June 2, 1947, a Monday, at the Windsor Hotel in Montreal. In the season just completed, the Canadiens had finished first and the Leafs a close second. Montreal's Bill Durnan was the top goaltender and Chicago's diminutive centre Max Bentley— the 155-pound Dipsy Doodle Dandy from Delisle, Saskatchewan—had edged the fiery Maurice Richard by a single point to win the scoring title, even though Bentley's Black Hawks had finished last and earned a hair over half as many points as Richard's Canadiens. Toronto and Montreal had met in the first all-Canadian Stanley Cup final in thirteen years and the Leafs prevailed by four games to two.

Campbell opened the meeting by presenting a state-of-the-union report on the league and its second, 180-game, postwar season, and he put smiles on the faces of the six stern figures seated around him. For the first time since the NHL was formed on that November day in 1917, amid the darkness and uncertainty of World War I, there wasn't a hint of trouble or discord—in the room or on the horizon.

Attendance for the entire league, for the full schedule, was 96.6 per cent of capacity. "From this," Campbell concluded, "it's clear that, assuming ticket price scales at all rinks remain the same, we have reached the maximum possible revenue for the six-club league. If there is to be any further expansion, it will have to take the form of further clubs."

That wasn't on the agenda for the moment, but other leagues were on the move, just as Merv Dutton had predicted. "The expansion of professional hockey is proceeding rapidly," Campbell reported. "New clubs are being formed and rinks planned and built in other cities of the United States. They will have to be accommodated in some league and I feel the dominant position of the National Hockey League will not remain unchallenged if all this expansion takes place in other leagues."

There were no immediate threats from outside. Relations with the other professional leagues had been "very cordial," he noted, while all dealings with the governing bodies of amateur hockey had been "most amicable."

Harmony prevailed within the NHL household as well. Player salaries had gone up—though he didn't specify by how much—and bonuses for player awards, league championships and winning the Stanley Cup had been "greatly increased." Neutral linesmen had been used in forty-five per cent of the games played, which was a new development and a notable success. Campbell had been compelled to lease more office space in the Sun Life Building—across Dominion Square from the Windsor—and to hire several new employees to keep pace with the increased services provided to the six member clubs. A publicity department had been created as an integral part of the league headquarters.

The governors adopted the report—without quibble or question—and James Norris added his own hearty endorsement. "It is the best report we have ever received," he stated. "It is very comprehensive and very excellent."

So began the long reign of Clarence Campbell.

CAMPBELL WAS FORTY-ONE WHEN he became president of the NHL. He was a bachelor and lived frugally. He boarded with a family in Mount Royal, the wealthy Anglo enclave that overlooked downtown Montreal. He was new to the city and could walk the streets unrecognized. He was no better known elsewhere in Canada, except perhaps in the hamlet of Fleming, Saskatchewan, where he was born and raised, or the city of Edmonton, where he had attended university and practised law before enlisting.

Campbell's hometown was one of dozens of tiny, nondescript communities that sprang up along the mainline of the Canadian Pacific Railway in the 1880s.

The original settlers, mostly Mennonites, chose a townsite nearly four miles west of the future border between Manitoba and Saskatchewan, and they named the place after Sir Sandford Fleming, the railway's surveyor and the inventor of standard time. The broad, unpaved main thoroughfare was called Sandford Street, and the Campbells lived there, in a two-storey, L-shaped shingle-board home.

George Campbell was the local agent for the Beaver Lumber Company, and his wife, either Annie or Anna, managed the household and raised her children, Clarence and his five younger siblings. Fleming's population peaked at 310 in 1916—when Clarence was eleven and a student in a one-room schoolhouse where he undoubtedly outshone every other kid.

He was a sports-minded youth who played goal in hockey and catcher in baseball, but brought more enthusiasm than ability to both. He was also industrious. Later in life, Campbell liked to recount how he had used a sixty-dollar inheritance from his grandmother and a forty-dollar gift from his father to purchase a cow. By the time he left home, at age fourteen or fifteen, to continue his education in Edmonton, he had a herd of five cattle, which he sold to help finance his studies.

Campbell took one year of high school before being admitted to the University of Alberta in 1921 at age sixteen. He breezed through two post-secondary programs, seemingly on fast forward. He received a Bachelor of Arts degree in 1923, when he was eighteen, making him one of the university's youngest graduates. Three years later, he had finished law school—near the top of his class, as usual.

In addition, he had a resumé leavened by extracurricular activity. He served as secretary of Edmonton's largest Sunday school, and at nineteen he and a friend organized the Edmonton District Hockey Association. He had a hand in creating the city's independent baseball league and played for the rugby team that won the provincial championship in 1925.

Campbell's academic achievements and community involvement earned him a Rhodes Scholarship. He enrolled at Oxford University in England in 1926 and studied jurisprudence. He played field lacrosse and tended goal for the university hockey team, and during a European tour in 1928 he refereed his first game—a contest between two local squads in Muerren, Switzerland. He must have enjoyed the experience, because that summer he was named the chief referee for lacrosse at the Olympic Games in Amsterdam.

Campbell returned to Edmonton in the spring of 1929 to practise law. He was just twenty-four and as civic-minded and sports-mad as ever. He was a member of a committee that built a three-thousand-seat baseball stadium. He served as secretary-treasurer of the Edmonton District Hockey Association and he was on the executive of the Alberta Amateur Hockey Association.

He was such a whirlwind that a columnist with the *Edmonton Bulletin* would later write: "No man connected with amateur sport in Edmonton has done more toward its promotion and development than Clarence Campbell. The young barrister is the czar of local sports circles, known by every enthusiast from the smallest lad to the oldest dad."

Campbell also distinguished himself as a referee. He was frequently assigned playoff series and championship games, and in the spring of 1934 he handled the Allan Cup final between Moncton and Fort William at Maple Leaf Gardens. This was the first time he had worked in the East, and he had to get used to a new item of equipment very quickly, as he told the *Hockey News* some years later. "I was told that the old cow bell was out," Campbell said. "We didn't use whistles out West because most of the rinks . . . were unheated and so cold a whistle wouldn't work. Saliva would freeze in the mouthpiece and you had to wear gloves to protect your fingers."

Campbell officiated at the 1935 Allan Cup series between Halifax and Port Arthur, and his work caught the attention of NHL officials. He began working their games in 1936 and, as usual, quickly established himself as one of the best. Campbell had good judgment. He was completely impartial and fair to a fault. He demonstrated the latter quality after a game between the Montreal Maroons and Boston Bruins on January 29, 1938. Two veteran players, Boston's Dit Clapper and Montreal's Dave Trottier, dropped the gloves and went at it. Campbell intervened and pushed the two apart. Clapper got an arm free and landed one more and flattened Trottier. Campbell and Clapper exchanged words, and then Clapper belted Campbell hard enough to blacken both eyes.

Frank Calder investigated, and Campbell provided a truthful account. "I talked out of turn," he told Calder. "I called Clapper a son-of-a-bitch. He asked me to repeat it. I did, and got what was coming to me." Calder settled on a $100 fine rather than a long suspension.

At the end of the 1938–39 season, Calder offered him the position of referee-in-chief, but Campbell opted to return to Edmonton and his law practice. His career took another turn a few months later, when Canada declared war on Germany. He was then thirty-four and determined to serve.

In the summer of 1940, Campbell enlisted, was assigned to the Second Battalion of the Edmonton Fusiliers and given the rank of second lieutenant. He trained in a number of different branches of the military over the next four years and in 1944 was assigned command of the Headquarters Squadron of the 4th Canadian (Armoured) Division. The Division crossed the English Channel and landed at Normandy in late July 1944, and over the next several months was engaged in heavy fighting. Campbell's squadron faced sniper fire, German artillery barrages and other assaults.

One month after V-E Day in May 1945, Campbell joined the Canadian War Crimes Investigation Unit and served as an associate prosecutor at the trial in Aurich, Austria, of Brigadefuehrer Kurt Meyer, who was accused of ordering the execution of Canadian prisoners of war. Meyer was convicted and sentenced to death, although the sentence was later commuted to life in prison.

Conn Smythe recommended Campbell to Merv Dutton, who hired him as his assistant in June 1946. Three months later, he was elevated to the top job, and on the day of his appointment, he told Ferguson: "I'm a bit dazed by the speed of the whole thing. I won't say I wasn't aware certain negotiations were underway whereby I might, at a future date, become president. But I expected to spend at least a season under Red Dutton. Now all of a sudden I find myself president.

"Do you know where a man can rent an apartment in this city?"

ON SEPTEMBER 2, 1948, the board of governors passed a motion that set the stage for extending the regular season to seventy games from sixty. The motion directed each club to submit to Clarence Campbell by December 1 a list of dates when their arenas would be available during the fall and winter of 1949–50. Campbell was instructed to develop a schedule of thirty-five home games per team based on the lists.

That proved to be far more difficult than anticipated, as he told the governors when they met on March 11, 1949, at the Royal York Hotel. "I was asked to see if it was possible to get a seventy-game schedule into twenty-three weeks, which is the normal playing season," Campbell said. "After working a very long time on it—almost two months—I concluded . . . it was physically impossible . . . so I took the liberty . . . to extend it one more week. Physically it can be done."

The debate that followed proved to be more divisive than any that had taken place on Campbell's watch up to that point. The issue split the board evenly, according to the minutes of the meeting. What follows is an abridged version of the discussion.

ART ROSS: We have given a lot of serious consideration to this and we go on record [that] we are positively against any further extension of the present schedule.

BRIGADIER GENERAL JOHN R. KILPATRICK: We are definitely limited, with our circus lease, to give them possession [of Madison Square Garden] in early April. Extending the season would completely eliminate us from any playoff possibility, which our fans would not stand for.

WILLIAM TOBIN [CHICAGO]: We are reaching the point now that we just cannot accommodate the people who want to see hockey. What are you going to do? If you are in business and cannot accommodate your trade, you are going to find some way to accommodate [it].

WILLIAM NORTHEY: I think the disadvantages outweigh the advantages so far as Canadiens are concerned. We are opposed until such time as there are more teams in the league.

CONN SMYTHE: I have not heard a decent argument come out of the people who are against it.

KILPATRICK: Is not the fact that you would eliminate us from any playoffs a factor?

WESTON ADAMS: We cannot stand any more games. Boston is entirely different than Toronto.

SMYTHE: The best hockey city in the whole world.

ADAMS: We have all kinds of school hockey and basketball and baseball all over our papers. We have more competition in Boston than any other city in the league.

SMYTHE: Is it not a fact, [based] on this year's figures, that we would draw $80,000 to $100,000 for the five games? What are the gates averaging this year?

ADAMS: Around $20,000.

SMYTHE: Here is a chance of making another $100,000 and you are going to lose $100,000.

ROSS: We don't get all of that. We have to pay $8,000 a night for rent. You don't pay any of that.

SMYTHE: We put a feeler out in the paper and we had hundreds of letters asking if we would get five extra games.

KILPATRICK: You never get the subscription [season-ticket] demand in New York that you have in Toronto where the only thing to do on Saturday night is the hockey game. New Yorkers do not like subscription seats . . . they want to go to the theatre one night and will not obligate themselves to go to a game every night.

SMYTHE: We have fifty per cent of our subscribers who are firms who have people come from out of town and go to the game.

KILPATRICK: When a man comes from out of town to New York, he does not want to see a hockey show.

SMYTHE: What do we have to do to decide on the policy of sixty or seventy games? Has it been laid down?

CAMPBELL: No, we have an even split of opinion as to what should happen.

SMYTHE: Are the Canadiens against it?

NORTHEY: Absolutely.

ADAMS: I make a motion that the NHL schedule remain at sixty games.

NORTHEY: I second that.

There was another prolonged discussion, the governors remained dead-locked and Campbell became increasingly uncomfortable because the league constitution stipulated that the president should cast a vote, even if it was the deciding vote. "I don't think it would be normal," he said, "for a person in my position—not having an interest—to make a decision that would amend the current regulations."

Ross replied: "You won't have to make a decision. Take a vote and see. You have to have a majority to get the seventy games and you won't get it."

He was right. Kilpatrick sided with Adams and Northey. Smythe, Tobin and Detroit's Jack Adams went the other way. Then Tobin put forward a motion to extend the schedule and it produced another three-three vote, though the yeas and nays had switched sides. Campbell, meantime, voted against both motions.

The issue was resolved in favour of the longer season when the owners met a day in advance of the annual general meeting, held June 1, 1949, at the Windsor Hotel. That was not the final word on the subject, though. Campbell developed the schedule over the summer and it was up for approval when the governors gathered on September 7 in Montreal.

"We have to be consistent," Ross said. "We were against the seventy-game schedule and whether we were wrong or not you are giving us the opportunity to vote against it."

"Regardless of the official objection," Campbell replied, ". . . I would like to request . . . that it be a definite instruction given by all club managements that there is to be no public criticism."

"We can assure the president that we have recorded our vote against it and we will not knock it," Ross added. "It will knock itself."

"What is the release date?" Weston Adams asked.

"September 13," Campbell replied. "Afternoon papers."

"We cannot control it," Ross interjected, "when the papers say it is a terrible schedule."

ROSS HAD A POINT. Campbell had stuck the Bruins with too many home dates in the opening weeks of the season, well before Boston's boisterous sports fans normally tuned in to hockey. But there wasn't a peep of protest in the papers—on the Canadian side, at any rate. They merely noted that the Bruins and Red Wings would square off in Detroit on October 12—the earliest-ever opening night. The 210-game schedule would conclude March 26 with all six clubs in action.

The weekend doubleheader—three games Saturday evening and three on Sunday—would be the cornerstone of the schedule and a change introduced in order to cram seventy games into twenty-four weeks. As well, the Leafs and Canadiens were given Saturday as their home date. Sunday was reserved for the U.S.-based franchises.

With the passage of years, the doubleheaders contributed significantly to the lore and legend of what has come to be known as the Original Six era. Home-and-home weekend sets became commonplace. The Canadiens and Red Wings, for instance, would play in Montreal on Saturday and Detroit on Sunday, and this gave rise to all those stories about overnight train rides with one group of bruised and battered athletes bunked down in a car up front and their rivals in another at the back with the diner in between, just to be sure their paths did not cross.

Some observers from that era contend that the doubleheaders inevitably led to an increase in rough play and violence in the compact, six-team circuit where each club played each opponent fourteen times. "As often as not, the second game was a war," recalled Frank Selke Jr., director of English-language public relations for the Canadian Arena Company, which owned the Canadiens. "Something would start on Saturday night and it would be finished on Sunday."

Nobody anticipated this problem when the schedule was released in the fall of 1949. By then, there were other things to command the attention of fans and sportswriters alike. Training camps opened one by one, teams began to take shape and the beat writers and wisecracking columnists of the six NHL cities felt compelled—as they did every autumn—to predict where the clubs would land several months and many dozens of games later.

The *Hockey News* queried fifteen pundits and the consensus was that the reigning Stanley Cup champion Maple Leafs would finish first and the Wings second. "Back of the Leafs and Wings," the weekly journal continued, "the writers ruled Montreal Canadiens favorites to hang onto the third playoff rung they held last year. In fourth spot they named Chicago Black Hawks. Boston Bruins, last spring's second-place finishers, were rated no better than a fifth-place prospect for this campaign. . . . The unhappy New York Rangers ruled an almost unanimous choice to bring up the rear."

Having rendered their judgments, the Toronto hockey writers immediately sought out Conn Smythe, and he was delighted to make his own predictions. The Bruins: anybody's guess how they would perform. Rangers: they had to be better than last year, and would be if the rookies came through. Hawks: a playoff team if coach Charlie Conacher could keep his scorers focused on scoring rather than fighting. The Wings: well, even the perpetually puffed up Smythe was wise enough to be circumspect. No need to give Jack Adams a reason to erupt, or to put any more fire in the eyes of Sid Abel, Gordie Howe, Ted Lindsay and the rest of these as yet Cup-less but powerful Wings. His Leafs: they should be a playoff contender, but the lack of real goal-scoring punch could hurt. Canadiens: the team to beat.

Then he added—in jest—that the Gardens should offer a prize to the sportswriter who most accurately predicted the date of the first, full cry of "What's wrong with the Leafs?" That occurred on or about November 23, after the team had lost three straight. When the winless streak hit five games, a loud, anguished wail arose among the writers and the hordes of faithful. When the Leafs lost on November 27 to the Hawks, who had already sunk to their habitual place at the bottom of the standings, Smythe snapped. The Leaf boss had worked himself into a righteous wrath, and he expended it on the guy the writers called the "fabulous fat man," the team's jovial, slightly rotund, five-foot, seven-inch goaltender, Walter (Turk) Broda, who had backstopped the team to Stanley Cup championships in 1947, 1948 and 1949. "We are not running a fat man's team," Smythe bellowed at the Monday morning practice after the debacle against Chicago. "Broda is way overweight at 197 pounds. He is off the team until he shows some common sense. He's been ordered to reduce to 190 pounds."

Smythe's tantrum produced an unexpected public-relations triumph. Toronto's three ultra-competitive daily papers forgot for the moment how awful the Leafs had been and, instead, gleefully covered the Turk's race to reduce. They ran photos of workouts in the gym and the Broda family at the dinner table. One paper produced a chart plotting the thirty-six-year-old goaltender's weight from the time he joined the Leafs in 1937. (He had weighed 167 pounds as a rookie.) Betty Broda—dubbed Mrs. B, and described by the *Toronto Star* as "a compact, five-foot, three-inch bundle who weighs 128 pounds"—provided the papers with a detailed daily account of her husband's diet. He shed the excess weight almost as quickly as he peeled off his equipment after a tough game. On December 1, a page one *Star* headline declared, in type two inches high:

BRODA GETS DOWN TO 189 POUNDS

The Red Wings were the toast of the league that season. Lindsay, Abel and Howe finished one-two-three in scoring. Harry Lumley was the second-ranked goaltender and the Wings were grooming Terry Sawchuk, who was destined to be one of the all-time greats. Their defence included two future Hall of Famers: Jack Stewart, a punishing and intimidating checker who had joined the Wings in 1938, and Red Kelly, who passed with great precision and could carry the puck as well and had established himself as one of the best young defencemen in the game.

The Wings were about to eclipse the Leafs as the NHL's dominant team. But the reigning champs would not surrender without a fight. The Leafs recovered from their first-half swoon and finished third. They met the Wings in the opening round and pushed them to a seventh game, and then lost only in overtime. Those who witnessed that series long remembered it for a dreadful incident that occurred late in the first period of game one.

Leaf captain Ted Kennedy had the puck. He carried it through the neutral zone. Howe and Stewart chased him. Howe was going to run Kennedy into the boards, but, as he later told the writer Brian McFarlane: "I was leaning forward, my head low, when Kennedy passed to Sid Smith. Kennedy came around with the stick and spiked me right in the eye. The real damage came a second later when I crashed into the boards."

The impact knocked him out. The team doctor's on-the-spot diagnosis included a broken nose, possible broken cheekbone, an injury to one eye and a concussion. He called for a stretcher. Howe was rushed to hospital by ambulance. "I'll never forget that horrible ride," Howe recounted. "People around me were saying, 'You're okay, Gord.' But I didn't feel okay. I felt terribly sick. At the hospital somebody gave me a glass of water and I vomited."

A neurosurgeon took one look, realized Howe had a fractured skull and summoned an anaesthesiologist. "They rushed me into the operating room," Howe continued, "and I remember getting upset when they shaved my head. . . . I recall the shock of having the drill put to my head and feeling the pressure and hoping they knew what they were doing and when to stop."

Howe was still lying in a hospital bed when his teammates finally subdued the Leafs, and he remained there through most of the final against the upstart New York Rangers—the league's big surprise in that initial seventy-game season. The Rangers were in second place at midseason. They slipped to fourth by season's end, but eliminated Montreal in five and earned admiration all round that spring by advancing to the final—largely without the support of loyal home fans.

They played two games of the opening round at Madison Square Garden. Then the circus moved in. The Rangers finished off the Canadiens at the Forum. They adopted Maple Leaf Gardens as their home for the final and drew capacity crowds for the two games played in Toronto. They took a three-two series lead and came within a whisker of being Stanley Cup champions.

That honour went to the Wings. They beat the Rangers in the second overtime of the seventh game. The crowd erupted. The Detroit players vaulted over the boards. "In the view of 13,095 fans," Paul Chandler wrote in the *Detroit News*, "weary, worn and aching Red Wings kissed and embraced, threw equipment to the ceiling and hoisted coach Tommy Ivan to their shoulders."

General manager Jack Adams and owner James Norris joined the melee. Clarence Campbell presented the Stanley Cup. Then a chant arose from the crowd—"We want Howe! We want Howe!"—and Detroit's newest sporting hero stepped on to the ice in a suit, a fedora and a big smile on his broad, handsome face.

GORDIE HOWE WAS TWENTY-TWO that spring. He had just completed his fourth full NHL season. He had scored thirty-five goals and accumulated nearly a point a game, and much bigger accomplishments lay ahead—four consecutive scoring titles and three straight years as the league's top goal scorer. Howe—along with linemates Ted Lindsay and Sid Abel, defenceman Red Kelly and goaltender Terry Sawchuk—formed the powerful nucleus of one of the best teams in NHL history. The Red Wings of the postwar years finished first seven times in a row (1948 through 1955) and won four Stanley Cups.

The Leafs were the first powerhouse of the day. They won three straight Cups—something no other NHL team before them had done—and they added a fourth in 1951. And while the Wings and Leafs were enjoying life at the top, the Canadiens' cross-country network of sponsored junior teams began to produce the formidable array of talent that would, by the mid-1950s, propel Montreal past Detroit and Toronto.

And then there were the Rangers, the Bruins and the Black Hawks—the league's poor cousins. The Rangers' near-win in 1950 was as close as any of those teams would come to a championship in many years. Something had to be done to correct the NHL's competitive imbalance, though the league was slow to address the problem.

The first tentative move toward a solution occurred during a governors meeting that stretched over two days, January 30 and 31, 1950. The board was discussing the cost of developing players through sponsored teams and whether they should continue signing kids at age sixteen or wait until they turned eighteen. Amid the back and forth, Chicago's Bill Tobin suggested—seemingly out of the blue—that the fifth- and sixth-place clubs be given the opportunity, at the annual general meeting, of taking two players from any sponsored club at a price of $5,000 to $7,500.

"In the form of an official draft?" Clarence Campbell asked.

Conn Smythe immediately objected. "We do the work," he snapped, "and you get the players?"

Weston Adams suggested that each team draw up a reserve list of twenty-five top prospects. "If players are not good enough to list as untouchables, take a chance on selling them to weaker clubs," he said.

"That is my suggestion," said Tobin.

"I like that," added General John Kilpatrick.

"I am against it," Smythe said.

"What would be wrong," Tobin asked, "with having a list of forty reserves at the annual meeting? Put your finger on twenty-five and leave fifteen open?"

"What is the advantage?" Smythe asked.

"It's good for the league, whatever the agreed price is," Tobin replied.

This caused Smythe to pause, think, and then ask: "What price?"

Tobin suggested $10,000.

"That is not a good price," Smythe said.

"What would you think a fair price?" General Kilpatrick asked.

"Anywhere from $25,000 to $50,000," said Smythe.

"Twenty-five thousand would be about right," Kilpatrick said. "A man that would help your club when you are in trouble would be worth about $25,000."

A short time later, the governors adjourned for the day. By then, Smythe had agreed to consider the intra-league draft, provided the reserve list was raised to thirty players. Campbell, meantime, thought the idea had considerable merit. He spent the evening devising the mechanics for such a draft and presented them the following morning.

Each club would prepare a reserve list and submit it to the league office by April 30. Campbell would compile the names of all the players not listed and therefore eligible for the draft. They could be acquired for a flat fee of $25,000. Selections would be made according to the following formula: 6–5; 6–5; 4–3–2.

That is, the sixth-place team would choose a player, followed by the fifth-place club. They would go again, and then the teams above them would select in the reverse order of the final standings. They could only draw from clubs ahead of them, meaning the league champion would not draft.

Campbell's plan provoked a long but reasonable discussion and emerged intact except for two minor amendments: the clubs would be allowed to claim any unprotected player and the first-place team would participate.

"Are there any other aspects of the cost of acquiring players that anyone wishes to discuss or comment on now?" Campbell asked. "If not, we can pass over this item and consider it concluded?"

BY THE FALL OF 1952, the NHL had introduced an intra-league draft. That year, it was held October 5, a week before the season opened. Each club could protect twenty-two players, including a pair of goaltenders, and the price per pick was set at $10,000. The board tinkered with the format through the early 1950s. By 1954, the protected lists had been trimmed to eighteen skaters and two netminders, the price bumped to $15,000, and junior players were ruled ineligible.

But the draft didn't help. Nor did anything else. The Rangers, Bruins and Hawks made trades. They brought players up from the minors and sent them back. They hired and fired coaches. They launched rebuilding programs and abandoned them. One of the three—the Bruins, more often than not—made the playoffs because four of the six clubs qualified. Nevertheless, the little six-team circuit remained a lopsided league with three strong and three weak members.

Inevitably, attendance dropped, particularly in Boston and Chicago. On November 8, 1951, the Leafs and Black Hawks played before 4,102 fans, the smallest crowd in Hawk history. Two weeks later, the Bruins and Rangers drew only 4,888 fans to Boston Garden, the poorest turnout in seventeen years. There was worse to come. A mere 3,128 Chicago diehards—an all-time low—watched the Hawks and Bruins skate to a scoreless draw on January 31, 1952.

Five years earlier, on February 23, 1947, the same two teams, playing in the same building, had drawn 20,004 fans and established an NHL attendance record. That season, 1946–47, the Hawks had drawn a total of 500,681, or 17,000 per game. And in March 1946, when the Hawks last made the playoffs, their loyal supporters began lining up eighteen hours before the opening faceoff just to get seats in the upper bowl of the vast amphitheatre. "They played poker under streetlights in shivering weather," journalist Bud Booth later wrote in the *Hockey News*, "and took turns going for hot coffee and sleeping in each other's cars. They were hockey NUTS!"

Six straight losing seasons changed that. Most of the fans had fled, and those who had stuck with the team were deeply disenchanted, as a *Chicago Herald-American* reporter discovered when he canvassed a number of spectators during a game in February 1952. "I blame the management," declared housewife Myrtle Ellerman, "and by that I mean Bill Tobin. I've been a Blackhawk fan for ten years and, believe me, all he'd need would be a winning team and he could forget about Sunday afternoon games to get crowds."

"This is the eighteenth season I've been watching the Hawks," added Theodore Sujdak, an employee of the Superior Match Company. "All I can do is recall the good teams with fellows like Johnny Gottselig, Earl Seibert, Mush March and so on."

With falling attendance came mounting losses, and old ownership gave way to new in Boston and Chicago. On October 12, 1951, following months of negotiation, Weston Adams, son of Bruins founder Charles F. Adams, sold his sixty per cent interest to the Boston Garden-Arena Corporation—reportedly for $179,520. It was a painful parting. Adams and his father had sat side by side at home games when Weston was a boy. He had played hockey as a youth—first at the Arena, and then at the Garden—and later tended goal for the Harvard Crimson varsity team. In 1936, he had become president and governor of the Bruins.

"I'll always be a Bruins fan," he said after closing the deal. "I'll still be nervous before the start of a game."

Adams could take comfort, however, in the knowledge that the team was in good hands. Walter Brown was president of the Garden-Arena Corporation—so named because the company owned both the Garden and the older, smaller Arena, where the Bruins had started—and he became president and governor of the Bruins. He and Adams had known each other, through their fathers, since boyhood. Gordon Brown had managed both buildings and had brought Walter into the business. Walter Brown had become a successful and celebrated promoter—one of the best in America. He was president of the Arena Managers Association, president and part owner of the Boston Celtics of the National Basketball Association, president of the Boston Amateur Athletic Association, sponsor of the famed Boston Marathon, and founder and president of the Boston Olympics, a team of barnstorming American college hockey players.

All that made him a welcome addition to the NHL. "The sale of the Bruins was the best thing that could have happened to the club," the *Hockey News* declared in a front-page editorial. "There is absolutely a new spirit in the Bruins camp and it's found its way from general manager Art Ross down to the assistant equipment manager. The team is full of pep and bounce. Optimism has become the keynote whereas gloom and misery were predominant last year."

The Hawks changed hands in the fall of 1952. General manager Tobin and a group of investors had purchased a controlling interest from the heirs of Major Frederic McLaughlin after his death in December 1944, and the family had kept a minority stake. Tobin and his partners did not have deep enough pockets to shoulder the annual losses and the McLaughlin heirs had no desire to squander their inheritance on a losing hockey team. They sold to the only possible buyers: Arthur Wirtz and James Norris, the team's landlords and the owners of Chicago Stadium for almost twenty years. Three months later, Norris died and his older son, James D., became the governor of the Hawks.

The new owners had scarcely assumed control when rumours surfaced that they would either move the Hawks to St. Louis, where they also owned the arena, or would fold the team altogether. James D. quickly squelched the speculation. He was a big man. He had a king-size personality and an appetite for drink to go with it, and he boasted that he was wealthy enough to keep the Hawks afloat even if they lost $1 million a year for the next two or three centuries.

"I know $100 million I can put my hands on," he said. "For sure there's $200 million and I'm probably worth $300 million."

The older, wiser, more pragmatic Wirtz wasn't happy losing $300,000, let alone $300 million, and said so in an interview, granted in early December 1953, while in Milwaukee to attend a professional ice show. (He and the Norrises owned the travelling production.) "I'd like to pull the Black Hawks out of Chicago," he told a reporter from the *Chicago American*. "The team has lost $350,000 already and the future isn't bright, all because we can't get players regardless of how much we're willing to spend.

"I wonder how the league would like to operate with just four teams, just in case the Hawks and Rangers folded," he continued. "That's the way things are headed unless they . . . assure equitable division of players, especially the younger ones . . .

"I refuse to continue to spend good money on behalf of a losing venture," he concluded. "If they can't take immediate action, I will—and they won't like what I'm going to do."

Having got all that off his chest, Wirtz was unprepared for the sudden burst of publicity that followed. "Misquote," he told the reporters who descended after his intemperate remarks hit the newsstands. "I've never heard of anything like that. I have no thought of that. The Black Hawks can't be taken out of the league. It's absurd."

That settled the matter. The Hawks weren't going anywhere, though they were, as usual, having another miserable season. By the midpoint of the 1953–54 campaign, they were deep in the cellar with a mere seven wins, twenty-five losses and five ties. Clarence Campbell and Conn Smythe conferred with Wirtz about the plight of the Hawks—and how to get them some players— but there were no quick and easy solutions. The league's sad-sack club finished with a measly twelve wins, a whopping fifty-one losses and seven ties and missed the playoffs for the seventh time in eight seasons.

Meantime, the new owners of the Bruins weren't any happier than Wirtz. At the annual meeting of the Garden-Arena Corporation in August 1954, the board of directors unanimously approved a revenue-sharing motion, which read, "Resolved, that for the 1954–55 regularly scheduled games the visiting clubs will receive 10% of the net box office receipts after deduction of 5% to the National Hockey League."

Art Ross presented the motion at an NHL board meeting held September 15 at the Park Lane Hotel in New York, but was unable to muster much support. "The pressure in the last three years has been terrific," he said. "I don't know how they [Bruins] are going to keep on going."

"I think it is very detrimental to hockey to bring this forward," Conn Smythe said.

"So helping your weak partners is detrimental?" Ross asked.

"There should be no handouts," Smythe replied. ". . . I don't agree with dishing out the dole. I prefer to see a man standing up and trying to make a success of it."

"That is what I am trying to do in Boston," said Brown.

"Have you ever found Canadiens lacking to help Boston?" Frank Selke asked. "I can remember when we were getting peanuts and Boston was getting much."

"Look up your records," Ross snapped, "and you will see that Canadiens did get money."

Clarence Campbell asked if someone would second the motion. Nobody volunteered. Campbell stated that the matter could not be put to a vote. That brought General Kilpatrick into the discussion. He disagreed with the Boston proposal, but thought there was merit in the concept of revenue sharing.

"I don't think this plan . . . should be abandoned for all time," he said. ". . . I think it should be open for re-examination."

"Is it a matter of record that any money has been given to clubs in this league?" Smythe inquired.

"We had a special assessment which was distributed to Chicago and Boston amounting to $73,000," Campbell replied.

"And that is the thanks you get for it," Smythe snapped.

"Is that not what always happens?" Selke added. "When you lend a friend a thousand dollars he becomes your enemy."

"I would like to say something," Brown interjected. "I have not been in the league very long, but I have been watching hockey since 1924 and have seen a lot of teams come in and go out. All the clubs should consider this question. You are at the irreducible minimum with six clubs . . . and I would not like to believe that if a club gave any indication of a reasonable ability to operate . . . that it should be allowed to go down the drain."

Still, there were no seconders. Ross withdrew the motion. That ended the discussion—and the possibility of a revenue-sharing agreement—and Campbell directed the board to the next item on the agenda.

———

THE NHL HAD BECOME A lopsided league because three organizations—
the Leafs, Canadiens and Red Wings—had built productive farm systems,
while their partners—the Rangers, Bruins and Hawks—had failed to keep pace.

The Leafs were first to begin developing talent by sponsoring junior teams,
meaning they either owned or subsidized them. In return, the players, initially
as young as sixteen, affixed their signatures to one of three forms—option
form A, B or C—and thereby assigned their professional rights to the Leafs in
perpetuity. Once they had graduated from junior, the most promising prospects moved on to a minor-pro affiliate, while the very rare one went straight
to the Leafs.

All this began during World War II, in the absence of Conn Smythe, who
was in Europe commanding an anti-aircraft battalion. Smythe had entrusted
day-to-day operations to his resourceful and reliable all-purpose aide, Frank
Selke. Sponsorship was Selke's idea, and he put it in place almost by stealth, as
he tells us in his autobiography, *Behind the Cheering:* "Before the other NHL
clubs caught on, we had signed most of the good lads in Canada."

This may have been a slight exaggeration. Nevertheless, Selke struck sponsorship agreements with the Toronto Marlboroughs and the St. Michael's
College Majors—the former for kids of the Protestant faith, the latter for those
who were Roman Catholic. He also established a Leaf presence in the West by
sponsoring the Winnipeg Monarchs of the Manitoba Junior Hockey League.
Selke's efforts paid off handsomely. The prospects groomed on those junior
teams formed the nucleus of the great Leaf clubs that won three consecutive
Stanley Cups in the late 1940s.

Selke wasn't around to enjoy those triumphs, however. Smythe had returned
from Europe. He had recovered from serious war wounds and he was running
the Gardens like a little tyrant, something Selke could not abide. He quit in the
summer of 1946 and quickly landed the general manager's job in Montreal. On
the opening day of training camp in September, Selke watched fifty-eight veterans and hopefuls work out. He was not impressed and immediately asked to
meet with the directors of the Canadian Arena Company, owner of the Forum
and the Canadiens.

He told them the Canadiens had six players who were as good as any in the
game: goaltender Bill Durnan; defencemen Emile Bouchard and Ken Reardon,

and the forward line of Maurice Richard, Elmer Lach and Toe Blake. But the supporting cast was weak and the pipeline all but empty. The Canadiens' only affiliate, the senior Montreal Royals, had an aging lineup with few good prospects.

Senator Donat Raymond, president of the company and the team, asked Selke what he proposed to do. "I'd like to inaugurate a farm system with a team in every province to build up young reserves, as in Toronto," he said.

The senator asked how much it would cost. At least $300,000 just to get started, Selke said, and without flinching or hesitating, Raymond said, "We owe the people of Montreal a good hockey team. Go ahead and build an empire."

Selke began signing sponsorship agreements and before long had built something that far exceeded anything his competitors were doing. The Canadiens' lineup of affiliates changed periodically, but over the years they had as many as thirteen teams sprinkled across the country—from Halifax to Edmonton. By the early 1950s, the Canadiens were spending $150,000 a year on player development.

They could do that because Senator Raymond and the directors of the arena company used the Forum to support the team. Monies earned through ice shows, boxing, wrestling and other forms of entertainment funded Selke's network of sponsored and affiliated teams. This economic model was reversed in New York, Boston and Chicago. The Rangers, Bruins and Black Hawks were merely sources of revenue used to support stadium corporations. Nevertheless, all three clubs had to invest, however modestly, in player development, and the Rangers made a bigger commitment than either the Bruins or Hawks.

According to a report that appeared in the *Hockey News* in October 1948, the Rangers had affiliation agreements with four minor-pro teams—the New Haven Ramblers, New York Rovers, St. Paul Saints and Tacoma Rockets—and Ranger alumni were coaching in each venue. New York also sponsored three junior teams, the Verdun Cyclones, Guelph Biltmores and Lethbridge Native Sons, and these clubs produced a number of bona fide NHLers, including goaltender Gump Worsley, defenceman Harry Howell and forwards Andy Bathgate and Dean Prentice.

A *Hockey News* report of January 1948 announced that the Bruins had hired their first full-time scout, the retired Leaf Harold (Baldy) Cotton, and he had been instructed "to have an eye for aggressiveness and will to win—not just ability." The Bruins had also established a farm system. It included a working arrangement with the Hershey Bears of the American Hockey League and a similar agreement with the Boston Olympics. As well, they were sponsoring the St. Catharines TeePees and the Port Arthur West End Bruins, both Junior A teams, and the Junior B St. Catharines Toledos.

The Hawks lagged far behind the rest of the league. Bill Tobin and his partners were either unwilling to invest in a farm system or, more likely, simply lacked the financial wherewithal. In any event, under their ownership, the Hawks had a working arrangement with the Kansas City Mohawks of the United States Hockey League and in July 1950 signed an affiliation agreement with the St. Louis Flyers of the American Hockey League.

That was it until the franchise changed hands. Wirtz and Norris—while complaining loudly about their inability to acquire talent—recognized that they had to catch up. In March 1954, the *Hockey News* reported that the Hawks had working agreements with two senior teams, the Quebec Aces and Chatham Maroons; the junior Galt (Ontario) Black Hawks; and the minor-pro Calgary Stampeders of the Western Hockey League. They were also forming an AHL team to be based in Indianapolis.

Then, in January 1955, Norris announced that the Hawks had paid $150,000 to acquire the AHL's Buffalo Bisons. As part of the deal, the Hawks got the St. Catharines TeePees, who had severed their ties with Boston and aligned themselves with the Bisons. "Norris is determined to make the Hawks contenders again," the *Hockey News* reported. "His latest move certainly indicates that he means business."

By then, however, the Canadiens had assembled a formidable team due principally to Selke's prolific, all-bases-covered farm system. Montreal's sponsored and affiliated clubs had produced in quick succession a startling number of players who were destined to become stars in their day and legends with the passage of time. Defenceman Doug Harvey arrived in the fall of 1947. Right winger Bernie Geoffrion broke in in 1950. Left winger Dickie Moore began his rookie campaign in 1951. Jean Béliveau donned the *bleu, blanc et rouge* in 1953. Jacques Plante became the starting goaltender in 1954.

In the final weeks of the 1954–55 campaign, Selke's mighty Canadiens were performing like a beautifully designed, perfectly assembled machine. They were strong in goal, on defence and up front, lethal on the power play and stingy on the penalty kill. Maurice Richard, Bernie Geoffrion and Jean Béliveau were first, second and third in scoring and the Canadiens were in top spot. Then, on the evening of Sunday, March 13, a stunning outburst of violence at Boston Garden nearly wrecked it all.

COINCIDENTALLY, THE NHL BOARD MET the next morning at the Commodore Hotel in New York. Among other things, the governors set dates for the three upcoming playoff series, agreed upon the opening and closing dates of the 1955–56 season and received a report on balloting for individual trophies and all-star ballots. At the conclusion of the day's business, Clarence Campbell said, "Anything else?"

"May I bring up some reference to the game in Boston last night?" Walter Brown asked. "I have been pursued by newspapermen ever since I arrived. We had six minutes to go and the Canadiens had pulled their goalkeeper and we had three defencemen on. I don't know how this thing started because I sit in one corner of the rink at the other end of the building.

"I am perfectly willing to base my case on whatever the referee reports. The only thing I want to say is that in the interests of the league, something should be done. We have made some progress in bringing Boston back to hockey and we are going to make some more fans. But . . . unless some pretty strong measures are taken in this case it is going to nullify what has been done because our fans don't like brawls on the ice.

"Richard went berserk and it is all in the papers and what made it look so bad was that two or three times he was disarmed but picked up a stick again and went after [Hal] Laycoe and the linesman."

"Have you got the referee's report?" James Norris asked Campbell.

"I have a verbal report from the referee-in chief . . . and a hearing will be held in Montreal on Wednesday morning," Campbell replied.

"It was really so rough," Brown added, "that the police wanted to arrest Richard and also [Dick] Irvin, but we were able to stop that."

"I will not be there, so you can conduct your inquiry without me," Frank Selke told Campbell. "As a matter of fact, I am not going to make any comment, either. If you all knew how sorry I am because that fellow is playing his best hockey and you fellows thought he was finished. Now he has thrown it all out of the window . . . none of you can appreciate what I feel because away from the rink he is such a decent guy."

"What I have said is in full recognition of the fact that he fills our rink," said Brown. "We had almost twelve thousand there."

CAMPBELL SET THE HEARING FOR 10:30 A.M., Wednesday, March 16; league headquarters; sixth floor; Sun Life Building; corner of Dorchester Boulevard and Metcalfe Street in the heart of downtown Montreal. That gave him time to study the reports of the game officials. It also gave the newspapers an opportunity to conduct their own haphazard inquiry.

The Boston sportswriters questioned Hal Laycoe, who admitted to striking Richard on the side of the head with his stick, but insisted that Richard, not he, had struck the first blow. As the *Globe*'s Tom Fitzgerald reported: "Laycoe said he was skating alongside the Rocket after a faceoff, following the puck when all of a sudden the Rocket brought up his stick like a pitchfork. He said it was just as if the Rocket was pitching hay. The stick hit him on the bridge of the nose."

Globe columnist Dave Egan offered a more skeptical take on the Boston player: "Hal Laycoe's first name is not spelled Halo, nor is there anything angelic about him. He plays needling hockey behind his eyeglasses. He hands out plenty of bumps, sometimes skating out of his way to do so. He has been in the league long enough to know that Richard erupts like Vesuvius. . . . So the inevitable inevitably happened and Hal Laycoe, I suppose, should be considered an accessory before the fact."

The French-language daily *La Presse* gave its readers a good look at the damage Laycoe had inflicted on the Rocket. The paper ran a large photo of Richard, his head tilted to the right and his left index finger pointing to a spot just above his temple that had been shaved to the scalp so a wound could be stitched. The Montreal *Gazette* reported that Richard was suffering from severe headaches and had spent a night at a city hospital.

Inevitably, there was a review of the Rocket's past transgressions. The

Gazette estimated that Richard had accumulated fines of $2,500 during his thirteen-year career and had twice been involved in altercations with officials.

On the morning of March 4, 1951, in the lobby of a New York hotel, he had confronted referee Hugh McLean and berated him over a penalty McLean had assessed the previous evening in Montreal. The second incident had occurred December 29, 1954, at Maple Leaf Gardens. A minor-league call-up named Bob Bailey ran Richard into the end boards. Richard gave chase, slammed into Bailey just outside the blue line and clipped him with his stick. A fight ensued. The linesmen intervened. Richard broke free. He grabbed a discarded glove and whacked one of the officials in the face with it.

Yet there were those who argued for lenience—none more eloquently than columnist Egan, who wrote: " . . . it would be a grave injustice to Maurice Richard to ride him out of hockey on a rail. . . . Much must be forgiven a man like Richard, not because he is an immortal hockey star, but because he is one of those few men whose value never can be measured by the . . . salary he receives. He is one of the remarkable ones who spend more in genius than he ever can get in money."

But, in the mind of Clarence Campbell, the time for forgiveness was long past.

BY THE MORNING OF THE HEARING, the entire city of Montreal was transfixed by the Richard affair. "It was the talk everywhere," the *Gazette* reported, "on the streets, in offices, on street cars and in homes."

Richard arrived at league headquarters along with Dick Irvin and Ken Reardon, by then retired and serving as the team's director of player development. Laycoe and Bruins general manager Lynn Patrick flew in from Boston. Referee-in-chief Carl Voss attended with the three game officials, referee Frank Udvari and linesmen Cliff Thompson and Sam Babcock.

The hearing lasted three hours and thirty-five minutes. Newspapermen, photographers and radio and television reporters jammed the reception area outside Campbell's quarters. Crowds gathered in the sixth-floor corridor. Stenographers, office boys and middle-aged businessmen came and went throughout the proceedings, hoping for a glimpse of the Rocket or a scrap of news about the proceedings.

The afternoon was nearly spent before Montrealers learned the outcome. At 4:25 p.m., Campbell met the press. He sat at a desk and read from a series of typewritten pages. "There is some doubt as to who actually had the puck, but it was either Laycoe or Richard," Campbell stated, "and as Richard skated past Laycoe, the latter high-sticked Richard on the side of the head. The referee promptly and visibly signalled a penalty to Laycoe, but permitted play to continue as Canadiens were still in possession of the puck."

Richard skated behind the Boston net and had almost reached the blue line before Udvari blew the play dead. Montreal's tempestuous star felt blood oozing from the wound to his scalp. He spotted Laycoe nearby. "Suddenly, he skated toward Laycoe . . . and swinging his stick over his head with both hands he struck Laycoe a blow on the shoulder and face," Campbell stated.

The linesmen took hold of the players, and one managed to yank the stick from Richard. He got loose, grabbed another and delivered a pair of one-handed blows across Laycoe's back. Thompson seized Richard a second time, but could not hold him, and the Rocket landed one more blow with a stick.

"Linesman Thompson again got hold of Richard and forced him to the ice and held him there until a Canadien player pushed him away and Richard gained his feet. When he did so, he punched Linesman Thompson two hard blows on the face."

Richard admitted these misdeeds, but maintained he was not aware of what he was doing due to the injury to his head. Campbell dismissed that defence. "The only person Richard had to contend with when trying to get at Laycoe was the official," he told the press. "He had no difficulty locating Laycoe when he was making his attacks. Furthermore, the base color of the Boston uniform is white and the officials' sweaters are a deep orange color.

"I have no hesitation in coming to the conclusion . . . that the attack on Laycoe was not only deliberate, but persistent. . . . I am also satisfied that Richard did not strike Linesman Thompson as a result of mistake or accident as suggested."

RICHARD, IRVIN AND REARDON left the hearing after all the evidence had been presented. Irvin and Reardon went back to the Forum. They were hanging around Irvin's office with Elmer Lach and the *Herald*'s Elmer Ferguson when Campbell read his statement. A few minutes later, Richard arrived, and by then, Montreal radio stations had interrupted their regular programming to deliver the news.

"Is the ruling out?" Richard inquired.

"Be prepared for a shock, Rocket," replied Irvin. "You're out for the season, including the Stanley Cup playoffs."

Richard was stunned. "You're kidding," he said. "Now tell me the truth."

"Sorry," said Irvin. "That's the way it is, Rocket. No kidding."

MOST OF RICHARD'S PEERS in the hockey world—teammates excepted—agreed with the decision. Montrealers of every stripe were appalled and outraged. Radio station CKAC asked listeners to voice their opinions. The switchboard was immediately jammed. Enraged fans phoned the league offices and left messages, which under normal circumstances would have led to criminal charges.

"It's unfortunate for Mr. Campbell," said one. "I will kill him at the first opportunity."

A female caller warned: "He will be assassinated. It would be best if he didn't show up at the game Thursday night against Detroit."

A third caller warned, "You can be assured that Clarence Campbell will be dead before the end of the week."

Even Mayor Jean Drapeau weighed in. Rather than appeal for calm, he denounced the decision as too severe and a blow to the entire team as well as the city. "It wouldn't take too many decisions like that to kill hockey in Montreal," he declared.

All of this was a mere prelude for what was to come.

THE CANADIENS WERE SCHEDULED to play the Wings on the evening of Thursday, March 17. The teams were tied for first. Each had three games remaining. That hardly mattered to many Montrealers. They were preoccupied with Clarence Campbell. The phones rang all day at league headquarters.

There were more death threats. Young men, some bearing placards denouncing Campbell, hung around the Forum all afternoon. Producers at radio station CKVL sensed trouble and set up a mobile broadcasting unit in a service-station parking lot across the street. By 8 p.m.—thirty minutes before the opening faceoff—a crowd numbering at least five thousand had taken over St. Catherine Street.

Inside the Forum, the Wings and Canadiens warmed up and spectators slowly filled the seats. The public address announcer advised in a booming voice that anyone caught throwing objects on to the playing surface would be ejected—permanently if they happened to be season-ticket holders. The anthems were sung, the game began, and for a few minutes, the crowd forgot about Clarence Campbell and Maurice Richard, though the latter happened to be standing at one end of the rink, next to the goal judge and team physician Dr. Bill Head.

Detroit's Red Kelly opened the scoring five minutes in. Teammate Earl Reibel added another at the eleven-minute mark. Moments later, there was a commotion in one section. Campbell had arrived with his secretary, Phyllis King, and two other women from the office. They made their way to seats a few rows up from the ice. They had scarcely taken their places when Kelly scored again at 12:58. Twenty seconds later, Montreal's Calum MacKay put one past Terry Sawchuk.

But the crowd was oblivious. Every voice in the big building, it seemed, united to produce one roof-raising roar of "Shoo Campbell. Shoo Campbell. *Va t'en. Va t'en.* [Go away. Go away.]" Those seated above him hurled eggs, tomatoes and other debris—splattering the intended target and those around him. As all this happened, Richard turned to Dr. Head and said, "This is a disgrace."

The period ended. By then, Detroit led four-one. Campbell and his guests stayed seated. A young man skirted the ushers, approached Campbell and extended his right hand as though to congratulate him for having the courage to show up. Campbell reciprocated and the man slapped him hard across the face. Another got close enough to crush two large tomatoes against his chest.

Then someone from an upper row tossed a canister that landed near ice level, about twenty-five feet from the NHL president. There was a small explosion. A plume of thick, putrid smoke arose and people in the sections nearby began coughing and gasping and hastily vacated their seats. Campbell and his party slipped unnoticed to safety under the stands. Most of the crowd stayed put even as the smoke and stench spread.

Campbell conferred with Frank Selke, police chief Tom Leggett and fire chief Raymond Paré. Paré ordered the evacuation of the building. Campbell decreed that the Canadiens must forfeit. Selke wrote a short note conceding the contest—and with it first place—and handed it to an assistant to deliver to his Detroit counterpart, Jack Adams, and the decisions were announced over the public address system. Fans headed for the exits and the Forum organist played a tune called "My Heart Cries for You."

And pandemonium erupted when the Forum crowd met the mob in the street. Those who had stood outside all evening—chilled and bored, their fury simmering—began throwing stones, pop bottles and chunks of ice. They broke nearly every window in the facade of the Forum, as well as those of a nearby bank and jewellery store. Others set a newspaper kiosk on fire. Dozens of police officers formed a line to prevent the mob from moving. They seized the most flagrant lawbreakers—some seventy in all—and hauled them off to paddy wagons.

Repeatedly, the police tried to disperse the crowd—to no avail. Both sides stood their ground. The stalemate lasted till shortly after midnight. Then the police began to advance and the crowd slowly retreated east along St. Catherine Street, anything but peacefully. Young rowdies smashed storefront windows and looted display cases. They knocked over mailboxes, emptied garbage cans, overturned a police car, broke windows in streetcars and, as one merchant put it the next morning, left Montreal's main commercial thoroughfare looking as though a hurricane had hit it.

THREE DAYS LATER, THE SEASON ENDED. The Canadiens finished second. They had earned ninety-three points, two fewer than the league champion Red Wings, but twenty-three more than the third-place Maple Leafs; twenty-six more than the Bruins, whom they would meet in the opening round of the play-offs; forty-one more than the fifth-place Rangers; and fifty better than the Black Hawks, who had come last for the seventh time in ten years.

There were no upsets and not many surprises in the playoffs. The Wings dispatched the Leafs in four games and the Canadiens eliminated the Bruins in five. The final began April 3 in Detroit. The Wings had won or tied twenty-three straight games at the Olympia dating back to December 19, and they had a thirteen-game winning streak going for them as they prepared to face Montreal. They promptly added two more victories and grabbed a commanding lead, but Canadiens coach Dick Irvin boldly predicted, "We'll make it an interesting series yet."

And they did. The Canadiens swept the two games played at the Forum. The teams went back to Detroit and the Wings pulled ahead three-two. The Canadiens evened it with another win in Montreal, but the Wings remained formidable at home. The Montreal newspapers would later note that the temperature inside the Olympia was a steamy eighty degrees Fahrenheit for the seventh game and the ice soft, but both sides had to compete under the same conditions and the Wings won by a score of three-one. The star of the evening, with two goals, was another promising young product of Detroit's farm system—twenty-three-year-old Alex Delvecchio from Fort William, Ontario.

Clarence Campbell presented the Cup to captain Ted Lindsay and he held it aloft as the adoring crowd of 15,141—the largest of the season—roared its approval. The triumphant Wings lugged the big silver mug off to their dressing room, plunked it on to a massage table and Lindsay yelled, "Where's the beer?"

"They never got the beer," Joe Falls of the Associated Press wrote. "They got champagne instead."

The 1955 Stanley Cup final had proved to be a fine showcase for the NHL's two best teams. But the season that preceded it had exposed all that was wrong with the league. The strongest and weakest clubs remained light years apart. The Black Hawks and Rangers could not compete with the Wings and Canadiens, and the Leafs and Bruins couldn't do much either, except put up the occasional good fight.

The governors were desperate to close the gap between top and bottom. They wanted something done to improve the league's competitive balance. But things were moving in the opposite direction, and that became apparent the following season.

6

NO QUICK FIX (1955-1963)

TRAINING CAMPS WERE FINISHED. Starting rosters had been set. The 1955–56 season was about to begin. But first—as was the practice at the time— the defending Stanley Cup champions would square off against an assortment of the league's best in the annual all-star game. It was played Sunday, October 2, at the Detroit Olympia before 12,178 fans. Dick Irvin, who had signed with the Chicago Black Hawks during the off-season, coached the All-Stars. They were no match for the champs and lost three-one. Irvin, a famously sore loser who normally brooded over every defeat, shrugged off the loss and was at his witty best the next day when the stars, the Wings, league officials, team executives and representatives of the press converged on a downtown Detroit hotel for a postgame luncheon.

Clarence Campbell, the emcee, thanked the participants, wished everyone well in the upcoming season and called a few people up to the head table for photographs and the presentation of small commemorative gifts. Irvin received a set of steak knives that came in a fancy case with gold lettering that read R.D. (DICK) IRVIN.

"Look at that," he said to those seated at his table, among them Montreal *Gazette* columnist Dink Carroll. "I've only been in the league twenty-seven years and they can't get my name right. That R.D. should read J.D. [James Dickinson]."

"The league has provided you with an easy out," said Boston Bruins general manager Lynn Patrick. "If you don't win with the Black Hawks you can cut your throat."

"I thought of that," replied Irvin. "Pretty near told Mr. Campbell that when I was up at the head table."

"Maybe you'll get lucky this year," said Patrick. "You didn't have a single injury at your training camp."

"There's another way of looking at that," Irvin said. "None of them were going hard enough to get hurt."

Later, a reflective Irvin said: "You know, I was looking at my guys at the station just before we left Welland for Syracuse to play the exhibition game with the Bruins. They looked the same to me as the Canadiens or the Detroit Red Wings. They were all healthy-looking fellows. . . . They eat steaks too, just like those other two clubs. There can't be so much difference."

"Not until they put on their skates," someone quipped.

Irvin wouldn't deny that. He had been asked during training camp how he saw the season unfolding. The Canadiens would finish ten games ahead of their nearest rival, he had replied. Patrick was of the same opinion and had said so publicly.

And they weren't far off. The Canadiens led from the start and never looked back. They began by shutting out the Leafs and Bruins. They were in first place at the end of October. By November 20, they were eight points ahead of the second-place Rangers and riding a ten-game unbeaten streak. By the middle of December, Jacques Plante had blanked the opposition six times. At the midway point, a few days after Christmas, the Canadiens had extended their lead over New York to thirteen points and they were thirty-five ahead of last-place Boston.

Their supporters were thrilled, of course, as columnist Jerry Trudel noted in the December 25 edition of the French-language daily *La Patrie*. "With all due respect to Bing Crosby and the nine million copies of 'White Christmas' that he has sold," Trudel wrote, "it's a *bleu, blanc, rouge* Christmas that sports fans in Montreal and the province of Quebec are celebrating today."

He attributed the team's early success to its new coach, Toe Blake. "He directs them without dominating them, moves them without whipping them." said Trudel. "He has ignited the aspirations and ambitions of the rookies as well as the veterans. He has moulded the great individual talents of his players into a dynamic and powerful machine."

A few days earlier, Lester Patrick had offered his perspective. Patrick, then retired and living in Victoria, British Columbia, told a hockey writers' luncheon in New York: "There is no doubt about it, this is a tough league and that Montreal team is one of the greatest I've seen. Their power play is without equal."

Bruins coach Milt Schmidt was of the same opinion and said so during a stop in Montreal. "You guys up here are spoiled," he told a group of sportswriters. "The Canadiens have the greatest power play in hockey. Because other teams can't stop it, you say they can't kill penalties. . . . They've got a guy like Harvey on one of the points and he handles the puck like a forward. They've got Geoffrion, a good stickhandler with a hard shot, on the other point. And they've got Béliveau, the Rocket and Bert Olmstead on the forward line. Olmstead can dig the puck out of the corners and the other two guys can put it in the net. They make plays that would be a joy to watch if they weren't making them against you."

Among the owners, though, another conversation was taking place. They took a dim view of the chasm emerging between the Canadiens and the rest of the league and concluded that something must be done.

THE OWNERS HAD MET ON DECEMBER 14. They had discussed the lack of parity—a problem that had perplexed them since the end of the war. They had searched for solutions and had left no stone unturned. They talked about sponsorship, scouting and the inter- and intra-league drafts. They explored alternatives to the existing methods of acquiring and developing players, but at length decided these were questions best left to the general managers.

They instructed Clarence Campbell to convene a meeting, and they gave him a mandate. He and the general managers were to develop a new program of player development and distribution that would: (a) improve the competitive balance; (b) ensure that the weak teams got first call on top-notch new talent; and (c) reduce their costs without affecting the supply of high-quality young players.

The general managers met on January 5, a Thursday, at the Windsor Hotel in Montreal. Campbell apprised them of the owners' directives and stressed the urgency of the task at hand. Two clubs, the Bruins and Black Hawks, desperately needed players. The situation in Chicago was especially grim. The crowds were so sparse that the Hawks had shifted seven home games in 1954–55 to other cities—namely St. Louis, Omaha and St. Paul—and in 1955–56 they were going to play six more in those venues. The Hawks had lost $750,000 over the previous two seasons and Arthur Wirtz and James Norris were again threatening to fold the team.

"I cannot visualize the present owners of Chicago agreeing to expose themselves to losing another $300,000 if they cannot get a hockey team that can sell tickets in their building," Campbell told the general managers.

All agreed that the intra-league draft was not working as intended. Boston's Lynn Patrick pointed out one shortcoming. "The draft was put into effect so that all other players except the protected ones were going to be free agents," he said, ". . . and it was no sooner in effect than Mr. Smythe and others got together and said we won't touch yours if you don't touch ours."

Chicago's Tommy Ivan spoke to another deficiency. "Our experience of the draft up to now has not been too good," he said. "The big reason is that if [a player] has been with his club for eight or six or ten years . . . if we draft such a player . . . nine times out of ten he is still thinking about the club he used to play for. They are not doing us any good."

Despite its inherent problems, the draft survived. Campbell put forward a motion reading, "This meeting is of the opinion that it would improve the competitive balance of the league if the spirit of the legislation covering waivers and the drafting of players was lived up to." It passed unanimously.

Sponsorship proved to be a far more slippery issue. The six NHL clubs were, at that moment, sponsoring forty-five junior teams: twenty-four in Ontario, nine in Quebec and twelve in the West. Montreal was supporting thirteen, New York and Detroit seven each—and both were funding a portion of an eighth—Boston and Chicago were backing six apiece and Toronto five.

Everyone agreed that doing away with sponsorship altogether would be too radical. But how to modify the system—that was the problem. Campbell stated his position at the outset. "I am satisfied that the two weak clubs should have two bonus choices of any hockey players in any place in the world," he said. ". . . We have got to get down to brass tacks and say unless they get a solid shot in the arm of the four best prospects . . . they are going to be in serious trouble."

The general managers spent the better part of the day wrestling with the issue. Everybody made suggestions except Montreal's Ken Reardon. He raised two objections. First, the Canadiens were spending $184,000 that year supporting junior clubs, far more than anyone else. If they allowed their rivals to pluck the best prospects, the Canadiens would be compensated to the tune of $15,000 per draft pick—a poor return on investment. His second objection sprang from a belief that junior hockey would not survive without NHL sponsorship money. "What you are asking me is to reduce the number of sponsored teams or to release sponsored players," he said. "I would do it in a minute if you told me these [junior] teams were going to continue to operate."

Several times, Campbell responded directly to Reardon, and he repeated the same point. "What you are losing sight of," is how he put it at one point in the discussion, "is that you are not going to have anyone to compete with in this league very shortly, and I mean shortly, unless some realistic steps are taken to share the available material."

Despite such admonishments, Reardon did not yield. Campbell put the issue to a vote. Reardon abstained, but his counterparts adopted a weak motion to the effect that "The extension of the intra-league draft to sponsored players and to players on the NHL negotiation lists would be helpful in improving the competitive balance of the league . . . and it is recommended to the owners that legislation to this end be enacted."

THREE WEEKS LATER, ON JANUARY 25, the general managers met again, this time at the Royal York in Toronto. Their primary purpose was to devise a fair and workable system for drafting players off sponsored teams. Several times, Clarence Campbell had to push the managers for a decision. "We have got to tell [the owners] what we think," Campbell said near the end of the morning session. "We were delegated to do a certain job and consider certain objectives. . . . I don't want the owners to feel that we have simply passed the ball back to them."

"I thought this was all right in Montreal," Toronto's Clarence Day said, "but having time to think it over, there are some bugs I could not approve of."

"That is quibbling," Campbell replied. "You, as the general manager of an organization, represent your club here and should say you are in favour of that resolution or not. . . . Do you want me to say you could not make up your mind?"

"Is that so awful?" Day shot back. "The owners haven't any ideas?"

"That may be," responded Campbell. "But they are paying our respective salaries and they expect us to come up with answers. You have to recommend a course of action and be prepared to stand by it."

"We can't make the decision," Montreal's Ken Reardon interjected.

That brought Chicago's Tommy Ivan into the discussion. "My problem is getting National League–calibre players for 1956–57," he said. ". . . I am unable to obtain players from National League clubs of the calibre that will help us. . . . The draft that has been suggested would help because there are three or four top amateurs who would help us right now."

"And if the provisional recommendation of the January 5 meeting is abandoned, then you have lost the one thing which you thought would be helpful?" Campbell inquired.

"Yes, I have lost unless someone has another suggestion," Ivan said.

There were, however, several legitimate problems that would have to be solved before the draft could be extended to sponsored teams. Would the players be required to sign with the NHL club that chose them? Could they remain in junior? What would a player's status be if the NHL team didn't want him after all? Would an NHL club have to pay for a draft pick in full immediately? Or would the money be due in instalments?

During the afternoon session, a testy exchange occurred between Reardon and Lynn Patrick of the Bruins. "You are not developing hockey players for the rest of us, you are developing them for Montreal and Montreal alone," Patrick said.

"You can talk all you want," Reardon snapped. "The club developing the players should get first pick of the players."

"Then we are wasting our time completely because you cannot have a league based on that philosophy," Campbell said. "It is impossible."

And Patrick added a rejoinder of his own: "If your contention is that the team that goes out and finds players and puts them on teams, in which they invest some amount of money, and they are entitled automatically to the first choice of all those players, you are simply saying the American clubs are not going to have a chance to compete. It is automatic."

And so it went. Back and forth. But no consensus emerged. The owners met in mid-February and considered the issue, but no more successfully than their general managers, and that ended any prospect of reforming the sponsorship system.

CLARENCE CAMPBELL CALLED A MEETING of the board of governors for mid-March, as he did every year, to set the dates for the upcoming playoffs and to select the officials who would handle the three best-of-seven series. On the day the governors gathered, at the Commodore Hotel in New York, 197 of 210 games had been played and, aside from the problems in Chicago, Campbell had some good news to report.

Gate receipts leaguewide were up $402,900 and it looked as though they would reach their targeted increase of $441,700. Almost as an afterthought, Campbell added, " . . . in recent years, the percentage of our earnings which have been paid out in salaries has been declining constantly."

"That is not unusual," General John Kilpatrick of the Rangers replied. "Some who have been in the red are getting back in the black."

Campbell noted that a few years earlier baseball's National and American Leagues had submitted a report to the U.S. Senate which stated that their players were receiving twenty-three per cent of that sport's total gate. "Ours was between twenty-six and twenty-seven at the time," he added. "I cannot accurately forecast what it will be this year, but it will be four or five per cent below that."

"The average [salary] of hockey players today is $9,280," New York's Murray Patrick said.

That brought a word of caution from Toronto's Clarence Day. "Fantastic statements get out that a player is going to get $7,000 or $8,000 more than that," he said. "We should try and keep these boys from telling everyone their business."

Financially, the league was relatively robust at that moment—Chicago excepted. From a competitive standpoint, it was anything but. The Canadiens had clinched first place on February 25—three weeks before the end of the season. They finished with one hundred points—twenty-four better than runner-up Detroit and fifty ahead of Dick Irvin's sixth-place Black Hawks. Jacques Plante posted the lowest goals-against average—1.86 in sixty-four starts. Doug Harvey was voted the league's best defenceman and Jean Béliveau won the scoring title.

And hockey fans in Canada were eager for the playoffs to begin. That became apparent when the CBC announced that it would only televise Saturday night games or those that might determine a Stanley Cup champion. Angry viewers flooded the network's Toronto switchboard with more than a thousand calls in a single evening, and CBC quickly decided that all the games would be available on television.

The Canadiens waltzed through the playoffs. They beat the Rangers in five and the Red Wings in five to claim their eighth Stanley Cup, and Montrealers were thrilled. The city held a victory parade and somewhere between 250,000 and 500,000 people—a quarter to half of the populace—lined the thirty-mile route. The crowds repeatedly converged on the players, who were seated in open convertibles, and a planned four-hour tribute turned into a six-and-a-half-hour marathon.

The faithful went home happy on that chilly April day, and their happiness sprang from a profound confidence that this team would be a force for years to come. But the Canadiens would have their sails trimmed ever so slightly when the board of governors met on June 4, 1956, for the league's thirty-ninth annual general meeting.

THE YEARLY POSTSEASON CONCLAVE was held at the Windsor Hotel, and the seventh item on the day's agenda was a report from the rules committee. The members recommended two changes of note, both of which were accepted by the board. First, the neutral zone on either side of the centre-ice red line was to be a no man's land during pre-game warmups. On several occasions during the past season, heated words had been exchanged while the players loosened up, and the hostilities had escalated, but the league wanted no part of fights or brawls before the puck even dropped.

The second amendment pertained to power plays. At the time, a player sent off for a minor infraction had to serve the full two minutes no matter how many times the opposition scored. The committee recommended that the offender be allowed to return after his team had given up one goal. The board voted five-one in favour, the only dissent coming from the Canadiens' Frank Selke, who had previously expressed his opinion in no uncertain terms.

"You might outvote me," he had told two fellow executives, Lynn Patrick of the Bruins and brother Murray of the Rangers, during the Stanley Cup playoffs, ". . . but you'll never convince me of its justice. In all the years of Detroit's dominance and their almighty power play there was no suggestion of such a change. Now Canadiens have finally built one and you want to introduce a rule to weaken it. Go get a power play of your own."

The Montreal sportswriters concurred with Selke and saw the change as a jab at the Canadiens. Not so, said retired Ranger Frank Boucher, who was coaching in the Western Hockey League. "The new rule makes sense," he told the assembled scribes. "We tried it last winter and everybody liked it."

The WHL had amended the rule on power plays, Boucher added, and so had the American Hockey League. But Lynn Patrick left no doubt that the dominance of the Canadiens had influenced the NHL decision-makers. "I can remember a night in the Forum last season when we had a two-nothing lead over the Canadiens," Patrick said. "Then we got a penalty and while we were shorthanded Jean Béliveau scored three goals."

The annual general meeting concluded the business of the NHL season. Three weeks hence, Clarence Campbell would close the league office for the month of July, as he had done each year since becoming president, and he and his staff would take their vacations. But one restless member of the hockey fraternity, Detroit's Ted Lindsay, would spend the off-season brooding over the near-dictatorial power the teams wielded over the players, the inevitable inequities it created and what could be done about it.

BY THE SUMMER OF 1956, Ted Lindsay was approaching the end of a great career and preparing himself for life after hockey. He and teammate Marty Pavelich owned a sales company, which they called Lindsay and Pavelich to capitalize on their prominence as members of the Red Wings. They represented auto parts manufacturers, and they spent the summer and what little time they could spare during the season pitching these goods to the Big Three—General Motors, Ford and Chrysler.

Lindsay was thirty-one. He had played twelve seasons and had jumped straight from the Junior A St. Mike's Majors to the Wings as a nineteen-year-old. He was small for the NHL, standing five foot eight and weighing 168 pounds, but what he lacked in size, he made up for in spirit. "I've really got one fault," he once told the *Hockey News*. "I can't back away from trouble. At times, I wish I could. But I can't and that's all there is to it."

Initially, the Wings saw him as a defensive forward who could be used to check Maurice Richard and other offensive stars. But he had become a prolific and consistent scorer while playing on a line with Gordie Howe and Sid Abel. Lindsay reached the hundred-goal plateau in February 1949. He won the NHL scoring championship in 1949–50 and was made team captain in 1952 after the Wings traded Abel to Chicago. In early November 1955, he scored goal number 271, surpassing the record for left wingers established two decades earlier by the Canadiens' Aurèle Joliat.

By the summer of 1956, Lindsay had been around long enough to understand that the players had no voice in running the league. They were not consulted or even considered, for example, when the owners extended the schedule from sixty to seventy games. Management set the terms and conditions of employment, which were encoded in the standard player's contract, a document that had not been significantly revised or upgraded since the last days of Frank Calder's tenure as president. The players had next to no bargaining power when it was time to sign. They were expected to play hockey and keep quiet. Troublemakers were liable to be buried in the minors or find themselves unemployed altogether because the standard contract allowed a team to terminate a player, without cause, on two weeks' notice.

Lindsay also observed that the owners, who were essentially competitors, met several times a year to discuss their mutual interests and to resolve common problems. So did the general managers. The players, on the other hand, barely spoke to their counterparts on other teams and were, in fact, discouraged from fraternizing. As Lindsay would later recall: "We'd ignore each other if we met on the street. We'd cross the road to avoid one another."

The fiery little left winger decided something had to be done, and he turned to another sport for guidance. Two years earlier, major-league baseball players had formed an association to give themselves some collective strength and clout when dealing with the owners. Cleveland Indians pitcher Bob Feller was serving as president in 1956, and Lindsay arranged a meeting through a mutual acquaintance while the Indians were in Detroit to play the Tigers. Fuller referred Lindsay to two New York lawyers, Norman Lewis and Milton Mound, who had helped the ballplayers organize.

Lindsay made three trips to New York that summer to consult with Lewis and Mound. They provided a blueprint, and Lindsay went to work. He lined up support among his fellow Red Wings at training camp. The NHL All-Star Game, held in Montreal on October 9, presented an opportunity to reach out to opponents.

Players from the other five teams supported the idea and agreed to confer with their teammates. Lindsay cautioned that secrecy was essential. If a coach or manager got wind of the association, they would kill it before it was ever formed. He asked everyone to contribute one hundred dollars as a sign of good faith and to cover the lawyers' fees. He consulted, clandestinely, with members of each opposing club when they visited Detroit that fall, and by early 1957 he had all but one player onside and they were ready to go public.

ON THE EVENING OF FEBRUARY 10, 1957, a Sunday, the Canadiens were in action in New York, the Leafs were in Boston and the Red Wings in Chicago. Monday was a day of rest, as it usually was in the six-team league. The hired hands were allowed twenty-four hours to recuperate from the wars of the weekend, but this would be a black Monday for their overseers.

On that day—February 11, 1957—Ted Lindsay and a single representative of each of the other clubs held a press conference at the New York offices of Norman Lewis and Milton Mound. They stood before microphones, cameras and notebook-toting reporters and announced the formation of the National Hockey League Players' Association. Lindsay was president. Doug Harvey was first vice-president. The Bruins' Fern Flaman was second vice-president. Gus Mortson of the Hawks was third vice-president. The Leafs' Jim Thomson was secretary and Bill Gadsby of the Rangers was treasurer. Their objectives were modest, to say the least.

"We are very happy," Lindsay said. "Each of us might have individual problems, but we have not a group complaint right now."

Lindsay stressed repeatedly that, generally speaking, the players were content. The NHL base salary was $6,500 per year—$500 above the minimum for major-league baseball. They had a pension plan that had been established in 1947. Every player contributed $900 per season, while the league added two-thirds of the proceeds from the annual all-star game as well as twenty-five cents for every Stanley Cup playoff ticket sold.

In fact, the hockey fraternity seemed only to be following the lead of the other team sports. Baseball players had organized in 1954. Their National Football League counterparts had formed an association in December 1956, though the owners were refusing to recognize it. And the players of the National Basketball Association had threatened to join an industrial union, but league president Maurice Podoloff had asked for three months to set up a system for dealing with grievances.

The announcement of the players' association caught owners and managers off guard. "I didn't know anything about it," Conn Smythe admitted when reached at his winter retreat in Palm Beach, Florida. "Undoubtedly it was the best kept secret in hockey."

"I'm completely surprised," said Boston general manager Lynn Patrick. "I honestly don't see where the players have a grievance. I know they're fortunate to have the pension plan they have. I wish I was in it."

Clarence Campbell insisted he would remain "completely neutral," but went on to say that "there was nothing which the players of the NHL could accomplish through a union or association which could not just as easily be secured by direct, informal representations to the league or its member clubs."

Campbell's cautious remarks may have assured some people that nothing much had happened or would happen. But Lindsay and the player representatives knew, as they headed back to their teams, that they were in for a fight.

THE LEAGUE'S CAMPAIGN AGAINST the association began immediately, and Clarence Campbell and the owners employed two tactics. They attempted to intimidate individual players and they refused to negotiate with the newly formed organization. Nevertheless, the fight lasted a few days short of a year due to the courage and resolve of the players.

Campbell embarked on a fact-finding mission the same week that the players held their New York press conference. He met with the Wings and Canadiens on the pretext of reviewing the status of the league's pension plan. "At the Detroit meeting, I got a completely negative response," Campbell stated in a report to Leaf president Conn Smythe. "Nothing but the usual type of inquiry about the pension affairs and nothing about the players' association."

In Montreal, Campbell brought a report prepared by the auditors for the pension society and read it to the players, though that did nothing to quell their doubts. "Another point raised," he informed Smythe, "is the complaint that the hockey players after ten years are allowed to be sent . . . to the minor-league teams without having any choice on where they wish to go. In baseball if you are in ten years and waived out of the league you are free to bargain with whoever you please."

The harassment and intimidation of some of the ringleaders in the association began at the same time. Jack Adams publicly denounced Ted Lindsay's treachery and ingratitude. He told one friendly reporter that Lindsay was making $25,000 a year when the actual figure was half that, and that he lived in a lavish $40,000 home. Adams unleashed his invective near the end of a season in which the left winger became the fourth NHLer to notch three hundred goals and would finish second in scoring behind Gordie Howe.

The Leafs took a different approach with the insubordinate Jim Thomson, a defenceman who had spent twelve seasons with the team and had been a stalwart member of four Stanley Cup champions. The thirty-three-year-old native of Winnipeg had succeeded Ted Kennedy as captain, but graciously turned over the coveted *C* when Kennedy returned to the Leafs in midseason.

None of this mattered. Smythe traded Thomson to Chicago shortly after the season ended and took a jab at him in his annual year-end press conference. "I find it very difficult to feel that there is time during a hockey season for the captain of my club to influence young players to join an association, which has, as far as I can find out, no specific plans or ideas how to benefit hockey," he said. "I also feel that anything spawned in secrecy . . . has to have an odour to it."

Smythe and Adams continued to lead the fight during the off-season. On the afternoon of April 22—Easter Monday—Leaf lawyer Ian Johnston spoke at length over the phone with Clarence Campbell, and in a follow-up memo to Smythe he wrote: "During this conversation, we agreed to recommend . . . that the league . . . cannot ignore the existence of the association, but you should avoid any formal step of recognition such as asking the association to prove whom it represents and how and in what capacity. There should be no formal recognition to the extent that any contract is signed or representatives admitted on any league committee."

Meantime, Adams hinted at his next move during a postseason press conference. The Wings had finished first, but the Bruins had eliminated them in five, and the Detroit general manager promised a big shakeup. The only untouchables on the team, he declared, were Gordie Howe, Alex Delvecchio, Red Kelly, Marcel Pronovost and Al Arbour. Reporters immediately noted that Lindsay had been omitted, and *Detroit Free Press* reporter Marshall Dann wrote, "It'll be the biggest surprise of the summer, however, if he should trade Lindsay."

In fact, Adams shattered the off-season calm by doing just that. He sent Lindsay and the promising young goaltender Glenn Hall to Chicago in exchange for Forbes Kennedy and John Wilson. Shocked Red Wing fans bombarded the Olympia switchboard with calls of protest and sent dozens of letters to the city's newspapers.

Lindsay, who had previously told friends he would quit before accepting a trade, did the unthinkable: he held a press conference and complained of Adams's shabby treatment. "I wanted to close my hockey career in Detroit," he said. "But the derogatory remarks about myself and my family showed me that the personal resentment on the part of the general manager would make it impossible for me to continue playing in Detroit."

Adams, completely unaccustomed to backtalk from his players, replied in kind. "There is no place in sport for a disloyal or selfish athlete," he said. "And it would appear from Lindsay's statements, which are vindictive and untrue, that he is apparently putting himself above hockey."

THROUGHOUT THAT OFF-SEASON, Milton Mound attempted to advance the players' cause and managed to get a meeting with two lawyers representing the league. It was held on June 14, 1957, and the agenda included: compensation and other benefits paid to all players during training camp; regular-season travel expenses; reimbursement of moving expenses when a player was traded or sent to the minors; reasonable contributions to the players' pension fund from television, radio and other sources; and modifications to nine clauses in the standard player's contract.

The discussion yielded nothing. However, the lawyers forwarded the player demands to Campbell, and later that summer Mound wrote to ask for a meeting with the board. Campbell apprised the governors of all these developments when they met on September 23 at the Commodore Hotel in New York, and his report prompted a vigorous, if one-sided, exchange.

Smythe spoke first. "We should just tell these people to go and jump in the lake," he said. "This has been going on all summer. I called in my players and told them, 'You have to declare yourselves.' Having signed all players to contracts, there is nothing to negotiate."

"I really feel that apart from Lewis and Mound . . . the association is as close to being kaput as you can get it," Campbell said. "I don't think there is any substantial group of players for it at all. But whether the best way to handle them is to hit them on the nose and secure a knockout, or let them die out is a matter for your decision."

"I think the best way will be to let the Canadian clubs take the lead and say they won't be bound by U.S. laws," said Chicago's Arthur Wirtz.

"I have contracts signed willingly," said Detroit's Bruce Norris. "What is there to negotiate?"

"I think we are winning fast and there's no sympathy with them," added General John Kilpatrick of the Rangers. "We must watch our public relations and what we do and say very carefully."

Montreal's Frank Selke provided the wording of a motion, Campbell polished it and the board accepted it unanimously: "In view of the statements of the Toronto and Montreal clubs that they are operating under Canadian laws and cannot concede to the National Hockey League the right to conduct any negotiations on their behalf with the players' association under any other laws, the meeting takes no action on the association proposal."

JACK ADAMS HAD A MISERABLE OCTOBER. His hastily rebuilt Red Wings had eight new faces in the lineup. They lost their first three home games. Attendance dropped to its lowest level in several years. The Black Hawks paid their initial visit on a Sunday evening, October 28, and the return of Ted Lindsay was enough to draw a crowd of 11,828—the largest to that point in the schedule. Glenn Hall earned a shutout. The Hawks scored three times and the fans cheered each Chicago goal.

To make matter worse, the players' association wasn't going away. In fact, the players went on the offensive following the board's flimsy and cavalier dismissal of their association at the September 23 meeting. On October 12, Milton Mound filed in a New York court a $3 million lawsuit against the league, its six clubs, Campbell and each owner. The suit alleged that since 1926, when the Western Hockey League folded, the NHL had monopolized and controlled the sport, contrary to the U.S. Sherman Anti-Trust Act.

The players further alleged that they had been "deprived of their natural and lawful right to sell their services to the highest and most acceptable bidder." They also contended, "As a result of the defendants' monopolistic position, their economic power and control over this important industry, and over all who labor in it, is complete and absolute."

The news hit with an impact akin to an unexpected and back-wrenching rear-end collision, and hockey writers around the league scrambled to get answers to two questions: What, on earth, were the players thinking? And how would the powers that be react?

"I feel, and I know a lot of other players do too," Leaf captain George Armstrong said, "that this suit is just a way of forcing the league to recognize our association. I don't know anyone who is really interested in getting the money."

Montreal's Doug Harvey said, "We had to do something like this or the association would die."

Stafford Smythe, who was slowly emerging from his father's tutelage, undoubtedly spoke for many on the other side of the chasm when he said: "It's inconceivable to me that hockey players would try this. . . . That $3 million could mean the end of the NHL."

Reporters in Detroit caught up with Campbell at the Olympia while he was watching the Wings and Rangers, and one asked if he thought the suit was ridiculous, to which Campbell replied, "Anytime you're being sued for $3 million it isn't ridiculous."

In fact, the players appeared to have a strong case, but this was no assurance of victory. For one thing, the U.S. Supreme Court in 1922 had set a precedent by exempting baseball's National and American Leagues from antitrust laws. The players also faced the daunting prospect of spending months, if not years, fighting the league in court, and they might not get a clear decision on their principal objective: recognition of the association. Therefore, Mound asked labour relations boards in Ontario, Quebec, New York and Massachusetts to certify the association.

The hearing before the Ontario board was scheduled to start first, and the Leaf players agreed to meet on the evening of November 5 at the Gardens in order to confirm their support. That morning, prior to practice, Conn Smythe barged into the dressing room along with son Stafford, Clarence Campbell and Ian Johnston. The four of them worked on the players for two hours—to no effect. The players held their meeting and ran a gauntlet of newspaper photographers on the way into the Gardens. Mound and Johnston each spoke. An expert in labour law, Ted Nobbs, was on hand to provide neutral advice. The discussions lasted three hours. A vote was called, and every player supported the association.

Adams had better success with his players. The following week, he convinced them to pull out. Red Wing captain Red Kelly issued a statement saying that he and his teammates had not been informed of the lawsuit and disagreed with it, although they supported the aims of the association.

In any event, the developments in Detroit were little more than a distraction. The certification hearing before the Ontario Labour Relations Board proceeded as scheduled, and the board heard four full days of evidence before adjourning in mid-December. The proceedings resumed January 8, 1958, and both sides presented closing arguments. A similar hearing was slated to begin in New York that week, and in mid-February a court was slated to begin dealing with the lawsuit.

But two unexpected developments changed the dynamics of the dispute. First, New York Congressman Emanuel Celler and California's Patrick J. Hillings introduced a bill in the House of Representatives that, if passed, would exempt all professional sports leagues, not just baseball, from antitrust laws. "This pretty well pulls the carpet out from under the players' lawsuit," Leaf lawyer Johnston told the *Toronto Telegram*.

Mound, naturally, disagreed. "This doesn't adversely affect our lawsuit one iota," he told the paper. ". . . The law as it exists now is the law of the land."

Next, a moderate voice suddenly emerged among the otherwise intransigent owners. The previous September, Senator Hartland de Montarville Molson and his brother Thomas had acquired the Canadian Arena Company, owner of the Montreal Forum and the famous team that called the building home. Senator Molson had hitherto been silent. But early in January he met with his players— not to badger, berate or intimidate, but to listen. And he wasn't startled in the least by what he heard, according to Doug Harvey's account of the meeting.

"We presented a list of twenty-four demands," Harvey later told reporters. "He said a couple of them seemed a little unreasonable, but nothing that couldn't be discussed. He also saw nothing wrong with meeting with our association. He said many of his other employees belong to unions, others just to associations. . . . His main concern is to keep his workers happy."

The Senator proved to be a peacemaker. He adopted an idea that Harvey and some of his peers had floated two months earlier: the formation of a player-owner council that would meet annually or semi-annually. At the time, Smythe had categorically rejected the proposal, but now Senator Molson persuaded his counterparts—Smythe included—to give it a try, and they scheduled a meeting for February 4 in Palm Beach, Florida.

That day, the owners and two player representatives from each club met for eighteen hours. Campbell did not participate, nor did Mound. The players had made significant concessions to get to the table. They had agreed to withdraw their lawsuit and had asked the Ontario Labour Relations Board to hold off on its ruling. The owners had made a substantive gesture as well: they had completely abandoned their steadfast and adamant opposition to such a meeting.

The players did not get everything they wanted, but they got plenty. The owners refused to recognize the association, but did agree to establish a council. The owners confirmed the minimum annual salary of $7,000, which was better than baseball's entry-level compensation. They agreed to match, dollar for dollar, player contributions to the pension plan and agreed to an independent review of the plan. They agreed to increase the playoff bonus pool to the point where winners of both the league championship and the Stanley Cup would be entitled to $4,000 per player. They agreed to provide better hospital benefits, schedule fewer exhibition games and would henceforth cover moving expenses of players traded or sold during the season.

Many observers have seen these events as a resounding victory for the owners and a crushing defeat for the players. Such conclusions are fundamentally inaccurate. At a crucial moment in the year-long fight, the players chose compromise over confrontation and evolution over revolution.

Furthermore, the uprising of 1957–58 permanently changed things. Hitherto, the owners had run their teams and the league as if by divine right and had never sought the advice or views of the athletes they employed. Henceforth, the athletes would have a voice—first through the player-owner council, which met at least once a year until 1966, and beyond that, through the second NHL Players' Association, which was formed in 1967 and was recognized by the league.

The real losers were Smythe and Adams—the most ardent, vocal and vociferous advocates of an old order that had suffered a mortal blow.

IT MAY HAVE BEEN POETIC JUSTICE, one of life's cruel ironies or nothing more than coincidence, but the two teams that fell the furthest immediately after that epic upheaval were Conn Smythe's Maple Leafs and Jack Adams's Red Wings. The Wings finished third in 1957–58, their worst result in a decade, and then endured the ignominy of being swept out of the playoffs four straight by their archrival Canadiens. As for the Leafs, they finished last—a calamity that hadn't befallen them since 1927.

The troubles and travails of both continued in 1958–59. The Wings started strong and stayed close to the front-running Canadiens through the first half, and then ran out of gas and by March 1 had tumbled to fifth. The Leafs spent most of that season at or near the bottom, and in mid-March, with a mere five games remaining, were seven points back of the fourth-place Rangers. Practically everyone had left them for dead, except for Punch Imlach, their brash coach and general manager. He was still boasting that the Leafs would make the playoffs, and he saw an opportunity others had overlooked: a

Saturday–Sunday doubleheader against the Rangers. The Leafs won both ends and cut the spread to three points. Next, they won a midweek contest and reduced it to one. That set up a climactic final weekend. Both the Leafs and Rangers played on Saturday night, and both won. That meant that two seventy-game seasons would be decided on the basis of two Sunday matches.

The Rangers played in the afternoon at home against the Canadiens, the Leafs that evening in Detroit. While his players dressed, a nervous Imlach paced up and down a corridor and every few minutes checked the telegraph updates arriving in the Red Wings office from New York. He knew as the Leafs sprinted on to the ice for the opening faceoff that the Canadiens were ahead by a goal. Then, late in the first, there was an announcement. The New York game was over. Final score: Canadiens four, Rangers two.

The Leafs beat the Wings. They captured the fourth playoff spot, and after the game there was an aircraft waiting in Windsor to fly them to Toronto and on to Boston, where the semifinal was set to start two nights later. "We're the hungriest team in the world," a jubilant Imlach told reporters. "We're just getting started."

The Leafs upset the Bruins, though it took seven games, and advanced to the final against the Canadiens. Imlach was now brasher than ever. "We're going to beat them in six games," he boasted, but nobody was going to subdue Montreal's mighty Canadiens with bluff and braggadocio, and the Leafs didn't.

They won in overtime in game three, and that was it. The Canadiens rolled over them in five. They became the first team to win four straight Cups, and they celebrated accordingly. "It was one of the wildest dressing room scenes in Canadiens history," Red Fisher wrote in the *Montreal Star*. "Hordes of newspapermen and photographers and newsreel men clamoured for photos. A television camera was moved into the room to record the festivities. Champagne appeared as if by magic and was poured liberally into the Stanley Cup. Everybody satisfied their thirst."

THE CANADIENS REMAINED THE LEAGUE'S dominant team again in 1959–60. They finished first, thirteen points ahead of the second-place Maple Leafs and twenty-three better than the third-place Black Hawks. In the playoffs, they dispatched the Hawks in four and the Leafs in four and were again champions. They outscored their opponents by a cumulative score of 29–11, and Jacques Plante earned three shutouts. Small wonder, then, that the Canadiens' post-Cup celebration was quieter this time around.

"When you win . . . in four games after four previous Cup titles," said Doug Harvey, "you don't get too excited."

That playoff was the end for Maurice Richard. He retired in September 1960. He was thirty-eight. He had had a dazzling eighteen-year career. He was the game's greatest scorer and its most riveting performer, and he would be remembered—forever, as it turned out—but Frank Selke's formidable organization ensured that the team could carry on without his fiery presence.

The Canadiens won the league championship for the fourth consecutive season, but in the playoffs they received a rude surprise from the third-place Chicago Black Hawks. The long-moribund Hawks were an emerging powerhouse. They had superstar-calibre players throughout their lineup: Glenn Hall in goal, Pierre Pilote on defence, Stan Mikita at centre and Bobby Hull on left wing. The secondary talent included half a dozen skaters who had once been in the Canadiens system: the defenceman Dollard St. Laurent and the forwards Murray Balfour, Ed Litzenberger, Red Hay, Reggie Fleming and Ab McDonald.

The resurgent Hawks toppled the Montreal dynasty in the sixth game of the Stanley Cup semifinal, played April 4, 1961, at Chicago Stadium before more than eighteen thousand jubilant fans. "The Canadiens fought hard until the last two minutes when frustration, augmented by the wild victory cheers of the crowd, smothered them," the *Chicago Tribune*'s Ted Damata wrote.

The final was an all-American affair: Chicago versus Detroit; Jim Norris's Black Hawks against stepbrother Bruce's Red Wings. The teams traded wins through the first four games. The Hawks won game five at home and went back to Detroit with a chance to win it all.

For two periods, it was close—so close that Jim Norris was too nervous to watch the start of the third. He and general manager Tommy Ivan went for a walk outside the Olympia and returned to find that the Hawks held an insurmountable lead. Afterward, it was younger brother Bruce who had to trudge down the hall to the visitors' dressing room to congratulate his victorious sibling.

The Hawks flew home the next morning. A city that had ignored them through a long, dreary decade of mediocrity now thoroughly embraced them. A banner headline in the *Tribune* declared:

OUR BLACK HAWKS ARE WORLD CHAMPS!!!

Hundreds of fans greeted the players when they arrived at O'Hare Airport, toting the Cup and bleary-eyed from a postgame celebration that lasted till 4:30 a.m. A motorcade escorted them to City Hall and a civic reception in the council chamber. Bobby Hull, twenty-two, muscular, exceedingly handsome and loaded with confidence, mounted the rostrum, rapped the gavel and called for order. A fan asked if he'd like to be mayor and Hull replied: "I wouldn't mind. When do I run?"

A seven-piece Dixieland band, playing a robust rendition of "When the Saints Come Marching In," announced the arrival of Mayor Richard Daley and Cook County president John J. Duffy. The mayor praised the Hawks for their unsurpassed "ability and agility" and then proclaimed them "the greatest hockey team ever put together anywhere."

That was a stretch, of course. Nonetheless, the Hawks would remain a playoff team and Stanley Cup contender for several years to come. The fans were back. Chicago Stadium was once again the loud, raucous, zany place it had been in the late 1930s and early 1940s. The wobbly, money-losing franchise would survive. Furthermore, the resurrection of the Hawks had altered the league's competitive balance. There were now four strong and two weak teams, the weak links being the New York Rangers and Boston Bruins. It was not perfect, but much better than having three perennial underachievers—the problem that had dogged the league and resisted resolution since the end of the war.

SIGNIFICANT OFF-ICE CHANGES were occurring around the league as well. On November 23, 1961, Conn Smythe announced that he was selling his Maple Leaf Gardens shares to son Stafford and a group of partners that included Harold Ballard and John Bassett, publisher of the *Toronto Telegram*. Smythe immediately resigned as president and managing director of the Gardens, and on February 5, 1962, he retired as a governor of the NHL, a position he had held since 1927.

Three months later, Jack Adams announced that he was retiring—though, unlike Smythe, he did not go voluntarily. Bruce Norris wanted a man of his generation running the team. He gave the general manager's job to coach Sid Abel, who was forty-four. "I had hoped I would be able to name my successor," Adams said in an interview. "But I wasn't even consulted. I left them a good organization and only hope they don't destroy it."

Adams was in a more gracious mood that fall when two testimonial dinners were held in his honour. The first was a civic event in late October. Over four hundred guests—friends, business executives, politicians and government officials, as well as members of the Red Wings, baseball's Detroit Tigers and football's Lions—turned out to salute the man known locally as Mr. Hockey.

Prime Minister John Diefenbaker, U.S. Supreme Court Justice Byron (Whizzer) White and Clarence Campbell sent congratulatory telegrams. And Ted Lindsay, who had bitterly denounced Adams five years earlier after the Chicago trade, thanked his old coach "for making me play hard every game and for making me realize when I was near the end of the line in hockey and that I should get into something tangible while I still had my head and my health."

The second dinner, held a month later, was a hockey tribute and drew a crowd of 225. Owners or governors of the six NHL teams attended, as well as executives of other leagues and retired players, including Maurice Richard, Aurèle Joliat, King Clancy and Dit Clapper. Gordie Howe spoke for the Red Wing players. "He ruled with an iron fist and a sharp tongue, but also with a golden heart," Howe said. "Sometimes he'd come in the dressing room and the air literally would be blue."

And Howe concluded with a moving testimonial: "If the world hadn't given me two such fine folks for parents, I'd be very happy to say I was the son of Jack Adams."

Many years later, long after Adams was dead, spiteful revisionists attacked the man and sullied his reputation. There were several pretexts for their posthumous assault. He had opposed the players' association. He had bullied and intimidated the athletes, famously walking around the dressing room with train tickets to Omaha or some other minor-league destination protruding from the breast pocket of his jacket. Finally, there was the seemingly schizophrenic split between the private and public Adams: the former a dressing room dictator, the latter an amiable and convivial bon vivant whom sportswriters nicknamed Jolly Jawn.

Adams had many deficiencies. But consider his achievements: he was a foundational figure in the advancement of professional hockey; he was as important to the Red Wings as Smythe was to the Leafs, Lester Patrick to the Rangers or Art Ross to the Bruins; James Norris Sr. provided the money, but Adams built the franchise and the audience, in no small part because he had a king-size personality, commanded attention and kept the Red Wings in the news.

He was a superb judge of talent. He moulded champions and won championships. His teams made the playoffs every single season from 1939 to 1958. They finished first twelve times. They won seven Stanley Cups. The Wings were the best-known hockey team in the United States by the time he retired. And only one other executive, Frank Selke, had come close to matching his record.

CLARENCE CAMPBELL WELCOMED two new members when the board of governors assembled on June 6, 1962, at the Queen Elizabeth Hotel in Montreal for the forty-fifth annual meeting of the National Hockey League. The first, Stafford Smythe, had frequently attended such gatherings with his father or had filled in for him and therefore needed no introduction. The second was William Jennings, the recently appointed governor of the New York Rangers. He had arrived from outside the hockey world—more by chance than by design—but would serve for nearly two decades, until he died of cancer in August 1981, and would become enormously influential in the affairs of the league.

Jennings was forty-one. He was born in New York City, earned an undergraduate degree from Princeton and, in 1943, a law degree from Yale, and then joined a prestigious old Manhattam firm, Simpson, Thacher & Bartlett. By the late 1950s he was a partner, and one of his clients was the Graham-Paige Corporation, a former automaker that had focused on real estate investments since the late 1940s. In February 1959, Graham-Paige had acquired a controlling interest in Madison Square Garden Corporation and, with it, the Rangers and the New York Knicks of the National Basketball Association.

Jennings began handling legal affairs for the building and the two teams, and two years later was named president of Madison Square Garden and the Rangers. His first challenge was to rebuild the front office of the Rangers, a sad-sack club that hadn't been to the Stanley Cup final since 1950 and hadn't won it since 1940. But Jennings's ambitions did not stop there. Within months of joining the NHL board, he had concluded that the league needed to grow beyond its regional base in order to keep pace with the development of professional sport in North America, and he became the prime advocate for expansion.

7

COUNTDOWN TO EXPANSION
(1963–1967)

SOMETIMES, THE SEEDS OF GREAT UNDERTAKINGS—those that change the shape and the character of an organization—are sown in odd and unexpected circumstances, and so it was with the great expansion of the National Hockey League that occurred in 1967–68. The inquisitive student of the game who sets off in search of the first stirrings of this audacious enterprise—audacious because no other major North American sports league had ever doubled in size between the end of one season and the start of another—might well wander back in time to September 1960, to Peterborough, Ontario, and the training camp of the Toronto Maple Leafs, which was, in its first two weeks at least, a very poor camp indeed. One veteran (snarly left winger Bert Olmstead) was sitting at home in Sceptre, Saskatchewan, grousing about the lousy contract he had been offered. Three others (Dick Duff, Ron Stewart and Billy Harris) were unsigned. The team had lost four consecutive starts, the last being a four-nothing thrashing at the hands of the Chicago Black Hawks on the evening of Saturday, September 17. Three days later, Punch Imlach and his still-winless Leafs boarded a bus outside the Peterborough Memorial Centre and embarked on a road trip that took them to Malton Airport—now Pearson International—and a flight to Chicago, then a second to Los Angeles and two exhibition games against the Boston Bruins, though there was one unpleasant hiccup along the way. Five minutes before departing from Malton, Tim Horton walked out.

The first game at the Los Angeles Memorial Sports Arena drew 9,861 spectators, the second 10,742. The Leafs won both, not that it mattered. The primary objective was to test the market for major-league hockey in southern California and, based on the Leaf–Bruin tilts, the region passed with flying colours. The rink was a "modern marvel," according to the *Toronto Telegram*, built for $6 million and with nearly fifteen thousand upholstered, armchair-style seats. The setting was unusual, though. Stately palms lined the perimeter of the parking lot. Temperatures hovered in the mid-eighties Fahrenheit. Fans arrived in summer suits and light dresses, but they were loud and enthusiastic and cheered every goal, every dashing rush and each stiff bodycheck.

"One game can't mean love at first sight for these rambunctious sports fans," the *Telegram* reported after the initial contest, "but an honest appraisal has to be—they and hockey are solid friends."

Conn Smythe and Clarence Campbell both made the trip west, and the former gushed, "This is a hockey gold mine," while the latter declared, "The rink is too good to ignore." And Imlach boldly predicted: "By the '62–63 season NHL clubs will be playing regularly scheduled games out on the California coast. They can't miss making it."

Two full seasons later, though, there was still lots of talk, but no action, as New York writer Stan Fischler noted in the May 1962 issue of the *Hockey News*. "Now that the Stanley Cup shenanigans are over, hockey minds are again turning to the puzzling question of expansion," Fischler wrote. "Topic A at the recent Cup finals was the possibility of the NHL pushing its frontiers beyond the present six cities."

Everyone Fischler consulted agreed that hockey was good enough to be a major-league attraction from New York to Los Angeles. However, nobody thought that expansion was imminent, and two comments seemed to sum up the prevailing outlook. "The league is prepared to consider each individual application on its own merits," Campbell said. Harold Ballard, then a vice-president of Maple Leaf Gardens, added, "If the right people come to us with five million dollars and the right kind of plans, we'll listen."

And that was the hitch: most of the league's movers and shakers were content to wait till the right people came knocking. But not Bill Jennings.

JENNINGS BELIEVED THE LEAGUE had to be proactive. It had to grow beyond its regional base in Toronto, Montreal and the northeastern United States and become truly national, which meant adding franchises on the West Coast. For one thing, there were rumblings that the minor-pro Western Hockey League had major-league ambitions. But, more important, the NHL had been shut out of network television in the U.S. since 1959–60. Baseball, football and basketball, meantime, had signed lucrative TV contracts, and Jennings foresaw bigger things ahead. In this, he was prescient. The National Football League in January 1966 would sign a two-year deal with CBS for $37.6 million and an option for a third at $18.8 million. To put those numbers into perspective, the NHL's gate receipts in 1965–66—regular season and playoffs—amounted to $10.7 million.

In any event, Jennings made his first decisive move at the 1963 semi-annual meeting, held on October 4 at the Royal York Hotel in Toronto. He presented a memorandum on expansion that prompted a prolonged exchange among the governors. "The meeting discussed in general terms the relative merits of expansion to eight clubs or ten clubs or even twelve clubs," according to the minutes, "[and] if the expansion should include one or more eastern or mid-western teams. No conclusion was reached."

At some point over the next twelve months—the minutes of various meetings do not say when—the issue became a priority. The board formed an expansion committee comprising Jennings and Montreal governor David Molson, and by late February 1965 Molson had prepared a proposal—three pages in length—that addressed many of the major issues. The league could either add teams to the existing six and play a fully integrated schedule, or create six new clubs in a separate division with only a limited number of interlocking games. He recommended the latter as more practical and workable because the newly created teams would inevitably be weaker than their established rivals. He suggested four cities—Los Angeles, San Francisco, Pittsburgh and St. Louis—with two others to be selected.

"Perhaps the most important factor of all is who will represent the chosen cities," Molson wrote. "Partners . . . must firstly be dedicated hockey men as it is not a 'get rich overnight' proposition. Secondly, new partners must have sufficient capital and be prepared to accept losses in the initial stages. This points up the need for true partners, NOT PROMOTERS."

He suggested a draft to stock the new teams. Each existing club would place thirty skaters and three goalies on a reserve list. Twenty would be designated protected, but only the top fourteen would be untouchable. Thus the original six would be making available nineteen players apiece, or 114 all told. The newcomers would be allowed to claim ten each from the pool. This would permit them to start with a nucleus of NHL-calibre talent while completing their rosters with players purchased elsewhere, primarily from minor-league teams.

Then there was the question of franchise fees. Molson began by placing a value on what today might be called the NHL brand. The six clubs were all financially sound businesses. League revenues from gate receipts had risen annually for twelve straight seasons, from $3.6 million in 1952–53 to $8.6 million in 1964–65. That success, he argued, had been hard won through years of collective experience, distinguished by trial and error, as well as advances and setbacks.

"New partners should expect to pay for this experience," he reasoned. ". . . It is a fact that present and past owners have spent millions bringing the NHL to where it stands today while still others have lost their proverbial shirts in unsuccessful attempts. A heritage such as this cannot be worth a penny less than $750,000 to each new entry."

Secondly, the league itself, as opposed to its member clubs, boasted cash and assets worth $1 million, consisting of a $600,000 investment in the Hockey Hall of Fame, $350,000 in reserve funds and $50,000 in office and administrative facilities. Based on a league of twelve, each club's share of these assets would be worth about $90,000, which would be added to the franchise fees.

The new entries would also be expected to pay for drafted players on the following basis: the top two would cost $100,000 apiece, the next four $75,000 each and each of the last four $40,000, for a total of $660,000. Therefore, the franchise fee would be $1.5 million based on the value of the NHL brand, league assets and players picked in the draft. Molson added that "the new entries could complete their rosters and equip each club for less than $500,000 additional which, in effect, would produce a full-fledged NHL club costing under $2,000,000. It is doubtful if any of the present franchises could be purchased for this modest amount."

There was one other sweetener that would, in his opinion, take the edge off the startup costs. "It is most likely that national television in the U.S. would result from expansion which, in turn, would represent substantial additional revenue to both existing and new franchises," he wrote.

The league announced its plan to expand—to no great fanfare—following a five-hour meeting in New York on March 11, 1965. This was one of the biggest developments, if not *the* biggest, in the NHL's first fifty years, but the Canadian newspapers did not have reporters on hand to cover the announcement. Many placed the story on the back pages of the sports section, and the reaction from the writers ranged from indifference to skepticism.

"The National Hockey League's board of governors made a decision yesterday at New York that may be heralded in some corners as a startling step forward," the *Toronto Star*'s Paul Rimstead wrote. "But the truth is the NHL may be as far from expansion now as it was going into the meeting. They have to find six cities with suitable arenas and six groups able to meet the stiff financial requirements."

But events would prove the skeptics wrong. Over the next several weeks, Clarence Campbell received inquiries from interested parties across Canada and the United States. In late June, the board released a six-page "Outline of Expansion," drafted by Jennings, which set out the terms and conditions for acquiring a franchise. The fee had been bumped up to $2 million, and, as the outline stipulated, this was "exclusive of all other obligations in respect of the franchise, including the acquisition and operation of at least one minor-professional team, the conduct of junior player development, the payment for territorial rights where applicable and necessary working capital."

The response convinced some of the governors that they had underpriced their product. On January 31, 1966, Campbell informed them he had received thirteen applications, all with the non-refundable $10,000 deposits: one each from Baltimore, Buffalo, Minneapolis-St. Paul, Philadelphia, San Francisco and Vancouver; two from Pittsburgh; and five from Los Angeles.

Campbell called a board meeting to conduct interviews with the applicants and to award franchises, and it was, undoubtedly, the biggest gathering to that point in league history.

THE GOVERNORS, ALONG WITH some of their alternates, met at the St. Regis Hotel in midtown Manhattan on February 7, a Monday. They started at noon, had lunch among themselves in a second-storey boardroom overlooking 55th Street, and at 2 p.m. the interviews began. Each party was given thirty minutes to make their pitch and answer questions.

First up was a group of eight investors—a Hollywood contingent drawn from the movie and television industries. Lawyer Greg Bautzer and TV producer Tony Owen represented them. Owen had made a similar presentation on behalf of another Hollywood group in June 1946. Then, he had spent two months preparing a leather-bound briefing book, but never received a formal response. This time, he kept it light. "I told them I had brought myself, a piece of paper and my associate," Owen told the mostly Canadian reporters he encountered upon leaving the meeting room. "I don't think we exactly bowled them over."

The board heard from five other parties that day—five on Tuesday morning and two on Tuesday afternoon, the last one representing Vancouver. Cyrus McLean, chairman of B.C. Telephone, and Foster Hewitt, the "man who put hockey in every household from Newfoundland to Victoria," as one sportswriter put it, stated the case for Canada's third-largest city. McLean and Hewitt were two of ten shareholders in Burrard Hockey Club Ltd., the company that would own and operate the franchise. The team would play in a new building erected by the Pacific Northwest Exhibition and funded jointly by the city, the province and the federal government. Shortly after that presentation, the board adjourned for the day.

At 9:30 the following morning, Wednesday, February 9, Clarence Campbell stepped off an elevator at the St. Regis, his shoulders stooped from the weight of the two bulging briefcases he was carrying, and walked the short distance to the boardroom, pestered every step of the way by inquisitive reporters, all wondering, Would the board be awarding franchises today? And Campbell coyly replied, "Do not expect immediate news on expansion, because the governors do not always act with finality or expedition."

But the six men who ruled hockey did act decisively that day, and at 12:40 p.m. Campbell walked up one flight of stairs to the room where the press waited and announced that the governors had voted and the league would expand. Los Angeles was in, which surprised no one, given the city's size, explosive growth and geographical location. The board had rejected bids from the Hollywood group; from Detroit businessman Ralph L. Wilson, owner of the Buffalo Bills football team; from the company that owned the Ice Capades skating show; and from the co-owners of the WHL's Los Angeles Blades, who had sunk a lot of money into the Blades and, by their own admission, had lost some $235,000 over five seasons.

The successful applicant was the expatriate Canadian Jack Kent Cooke, and he was thrilled. "Happiest day of my life," said Cooke, a man with deep blue eyes, a high-voltage smile and off-the-scale confidence. "I haven't slept for twenty-four hours from sheer excitement."

Cooke had made a small fortune in publishing and broadcasting in Canada and substantially increased his wealth through the ownership of cable television companies in the U.S. In his presentation, he had wisely included references from California governor Jerry Brown, Canadian finance minister Walter Gordon, two U.S. senators and several prominent sports figures, and had circulated a letter from Security First National, the Beverly Hills bank that held his personal accounts. "Mr. Cooke's balance on deposit currently averages in low seven-figure proportions," the letter stated, adding, "Mr. Cooke has a net worth of eight figures."

He was also an experienced sports promoter. He had owned baseball's Toronto Maple Leafs of the International League for most of the 1950s. He held a twenty-five per cent interest in the National Football League's Washington Redskins and had recently acquired the Los Angeles Lakers of the NBA. Furthermore, he planned to erect a new rink, whereas the other bidders all planned to use the existing Los Angeles Sports Arena, and he brought along two architects to exhibit drawings of his proposed building.

San Francisco was the second automatic choice. The league needed two West Coast teams in order to make transcontinental travel more economical. Furthermore, CBS had informed the NHL that a Bay Area team would help secure a national television contract. There was only one applicant for the franchise: a young, well-connected Princeton University graduate named Barend van Gerbig, who came from a wealthy family, who had grown up on Long Island and in Palm Beach, who was married to the daughter of Douglas Fairbanks Jr. and who had gone to work on Wall Street after graduating.

Van Gerbig was a personal friend of Bruce Norris, Bill Jennings and Charles Mulcahy, the lawyer for the Boston Bruins. He had learned of the NHL's impending expansion while playing a round of golf with Mulcahy in the summer of 1965, and Mulcahy had suggested he would be well positioned to get the San Francisco franchise if he were to purchase that city's WHL team, the Seals, who were a Bruins affiliate. Van Gerbig took his advice, and in order to gain admission to the NHL he assembled a limited partnership of fifty-two investors, including George C. Flaherty, president of the company that owned the Ice Follies skating show; John Brodie, quarterback of the NFL's San Francisco 49ers; and Bing Crosby, his godfather.

Minnesota's Twin Cities—Minneapolis-St. Paul—were not an automatic choice, but a sound one. They were situated in the Midwest, on opposite banks of the Mississippi River, in the heart of one of three hockey hotbeds in the U.S. (the other two being Massachusetts and Michigan), and there was a solid eight-member group behind the bid, four from Minneapolis and four from St. Paul. Walter L. Bush, a real estate lawyer with impeccable credentials as a hockey organizer at the state and national levels, had assembled the partnership and recruited young men from some of the state's most prominent business families. It also didn't hurt that six of the eight had gone to Yale University, Bruce Norris's alma mater, and some of them knew him personally.

The only drawback was that Minneapolis-St. Paul did not have an acceptable arena. Bush and his partners intended to lobby the municipal governments to build one for them, and the board granted a franchise on condition that the rink would be finished in time to start the 1967–68 season.

Two cities in the eastern U.S. gained admission that day—Pittsburgh and Philadelphia—and both had impressive local ownership. The Pittsburgh representatives had the earnest, clean-cut, youthful look of a high school debating club, as one writer put it, and their group included state senator Jack McGregor, H. John Heinz III, whose family owned the ketchup company; Russell Byers, son-in-law of General R.K. Mellon; and Art Rooney, owner of the NFL's Pittsburgh Steelers.

Banker Bill Putnam spoke for the four-man Philadelphia partnership, comprising building contractor Jerome Schiff; property developer Jerry Wolman— the "rich young sultan of the NFL's Philadelphia Eagles," according to one newspaper account; and Ed Snider, a lawyer and Eagles vice-president. Their city did not have an adequate arena, but Wolman boasted, before the board voted, "We don't have any land or an arena in downtown Philadelphia, but if we get a franchise we can buy both."

The governors made one unexpected and controversial decision that day: they agreed to put a team in St. Louis even though nobody from that city had applied. They did so to win over Jim Norris, a staunch opponent of expansion. "We can't make a nickel by expanding," he said. "So the new guys cough up two million for a franchise and players. How much will we see after taxes?" Nor was he swayed by the prospect of a national TV contract. "The Hawks already get $200,000 for televising thirty-five away games," he pointed out. "How much more can we expect?"

But Norris and his partner, Arthur Wirtz, had a problem in St. Louis. They owned the St. Louis Arena, which was built in 1929 and was rundown and needed a facelift. They had lost money on it for years and wanted to sell and reckoned it would be a lot easier to unload as a package that included an NHL franchise.

And so Norris reluctantly voted for the motion—moved by stepbrother Bruce, seconded by David Molson—that the league should add six teams. Norris assured his fellow governors that he had four prospective buyers lined up, and the board gave him sixty days to come back with a firm offer. Failing that, the franchise would go to Baltimore.

Two cities, Buffalo and Vancouver, were left out completely. Seymour and Northrup Knox had applied for a Buffalo franchise. Press reports described the brothers as the "five-and-dime heirs" because their grandfather had made the family fortune in 1911 when he and three other retailers agreed to merge their department store chains with a larger rival—F.W. Woolworth—to create the F.W. Woolworth Company. The Knoxes had spent between $5,000 and $10,000 on a glossy, full-colour brochure touting the benefits of Buffalo. The city had one drawback, however. It was too close to Toronto, according to Stafford Smythe. "Buffalo is only twenty miles from us across the lake," he said. "We might as well just put another franchise in Toronto. It wouldn't have intruded on our TV any more than Buffalo."

Smythe also opposed Vancouver and made some unflattering remarks about the city's bid. "There are too many ten per centers in their makeup," he said after McLean made his pitch. "It's stupid to make a presentation where no one man has complete control. Vancouver is the smallest of the cities seeking admission and we'd get no more TV customers by letting them in. We've got them all now with our Saturday night telecasts." After the board announced its decision, he added, "I don't think Vancouver will get NHL hockey for a generation."

Anger over Vancouver's rejection erupted immediately. Foster Hewitt complained that the interviews with applicants had been a waste of time. The decisions were all made in advance, he charged, and then stated what many Canadians felt: "This is Canada's national game and to be completely ignored is just too much."

Newspaper columnists across the country scorned the league and its governors. "No matter how vigorously they may deny it," the *Ottawa Citizen*'s Jack Kinsella wrote, "the NHL has sold its soul to television in exchange for the silver of expediency." The *Lethbridge Herald*'s Don Pilling added: "Let's go American, rah, rah, rah. And let's name Stafford Smythe the number one cheerleader." And from the *Vancouver Sun*'s Denny Boyd, there was this: "Suddenly you feel the whole two years we have been hoping for a big-league franchise was nothing but a put-on."

The issue also caused an uproar in the House of Commons. B.C. New Democrat Robert Prittie urged the government to subject the league to an inquiry under the Combines Investigation Act. Social Credit MP Gilles Grégoire called for a law "to protect the rights of hockey players who would prefer to play in Canada rather than be obliged to go to the United States." But Prime Minister Lester B. Pearson deftly turned aside these calls to action. "I have a good many problems facing me," Pearson said. "I hope I don't have to take on those of the NHL."

Speaker Lucien Lamoureux urged the members to turn their attention "to matters which are of a little more urgent and immediate national importance." And with that, the political furor subsided, but in British Columbia, public anger continued to simmer. Fans in the Lower Mainland circulated a petition calling for Vancouver's inclusion and quickly collected over five thousand signatures. They sent it to league headquarters in Montreal and received no more than a polite, formal acknowledgement.

JIM NORRIS WASN'T AROUND TO finish the business of bringing St. Louis into the league. On February 15, 1966, he checked into Presbyterian-St. Luke's Hospital "for treatment of heart disease and repeated disturbance of the heart," as the *Chicago Tribune* put it. He had previously suffered two heart attacks. He had a third while in hospital and died on February 25 at the age fifty-nine, leaving behind his wife, a daughter and a rather hefty estate.

Newspaper reports described Norris as one of the fifty richest men in the U.S. and estimated his net worth at $250 million, though the lawyer handling the estate insisted that such stories were exaggerated. In any event, he had inherited parts of the vast grain, shipping and cattle ranching empire his father had built, and he and Arthur Wirtz were partners in a company called Consolidated Enterprises, which invested in real estate, hotels and arenas, among other assets.

But Norris was known for his sporting interests. He owned thoroughbred racing stables. He and Wirtz had controlled professional boxing for roughly a decade, from 1948 to 1958, and he had rubbed shoulders with known mobsters and shady underworld figures who controlled most of the fighters, including one notorious character who was twice tried for murder and once convicted. He had been governor and co-owner of the Black Hawks since the fall of 1952 and insisted that hockey was his real passion. "I live and die with the Hawks," he once said. "I'd much rather win the Stanley Cup than the Kentucky Derby."

Canadian sportswriters had come to know him as a big, amiable, gruff-voiced, hard-living man who had a penchant for drink. Indeed, on day three of the New York expansion meeting, the *Globe and Mail*'s Dick Beddoes took note of his appearance and wrote: "Big Jim's eyes were poached, the bags under his eyes about a four-suit size. He had a rumpled, unslept look."

It was said, and said often, that Norris ran the NHL because he could always count on the support of stepbrother Bruce at board meetings, and until 1958 he and Wirtz held a controlling interest in Madison Square Garden and, presumably, exercised some sway over the Rangers. But his influence, like his wealth, was greatly exaggerated. On expansion, the biggest single issue in his fourteen years as a governor, he was opposed, while the rest of the board—even Bruce Norris—was in favour. And he had spent most of the 1950s pleading for players, not pushing his fellow governors around.

Clarence Campbell, Conn Smythe and others long associated with the NHL often said he saved the game in Chicago, and this was essentially true. He and Wirtz had acquired a dreadful team. They had absorbed enormous losses in the early years. Wirtz repeatedly argued for folding the club, but Norris insisted on continuing and, it was said, put upward of $2 million of his own money into the Hawks.

The *Toronto Star*'s Milt Dunnell speculated after Norris's death that the board had gone along with him on the St. Louis deal as a repayment of sorts for all he had done to keep hockey going in Chicago. And even the normally sharp-tongued Beddoes, who was rarely more than parsimonious with praise, had some kind words for Norris. "One can show respect for the dead without starting canonization proceedings," he wrote. "It is no attempt to fit Big Jim with a tin halo and paper wings to say that he was a factor for good in the NHL."

TWO GROUPS APPLIED FOR THE St. Louis franchise, and the board met at the Plaza Hotel in New York on April 5, 1966, to decide which would get it. One was from Chicago, the other from St. Louis. Both made presentations, and the governors reached a consensus quickly and easily and with minimal debate. The franchise went to Sidney Salomon Jr., his son Sidney Salomon III and eight associates, described by one journalist as "a gold-plated batting order of St. Louis's fiscal society."

The elder Salomon was fifty-five and had built a modest fortune in the insurance business. The younger Salomon, not yet thirty, worked for his father and was a smartly dressed, smooth-talking salesman who sold more than $1 million worth of policies annually. Both were sports fans. Sid Jr. had started his career as a sportswriter at a local paper and had briefly been a part owner of the St. Louis Browns of major-league baseball. His son, known as the Third, was an excellent amateur golfer and had talked his father into making a bid for the franchise.

The elder Salomon had impressive political connections as well, and that caught the attention of the NHL board. He was a leading Missouri Democrat. He was credited with putting Harry Truman on the 1944 ticket as Franklin D. Roosevelt's running mate, and he had been chairman of John F. Kennedy's

1960 campaign committee. "In Salomon, we've got a genuine kingmaker," Clarence Campbell boasted to reporters after the meeting. "This you can bet on. He's the only guy in the NHL who can walk in the White House door without an invitation."

The board asked Salomon to address the assembled scribes, but the question was: What to say? A hurried discussion took place behind closed doors, and he recounted the gist of it several years later in an interview with *Sports Illustrated:* "I said, 'Gentlemen, we have only two or three minutes, but it would be to our advantage if we could name this team right now. Nobody else has come up with a name and those fellows out there need something to write about.'

"We started kicking names around fast—mostly space names like Mercurys and Apollos, things like that, since McDonnell Aircraft [was] the biggest employer in the state. Nothing clicked. It was time to go outside. Then it hit me. I said, 'What about the Blues—the St. Louis Blues?' It had a great identity with the city and it gave us an instant theme song. It was a natural. We all liked it, but then our lawyer, Jim Cullen, said: 'Sid, you could be asking for a lawsuit. I think we should clear it with the [composer W.C.] Handy estate first.'

"I said: 'Jim, if that's the way your mind reacts, then we've got to use the Blues. The publicity surrounding a lawsuit like that would be priceless.' So we went out and told everybody that the last city to get a team was the first to have a name for it, and the next day papers all over the country had headlines like: The Blues Are Reborn, The Rebirth of the Blues, St. Louis Is Blue Again."

CLARENCE CAMPBELL HAD SOME GOOD NEWS for the governors when they gathered for their 1966 annual general meeting, held at the Queen Elizabeth Hotel in Montreal in early June, and he delivered it in a twenty-three-page report that began with the happy declaration that the season just concluded had been "the most outstanding year in the history of the league."

The hockey, most nights, was blazing fast and played with searing intensity, though Campbell acknowledged that the league was "virtually a '4–2' operation throughout the season." The Canadiens had finished first, the Hawks second, the Leafs third and the Wings fourth. The Bruins had overtaken the Rangers on the final day of play, but both spent the postseason on the sidelines for the fourth consecutive year, and the point spread between the top four and bottom two was so large that "there was very little challenge for playoff positions beyond the half-way mark of the schedule."

The Canadiens swept the Leafs in four. The Wings eliminated the Hawks in six and then won the first two games of the final at the Montreal Forum. That embarrassed the Canadiens and pricked their enormous pride. They were determined to bury an opponent they viewed as a lesser team, and they did. The Montrealers won the next four contests to capture their fourteenth Stanley Cup.

There may have been a dearth of suspense and drama, but it didn't matter. The quality of play was apparently sufficient to hold the interest of the fans. All 210 league games and sixteen playoff contests were virtual sellouts. Two clubs, Toronto and Detroit, had each added several hundred new seats to their rinks, and the average price of a ticket, leaguewide, had risen to $3.25 from $3.05.

Campbell proudly reported that total attendance for league and playoff games had hit an all-time high of 2,941,164. Likewise, gate receipts for the season and postseason combined had reached a new record of $10,722,587. Campbell also compiled the following list of gross gate receipts dating back to 1946–47, and they provide a revealing snapshot of an era fast coming to an end.

Season	Games	Receipts	Season	Games	Receipts
1946-47	180	$3,681,000	1956-57	210	$4,282,000
1947-48	180	$3,840,000	1957-58	210	$4,909,000
1948-49	180	$3,934,000	1958-59	210	$5,245,000
1949-50	210	$4,050,000	1959-60	210	$5,587,000
1950-51	210	$3,617,000	1960-61	210	$5,777,000
1951-52	210	$3,425,000	1961-62	210	$6,356,000
1952-53	210	$3,605,000	1962-63	210	$7,090,000
1953-54	210	$3,688,000	1963-64	210	$7,827,000
1954-55	210	$3,689,000	1964-65	210	$8,603,000
1955-56	210	$4,138,000	1965-66	210	$9,568,000

Campbell's figures show that between 1946–47 and 1956–57, gate receipts were basically stagnant once inflation, increased player costs and the added expenses of the seventy-game season are factored in. The 1957–58 season was a turning point, and from then on receipts grew by leaps and bounds.

The president was less forthcoming about player compensation and the players' share of revenues. The average base salary in 1965–66 had risen to $16,360 from $14,386 the previous year, an increase of nearly fourteen per cent, and Campbell added, "For the first time in ten years the players' share of income, expressed as a percentage of the league's total gate receipts, both league and playoffs, has shown a modest increase."

He disclosed those numbers in a separate letter to the governors, and therefore the exact number must remain a mystery. Nevertheless, it is possible to calculate a reasonable estimate of the players' share of revenue by extrapolating from the figures that are available.

There were that season 103 regulars and 74 call-ups, and the latter played a cumulative total of nearly 490 games. Given the average base salary for a regular, and assuming that call-ups were paid $100 per game—since the minimum salary was $7,000 for a seventy-game season—it would appear that the athletes earned about 18.1 per cent of the total regular-season gate receipts. Applying the same assumptions, their share of the 1964–65 regular-season gates would have been 17.3 per cent.

These figures appear at first glance to confirm the conventional wisdom, now deeply entrenched in the minds of players past and present—as well as a good number of hockey writers—that the owners were pocketing great gobs of money and enriching themselves at the expense of the athletes. However, the closer we look, the less certain this becomes. In fact, the most that can be said is this: while it may have been true in some cases, it was certainly not true in all cases.

The evidence can be found in a set of Montreal Canadiens balance sheets from this era that are safely stowed in the Molson Fonds at Library and Archives Canada in Ottawa. The following summary is drawn from those documents:

	1958–59	1961–62	1964–65
Revenues	$910,779	$1,094,882	$1,422,166
Salaries	$342,942	$357,849	$349,983
Scouting and Development	$140,681	$269,824	$279,909
Total Expenses	$772,307	$971,429	$1,086,805
Net Profit After Tax	$77,637	$64,453	$136,627
Salaries as a Percentage of Revenue	37.6%	32.6%	24.6%
Net Profit as a Percentage of Revenue	8.5%	5.8%	9.6%

These figures clearly demonstrate that in a well-run organization, in which there was a serious commitment to product development, the players were fairly compensated and the owners earned a reasonable return on their investment.

In any event, all of this was beyond the purview of Campbell's report, or the discussions that took place among the governors on that sunny June day in 1966. There was good news beyond that pertaining to attendance and gate receipts. For the first time in six years, the league had made a modest breakthrough with network television in the U.S. NBC had televised four Sunday afternoon playoff games in colour—two from Chicago, one from Detroit and one from Montreal—and had paid the clubs $50,000 per game.

Finally, expansion was proceeding on schedule and the new members were meeting their commitments. "This decision to expand has already generated a new set of problems which will require the best judgment and the sincere good will of everyone," Campbell concluded. "It will be the measure of our collective capabilities to bring this great project to a successful conclusion in a reasonable period of time."

THE FINAL SEASON OF THE six-team league was filled with strange twists and pleasant surprises. The Canadiens returned with virtually the same lineup and were expected to finish first again by a comfortable margin. The Hawks were pegged as "the best of the rest" by one sportswriter. The Leafs and Wings seemed set to duel for third and fourth, and everyone figured the Bruins and Rangers would land where they usually did—fifth or sixth.

These appeared to be safe assumptions. There had been just one off-season coaching change: Hall of Famer Milt Schmidt had stepped aside in Boston and a more youthful Harry Sinden had taken over. And coming out of training camp, the six clubs had a grand total of eight rookies on their rosters. The Canadiens signed goaltender Rogatien Vachon. Chicago defenceman Elmer Vasko had retired and Ed Van Impe had taken his place. The Leafs added two new forwards: Mike Walton and Lionel Conacher's son Brian. The Wings' one newcomer also had a famous name. He was Peter Mahovlich, younger brother of Leaf star Frank. The Bruins made more changes than any of their rivals. Their freshman contingent included forward Wayne Connelly, defenceman Joe Watson and eighteen-year-old Bobby Orr, the most highly touted prospect since Jean Béliveau fifteen years earlier.

Orr was a prodigy. Playing Junior A when he was fourteen and in grade eight and living at home in Parry Sound, Ontario, joining his Oshawa Generals teammates for weekend games. Appearing between periods on *Hockey Night in Canada* when he was fifteen and responding respectfully to the questions of host Ward Cornell. Making the cover of *Maclean's*, then a biweekly, when he was sixteen and "the finest professional hockey prospect in Canada today," according to the sportswriter Trent Frayne. Finishing third in scoring in his final season in junior and then leaving for Boston, the NHL and the big time.

Orr broke with tradition before signing. Whole generations of players before him had meekly accepted the entry-level minimum salary. Orr allowed a brash, ballsy Toronto lawyer named Alan Eagleson to represent him, and Eagleson wrangled between $40,000 and $50,000 a year—unheard of for a rookie—out of a desperate organization that hadn't made the playoffs in nearly a decade and hadn't won the Stanley Cup since 1941.

That made Orr one of the highest-paid and most closely watched players in the game. "I'm nervous, sure," he told the *Boston Globe* on the day before his debut, "but I'll just do the best I can. I missed four exhibition games with this injury [a slight shoulder separation] and can tell you it's sure a lot tougher watching than playing."

Orr collected an assist in that initial outing—a six-two win over Detroit—and some of the wise old men of Boston hockey were starstruck. "Did you see how smart he is?" Schmidt said. "When he had nobody to pass to to get the puck out of his own end, he nonchalantly flipped it into centre ice instead of icing it." Former Bruin Bill Quackenbush added: "Why, he passes better than most players in the league now. He doesn't hesitate a moment to give it to the man in the clear."

Orr's magic in itself was not enough to make the Bruins a contender, but the dazzling teenager inspired hope among the Bruins faithful for the first time in years. The Gallery Gods—the loud, boisterous, knowledgeable fans who sat in the upper echelons of Boston Garden—chose Orr as their favourite player of 1966–67. And on the eve of the team's last game, a *Boston Globe* reporter wrote, "Any time you attempt to develop a really positive item on the Bruins in these waning days of the hockey season, you wind up spelling it out with three letters—O-R-R."

The Bruins finished last, exactly fifty points behind the Black Hawks, who won the league championship for the first time in their forty-one-year history. The Wings, battered by injuries, came fifth. The Rangers were the big surprise. They had been in the top four from the start and on March 1 had a comfortable hold on second, but fell into a slump and wound up fourth. The Canadiens claimed second, the Leafs third, and both rode winning streaks into the playoffs.

The Hawks were prohibitive favourites to win the Stanley Cup. Goaltenders Denis DeJordy and Glenn Hall had won the Vezina Trophy. Stan Mikita captured the scoring title, Bobby Hull enjoyed his third fifty-goal season and the team tallied a record 264 goals. But the Leafs beat them in six and advanced to the final against the well-rested and confident Canadiens, who had swept the Rangers in four.

The Leafs trumped the Canadiens in a hard-fought, six-game final and became one of the most unlikely Stanley Cup champions since the trophy was first awarded in 1893. Many of their key players were, by the standards of any era, too old. Goaltender Johnny Bower was forty-two. Defenceman Allan Stanley was forty-one. Centre Red Kelly was forty. Terry Sawchuk, who had split goaltending duties with Bower, was thirty-eight. Captain George Armstrong and defencemen Tim Horton and Marcel Pronovost were all thirty-seven.

Furthermore, their season had been marred by turmoil. Frank Mahovlich held out for more money in October. The Leafs lost eleven straight between mid-January and mid-February. The losing streak made a nervous wreck of coach Punch Imlach, who checked into a Toronto hospital suffering from stress and exhaustion and left his assistant King Clancy in charge until he returned March 18.

But all the turbulence and upheaval were forgotten during that sweet spring. Canada was celebrating its centennial. Montreal hosted Expo 67—a world's fair—and a million and a half people surged through the gates during the first three days. Toronto settled for a Stanley Cup parade. It began at Maple Leaf Gardens at 4 p.m. on May 5 and proceeded south on Church Street to Wellington, west to Bay, and north to City Hall and Nathan Phillips Square.

Thousands of smiling, cheering, delighted fans lined the route. A squad of mounted city police in white helmets came first, then a military brass band, and finally twenty white convertibles. Armstrong, his father, Fred, Stafford Smythe and his sidekick, Harold Ballard, all sat beaming and waving in the lead car. Imlach and his aging assistant, King Clancy, were in the second, and then came the players, each with a blue-and-white carnation pinned to his lapel.

Police had to clear a path through the adoring throngs at Nathan Phillips. Mayor William Dennison saluted these improbable champions, and Armstrong told the crowd: "All the experts said we could not win. They said Chicago had too much scoring and Montreal had too much skating. But they forgot the most important ability of all, the ability to work and dig when it counted."

And that ended Toronto's eleventh Stanley Cup celebration and, as of this writing, its last.

ELMER FERGUSON HAD SEEN MOST EVERYTHING in the half century or more that he had covered professional hockey. He had witnessed the demise of the National Hockey Association and the formation of the National Hockey League. The creation of franchises and the deaths of franchises. The arrivals and departures of the great players, coaches and general managers. But even after all that, the grand old man of Canadian sportswriters was readying himself for an entirely different spectacle as he sat before the typewriter and composed the column that would run in the *Montreal Star* of Thursday, June 1, 1967.

"Professional hockey, which in forty years has leaped from an all-Canada, leaky-roof circuit to international status, has never known anything like this," Ferguson wrote.

"The biggest show in town next week . . . outside Expo, will be staged Tuesday in the grand ballroom of the Queen Elizabeth. And it won't be a dance. It will be a high-flying poker game, with players for chips and a pool of $12,000,000 tossed on the gaming table from the chequebooks of owners of the six new teams entering the National Hockey League."

The long months of gestation were nearly complete. General managers, coaches and scouts had, for the most part, been hired and had spent the previous winter searching high and low, east and west for talent. New arenas were nearing completion in Philadelphia, in Bloomington, Minnesota—a suburb of Minneapolis-St. Paul—and in Los Angeles. Existing buildings in Pittsburgh and Oakland were being buffed and polished, and the St. Louis Arena was being refurbished at a cost of $2 million. Team colours had been chosen and nicknames bestowed. The expansion clubs would be the Flyers, Penguins, Blues, North Stars, Seals and Kings.

All they needed was players—twenty each—and those would be selected in the draft of Tuesday, June 6, which was sure to be the biggest gathering ever of hockey people. The established clubs were each allowed to protect one goaltender and eleven skaters, and they submitted their lists to Clarence Campbell at 6 p.m. Monday. He released them to the newcomers at 9 a.m. the following day.

One piece of business was transacted before the draft began. Representatives of each expansion franchise presented Campbell with a certified cheque for $2 million and signed over the money to one of the old clubs, and with that they became fully fledged rather than conditional members of the league. Afterward, a beaming Campbell held the cheques aloft for photographers and took several questions from the two hundred journalists covering the event. And then the day's events commenced.

The names of the incoming clubs were placed in capsules and deposited in the bowl of the Stanley Cup. Campbell drew them one by one to determine the order of selection, and each club was given three minutes to make a decision.

The Los Angeles Kings went first and chose goaltender Terry Sawchuk. The others also filled that vital position with their initial picks. Minnesota took Cesare Maniago from the Rangers. Pittsburgh selected Detroit's Joe Daley. Philadelphia grabbed the young and promising Bernie Parent from Boston. St. Louis took a veteran, Chicago's Glenn Hall, and the California Seals completed the round by taking Montreal's Charlie Hodge, a two-time Vezina Trophy winner.

A total of 120 players were chosen from the 404 deemed eligible, and they were an eclectic mix: spare defencemen, utility forwards, career minor-leaguers, bottom-of-the-barrel prospects and brand-name veterans who were past their prime but might yet have some box-office appeal. California was deemed to have drafted the most potent assembly of talent, while Los Angeles had chosen poorly. Philadelphia had opted for youth and vigour, St. Louis for age and experience. Pittsburgh had drawn heavily from the Rangers, perhaps because coach Red Sullivan had spent most of his career with the team, and Minnesota's Wren Blair had leaned heavily on the Wings and Hawks and added a sprinkling of talent from the Canadiens. One thing was certain: none of the new teams left the Queen Elizabeth a Stanley Cup contender.

This was due, in part at least, to the work of Sam Pollock, who had drawn up the rules of the draft at the request of the board. Pollock was general manager of the Canadiens and therefore guardian of the richest pool of talent in the league, and his objective was to protect Montreal's assets. He devised a clever approach that he called "pick and fill." That is, a new club picked an unprotected player from an established rival, and the latter was allowed to fill that spot by adding one of its prospects to the protected list. This and other measures worked wonderfully for the Canadiens, who were as mighty after the draft as they had been before.

Fortunately, the expansion clubs would only play the Canadiens and the other established teams four times apiece. The balance of their games would be against each other, and they would form a separate "western" division. "Several teams drafted with intelligence and foresight," concluded the *Montreal Star*'s Red Fisher, "while others may have established a lock on the lower reaches of the new division." And he threw in a few words of praise for the league: "This mammoth draft was the finest operation ever conducted by the NHL."

IN A SINGLE DAY and twenty rounds of player selection, the league had doubled in size, and this great gathering produced one additional game-changing development that occurred with remarkable swiftness the following day, June 7, 1967. The owner-player council, which had met once and sometimes twice a year since it was established in February 1958, was set to meet at ten o'clock that morning.

The owners or their representatives, all twelve of them, assembled first in a small boardroom at the Queen Elizabeth. The seven-member player delegation arrived a few minutes later, led by their spokesman, Bob Pulford of the Maple Leafs. They were scarcely seated when Pulford made the following short statement: "I have been directed to tell you that we want Alan Eagleson to speak on our behalf. A players' association has been formed and he is our executive director. Talk it over among yourselves. If you agree to meet with Eagleson, fine. If you don't, our meeting this year won't last five minutes."

The players then left. Thirty minutes later, Bruins lawyer Charles Mulcahy emerged and announced that the owners were prepared to recognize the association and he read a brief statement: "The expansion of the National Hockey League has made it apparent that many problems have to be dealt with on a different basis than formerly. With respect to the player-owner relations, both the owners and players desire to have any problems . . . resolved in a workable committee."

Mulcahy then invited Eagleson into the boardroom to begin the first formal discussions. Eagleson was thirty-three, a Toronto lawyer and a backbench member of Ontario's Progressive Conservative government. He had played lacrosse with Pulford as a teenager, and in the early 1960s had quietly advised him and other Leaf players during contract talks with Punch Imlach.

He had burst into the spotlight as a players' advocate over the previous nine months. First, he had landed Bobby Orr's precedent-setting deal. Then he had forced the Leafs to release defenceman Carl Brewer from his contract so he could play for Canada's national team. Finally, he had taken on Eddie Shore, the Boston Bruins legend and notorious crank who owned the Springfield Indians of the American Hockey League. In mid-December 1966, Shore's players had gone out on strike to protest his eccentric and abusive behaviour. Eagleson took up their cause. He convinced them to return to work and over the next month employed shrewd legal tactics and political pressure that eventually compelled Shore to announce that he was stepping aside—for health reasons—and would put the team up for sale.

In the midst of all this, Orr's Boston teammates approached Eagleson about starting a players' association. They met on the morning of December 28, 1966, in Montreal. Eagleson was in the city to meet with Clarence Campbell; the Bruins were there to play the Canadiens. After the morning skate, goaltender Eddie Johnston invited Eagleson up to his room. Every member of the Bruins was there and all were onside.

"As far as I'm concerned," Eagleson would later write in his autobiography, "right there in that room was the beginning of the National Hockey League Players' Association."

By the end of April, he had met with the rest of the NHL teams, and all but nine of 120 players had endorsed the idea. He also received pledges of support from overwhelming majorities in the American and Western Hockey Leagues, the two leagues that would be providing most of the talent for the NHL's expansion clubs. Money was a secondary issue. The average annual salary in the NHL had risen to $18,226 in 1966–67 (bonuses excluded) from $16,360 the previous season. That compared favourably with the Major League Baseball average of $19,000. However, baseball's biggest stars were drawing salaries in the neighbourhood of $100,000 a year, whereas Bobby Hull was reportedly getting $65,000 and Gordie Howe $50,000.

The standard player's contract was the real irritant. It imposed a multitude of restrictions and constraints on the players while conferring too much power on owners and managers who had, too often in the past, behaved in ways that were arbitrary, capricious and occasionally downright nasty. This archaic document needed an overhaul, but that would take time. Meanwhile, Eagleson coaxed a few modest concessions out of the owners in his first face-to-face meeting with them. They agreed to pay the players for exhibition games played in NHL cities and against league opponents, and they also increased the daily expense money by fifty per cent, to $15.

Later that day, the governors surprised many when they boosted the entry-level minimum salary by $3,000 to $10,000 without any prodding from the players' association. That was significantly better than baseball's $8,000 floor.

But it was less an outburst of generosity than a recognition of reality. According to Campbell, only one player had earned less than $10,000 the previous season.

That was the last significant announcement to come from the expansion meetings of June 1967. The delegations parted and returned to their respective domains to prepare for a season opener unlike any in the first half century of the NHL.

8

GROWING PAINS (1967–1972)

THEY KEPT THINGS SIMPLE at the Pittsburgh Civic Arena on opening night of the National Hockey League's fifty-first season—and the first for the league's six hastily assembled, untested expansion teams. At 7:59 p.m. on October 11, 1967, the booming voice of the house announcer signalled the start. "Ladies and gentlemen. The NHL presents the Montreal Canadiens and the Pittsburgh Penguins." The lights went down, the players were introduced, the anthems were sung and the starting six on each side took their positions. There were no speeches, no ceremonial faceoffs, no handshakes and photographs at centre ice, just the game—and an entertaining one—for the crowd of 9,307: a two-one win for the visitors. One of those three goals was a milestone: number 400 in the prodigious fifteen-year career of the Canadiens' elegant captain, Jean Béliveau.

The puck dropped one hour later in St. Louis by dint of the city's location in the Central time zone, and the Salomons—Sid Jr. and son Sid III—did put on a show for the 11,339 spectators who passed up game six of the World Series between their hometown Cardinals and the Boston Red Sox to witness the season opener between the Blues and Wren Blair's Minnesota North Stars. The Salomons staged a ninety-minute pre-game gala that featured performances by Guy Lombardo and His Royal Canadians; actress and singer Anna Maria Alberghetti, who had made some fifty appearances on *The Ed Sullivan Show;* and figure skater Aja Zanovo, a former world champion turned Ice Capades star.

The fans also got their first look at the refurbished St. Louis Arena, the thirty-eight-year-old structure known locally as the "Old Barn" because it had been used mainly for livestock shows. The Salomons had paid $4 million for the dilapidated, money-losing building and then spent $2 million upgrading the ice-making plant, installing new seats, overhauling the concession stands, cleaning up the washrooms and generally turning it into one of the classiest rinks in the NHL.

Clarence Campbell was on hand to preside over a ceremonial faceoff. The Blues and North Stars played a fast, tight game that ended in a two-two tie when St. Louis right winger Wayne Rivers fired a slapshot past netminder Garry Bauman with just under ninety seconds remaining.

The NHL became national in more than name only at 8 p.m. Pacific time when the California Seals lined up against the Philadelphia Flyers at the Oakland–Alameda County Coliseum. Bing Crosby attended. A Dixieland jazz band performed between periods. The 6,886 spectators filled just over half the building. The Seals, wearing what one press box observer described as "flashy green and blue uniforms that looked like something from a psychedelic tailor," dominated on both offence and defence and skated to an easy five-one win. Afterward, the club hosted a big banquet for investors and season-ticket holders.

The Kings opened at home on October 14, a Saturday, against the Flyers, though Los Angeles hardly felt like home to the players. They had trained in Guelph, Ontario, and had only arrived in southern California a week before the season began. Most were living in hotels until they could find apartments. "This club is great," centre Gord Labossiere told a *Los Angeles Times* reporter. "They've done nothing to help us get settled. We won't have an advantage over the teams coming here because we haven't been here long enough ourselves."

Furthermore, the $16 million Los Angeles Forum was still under construction and wouldn't be ready until December 30. The team's first seventeen home games would be played at either the Los Angeles Sports Arena or the Long Beach Arena, the latter located an hour's drive south of downtown, which was where they made their debut against the Flyers—a four-two win, as it happened.

Immense uncertainty surrounded the expansion, and two questions loomed above all others: Would the six new teams be competitive, and would local fans support them?

The Kings were picked in many preseason polls to finish last. Goaltender Terry Sawchuk was the only NHL veteran. The rest of the youthful roster had spent the previous season in the minors. Owner Jack Kent Cooke had skated with his players daily during the first week of training camp and happily pronounced the experts wrong. "There are going to be mighty red faces after we've been around the circuit for a while," he said. "We look like we have a very fine team."

At a minimum, they proved to be much better than expected. The Kings led the six teams that comprised the West Division at the end of October and through the first quarter of the seventy-four-game schedule. There were midseason rough patches, including an eight-game losing streak, but they recovered and finished second and earned praise from many quarters. As the *Hockey News* put it, "The experts underestimated Cooke's judgment of men, manager Larry Regan's ability to evaluate talent and [coach] Red Kelly's ability to whip talent into shape."

The Seals, picked to finish first, wound up last—and by a wide margin. They lost early and often and did not click with fans in either Oakland or San Francisco. The team drew, on average, 4,690 per night, whereas the San Francisco Seals of the Western Hockey League had drawn around 7,000 per game the previous season, playing in an aged livestock exhibition hall known as the Cow Palace, which the NHL had deemed inadequate for its Bay Area franchise.

Early in the season a debate arose over the team's Oakland home. Critics argued that the Seals should have been based in San Francisco. Nonsense, replied managing partner Barry van Gerbig. "The centre of population is right where our building is," he told a reporter in mid-November. "We have access to four million people within an hour's drive of our arena. We're in the right place."

But van Gerbig decided the team's name was wrong. In November, the California Seals became the Oakland Seals. Ticket prices were reduced as well. Nothing helped, though. One game in early December drew a mere 2,426 fans. By then, van Gerbig had held discussions with Labatt Breweries of Canada, which was prepared to buy a majority interest provided the Seals could be moved to Vancouver. The NHL rejected that option and instead advanced the franchise $700,000 to ensure that it survived the season.

The Penguins inherited a small, knowledgeable fan base from the Pittsburgh Hornets of the American Hockey League, but that didn't do them much good.

The Hornets had cruised to first place the previous season and won the Calder Cup. The Penguins were mediocre, and the crowds at their games let them know it. One such incident made a vivid impression on sportswriter Lou Prato.

"The fans unleashed a torrent of boos that might have shocked anyone seeing a hockey game for the first time," he wrote. "There were cries of 'Bring back the Hornets' and 'Go back to the Eastern League.'"

By mid-January, the Penguins had averaged 6,700 per game through twenty dates. They needed 9,000 to break even, club president Jack McGregor told a visiting Montreal *Gazette* reporter. He added that the team would likely lose $350,000 on the season. They were in fifth in early March and seemingly out of the playoff picture altogether. But they finished with a flourish—five straight wins that brought them to within a point of fourth—and they received a rousing standing ovation from the home crowd when the buzzer sounded to end their season.

The North Stars, Flyers and Blues built large, enthusiastic, even passionate fan bases in that inaugural season. The Stars drew almost 13,000 for their home opener and continued to attract decent crowds, but they were "deathly silent," as Wren Blair later recalled in a memoir. Media coverage was another challenge. "We had a tough time getting publicity in the Twin Cities because of the other big sports—basketball, baseball and football," Blair wrote.

Things changed, though. The North Stars sold out the 15,000-seat Bloomington Metropolitan Sports Center eight times and led the West Division with combined regular-season and playoff attendance of 487,859.

The Flyers won the division, were second in attendance and solidified a budding relationship with the public during a dramatic and exceptionally hard-fought playoff against the Blues. St. Louis took a three-one series lead. The Flyers rebounded to tie it. Two of those six games were decided in overtime. A brawl erupted in the third period of game five in Philadelphia. It lasted twenty minutes. Clarence Campbell witnessed it and later handed out fines totalling $3,800.

The Flyers hired two off-duty Philadelphia police officers to accompany them to St. Louis for game six and to stand guard outside their dressing room. It proved to be a quiet night for the officers, though they did see a dandy contest—a two-one overtime Flyer victory that sent the teams back to Philadelphia for a seventh game. The Blues won that night, but the Flyers had made their mark on the city. "Verbal and physical blasts flew back and forth like heavy artillery in this thrilling series," a local sportswriter concluded, "and when it was over the 14,646 who packed the Spectrum stood and roared. . . . They call this a tough town. But right now Philadelphia has a love affair with this hockey club."

The turning point for the Blues had occurred on a Saturday night in late January. The New York Rangers—one of the league's best—paid a visit. The Rangers roared to a three-nothing first-period lead. The Blues fought back and won four-three. "From then on, the Blues—and big-league hockey— were in like O'Flynn with the fans," Bob Broeg, sports editor of the *St. Louis Post-Dispatch*, later wrote. "They completely captivated a sizeable segment of St. Louis' sports following."

A remarkable playoff run turned infatuation into a deep and enduring affection. After dispatching the Flyers, the Blues beat the North Stars in seven. Four of the games, including the seventh, were decided in overtime. That triumph brought them face to face with Montreal's mighty Canadiens in the Stanley Cup final.

The Blues did not stand much chance. The Canadiens had been in last place in the East at Christmas, but lost just eight times in the second half and finished first overall. They beat Boston in four and Chicago in five and swept St. Louis in four. The best the Blues could do was keep it close and push two games into overtime.

It didn't matter to their supporters. They sang, chanted and repeatedly stood to applaud. "You get a fantastic feeling when you walk into the St. Louis Arena," marvelled NHL statistician and information director Ron Andrews. "It's the fans, of course. They're unlike the fans in any other city in the league, and I've seen them all."

THERE WERE SOME NOTEWORTHY individual achievements in that first expansion season and one terrible tragedy. Gordie Howe turned forty on March 31, the final day of his twenty-second season. He had scored thirty-nine goals and finished in the top five in total points for the nineteenth time. Glenn

Hall earned the seventieth shutout of his career. Frank Mahovlich scored his three-hundredth goal and Bobby Hull his four-hundredth. Tim Horton, George Armstrong and Ron Stewart all played their one-thousandth games.

And North Stars centre Bill Masterton became the only NHL player to die of injuries suffered on the ice. He was twenty-nine, a native of Winnipeg and the father of two preschool children. Masterton had been a star college player and afterward signed with the Canadiens. He quit hockey following an eighty-two-point season with the Cleveland Barons of the AHL, earned a master's degree at the University of Denver and went to work in the Twin Cities. Expansion gave him the opportunity to resume his playing career, and he appeared in thirty-eight games.

On the evening of January 13, in a home game against the Seals, he was checked heavily by two opponents simultaneously near the North Stars bench. The impact likely knocked him unconscious, and he went down hard. His head struck the ice, with no helmet to absorb the shock. Doctors kept him on a respirator for some thirty hours, long enough to determine that there was no hope of recovery.

"The NHL was shocked to its very foundations by the passing of Masterton in the early hours of January 15 from a massive brain injury," the *Hockey News* reported.

The shock subsided and the league moved on without rethinking player safety or making helmets mandatory. However, the NHL Writers' Association was moved to create a trophy—the Bill Masterton Memorial Trophy, awarded annually ever since to the individual who best demonstrates perseverance, sportsmanship and dedication to hockey.

THE LEAGUE HAD EXPANDED in more ways than one. The schedule had been extended from seventy games per team to seventy-four. The total number of games played had soared from 210 to 444. Three playoff rounds had grown to seven. Postseason bonuses, team and individual, had risen to a remarkable $567,000. Clarence Campbell had presented the Stanley Cup to Jean Béliveau at centre ice at the Montreal Forum on May 11, thereby concluding the NHL's longest season ever.

Nobody expected the new teams to be the equals of the old, and they weren't. The two groups played a total of 144 games against one another in 1967–68. The expansion clubs won forty, lost eighty-six and tied twelve, and the ownership groups behind the Penguins and the Seals weren't interested in sticking around until things improved.

The youthful luminaries who acquired the Pittsburgh franchise had run out of money before their opening game, in part because they had also invested in a pro soccer team. "Soccer didn't draw the ushers," recalls Jack Riley, the Penguins' first general manager. "It was really bad. As a result, they were looking for investors for the hockey club right away."

They held on for the season, but early in April 1968 team president Jack McGregor announced that he and his partners had sold eighty per cent of the Penguins to a nine-member group from Detroit headed by Donald H. Parsons, a thirty-seven-year-old lawyer and businessman. Parsons owned a thriving law practice and nineteen banks located in Michigan and several nearby states. He was an ambitious and innovative entrepreneur who had rattled the foundations of a staid industry through such novel practices as paying interest on chequing accounts and buying B-grade municipal bonds, which yielded better-than-average returns. Parsons was the only prospective buyer of the Penguins and, other than his out-of-town address, was deemed perfectly acceptable.

The Seals began the off-season in complete disarray. Head coach Bert Olmstead and his two assistants quit. Barry van Gerbig and his ownership group put the team up for sale. A buyer emerged from that unmanageable syndicate of fifty-eight geographically dispersed individuals. Potter Palmer, a thirty-two-year-old Harvard graduate whose family had owned the Palmer House Hotel, a Chicago landmark, was a minor shareholder, and he made an offer for the franchise along with two partners: his brother-in-law John O'Neil Jr. of Miami, who was thirty-seven and owned insurance and travel businesses, and George Gillett of Chicago, who was twenty-eight and president of the Harlem Globetrotters.

The triumvirate formed a company called Puck Inc. O'Neil became chairman, Palmer president and league governor, and Gillett vice-president. They brought in an up-and-coming Pittsburgh-based sports promoter named Bill Torrey to run the Seals day to day and they hired Fred Glover, a fiery but successful career minor-leaguer, to coach the team.

The Puck Inc. purchase was contingent upon a favourable tax ruling from the Internal Revenue Service, and this would give Clarence Campbell and the board a collective migraine when the IRS decision went against the company. Likewise, Parsons's involvement with the NHL would be short-lived and messy due to a fight with federal financial regulators that would sink his business empire and nearly take the Penguins down as well.

But no one could foresee such events. The two troubled organizations had been put aright. The league could move forward and did. At the annual general meeting, held in Montreal in mid-June 1968, Cyrus McLean, president of the minor-pro Vancouver Canucks, submitted a detailed and comprehensive application for a franchise, and the governors spent a day and a half reviewing it.

Afterward, Campbell announced that the board had formed a four-member expansion committee to decide how many new teams should be added and when. Campbell also reassured a city desperate for admission to hockey's premier league. "After due consideration of the excellent application for a franchise," he said, ". . . the board has voted that the Vancouver group will definitely be invited to participate in the next National Hockey League expansion."

THE COMMITTEE, COMPRISING DAVID MOLSON, Jack Kent Cooke, Minnesota's Gordon Ritz and Chicago's Bill Wirtz, had been given a mandate that appeared straightforward. It was anything but. They deliberated among themselves, consulted privately with individual governors and presented alternatives to the board.

All agreed that two cities should be admitted for the 1970–71 season. The result would be a fourteen-team league of six original and eight expansion clubs. The problem was how to mix old with new to create two divisions, each with seven clubs, while maintaining some semblance of competitive balance. The 1968–69 season came and went. The summer of 1969 passed, and still the question of divisional realignment remained unresolved. The governors finally reached an accord in mid-September. Chicago would play in the West Division with the teams of the 1967 expansion. The two new clubs would join the East, along with Montreal, Toronto, Detroit, Boston and New York. The schedule was bumped up to seventy-eight games from seventy-four, and the playoff structure was revised. The deadline for submitting applications was December 1 and the price of admission was hoisted to $6 million.

In Vancouver, there was consternation. Cyrus McLean and the board of the city's minor-pro Canucks balked. They couldn't come up with that kind of money. The response from the league was unequivocal: the fee was fully justified. "I know of two parties who are eager to get the franchise at $6 million," Cooke said. "Not just interested—eager. If I wasn't involved I'd be prepared to buy it myself."

Minnesota's Walter Bush concurred. "I know of several people, both in the United States and Canada, who would be interested in an NHL franchise in Vancouver or anywhere else," he said.

Vancouver risked being left on the sidelines again, but was rescued by Thomas Scallen, a forty-four-year-old Minneapolis lawyer and businessman. He owned several companies, including the Ice Follies ice show, a New York advertising agency and Medicor, short for Medical Investment Corporation, which leased equipment to doctors. Bush and his North Star associates had encouraged Scallen to pursue the Vancouver franchise, and he hadn't hesitated. He had visited the city with his skating show and was certain the NHL would be a hit. "I'll do it," he told his fellow Minnesotans. "We won't have any trouble up there."

The second franchise went to the Knox brothers of Buffalo—Seymour III and Northrup. Clarence Campbell had previously stated that the league had received "intimations of interest" from cities as scattered as Atlanta, Dallas and Seattle, but the league owed the Knoxes. They had acquired a twenty per cent interest in the Seals, a team that had improved greatly in its second season but had remained a box-office flop.

The brothers hoped they might use their investment as leverage to acquire the Seals outright and move them to Buffalo. The league vetoed that idea, but the Knoxes held on to their shares rather than dumping them and going home. That helped keep the team afloat, and the brothers were rewarded with a franchise of their own. "This fulfills a lifetime ambition for me," Seymour Knox said afterward. And his lawyer, Robert O. Swados, added, "No one will ever know how difficult, complex and at times, discouraging a road we've had to travel."

The league awarded the franchises at a meeting held in New York on December 2, 1969, and the board declared that the next round of expansion would happen five years hence, in 1974–75.

SEASON-TICKET SALES WERE BRISK in Vancouver and Buffalo, and that meant the two new franchises would get off to a roaring start regardless of the calibre or performance of their respective teams. This was good and welcome news for Clarence Campbell. He spent a good part of 1970 dealing with two troubled clubs—namely, Oakland and Pittsburgh. In both cases, the symptoms of the malaise were the same: poor attendance, big losses, unstable ownership.

The Seals had wound up back in the hands of Barry van Gerbig and partners after the IRS ruled against Puck Inc. and its three principals—Potter Palmer, John O'Neil Jr. and George Gillett. But van Gerbig's group wanted out, not back in, and the league found a buyer in Trans National Communications of New York, a holding company formed in 1968 by a number of partners to acquire and manage various assets.

Trans National had no track record to speak of, but had attracted several high-profile investors, including Whitey Ford, a retired New York Yankees pitching star; Dick Lynch, a former New York Giant; and Pat Summerall, then a prominent TV sportscaster. The company paid approximately $1.6 million for the Seals and assumed debts totalling some $3 million—and, in short order, defaulted on its payments.

Van Gerbig's group tried to repossess the team, but Trans National applied for a court injunction to stop them and also filed a bankruptcy petition. A judge would have to decide which party was the rightful owner and would oversee the sale of the franchise. The presiding justice conceded he knew nothing about hockey and agreed to let the league select the next owner. There were two candidates.

The first was Jerry Seltzer, who was thirty-eight, a Bay Area resident and owner of Roller Derby—a hugely popular though lowbrow sport in which five-member teams of padded, helmeted women raced around an oval on roller skates, bumping, jostling and sometimes knocking the daylights out of each other. Seltzer had gathered an investors group that included the owners of four

American Football League teams. He bid $4.3 million, submitted a detailed, 120-page application and enjoyed the support of the local newspapers as well as the civic administrators of the Oakland Coliseum.

The second candidate was Charles O. Finley, who was sixty-two, a resident of Chicago and had made a fortune selling group medical insurance to doctors. He had been just another wealthy, no-name businessman until 1961, when he purchased baseball's Kansas City Athletics and promptly rattled that staid, tradition-bound sport by introducing garish promotional gimmicks, by dressing his team in uniforms of kelly green and yellow and adding white cleats and, in 1968, by moving the franchise to Oakland. For this, Finley was denounced on the floor of the U.S. Senate by Missouri's W. Stuart Symington, who pronounced him "one of the most disreputable characters ever to enter the American sports scene."

None of this troubled the NHL board of governors. They awarded the franchise to Finley, even though he had apparently bid slightly less than Seltzer and submitted a bare-bones one-page application. They apparently preferred the fact that Finley was a sole proprietor and they shied away from any association with Roller Derby. Time would prove that the board had made a grievous error. Nonetheless, by late June 1970 Finley was the new owner of the Seals. He was asked about introducing white skates and said he had no plans to do so, though he might if it meant boosting attendance. However, he did rename the team. The Oakland Seals became the California Golden Seals and would wear his favourite colours: kelly green and yellow.

Six weeks after this ownership debacle was tidied up, another arose. A story in the *Wall Street Journal* of August 13, 1970, disclosed that Donald Parsons was dismantling his banking empire after a long, futile battle with federal regulators over his rule-bending investment and acquisition practices. Parsons was also resigning from his law firm, which had laid off one-third of its lawyers, and, according to the *Journal*, he was likely under personal financial pressure. These events put the Penguins in jeopardy because Parsons still owed Pittsburgh-based Mellon Bank $3.8 million on a loan taken out to acquire the team.

Rumours quickly spread about the fate of the Penguins, and Campbell was compelled to address the issue. "The Pittsburgh hockey club will play in Pittsburgh, period," he said during a late-August press conference. "There is no way the club is currently contemplating or planning to move elsewhere." Campbell immediately began looking for a buyer and devoted the next eight months to the search. Meantime, the Penguins were reportedly insolvent as they began the 1970–71 season.

THE PROSPECTS WERE ALTOGETHER DIFFERENT in Vancouver and Buffalo that fall. The Canucks played their home opener on the evening of October 9, a Friday, and there was a palpable sense of anticipation in the city leading up to that momentous and long-awaited event. One wrinkle threatened to dampen the party, however. General manager Bud Poile was wrestling till the last hour with unruly players who were reluctant to sign, and he was far from alone. "Most all of the National Hockey League's fourteen teams are caught up in contract squabbles of some kind or another," the *Hockey News* reported.

Rangers general manager Emile Francis had suspended his four best players—Jean Ratelle, Vic Hadfield, Walt Tkaczuk and Brad Park—all of whom had refused to play exhibition games till they had signed. Boston's Derek Sanderson was holding out for $40,000 or more. Eddie Joyal of the Kings wanted around $30,000. Leaf Captain Dave Keon was demanding $125,000— an astronomical sum—according to newspaper reports, but settled for $75,000.

Two forces were driving salaries upward. Bobby Orr's precedent-setting contract had awakened the established stars, who immediately insisted on the same or better. Bobby Hull had sat out the first fifteen games of the previous season until the Black Hawks coughed up $100,000 per year. Veteran Leaf defenceman Tim Horton, who did not belong in the same hallowed sphere as Orr and Hull, nevertheless held out for $92,000. And the Wings had in the fall of 1970 rewarded Gordie Howe with a two-year deal at $100,000 per annum, more as recognition for past service than any expectation that he would remain as prolific as he had been.

Lawyers acting as player agents were also roiling the hitherto placid business of contract negotiations. Alan Eagleson, who had formed the NHL Players' Association, pioneered the practice—in hockey, at any rate—and others quickly charged in. New York attorneys Steve Arnold and Marty Blackman of Pro Sports Inc. were acting for the Ranger holdouts as well as Carol Vadnais and Harry Howell of the Seals. Boston attorney Bob Wolff was speaking for Sanderson and fellow Bruins Wayne Cashman and Gerry Cheevers.

It mattered not that no one had ever played a two-point tilt for the Vancouver Canucks of the NHL. The hired hands demanded equal treatment. Defenceman John Arbour and left winger Ted Taylor had bolted from the Canucks camp and hadn't returned. Poile managed to reach agreements with Pat Quinn, Murray Hall and Len Lunde the day before the season opener, but four others remained unsigned.

The Canucks made their debut against the Kings, before a crowd of 15,062, a full house compelled to endure a prolonged pre-game ceremony. Canuck alumni of the sixties, the fifties, the forties and the thirties were introduced, and lastly, and to a loud ovation, the most famous player ever to represent the city in professional hockey: eighty-seven-year-old Fred (Cyclone) Taylor, a member of the 1915 Stanley Cup champion Vancouver Millionaires.

There were so many politicians and dignitaries on hand that some of the introductions had to be shunted to the first intermission. Among those who endured this indignity were the owner, Tom Scallen, league president Clarence Campbell and British Columbia premier W.A.C. Bennett. The home side lost, and that erased some of the sparkle from the evening, but not all, because Vancouver was, at last, an NHL town.

The Sabres spent their first week on the road and went home to face the almighty Montreal Canadiens. *Globe and Mail* reporter Dan Proudfoot arrived two hours before game time and observed a last-minute scramble to prepare the Memorial Auditorium. Workers were installing protective glass around the boards. The clock and scoreboard that hung over centre ice had been lowered so staff could replace the basketball PLAYER FOUL signs with PLAYER PENALTIES. And the building smelled of fresh paint.

The city had not completed the requisite expansion of the building, and the Auditorium seating capacity remained at 10,331. That was the announced attendance for the Sabres-Canadiens clash, though Proudfoot reported that at least four hundred additional spectators were packed into the aged and undersized arena.

The club had sold six thousand season tickets, a quarter of them to fans from the Canadian side of the border. They came from Welland, St. Catharines,

Hamilton and elsewhere in the Niagara Peninsula. On opening night, Dofasco, the big steelmaker, had chartered three buses for employees. Other companies, as well as social clubs, had done the same. Sabres coach and general manager Punch Imlach had placed an advertisement in a Toronto newspaper inviting readers to join him in Buffalo, but few did, and the league ordered the paper to pull the ad.

The Sabres, like the Canucks, lost their home opener, but they proved to be the better of the two expansion teams. Neither stood a chance of making much noise in a division that included the Canadiens, a powerful Rangers squad and the formidable Bruins—the defending Stanley Cup champions. Vancouver finished sixth of seven in the East, one point up on the Red Wings, who had been slipping for several years. Buffalo placed fifth, nineteen points out of a playoff spot, but the Sabres had a franchise player to build around.

Imlach had selected Gilbert Perreault of the Montreal Junior Canadiens first overall in the June 1970 draft. Perrault was a powerful skater and a prolific offensive centre, and he quickly endeared himself to the home fans. They gave him a standing ovation when he scored twice during a game in early March and set a new record for rookie goal scoring. Perrault finished with thirty-eight and was the runaway winner of the Calder Trophy as rookie of the year.

But the 1971 season belonged to the Bruins. They equalled or broke thirty-seven records. They won more games (57) and scored more goals (399) than any team in history. They boasted ten 20-goal scorers and four who topped the 100-point mark: Ken Hodge with 105; Johnny Bucyk with 116; Bobby Orr, the previous season's scoring champion, with 139; and Phil Esposito, who tallied an astonishing 76 goals, 76 assists and 152 points.

Nobody had ever seen anything like it, and some questioned the validity of the Bruins' staggering accomplishments. Maurice Richard, ten years retired, attributed it to expansion and the dilution of talent. Not so, replied Esposito. "You know what I really think about all the comparisons between our records and the older clubs'?" he said. "I think there's never been a hockey club that could tie our laces."

It was just the sort of triumphalism that precedes the fall, and the Bruins took a fall for the ages that spring. They lost to the third-place Canadiens in the opening round. It took seven games, but all agreed that the series turned on game two, played on a Sunday afternoon, April 8, before a rabidly partisan crowd at Boston Garden. The Bruins led five-one late in the second period, but the Canadiens won seven-five, tied the series and shattered the aura of invincibility that had surrounded Orr, Esposito and their teammates.

Montreal went on to beat Minnesota in six games in the semifinal and Chicago in seven to capture its seventeenth championship to that point.

BEFORE PUCKS DROPPED TO START the 1971–72 season, the fifth of the expansion era, the Canadiens dumped Al MacNeil, the coach who had guided the team to its most recent Stanley Cup, and there were coaching changes in Philadelphia and St. Louis as well. The Flyers fired Vic Stasiuk in favour of Fred Shero. The Blues sent Scotty Bowman packing and hired Sid Abel. The Canadiens, meantime, shunted MacNeil to their AHL affiliate, the Nova Scotia Voyageurs, and replaced him with Bowman.

There were big changes of a different sort in Pittsburgh. Clarence Campbell announced—with evident delight—that the Penguins had new owners, all of them local, all in their mid to late thirties. "Relieved," he said when quizzed by reporters, "I'll say. Finding a buyer for this team has been my main concern since last August 15. It ruined the winter for me."

There were landmark contracts for Boston's Bobby Orr and Montreal's Guy Lafleur. Neither Orr nor the Bruins would disclose the terms, in keeping with the practice at the time, but there was speculation that the deal was worth a million dollars and Orr's agent, Alan Eagleson, did not discourage such talk. "It is a safe assumption," Eagleson said, "that Bobby's contract is the richest in NHL history."

Lafleur, the top pick in the June amateur draft, was seen as the successor to Rocket Richard and the freshly retired Jean Béliveau, and the hopes and aspirations of every hockey fan in the province of Quebec immediately alighted on his shoulders. He expected to be paid accordingly, and he was. Lafleur signed a two-year deal reported to be worth $105,000 and described as the sport's richest rookie contract ever.

Amid all this movement, the great Gordie Howe retired after twenty-five seasons, 1,687 regular-season games, 786 goals, 1,023 assists and 1,809 penalty minutes. He was forty-three. He had a painfully arthritic left wrist and rightly reasoned he should exit gracefully rather than hang on. "I could play one more year and I could play badly," Howe said. "But what good would that do when it could undo twenty-five years of work?"

Such were the events that commanded attention that off-season. There was another: a new league called the World Hockey Association was being formed, and it aimed to compete for talent with the NHL. There would be fourteen teams and play would begin in the fall of 1972. News of this unlikely venture first surfaced in late June 1971 in the Hollywood *Sun-Tattler*, a Florida newspaper. The promoters were Dennis Murphy, a former municipal politician from Santa Ana, California, and Gary Davidson, a San Francisco lawyer, and they had filed articles of incorporation in the state of Delaware.

Murphy and Davidson didn't know the difference between hockey sticks and hula hoops. Nor were they fans of the game. They were opportunists. They were out to make a buck and they were treading a well-worn path. In 1960, the American Football League had been created to challenge the established National Football League. In 1967, the American Basketball Association had taken on the National Basketball Association, and Davidson had handled some of the legal work involved in forming the ABA while Murphy had managed four of its teams in as many seasons.

The pair worked behind the scenes all summer and into the fall before convening the first public meeting of their World Hockey Association. It was held in New York on the final weekend of October 1971, and on November 1, a Monday, they held a press luncheon to unveil their plans and introduce their franchisees. There were ten, representing New York; Chicago; Los Angeles; San Francisco; Miami; Dayton, Ohio; St. Paul, Minnesota; and three Canadian cities: Winnipeg, Edmonton and Calgary. (Later that month, the WHA announced two additional franchises, one to be based in Hamilton, Ontario, the other in New England, rounding out the roster of teams at twelve.)

There were plenty of questions from the sportswriters and an abundance of bluff and braggadocio from the franchisees. The NHL? No problem, replied Winnipeg's Ben Hatskin. "All I can say is, let the NHL try to fight us," Hatskin snapped, adding he had $100 million behind his venture. Players? Not a problem, either. They'd jump to the WHA if they could make more money or get more playing time. The WHA would be an attractive alternative for graduating juniors and would draw from all the minor leagues—the American, the Central, the Eastern and the International.

"We will ice competitive teams," declared Edmonton's Bill Hunter, who had long been involved in junior hockey in the West. "We will be at least as competitive and, we believe, better than the new division of the NHL."

Davidson and a team of fellow lawyers had developed a standard player's contract that was radically different than those of the NHL or the other North American professional leagues. The WHA's would not contain a reserve clause, which bound an athlete to his team in perpetuity. Nor would it have an option clause, which gave a club the right to offer a player a new deal or extend the existing one before he could negotiate with an opponent. In the absence of such provisions, a WHA player would become an unrestricted free agent once his contract expired. "It will revolutionize sports," said New York lawyer Steve Arnold, president of an agency that represented athletes.

The NHL could not ignore these developments. A rival league, however flimsy, frivolous or contemptuous, was invading several of its markets and intended to steal its players. No one on either side was calling it a hockey war, but that's what it was, and the NHL moved swiftly.

New arenas were under construction in Atlanta and in Nassau County on Long Island in the greater New York area, and both would be first-class, NHL-calibre buildings. Murphy and Davidson wanted WHA teams in those facilities. They had aggressively courted Tom Cousins, owner of the NBA's Atlanta Hawks and the real estate developer behind the $17 million arena. Likewise, Long Island lawyer Neil Shayne, the WHA's New York franchisee, had lobbied Nassau County officials for his as yet unnamed, newborn team.

But the county, as well as Cousins and his partners, wanted NHL teams. Clarence Campbell convened a meeting of the board for November 8, 1971, at a Howard Johnson Hotel near New York's John F. Kennedy Airport to consider granting two new franchises. The league constitution required a unanimous vote on the issue, but one member of the board, Charles O. Finley of the California Golden Seals, was opposed, and he had one, maybe two allies. Finley was understandably concerned that his already weak, money-losing club would have to surrender players in an expansion draft. He had another grievance—namely, the absence of a revenue-sharing arrangement in which visiting teams received a cut of the home side's gate, which was standard practice in the NFL and Major League Baseball.

Finley could not be persuaded to support the expansion. A one-day meeting spilled over to a second day, and late on the second afternoon Campbell emerged and announced that the board had voted twelve-two in favour of awarding franchises to Atlanta and Long Island, though he did not say whether the unanimity rule had been amended, revoked or merely ignored.

The Atlanta franchise went to a ten-member group led by Cousins, Long Island to a company called Long Island Sports Enterprises Inc., a syndicate of investors who also owned the New York Nets of the ABA. Both had paid a $6 million entry fee, and the Long Island interests also had to pay the Rangers $4 million for territorial rights. Campbell had scarcely finished announcing the two new clubs—the league's fifteenth and sixteenth—when the WHA fired its first shot at the NHL.

New York franchisee Shayne was furious at being shut out of the Nassau rink and was suing the county. "I do not intend to let this matter rest," he said in a press release. "I will ask the courts for a full and complete open hearing in connection with my suit against Nassau County and I intend to vigorously pursue whatever remedies are available under antitrust laws."

IN THE COMING MONTHS, the WHA moved franchises from here to there like the pieces on a checkerboard. The San Francisco entry was shifted to Quebec City. Ontario's relocated from Hamilton to Ottawa. One ownership group in Chicago fell apart and another took over. Dayton city council wouldn't build an arena, so the local promoter, Paul Deneau, took his team to Houston. Arena problems put Miami on the sidelines; Murphy and Davidson found investors in Philadelphia to take over. Calgary folded, but a brash, colourful Cleveland promoter named Nick Mileti stepped up and the WHA planted its flag in that Ohio city.

The whole rickety enterprise appeared doomed, but the prospect of jobs and big money proved powerful incentives for the players. The WHA held its inaugural draft over two days in mid-February 1972 at the Royal Coach Inn in

Anaheim, California. Twelve teams selected upward of a thousand players, and within two weeks the first bona fide NHLer—Toronto Maple Leaf goaltender Bernie Parent—announced he would jump leagues as soon as the season ended. The money, $100,000 annually for five years, guaranteed, was too good to turn down and far more than he could expect in the NHL.

Murphy and Davidson were good at public relations. They churned out press releases one after another to document player signings and commitments. A May 8 release announced that twelve players had signed, including Wayne Connelly from the Canucks, Larry Pleau from the Canadiens and Brad Selwood from the Leafs. By May 26, the number had grown to thirty-six. On June 13, another release boasted that seventy-two had signed, and two weeks later, on Tuesday, June 27, the Winnipeg Jets landed Bobby Hull.

The wooing of Hull had begun seven months earlier, when Hatskin boasted that he was prepared to sign the Chicago Black Hawk superstar for $1 million. The Jets selected Hull in the WHA player draft and the courtship began in earnest after the Hawks were eliminated from the playoffs, even though he would remain under contract until September 30. By the latter half of May, Hull and Hatskin had agreed verbally on the terms of a multimillion-dollar deal, according to the *Chicago Tribune*.

The Hawks and their owners, Arthur Wirtz and son Bill, hadn't commenced negotiations with the flamboyant and prolific left winger who had given fifteen years to the franchise and done more than any other player to revive its fortunes. "They haven't been in touch," Hull told the *Tribune*'s Bob Verdi. "Maybe they don't think the Winnipeg offer is serious. I'm not going after them [the Wirtzes]. They have to sign me. I don't have to sign them. Winnipeg has taken the initiative and that's why I've agreed to sign if they come up with the money. I'm not going to see their two million and then say, 'Wait a minute. I'm going to call the Wirtzes.' I'll just sign, and the next phone call I'll make to the Wirtzes will be to tell them I'm leaving."

That proved unnecessary, given the massive publicity surrounding his departure. There were two signing ceremonies. The first occurred in St. Paul, Minnesota. Hatskin and his entourage, a horde of journalists and the Hulls—Bobby, his then wife Joanne and three of their five children—took an early-morning charter from Winnipeg. The Hulls rode to the Minnesota Club in downtown St. Paul in a 1934 Rolls-Royce leased from a private owner for the occasion, and there Hull signed a $1 million certified cheque. It was a signing bonus covered by the league and its member clubs.

Then everyone returned to the airport and flew back to Winnipeg for a public signing at 4:30 p.m. at the corner of Portage and Main. That famous commercial crossroads in the heart of the Manitoba capital was packed with thousands of fans, and traffic was congested in all directions. Hull pulled on a Winnipeg jersey and promptly signed a $1.75 million cheque, which represented five years' salary at $250,000 per season and another five at $100,000 annually to serve as a team executive once his playing days were over. "This has been the greatest day, the greatest thrill of my hockey career," Hull told the adoring crowd. "The pressure is on me to help this league get off the ground and, believe me, I'll try."

Winnipeggers could hardly believe their good fortune. Their city had been producing hockey players for generations, but the best of them always had to compete for other cities and other fans. Now, one of the greatest ever would be playing for *them*. "Bobby Hull of Winnipeg Jets," wrote *Free Press* reporter Reyn Davis. "The sound has a majestic ring to it. . . . What a coup!"

Afterward, there were rumbles of discontent and muted threats from the NHL. Bill Wirtz said nothing and neither did his father, Arthur. Clarence Campbell told the *Chicago Tribune* that Hull had broken his contract with the Hawks and insisted they would win if they took legal action. "I don't think Mr. Hull will be playing for Winnipeg next year, nor do I think he'll be playing in the National Hockey League," Campbell said. "I certainly do not mean he will be blacklisted. I just don't think he'll return to the NHL as long as the WHA is in existence."

The Hawks did not sue. Hull did play for the Jets. His presence ensured that the WHA achieved liftoff with a modicum of credibility. The rebel league would survive seven tumultuous seasons. It would spawn no fewer than twenty-seven teams, steal established stars from NHL clubs, lure junior prospects with wildly extravagant contracts (many of which could not be paid in full) and, all in all, make the 1970s a calamitous decade for the National Hockey League.

9

WAR OF ATTRITION (1972–1977)

THE MOST IMPORTANT SERIES in the history of hockey opened on Saturday, September 2, 1972, at the Montreal Forum. Team Canada, a collection of the NHL's best, would face the Soviet Union Nationals for the first time. Eight games—four in Canada and four in Moscow—would determine whether the purported superiority of the NHL was real or bogus and whether Canada really was the world's leading hockey nation.

Some very informed observers made some extravagant wagers and predictions. Harold Ballard bet $640 that Canada would win the opener by three goals. Scotty Bowman put money on Canada and spotted the Russians forty goals, assuming that the NHLers would win by an average of five goals per outing. Jacques Plante watched the Russians practise before game one and afterward told a reporter: "I'd love to be in goal because there isn't going to be much for any goaltender to do. It would be a nice place to watch the game from."

Team Canada coach and general manager Harry Sinden, who had guided the Boston Bruins to a Stanley Cup championship in the spring of 1972, was more circumspect. But then, Sinden really had no idea what he and his players were up against. He acknowledged as much during a press conference at Maple Leaf Gardens shortly before they decamped for Montreal and game one.

They had watched a film of a world championship game between the Soviets and the Czechs and another of a game between them and the Canadian national team. But that was it. Sinden received plenty of advice from those who had seen the Soviets or played against them, but opinions were so divided that he concluded they were best ignored.

"We wanted to avoid going into the series with any preconceived ideas," he told the media. "We feared preparing for something that might not be there. We're going into this thing with the idea that we won't really know until we've played them a game. We have to leave ourselves open and be ready to make big and quick adjustments."

That approach failed badly in the opener. Russia won seven-three. The *Globe and Mail* described Canada's defeat as "a shocking and incredible result," while the Soviet news agency TASS declared that it had "destroyed the myth of invincibility of the best Canadian professionals."

A victory in game two in Toronto salvaged the country's reputation and restored confidence. A tie two nights later in Winnipeg provided a true measure of just how closely matched the teams were.

"Gentlemen," Sinden said at a postgame press conference, "aren't we all glad to be alive to see a hockey game like that?"

Do the Russians compare with the best in the NHL? a reporter asked.

"Absolutely," Sinden replied.

"As good as the Boston Bruins?"

"Yes, sir. As good as the Boston Bruins."

The Russians dominated game four in Vancouver and won handily, and the crowd booed Team Canada. It was a stinging rebuke, and there was more trouble when the Canadians arrived in Moscow. Three players who had been used sparingly or not at all—Vic Hadfield, Richard Martin and Jocelyn Guevremont—quit and went home.

A capacity crowd of fourteen thousand packed the Moscow Sports Palace for game five—including Leonid Brezhnev, general secretary of the Communist Party, Alexei Kosygin, the premier of the Soviet Union, and Nikolai Podgorny, the president. The Canadians carried a three-nothing lead into the third, but the Russians rallied. They tied it, then went ahead, and the normally dour, unsmiling party bosses stood with the rest of the partisan crowd and cheered wildly.

The loss triggered a collective shudder across Canada. Defeat—previously unthinkable—appeared inevitable. Among the players, however, a different mood took hold—anger at having let a sure thing slip away and a hell-bent resolve that it wouldn't happen again—and it launched the most memorable and celebrated comeback in the history of the sport. Three straight wins, all by one goal, and the winner in each case scored by Paul Henderson, a winger on the checking line. The last of those three miraculous tallies came with thirty-four seconds showing on the clock in game eight. "When Paul scored that goal, it was like an atomic bomb going off," Henderson's mother, Evelyn, told a reporter.

That may have been an understatement. A whole, immensely relieved country erupted with the joy of someone who has just survived a near-death experience. The players returned as heroes. Montrealers were the first to fete them, thanks to Mayor Jean Drapeau. He sent a telegram to Sinden imploring him to make a stop in his city rather than flying straight to Toronto as planned.

"I express the ardent wish," Drapeau wrote, "of all my fellow citizens to acclaim in Montreal . . . all Canadian players for whom Montrealers cheered with all their hearts. They justly demand their presence for a few hours on the streets of Montreal."

The Air Canada jet bearing the team arrived at Dorval Airport at 6:32 p.m., Sunday, October 1. Prime Minister Pierre Trudeau stood at the foot of the ramp rolled up to the door of the aircraft and shook hands with each player. Some ten thousand Montrealers—crammed into the departure lounge over-looking the tarmac—welcomed them with what one journalist described as "screaming adulation."

Drapeau spoke during a brief ceremony and so did the prime minister. "We bid you welcome in the name of all Canadians who open to you their hearts, who open to you their arms," Trudeau said.

The Montreal stop delayed by three hours the team's arrival in Toronto and the start of a similar ceremony at Nathan Phillips Square. It poured rain, but no matter. Between thirty and forty thousand people huddled under umbrellas, sought shelter under trees or simply got drenched. The 48th Highlanders military band played, the St. Andrews of the Apostle Folk Choir of London, Ontario, sang and the crowd sang with them.

The players finally arrived at 10 p.m. They shared the stage with the premier (William Davis), the mayor (William Dennison) and the leader of the federal New Democrats (David Lewis), among others. The jubilant onlookers drowned out everyone who spoke except members of Team Canada. "You people are remarkable," Sinden shouted. "Without you, we'd be nowhere." He concluded with a chant: "Ny-ET, ny-ET, so-VIET, da, da, ca-na-DA." And the people chanted with him.

It was over all too soon for many, and the throngs slowly dispersed and filled the soggy night with cries of "We're number one!"

SIX DAYS LATER, ON SATURDAY, OCTOBER 7, the NHL opened its fifty-fifth season. Fourteen of its sixteen teams were in action, including the two new clubs, the Atlanta Flames and New York Islanders. They squared off at the Nassau County Coliseum, before a crowd of 12,221, and the Flames went home winners by a score of three-two.

There had been the usual round of preseason predictions about who would finish first in the league's eight-team East and West Divisions, who would make the top four on each side and therefore qualify for the playoffs, who would miss the cut, who would rise and who would fall. There was a consensus that the Canadiens, Bruins and Rangers were the teams to beat. Beyond that, as the *Montreal Star*'s Red Fisher wrote, "It was anybody's guess."

So much had changed since the previous May, when the Bruins captured their second Stanley Cup in three years, and the debut of the Flames and Islanders was the least of it. The Canada-Russia series had forced the league and its fans to ditch their smug assumptions about the superiority of the North American professional game. There were already murmurs to the effect that perhaps NHL teams should adopt Soviet-style, year-round conditioning programs. The league could deal with such questions at a time and on terms of its choosing.

The more pressing and immediate problem was the World Hockey Association. Many of the sharpest minds in the NHL had dismissed the threat posed by the WHA, just as almost everyone had underestimated the Russians. It would never get off the ground, they scoffed. But they were wrong. For the first time since 1926, the NHL had a rival and, as the *Globe and Mail*'s Rex MacLeod wrote prior to the season opener: "These days, the NHL is doing more crying than laughing as it contemplates the WHA."

Some three hundred players had jumped leagues, including sixty-seven who defected directly from NHL rosters. WHA teams had raided indiscriminately from the strong and the weak. The Bruins lost six players, four of them key members of their championship teams: goaltender Gerry Cheevers, defence-man Ted Green and forwards John McKenzie and Derek Sanderson. The Islanders, having just paid a $6 million entry fee, lost five skaters acquired in the league's expansion draft. The California Golden Seals were hardest hit. They lost eleven, including five of their top six scorers from the previous season.

Money was the attraction. Cheevers, who had earned $80,000, plus bonuses, with the 1971–72 Bruins, signed with the Cleveland Crusaders for $200,000 annually over seven years. McKenzie, a thirty-four-year-old right winger, jumped to the Philadelphia Blazers as a player-coach for $100,000 per season. The Bruins had offered Sanderson $80,000. He spurned that for a ten-year, $2.35 million contract with the Blazers that paid $300,000 in each of the first two seasons. Lesser players received less, but still double or triple what they might have earned in the NHL.

Compensation in the NHL rose accordingly. The average player salary jumped to $44,000 in 1972–73, up from $31,000 the previous season, and some did a lot better. Ranger defenceman Brad Park signed for $200,000 annually over five years. Teammate Walt Tkaczuk got a deal worth $150,000 a year. Vic Hadfield, a fifty-goal scorer, received a WHA offer of $1 million for four seasons. That left Ranger manager Emile Francis with two options: match it or lose Hadfield. Salaries had escalated so quickly that Bobby Orr's $180,000 a year "now seems too low," one player agent said.

The fight for talent made a shambles of the established economics of pro hockey. For decades, the owners had held the high cards at contract time. Now the players had the upper hand. But as salaries were going up, the calibre of competition was going down. It had slid steadily as the NHL added teams. It dipped again with the advent of the WHA.

The gap between the first- and last-place teams, leaguewide, stood at 47 points at the end of 1967–68, the inaugural season of the expansion era. It widened in each of the next two years and jumped to 76 in 1970–71 when Vancouver and Buffalo debuted. It hit a staggering 90 points in 1972–73 when the Canadiens piled up 120 and the Islanders earned a mere 30 on the basis of the worst record of any expansion team to that point: twelve wins, sixty losses and six ties.

Maurice Richard, up against it in the 1950s, with Ted Kennedy and Tom Johnson: *Boston Globe* columnist Dave Egan said, "He is one of the remarkable ones who spends more in genius than he ever can get in money."

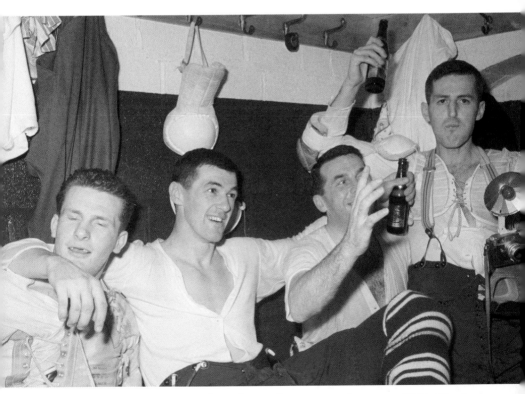

April 18, 1963: Kent Douglas, Ed Litzenberger, Ron Stewart and Billy Harris of the Toronto Maple Leafs celebrate the second of what would turn out to be three straight Stanley Cup victories.

Red Wings coach and GM Jack Adams, circa 1930: In his playing days he was once so badly hurt that his nurse took a while to recognize him as her brother. She said, or so the story goes: "Jack, hockey will kill you if you don't quit." He didn't.

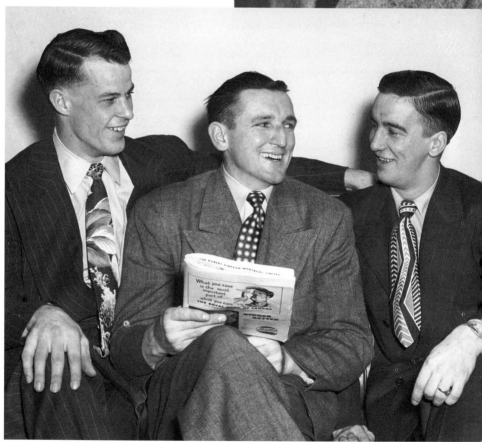

Gordie Howe, Sid Abel and Ted Lindsay—the "Production Line"—at Maple Leaf Gardens in 1948: The Red Wings had a good postwar, finishing first seven times in a row, from '48 to '55, and winning four Stanley Cups.

April 25, 1935: Red Dutton (left) signs a two-year contract to coach the New York Americans. With him is Bill Dwyer, son of the team's owner. Bill Dwyer Sr., a prominent figure in the city's criminal underworld, avoided cameras. For reasons lost to history, Bill Jr. sports a counter-clock-wise swastika ring.

Big Jim's big win, April 15, 1937: James Norris (left) celebrates Stanley Cup victory with left winger Herbie Lewis and James Norris Sr. The owner of the Detroit Red Wings took hockey seriously. His butler, gardener, handyman and other members of the household staff had to know how to skate and handle a puck in order to be hired.

Burying the hatchet, February 14, 1934: Ace Bailey (left) and Eddie Shore at a Maple Leaf Gardens benefit for Bailey that is now regarded as the first NHL all-star game. The two had been involved in a near-fatal on-ice incident the previous December.

A rookie's first training camp, 1966: Bobby Orr with Boston Bruins coach Harry Sinden.

Alan Eagleson, 1972: The bitterest feud in NHL history occurred not on the ice or in the dressing room but away from the rink altogether. It pitted player—Bobby Orr—against agent.

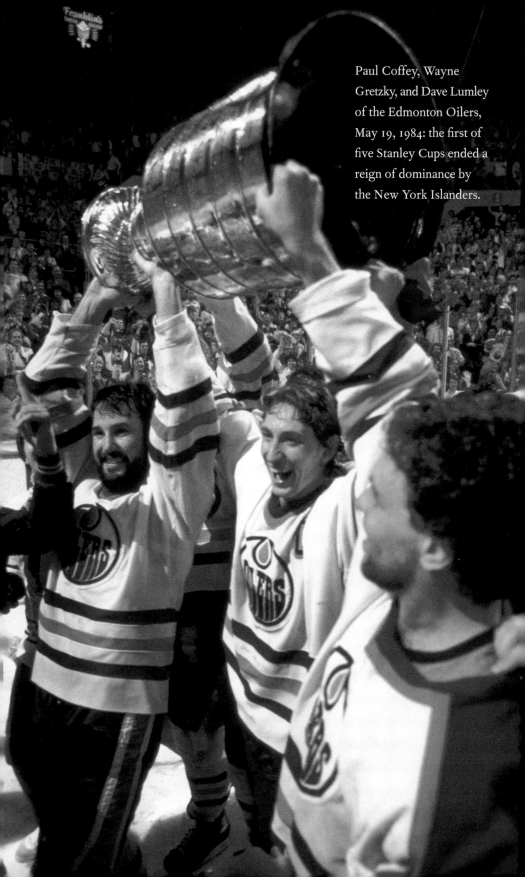

Paul Coffey, Wayne Gretzky, and Dave Lumley of the Edmonton Oilers, May 19, 1984: the first of five Stanley Cups ended a reign of dominance by the New York Islanders.

Ron Francis: He was a core member of the Carolina Hurricanes from 1998 until 2004 as they established themselves in an untested southern market and then captivated local fans with several stirring playoff runs. The Hurricanes officially retired his No. 10 jersey in 2006. Francis was inducted into the Hockey Hall of Fame the following year.

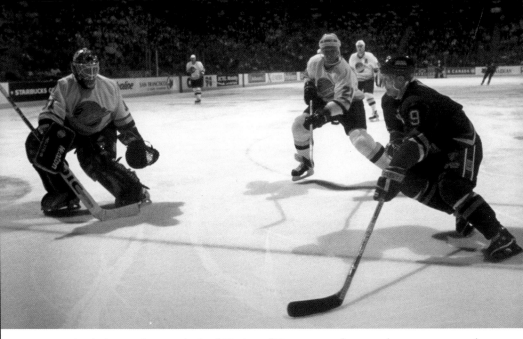

Anaheim Ducks captain Paul Kariya of Vancouver plays to a hometown crowd at General Motors Place, February 20, 1999: Bruce McNall, chairman of the NHL's board of governors, had conjured up the "Mighty Ducks" in 1993 in order to bring the Walt Disney Company into the league; not long after, he was in jail.

Brett Hull, Stanley Cup final, June 8, 2000: The Dallas Stars were one of four teams that moved from north to south in the 1990s and one of the three to capture the Stanley Cup in their new home (the others being the Quebec Nordiques, who became the Colorado Avalanche, and the Hartford Whalers, who became the Carolina Hurricanes).

In the East Division, Montreal, Boston and the Rangers were miles ahead of the rest and assured of playoff positions early on. That left five others chasing fourth, though it quickly became a two-team race, Buffalo versus Detroit, and Buffalo prevailed on the final day. Chicago finished first in the West even without Bobby Hull. Pittsburgh, Los Angeles and California remained the divisional doormats. The Atlanta Flames were a pleasant surprise. They earned sixty-five points and were better than the Seals, Islanders, Canucks and Maple Leafs, then in the early stages of a long slide into mediocrity. The North Stars made the playoffs for the fifth time in six years and the Blues were in for the sixth straight time. St. Louis nailed down fourth on the final day before a crowd of 20,009, an NHL record, and they drew 726,158 on the season, another record.

The Philadelphia Flyers, who finished second in the West and sixth overall, were the big surprise. They compiled their first winning record. They became the first NHL team to hire an assistant coach—a career minor-leaguer named Mike Nykoluk. Bobby Clarke—at twenty-three—became the NHL's youngest captain and the first player from an expansion team to accumulate more than one hundred points in a season. Fellow centre Rick MacLeish became the first to score fifty goals. Left winger Bill Flett contributed forty-three and the Flyers boasted two thirty-goal scorers, Gary Dornhoefer and the rookie Bill Barber.

Offensive firepower was one element of the Flyers' success. Solid defence was the second and intimidation the third. Head coach Fred Shero added that element to the mix. He had once coached a roughhouse minor-league team that became known as the Magnificent Malcontents. They cruised to a championship, and the experience shaped Shero's thinking. "Eighteen choirboys never won the Stanley Cup," he told a Philadelphia sportswriter, "and they never will."

Shero made room on his Flyers roster for Don Saleski, who earned 205 penalty minutes, André Dupont, who picked up 215; Bob Kelly, who accumulated 236, and Dave Schultz, who led the league with 256. Schultz had established AHL penalty records in consecutive seasons, and in this, his first NHL campaign, he earned a reputation as one of the league's most feared fighters. He beat up Terry Harper of the Los Angeles Kings and Bobby Schmautz of the Vancouver Canucks and soon complained about the lack of willing sparring partners when teams visited the Philadelphia Spectrum. "It's too bad these home games aren't exciting anymore," he said. "Nobody wants to fight back."

Five members of the Flyers were charged with assault and causing a disturbance after going into the stands and brawling with fans in Vancouver. Defenceman Barry Ashbee was suspended for eight games for punching a referee. After a chaotic game in Atlanta in early January 1973, Jack Chevalier of the *Philadelphia Bulletin* wrote: "The image of the fightin' Flyers is spreading gradually around the NHL and people are dreaming up wild nicknames. They're the Mean Machine, the Bullies of Broad Street and Freddy's Philistines." The story appeared under the headline BROAD STREET BULLIES MUSCLE ATLANTA and the name stuck.

Clarence Campbell, for one, was not impressed and ordered owner Ed Snider and general manager Keith Allen to control their players or face disciplinary action. But fans in Philadelphia loved the team, mayhem and all. That was evident when the Flyers advertised 1,500 general-admission seats for their first-round playoff against the North Stars. There was a lineup outside the Spectrum by ten o'clock the night before tickets went on sale. By the following morning, the crowd had grown to ten thousand.

The Flyers gave the fans value for their money in the postseason. They ousted the North Stars in six—the first playoff triumph for the franchise—and moved on to the Stanley Cup semifinal against Montreal's formidable Canadiens. This edition of the venerable old club was blessed with speed, depth and an extraordinary determination to win. They had won fifty-two regular-season games and lost just ten and did not lose two in a row until the opening round of the playoffs against the Sabres.

Nevertheless, the Flyers fought the Canadiens to a draw in games one and two. The Flyers won the first in overtime and lost the second and returned home for the third. They received a thunderous six-minute standing ovation when they took to the ice. "You couldn't talk over it," Dornhoefer later recalled. "I will never forget it."

The Canadiens won that night and swept the next two and sent their rambunctious rival home for the summer. They then dispatched the Black Hawks in six to win their eighteenth Stanley Cup. But one piece of silverware was awarded to the Flyers. Their captain, Bobby Clarke, won the Hart Trophy as the league's most valuable player.

That summer, they greatly improved their prospects by signing goaltender

Bernie Parent, who was a well-travelled twenty-eight. He had begun his career with Boston. Philadelphia acquired him in the expansion draft of June 1967, and then traded him to Toronto in February 1971. He jumped to the WHA's Philadelphia Blazers, but walked out over a contract dispute after sixty-three games and he was thrilled to be back in the Flyer fold.

"This is the first time I'll be playing for a team with a great chance at the Stanley Cup," he said upon his return. "I saw some Flyers playoff games at the Spectrum and it gave me goose bumps."

EVERY WAR HAS ITS HAWKS and its doves, and the one between the NHL and the WHA was no exception. Doves appeared among the owners before round two of the conflict commenced with a second off-season scramble for players. There were those on both sides who recognized—correctly, as time would show—that revenues could never keep pace with skyrocketing salaries. It was madness, they concluded, to allow the fight to continue.

The players were prospering as never before, while the teams were bleeding red ink. NHL losses were not disclosed, and those who were losing endured their pain in silence. But the *Hockey News* reported in early April 1973 that the twelve WHA clubs collectively had lost $11 million in their first season. Both leagues were selling an inferior brand of hockey, and that was apparent to every fan who had witnessed the magnificent and exhilarating Canada-Russia series. Common sense trumped pride among a handful of NHL owners. They sued for peace.

In early April, just as the playoffs were commencing in both leagues, Rangers governor Bill Jennings and Flyers owner Ed Snider arranged a secret weekend meeting at a New York hotel with a delegation of WHA owners, led by Winnipeg's Ben Hatskin. The two parties explored the possibility of a merger. A second, larger gathering was held a few days later. Seven NHL and eight WHA clubs sent representatives.

The talks were merely exploratory, given the extraordinary legal complexities of merging leagues, but the reaction among the hawks was swift and unequivocal. Alan Eagleson hired New York lawyer Ira M. Millstein, who had fought the amalgamation of the National and American Basketball Associations, and instructed him to prepare an antitrust complaint on behalf of his members.

"It's a heyday for the players," Eagleson said of the NHL-WHA battle, "and I want to keep it that way."

Meantime, Clarence Campbell convened a board meeting to deal with this unauthorized gubernatorial freelancing. He and the two leading hawks, Detroit's Bruce Norris and Chicago's Bill Wirtz, were furious with Snider and Jennings, according to Gil Stein, who was the Flyers' general counsel and attended with Snider. "Norris and Campbell excoriated [them] for what they had done," Stein tells us in an account written some years later, "and the board passed a resolution, moved by Norris and seconded by Wirtz, prohibiting all persons connected with NHL member clubs or the league from having any discussions with WHA representatives regarding a merger. . . . Snider and Jennings had been effectively silenced."

Campbell emerged from the conclave clutching a prepared statement confirming the decisions made behind closed doors. He read it to the press, and then sent a copy to Eagleson. This was far from the end of the matter, though. There were now pro- and anti-merger factions on the board. Relations between them grew distant and chilly. Distrust and animosity arose between Wirtz and Snider, and these dark sentiments would lead to further clashes. And in the short term, the war with the WHA continued, with all its calamitous consequences.

The NHL appeared to have the upper hand in the summer of 1973. By the end of June, NHL clubs had signed fifteen of the sixteen players taken in the first round of the amateur draft. Denis Potvin of the Ottawa 67's became a New York Islander. Tom Lysiak of the Medicine Hat Tigers joined the Atlanta Flames. Fellow Tiger Lanny McDonald became a Maple Leaf and Rick Middleton of the Oshawa Generals a New York Ranger. The only first-rounder who held out was Bob Gainey, a Peterborough Pete taken by the Montreal Canadiens.

By late August, NHL clubs had signed forty-two of the top sixty-four amateurs, Gainey included, but the rival league had achieved one resounding triumph. It occurred at the WHA draft, held in Toronto in late May, a few days after the Toronto Marlboros had won the Memorial Cup. In the opening round, Houston Aeros coach and general manager Bill Dineen stood in his turn and declared, "With their first pick, Houston takes Mark Howe." Later, Dineen struck again: "Houston takes Marty Howe."

A headline in the next issue of the *Hockey News* summed up the reaction:

HOUSTON ROCKS HOCKEY WORLD
BY LURING HOWE BOYS TO WHA

And a secondary heading posed a startling question:

WILL GORDIE FOLLOW SONS?

It took several weeks to negotiate a deal, but by the end of August all three Howes were Houston Aeros. Gordie was forty-five. He was two years retired and restless and discontented as a Red Wing front-office executive, a position that was more a sinecure than a job. In the last of his twenty-five seasons as a Red Wing, he had earned $100,000. The Aeros guaranteed him $1 million over four years. Mark and Marty each got $600,000 over the same period.

Campbell and others in the NHL were angry and alarmed. The elder Howe had spurned the league in which he had achieved greatness, and so had his sons, who were highly regarded junior prospects. Both had played for the Memorial Cup champion Marlboros and Mark had been tournament MVP. He was eighteen and Marty nineteen, and both were ineligible to play pro until they turned twenty, according to the rules of the day, which were spelled out in an agreement between the NHL and the Canadian Amateur Hockey Association.

Two other WHA clubs also signed underage juniors, which raised the spectre of an all-out assault on the established rules, one the NHL appeared to be powerless to stop. But the league did have one card to play: the agreement with the CAHA was about to expire. The NHL could have let it lapse and joined a bidding war for eighteen- and nineteen-year-olds. That was a sobering prospect for the WHA. It was facing myriad challenges and didn't need another, and so it fell into line and signed an accord with the CAHA.

"From a short-range view," WHA president Gary Davidson said, "we could have kept right on doing what we were doing, but we're in business to stay, so over the long run, it was just good business sense to make a deal."

THE NEW LEAGUE HAD TWELVE TEAMS in place for the 1973–74 season, its second, but the Philadelphia Blazers had moved to Vancouver and the Ottawa

Nationals took up residence in Toronto and became the Toros. Five games in, the New York Golden Blades (formerly the Raiders) were unable to meet their semi-monthly payroll of approximately $40,000 and the league took over. By the end of November, the Blades had been moved to a 5,500-seat arena in Cherry Hill, New Jersey, and renamed the Jersey Knights.

The NHL could hardly afford to sneer at its struggling rival. It had its own troubled franchises, and none were in worse shape than the California Golden Seals. Owner Charles O. Finley lived in Chicago and rarely saw a game. He fired staff with alarming frequency and refused to spend money on the team. He put his losses at $2.2 million over three seasons, and in June 1973 he proposed moving the Seals to Indianapolis. His fellow owners rejected that idea; instead, they decided to buy back the franchise to rid themselves of a troublesome and exasperating partner.

But with Finley, nothing was ever simple. He haggled and nitpicked over the summer and into the fall, and the Seals began the 1973–74 season under a cloud of uncertainty. New Year's came and went. Finley was still the owner and the team a mess. The Seals had the poorest attendance in the league—drawing fewer than three thousand many nights—and were buried in last place in the West Division. By mid-January, they had lost fifteen straight road games and the players were seething.

Most of them detested coach and general manager Fred Glover. He walked into the bar at a New York hotel late one night and found three members of the team—Walt McKechnie, Stan Gilbertson and Rick Kessell—with drinks in hand. They had broken curfew and Glover ordered them out. There was an argument, then a fight between McKechnie and Glover—player and coach were on the floor, wrestling, as hotel employees raced in to pull them apart. "We were embarrassing ourselves," Gilbertson ruefully told an *Oakland Tribune* reporter who got wind of the incident.

The players were delivered from their misery when the league finally reached a deal with Finley. It was announced on January 15, 1974, and closed in mid-February. The other fifteen owners had coughed up nearly $6.6 million, or some $400,000 apiece, and they immediately put the franchise back on the market. "Now that all the necessary paperwork has been completed," Clarence Campbell told reporters, "our first order of business will be to screen the various applicants and to accept as soon as possible an appropriate purchaser."

A full year would elapse before that "appropriate purchaser" appeared. Meantime, the league appointed an interim president to run the franchise. His name was Munson Campbell, a choice that added another curious twist to the Seals saga. Campbell was a close friend of Bruce Norris from their days at Yale. He rose through the ranks of the *New York Times* business development division and later spent six years as senior vice-president and director of the New York advertising firm J.M. Mathes Inc.

In the mid-1960s, Campbell had represented a Japanese manufacturer of athletic footwear, and this client wanted to introduce its white baseball cleats to the American market. Campbell approached Finley, and his Oakland Athletics became the first major-league team to wear white cleats. Campbell also introduced Finley to Norris when the NHL was looking for someone to take over the Seals from the van Gerbig group.

Not long after he acquired the team, Finley wanted to put his players in white skates—an idea that made them cringe. His general manager at the time, Bill Torrey, rightly pointed out that white cleats on green grass worked, but a white boot on white ice would not. So Finley compromised. The skates would be white and trimmed with kelly green and yellow.

The idea caught on elsewhere, and the Leafs, Blues and several other teams began wearing coloured boots. There were two unanticipated problems, though: trainers had to repaint them after every game to hide the scuff marks—a tiresome task that they disliked—and the players complained that all that paint made the boots stiff and heavy.

Coloured skates were the first thing to go when Campbell became president of the Seals. "Those white and green boots . . . made them look as if they were cut off at the ankles," he told a visiting *Toronto Star* reporter. "In Canada, only girls—and Lord knows I have nothing against girls—wear white skate boots. This has to give hockey players an inferiority complex."

Glover was the next to go, which meant the Seals needed a general manager and a coach. Campbell brought back former general manager Garry Young, and defenceman Marshall Johnston retired to take the coaching job. These measures had no discernible effect. The 1973–74 Seals achieved a new low: thirteen wins, fifty-five losses, ten ties and a league-worst thirty-six points.

THE BRUINS FINISHED FIRST OVERALL that season with 113 points, with the Canadiens and Rangers right behind them in second and third. And who could be surprised? After all, these same clubs had occupied the three top spots in the East in six of seven post-expansion seasons. There was also a dreary predictability at the bottom. The Penguins had failed to qualify for the playoffs six times, the Seals five and the Kings four. The Canucks hadn't made it in four attempts, while the Sabres had succeeded once. The Blues and North Stars assembled good, competitive teams, but that was as far as they got.

The league hadn't come close to achieving competitive balance, and the chasm between top and bottom reinforced what many were thinking: the NHL had expanded too quickly. The talent was spread too thin and the product badly watered down, problems that were magnified by the presence of the rival league drawing players from the same shallow pool.

The Flyers were the first of the early expansion teams to rise above the pervasive mediocrity and claim a place among the league's best. They began the 1973–74 season convinced they could win the Stanley Cup, and their confidence never wavered. Not with Bernie Parent in net. He earned five shutouts in the first twelve games and yielded 1.89 goals per game in forty-seven starts, inspiring a popular bumper sticker in Philadelphia: "Only the Lord saves more than Bernie Parent."

Their offensive leaders—Bobby Clarke, Bill Barber, Rick MacLeish and Ross Lonsberry—all enjoyed thirty-goal seasons. By Christmas, the Flyers had overtaken front-running Chicago in the West, and they kept the lead. They became the first expansion franchise to win a divisional title over a pre-1967 club, and one of six teams in the history of the league to win fifty games in a single season.

These were commendable achievements, but they were tarnished by the Flyers' style of play, which comprised equal parts brawn, brutality and beauty. The Flyers set a single-season record for team penalty minutes, and Dave (The Hammer) Schultz established a new individual mark. Bob (The Hound) Kelly went 14–1 in the fight department that year, leading one teammate to describe him as "the most dangerous eleven-goal scorer in the game." The Flyers didn't just fight, they brawled. Every man on the bench going over the boards. Littering the ice with sticks and gloves and their opponents doing the same.

Two donnybrooks erupted in a game against the Seals in early December. One lasted twenty minutes, the other twenty-five, and six players were ejected. Another occurred just before Christmas, this time between the Canucks and Flyers. The referee handed out ninety minutes in penalties and tossed four combatants. The wildest brawl of the year, according to newspaper reports, took place in mid-February against the Canadiens. Over ninety penalty minutes were assessed and three participants were banished for the night.

The Flyers frightened some of their lesser rivals. The odd player was known to contract the "Philly flu" on the day of a game at the Spectrum. After one particularly rough outing, Chicago coach Billy Reay complained, "[Dave] Schultz and [Don] Saleski don't belong in the league." Strangely, the animosity became part of the glue that bound the Flyers together. "We were hated everywhere we went," centre Bill Clement later told the writer Jay Greenberg. "So we began to feel like it was us against the world."

The Flyers toned it down for the playoffs, but retained several essential elements of their game. They checked ferociously, hit hard and often, jabbed, poked and slashed with their sticks and remained an intimidating physical force. That, combined with their undeniable skill and talent, worked. They beat Atlanta in four, the Rangers in seven and the mighty Bruins in six.

They won the Stanley Cup on a Sunday afternoon, May 18, in Philadelphia. The Spectrum was packed, raucous and sweltering. An estimated 1.5 million people watched locally on TV. MacLeish tipped in a shot from the point at 14:48 of the first period. Parent stoned the Bruins and the Flyers held on until time expired. The jubilant champions leapt over the boards and mobbed their goaltender and hundreds of youthful, mostly male fans joined them. Clarence Campbell presented the Cup, but the bedlam on the ice ruled out a victory lap.

So began what some described as the biggest spontaneous celebration in Philadelphia since the end of World War II. Tens of thousands of fans, waving Flyer flags or wearing the colours, converged on the city's downtown core and partied until well past midnight. A hastily arranged civic parade the following day drew a gargantuan crowd estimated at two million. The players rode in open convertibles that could hardly move through the throngs of delirious fans eager to touch hockey's newly crowned kings. The car carrying Clarke and defenceman Ed Van Impe never made it to the reviewing stand at Independence Park in the city's historic district.

Head coach Fred Shero did arrive, and he told the assembled multitudes, "You've got the greatest team in hockey and you're going to win the Cup again next year."

THE NHL HAD A NEW LOOK IN 1974–75. There were now two conferences—the Campbell and the Prince of Wales—and four divisions: the Patrick, Smythe, Norris and Adams, names that needed no explanation to anyone acquainted with the history of the league. The changes were made to accommodate the league's seventeenth and eighteenth teams—the Kansas City Scouts and the Washington Capitals.

Abe Pollin, who had made a substantial fortune in the construction industry, was the sole owner of the Capitals. Pollin and three others had acquired the Baltimore Bullets of the NBA in 1964, and he had subsequently bought out his partners. In the early 1970s, Pollin wanted to move the Bullets to Washington, but he had to build an arena and needed a second core tenant to make it viable.

He had never seen a hockey game and knew nothing about the sport when he applied for an NHL franchise in the spring of 1972, but he did know construction. He began erecting the $18 million Capital Centre in August 1972 and opened the doors on December 2, 1973, some ten months before the Capitals played their home opener.

Edwin Thompson, a youthful real estate developer, led a group of investors who brought the Scouts to Kansas City. The bustling Midwestern community had in the previous decade become home to three major-league franchises: baseball's Kansas City Royals, the Chiefs of the NFL and the Kings of the NBA. Thompson and his partners saw the NHL as a logical addition to the mix, and they, too, had to build an arena, though it wasn't completed on time, forcing the Scouts to play their first eight games on the road.

They opened at home on November 2 against the Black Hawks, but their dressing room wasn't ready and the players never set foot on the ice till they skated out for the pre-game warmup. "I'm nervous," coach Bep Guidolin told a *Kansas City Star* reporter. "I really am. There's new people, new faces and I'm anxious to see how we'll be accepted."

Clarence Campbell spoke briefly at the pre-game ceremony. So did Mayor Charles B. Wheeler Jr. There were 14,758 fans on hand and a good many were watching hockey for the first time. "I really don't understand the game," city manager Robert A. Kipps told a *Star* writer during the warmup, and the same journalist added, "Hockey, like escargot and Turkish coffee, is an acquired taste."

The Scouts fell to the Hawks that night. It was a shaky start and just the beginning of a typical, first-year performance from a wobbly, no-name expansion team of aging castoffs and youthful prospects. The Scouts won fifteen, lost fifty-four and tied eleven. The Capitals were beyond bad. They set records for fewest points (twenty-one), fewest wins (eight), most losses (sixty-seven), most home losses (twenty-eight), most road losses (thirty-nine), fewest road wins (one) and most goals against (446).

They went through three coaches, and after that lone road victory—a late-season win over the Seals—their third bench boss, Milt Schmidt, told reporters, "It was like winning the Stanley Cup."

SOME GOOD MEN TOOK UP the task of coaching and managing the NHL's expansion teams, but no matter how smart or well intentioned, they had steep hills to climb. Many were operating in markets where hockey was an exotic import and fans had to be educated. In Atlanta's first season, for instance, the public address announcer would inform the crowds that a stoppage in play was due to icing, offside, a two-line pass or some other minor infraction of the rules.

Fan bases had to be built from scratch, and the surest way to do that was to build a winning team. However, the new clubs got no help from established rivals, who stacked the deck in each expansion draft to protect their own assets and left the newcomers with the dross and dreck. Furthermore, there was no tried and tested approach to creating a winner.

Several managers opted for a shortcut. They traded future draft picks for established veteran talent that could step into the lineup and produce immediately. Too often, the results were disastrous. The veterans didn't perform as expected, while a lucky opponent later claimed a dazzling junior who lit up the NHL and haunted the expansion franchise for years to come.

The alternative was to build through the draft. New York Islanders general manager Bill Torrey and coach Al Arbour went this route, and they had a head scout named Jimmy Devellano who had an unusual ability to assess talent. In their first three seasons, the Islanders acquired, in the following order: Bill Harris, Lorne Henning, Bob Nystrom, Garry Howatt, Denis Potvin, Dave Lewis and Clark Gillies. These players quickly made the Islanders a contender. The expansion team that earned thirty points in 1972–73 accumulated eighty-eight in 1974–75, made the playoffs, eliminated the Rangers and the Penguins and pushed the pugnacious Flyers to seven games in the semifinal before surrendering.

The Flyers had also drafted smartly. They acquired Bobby Clarke in 1969, and he became the heart and soul of the team. Three years later, they got Bill Barber, one of their best offensive players, and two good defencemen, Jim Watson and Tom Bladon. Dave Schultz and Bob Kelly, the two fearsome punchout specialists, arrived as draftees and so did Don Saleski, a big, physical right winger, and Bill Clement, who provided depth at centre ice. All eight were members of the Flyers' 1974 Stanley Cup team.

The Buffalo Sabres were a third expansion team that had drafted well and reaped the benefits. General manager Punch Imlach took Gilbert Perreault in 1970. He acquired Craig Ramsay, Bill Hajt and Richard Martin, another Quebecer, the following year, Jim Schoenfeld and Peter McNab in 1972, and Danny Gare in the spring of 1974. With these youthful legs in the lineup the Sabres rose to the top.

Perreault, Martin and a third Quebecer, René Robert, who was acquired in a trade, formed the slickest and most productive forward line in the league in 1974–75 and became known as the French Connection. They combined for 131 goals. The Sabres accumulated 113 points and tied the Canadiens and Flyers for first overall.

Buffalo beat Chicago in the quarter-final and Montreal in the semifinal and then advanced to the final against the Flyers. This was a fortuitous development for the league. In the same season that the NHL had inflicted the Scouts and the Capitals on the sporting public, here were two expansion teams going head to head for hockey's most hallowed prize. It was a first, and it seemed to vindicate the whole program of expansion, the single most important development of the postwar era.

But there was a subplot, and it took some of the sheen off a triumphant moment for the league. The 1975 final was a clash of competing styles. The Flyers remained the fire-breathing dragons of pro hockey. They too often relied on havoc and mayhem rather than their abundant skill and admirable work ethic to get the job done. The Sabres beat opponents with speed, flair and finesse, and a Sabre championship would do wonders for the image of the game and the league.

The Flyers left some of their tools in the toolbox for the final. There were only two fights and no bench-clearing brawls. Nobody mugged Perreault or attempted to decapitate his wingers. Instead, the Flyers relied on short shifts, close checking, tight defence and hard hitting. They won in six, and centre Terry Crisp offered a concise explanation of what it all meant.

"When people think of hockey," he told a *Sports Illustrated* writer, "they think of everything being graceful and flowing. The Flying Frenchmen and the French Connection . . . then we come along. They used to call us goons because we weren't fancy, but now they have no excuses—none—because there was no gooning in those playoffs. The point we proved is that a working man's hockey team can win."

It was a good point, but did not change the fact that the Flyers were by then the most hated team in hockey.

CLARENCE CAMPBELL PRESENTED THE STANLEY CUP at the conclusion of the 1975 final, a ritual he had performed in each of his twenty-nine years as president. He had held the job longer than his predecessor Frank Calder and longer than anyone else who had served as head of a major North American sports league. He was seventy, but he had no intention of retiring, despite the heavy workload and incessant demands.

Each year until the early 1960s, he had closed the NHL offices in Montreal for the month of July. He had sent the staff home, save for a token employee who was there to answer the phones and sort the correspondence, and he had played golf or taken a good, long vacation. The leisurely summers had ended with expansion, and by 1975 even a short holiday was impossible.

Campbell and the governors had a heap of trouble looming over them. They were uncertain whether they would start the 1975–76 season with eighteen teams or be forced to go with seventeen or even sixteen. The Penguins were bankrupt. They owed a Pittsburgh financial institution, Equibank, $5 million. They owed the league $1 million in funds advanced to meet payroll, and the Internal Revenue Service was claiming $500,000 in unpaid back taxes.

On June 12, IRS officers raided the team offices and seized the player contracts (the team's only asset of any value), ordered the employees out and padlocked the doors. Equibank sued, and a court placed the Penguins in receivership. General manager Jack Button was appointed receiver and given till August 15 to find a buyer.

Campbell's assistant, Brian O'Neill, drafted a tentative schedule for a seventeen-team league, but by early July a minor miracle of sorts occurred: a three-member buyer group appeared unsolicited. Albert Savill, an Ohio banker and owner of the Columbus Owls of the International Hockey League, had partnered with Wren Blair, a part owner of the Owls and a former general manager of the Minnesota North Stars. They brought in Indianapolis-based banker Nick Frenzel, and the three of them offered $3.8 million for a franchise that had originally sold for $6 million. A U.S. Federal Court judge, who happened to be an ardent Penguins fan, approved their offer and ordered the IRS to return the player contracts.

That solved one ownership problem, but there was a second: the league still hadn't unloaded the Seals, and they had become a dreadful financial burden. Campbell acknowledged in an interview that the club had cost the NHL about $11 million. That was to buy out Charles O. Finley, subsidize operating losses and cover legal fees, and the owners were through pumping in money. "If no buyer is forthcoming," Campbell said, "we may have to disband that franchise or suspend or move it."

But a prospective buyer did emerge: a San Francisco businessman named Mel Swig. He was fifty-nine and a former owner of the WHL Seals, and his family owned the high-end Fairmont Hotel. Swig put together a ten-member investor group. They agreed to assume the league's debt to Finley—$4.5 million—and to pay it down in five years, and they promised to come up with $1.5 million cash as proof of their deep pockets and good intentions. The deal closed and was announced July 27, but as October 1 arrived and the season opener loomed, Swig and partners were short $600,000 on their guarantee. The league had to advance the funds as working capital.

FRANCHISE TROUBLES KEPT CAMPBELL FULLY OCCUPIED that summer, and so he took little or no part in negotiations that led to the league's first collective bargaining agreement with its players, an initiative that arose out of legal battles with the WHA.

The courtroom skirmishes between the leagues had begun in the fall of 1972, before the first WHA game had been played. NHL clubs applied for injunctions in fourteen jurisdictions to prevent their players from jumping. The applications were based on the reserve clause in the standard player's contract, which allowed a team to extend a contract year after year and effectively bind the athlete to the organization in perpetuity.

WHA lawyers argued that the clause allowed the NHL to monopolize players and prevented competitive bidding for talent—a clear contravention of U.S. antitrust laws. The WHA also contended that the NHL extended its monopoly over professional hockey through affiliation agreements with various minor leagues.

Most of the NHL applications were transferred to a U.S. District Court in Philadelphia and argued before Justice A. Leon Higginbotham Jr. He issued his ruling on November 8, 1972. It was a decisive defeat for the NHL. Judge Higginbotham refused to grant the injunctions the NHL had requested. To do so, he reasoned, would kill the WHA. Furthermore, he concluded that there was a "mutual understanding and conspiracy by the NHL and its affiliated minor leagues to maintain a monopolistic position so strong that the NHL precludes effective competition by the entry of another major professional league."

Emboldened by this victory, the WHA filed a $50 million antitrust suit against the NHL. The warring leagues settled out of court in March 1974, but the repercussions were profound. The reserve clause was no longer enforceable. Players would automatically become free agents when their contracts expired. They could sell their services to the highest bidder. For a league that had grown too quickly and had a number of struggling expansion franchises, the financial implications were potentially catastrophic.

"We knew we had to change our way of doing business with respect to player contracts," recalls John Ziegler, who was then Detroit's alternate governor and a member of the legal committee. "But we didn't know what to do."

The challenge was to maintain control over the movement of players once their contracts had expired—without running afoul of U.S. antitrust laws. The league's outside law firm, Washington-based Covington and Burling, proposed a solution. Labour agreements that had been collectively bargained between unions and management often included various constraints that, unilaterally imposed, would have been illegal. Such agreements had been tested and upheld in U.S. courts, and they served as a precedent.

"That was our only hope, and that's why we started trying to get a formal collective bargaining agreement with the players," says Ziegler.

The sides commenced their talks in the fall of 1974, and they built upon a solid foundation of rights, privileges and obligations previously bargained by the owner-player council. That body had met annually since the summer of 1958 and had continued to serve as a forum for negotiation after the formation of the players' association in 1967.

The five-year collective bargaining agreement (CBA) took effect September 15, 1975, and gave the players significant new rights. The widely despised reserve clause was gone, and with it a decades-old system in which the teams exerted tyrannical control over the players year after year until they retired. It was replaced by an option clause that allowed a club to extend a contract for one year. After that, the player could sign with a rival team, although the new employer had to compensate the former with a player or players of equal value—a concept borrowed from the NFL. Alternately, the athlete could negotiate a no-option contract and become an unrestricted free agent at the end of term, although most took the option because it more or less guaranteed them another year of employment.

These measures could hardly be called an Emancipation Proclamation. The owners, for all intents and purposes, still controlled the players and therefore could keep a lid on costs. Nevertheless, the CBA introduced a limited form of free agency and represented a first step toward a more equitable partnership.

The league made other significant concessions that helped level the playing field, as Ziegler points out.

"Under the old contracts," he notes, "there was a clause that said management could give a player two weeks' notice and fire him if they felt his play wasn't up to an acceptable standard. We struck that clause, and immediately every contract was guaranteed. It was a monumental change."

IN ITS ISSUE OF OCTOBER 24, 1975, the *Hockey News* described the deal as "the most significant piece of legislation formulated between the owners and players in the long history of the NHL." This was true, but scarcely anyone noticed. There were more pressing questions to engage the fans and those who covered the league: Would the Islanders continue to improve? Would the Sabres be back? Would the Canadiens smite the fire-breathing Flyers and deny them a third Stanley Cup? Would the warring leagues continue to lose frightful amounts of money?

Winnipeg's Ben Hatskin, chairman of the WHA, admitted that his members had lost $12 million to $15 million over three seasons. A report in the *Globe and Mail* predicted NHL losses of $2.7 million in the upcoming campaign and listed eight money-losers and their projected deficits: Kings, $100,000; Flames, $200,000; North Stars, $250,000; Penguins, $250,000; Scouts, $300,000; Red Wings, $400,000 to $500,000; Capitals, $500,000; Seals, $1 million.

Some teams were cutting their payrolls, while others were resorting to more desperate measures, according to Alan Eagleson. "I know for a fact," he told a journalist, "that certain clubs have tried to give players away for nothing just to free themselves from $100,000 contracts."

Trouble arrived in bunches that season. Bobby Orr, the most brilliant player of his generation and the reigning scoring champion, played a mere ten games. At training camp, he experienced chronic pain in his oft-injured left knee. On September 25, he acknowledged the problem and a Boston surgeon operated— the fourth such procedure in his ten years with the Bruins. On November 8, he was back in uniform, and on November 28, the knee locked up as he drove to the airport for a flight to Chicago. Another surgery was necessary, and Orr was done for the season.

In December, rumours surfaced that the St. Louis Blues would be moved. New Orleans, Seattle, Denver and Miami were all mentioned as possible destinations. Sid Salomon Jr. denied the reports, but admitted that the organization was losing money. The Blues were the most successful of the expansion franchises next to the Flyers. They were drawing close to 17,000 fans per game and the team itself was expected to turn a profit of $350,000. The St. Louis Arena was the problem. Salomon and his son, Sid Salomon III, had acquired the building in 1966, when they were granted the franchise, and had invested some $12 million to turn it into a showpiece. But revenues weren't sufficient to cover operating costs, debt-servicing charges and an exorbitant municipal entertainment tax. The shortfall that season was expected to hit $2 million, and in February the league gave the Salomons permission to relocate if necessary.

The Washington Capitals were as wretched as they had been in their inaugural campaign. The Caps won a game on November 26—American Thanksgiving—and then endured a record losing streak. They were winless through Christmas. Coach Milt Schmidt resigned on December 30, career minor-leaguer Tom McVie replaced him and the Caps rang in the new year with more losses. Montreal beat them three-two on January 14. That was their twenty-second game without a win—tying the existing record established by the 1943–44 Rangers and equalled by the 1950–51 Black Hawks. The Caps then proceeded to run their string to twenty-five.

The new record didn't last long. The Scouts beat the Seals on December 28 and the Capitals on February 7 and did not win in the final twenty-six games of the season. They were drawing fewer than eight thousand a night at home and playing in a 16,500-seat arena. The club was on a course to lose $1 million. The ownership group had twice put up funds to cover operating costs. In late February, Edwin Thompson attended a governors meeting in New York and pleaded for a rescue package to meet the payroll and cover operating expenses. He didn't get it.

"We won't commit a nickel to them," Clarence Campbell declared afterward. "We don't want to go through the same financial headache we did with Pittsburgh. If the Scouts fold, we have an emergency plan ready to help us finish the schedule."

Two weeks later, the board reversed itself. The governors approved a $300,000 loan, but attached conditions: the owners of the Scouts had to contribute $100,000 and they were to look for new partners, sell the franchise to local buyers or relocate. The season ended April 4. The league funds were exhausted a few days later and Thompson and his partners laid off the entire staff, including general manager Sid Abel and his assistant, Baz Bastien.

The Scouts had earned a measly 36 points, 4 better than the last-place Capitals. Five teams broke 100: the Islanders with 101, the Sabres with 105, the Bruins with 113, the Flyers with 118 and the Canadiens—a dynasty in the making—with 127. The spread between top and bottom was a monstrous and record-setting 95 points.

But there was one shining and transformative event in this otherwise troubled season. The Canadiens and Flyers survived the preliminary playoff rounds and advanced to the Stanley Cup final, which, that spring, became a showdown to determine which way hockey would go: with the speed and finesse of the Canadiens or the brawn and brutality of the Flyers, who had hit a new low in their seven-game quarter-final against the Leafs.

Toronto police laid nine charges against Joe Watson, Don Saleski and Mel Bridgman after game three, and the alleged offences included common assault, assaulting a police officer and possession of an offensive weapon, namely a hockey stick. In game six, a female usher was struck in the left eye by a glove hurled into the stands, and police later charged Bob Kelly with assault causing bodily harm.

Mayhem and intimidation would not work against Montreal's high-powered offence, and the games of the final were close, fast, hard-fought and clean. The Montreal *Gazette*'s Tim Burke described the opener—a four-three Canadiens win—as "one of the great hockey games I've witnessed in this decade. . . . What really piqued my interest was the marvellous, freewheeling style of both teams."

The Canadiens won the second by a two-one margin, and the teams headed south to Philadelphia and the Spectrum. Montreal hadn't won there in two and a half years, but they did on this occasion, and again by a one-goal margin. By then, the Canadiens were on a mission to send a message. "We were up three-nothing in the series and you'd have thought everybody would just be doing cartwheels," recalls left winger Murray Wilson. "But the dressing room was stone silent because we wanted to take it from them in their building in four straight. It was never broadcast outside the dressing room. It was closed door—'This is what we want to do.' . . . There was no way they were going to win the fourth game. . . . We thought, 'We can change hockey.'"

The Canadiens did accomplish their objective, and they took the game in a direction that was infinitely more appealing and sustainable. But there were no short-term fixes for the sport's many other afflictions, and that became apparent in the off-season.

Two sickly franchises—Kansas City and the Seals—had to relocate, and the league's deeply divided board had to elect a new chairman. James D. Norris had held the post at the time of his death in February 1966. It had then passed to his stepbrother Bruce for a two-year term (1966–68) and then on to Bill Wirtz and then Bill Jennings. In 1972, the rotation had begun again so that in June 1976 it was to have been Jennings's turn, but he had run afoul of the board over a conflict of interest and had to step aside. That caused some memorable political jousting.

The governors were essentially split into two camps, one led by Wirtz and Norris, the other by Philadelphia's Ed Snider. Snider coveted the chairman's job, while Wirtz and Norris wanted a candidate of their choosing. They disliked Snider for a number of reasons. He was the newcomer, whereas their families had been involved for nearly half a century. His Flyers had won back-to-back Stanley Cups, while Norris's once-mighty Red Wings had slid to the bottom of the league and Wirtz's Black Hawks were fading. Perhaps most important, Snider remained a leading advocate of making peace with the WHA—an idea that Norris and Wirtz abhorred.

The governors would vote on a chairman at the annual meeting in June 1976, but the infighting began much earlier. According to Gil Stein, then the Flyers' general counsel, Wirtz struck first. He called a board meeting for November 18, 1975, at the Harbour Castle Hotel in Toronto. The agenda that circulated in advance suggested that Wirtz and the committee chairs would update their partners on several routine business matters, and at least half the clubs sent alternates—and Vancouver was not represented at all. But the proceedings began with an announcement that caught many, Stein says, completely by surprise: Clarence Campbell was resigning.

"Lately," Campbell told his audience, "I have found that the demands of the office of president have become too much for me to handle. I have tried to cope with the ever-increasing workload, but my efforts have been in vain. I have given a great deal of thought to what I am about to tell you. After due consideration, I have concluded the course I must follow is to tender my resignation, which—with much regret—I do at this time."

Campbell finished quickly, and Wirtz struck again. He proposed Campbell for chairman in recognition of his years of service. This would require an amendment to the constitution, since the position was reserved for governors. Stein saw Wirtz's moves as a brazen attempt to control the board, and so did Montreal's alternate governor Sam Pollock, who was seated next to him. "My name is Tucker, not Sucker," Pollock whispered to Stein in order to convey his skepticism.

The full board took up the questions of succession during the all-star break in late January, and again at meetings in New York at the end of February, but resolved nothing. They could not agree on a suitable candidate to replace Campbell, and so they appointed a five-member search committee. They rejected the Wirtz amendment that would have made Campbell chairman, and the fight for the position began in earnest.

Snider trolled for the support he needed, and Wirtz and Norris beat the bushes for someone to stop him, but neither side had prevailed by early June, when the governors, their alternates, the general managers and entourages of lesser team officials converged on Montreal and the Queen Elizabeth Hotel for the annual meeting. The campaigning culminated in a few hours of frantic push and shove in the corridors and suites of the Queen E. on the eve of the vote. Wirtz and Norris recruited Buffalo's Seymour Knox as their candidate, and then matters turned murky.

Snider stunned his supporters by revealing that he would withdraw and back Knox in order to restore harmony. In return, he wanted to chair the finance committee. A meeting was arranged, and Knox agreed. Then he made the mistake of informing Wirtz and Norris. They were livid and, concluding that Knox was unreliable, launched a last-minute search for another candidate. They gathered in Norris's suite with Jennings and North Stars governor Bob McNulty, and in the course of their deliberations, McNulty said, "Why don't we nominate John Ziegler?"

Ziegler was a Detroit lawyer and the alternate governor of the Red Wings. He was a man of moderate stature with a handsome, boyish face, a sunny personality and a sharp mind. He had begun doing legal work for the Wings in 1958, shortly after graduating from the University of Michigan law school, and his relationship with the club and the Norris group of companies had grown and deepened over the years. Ziegler had begun attending board meetings with Norris in June 1966, and that happened to be an opportune time for a bright, ambitious young lawyer.

As the NHL grew with successive rounds of expansion and as it later contended with the WHA, the owners and governors needed advice at every turn to deal with the myriad and complex legal questions that arose, and Ziegler was always there with an answer. He had served on the legal committee. He had acquired a reputation for honesty and integrity and for providing sound advice. And thanks to his good humour and easygoing manner, he had made many friends—Norris, Wirtz, Jennings and McNulty among them—and they turned to him in their moment of need.

There was one hitch. He was only an alternate and therefore ineligible. But they devised a solution, and with Campbell's help, they sprang it on their unsuspecting adversaries the following morning. Campbell called the proceedings to order and asked for nominations for chairman. Three names were advanced: Knox, Ziegler and Snider, who had re-entered the running after learning of Knox's miscues and the machinations of his opponents. Knox immediately realized that both camps had abandoned him and he withdrew.

At that point, Stein intervened. "Point of order, Mr. Chairman," he said to Campbell. "I believe Mr. Ziegler is not eligible for this election since the constitution provides [that] only a governor may be elected chairman."

"Well, let us see, Mr. Stein," Campbell replied. "We certainly are obliged to follow the letter of the constitution."

He consulted the appropriate section, which confirmed Stein's point, and then pulled from his pocket a note on yellow legal paper and read it aloud: "I hereby appoint John A. Ziegler Jr. Governor of Detroit Hockey Club, effective this eighth day of June, 1976. Signed Bruce A. Norris."

Stein raised a second point of order, but Snider reined him in and he withdrew it. Campbell called for a vote, and Ziegler won by a margin of nine to eight.

The governors voted to keep Campbell as their president for another year, his thirty-first, to allow time to find a suitable successor, and they spent many hours deliberating over the future of the league's two deathly-ill franchises—the Scouts and the Seals—but concluded the meetings with those problems unresolved.

By the end of the summer, however, the landscape of the league had changed yet again: Kansas City and Oakland had been erased from the map. Hotelier Mel Swig uprooted the Seals, moved them to Cleveland and renamed them the Barons. Meantime, Edwin Thompson and his partners had sold the Scouts to Denver oilman John Vickers, who moved the club to the Mile High City and christened it the Colorado Rockies.

CLARENCE CAMPBELL'S FINAL YEAR as president was distinguished by conflict, turmoil and falling attendance. The season had barely begun when a crisis arose. On October 8, the Bruins filed a lawsuit against the Black Hawks in a U.S. District Court. Four days later, the Hawks filed a countersuit. The issue was free-agent compensation, and the player at the centre of the dispute was Bobby Orr.

Orr's contract had expired June 1. He and the Bruins failed to agree on a new deal and the Black Hawks signed him for five years and some $3 million. The collective bargaining agreement stipulated that a team that lost a player through free agency was entitled to compensation. Chicago owner Arthur Wirtz told an interviewer he had spoken to his Boston counterpart, Jeremy Jacobs, while the Hawks were negotiating with Orr, and Jacobs had agreed to waive compensation.

Not so, the Bruins replied, and they applied for an injunction to prevent Orr from playing for the Hawks until the matter was settled. The Hawks asked the court "to enter a judgment to restrain Boston from doing anything that would deprive the Black Hawks of the services of Bobby Orr." Orr's new teammates were outraged and threatened to strike if the court sided with the Bruins, and an exasperated Campbell said, "We need another lawsuit like a hole in the head."

Campbell had his hands full simply managing day-to-day operations. The league's head office staff was so small that every problem landed on his desk, and at age seventy-one he was still working fifteen to sixteen hours a day—a problem that had long concerned some governors. "I've said for ten years that the league lacks structure," Ed Snider told a reporter. "Clarence Campbell should have retired ten years ago. He's a fine man, but he can't do it alone. . . . The league needs more people—counsel, administrators, researchers. We play many more games than the NFL, we have minor leagues to worry about, a war with another league, yet we have about two per cent of the NFL's staff. This league is in the Dark Ages. It had better wake up soon."

Campbell received some unexpected help dealing with the Bruin–Black Hawk dispute. The league's new chairman, John Ziegler, forced a peace upon the warring parties, but it took considerable effort. "I was on the phone to Paul Mooney, who was president of the Bruins, and Bill Wirtz every day for hours trying to get this resolved," Ziegler recalled in an interview. "What I thought was going to be a part-time position turned out to be taking a huge amount of time. I was angry with both of them because they should have worked this out in-house, not in the courts."

Ziegler used the constitution to break the deadlock. He found a clause that directed member clubs to resolve disputes among themselves. If that failed, they could present their arguments before the board and let their peers decide. "I sent out a notice that I was calling a meeting, and Wirtz and Mooney reacted exactly as I thought they would," says Ziegler.

They agreed at a governors meeting on November 5 to drop their lawsuits and resume negotiations. The board gave them until June 1, 1977, to reach an agreement. Otherwise, an arbitrator would be appointed.

The Bruins paid a heavy price at the box office for letting Orr walk. They sold only 8,500 season tickets in 1976–77, down from 13,000. They drew 9,211 to their home opener, which broke a string of 117 straight sellouts. If Bruin management was miserable that fall, they had plenty of company. Attendance was down in a number of NHL cities, including St. Louis, Atlanta, Pittsburgh, Detroit, Chicago and Minnesota.

The league was no overnight hit in Denver or Cleveland, either. The

Rockies had sold a mere 1,600 season tickets, the Barons 2,000, and the *Hockey News* reported in late October that high school football games in the Cleveland area were attracting bigger crowds than the Barons. By early December, declining attendance was being openly discussed.

"I'm concerned about our sport and where it's going," Flyers captain and NHLPA president Bobby Clarke told an interviewer. "The crowds are down, and that's the first things you notice in the papers every morning. Boston is down, Chicago is down, and how much longer can teams like Cleveland and Colorado draw 4,000 and 5,000 before they fold?"

New York Islanders general manager Bill Torrey echoed that: "The first thing a lot of GMs and owners look for when they check the game sheets is that little line of type at the bottom that tells you the attendance."

The concerns were well placed. Attendance that season—regular-season and playoffs—totalled 9.2 million, down from a record 10.3 million in 1974–75. Inevitably, some teams listed and foundered, and the Flames sent out the first SOS. They were one of the league's best expansion clubs, but were drawing under ten thousand a night and needed thirteen thousand to break even. The ownership group claimed to have lost $5 million in five seasons, and they had paid only half the $6 million franchise fee.

In early December 1976, the team was running out of money and Atlanta mayor Maynard Jackson and Georgia governor George Busbee led a rescue effort. They convened a meeting at the governor's mansion with representatives of forty of the city's largest companies and asked them to buy blocks of tickets worth $25,000. "As I understand it," Governor Busbee said afterward, "there is a payroll due the fifteenth of this month and unless we take this action, that payroll can't be met."

The players stepped up and bought a $25,000 package and turned the tickets over to the governor, who distributed them to state employees as Christmas gifts. By the end of December, the campaign had generated $750,000 and the franchise was saved for the season.

Trouble arose next in St. Louis. The Blues had led the league in attendance the previous five seasons and were seen as a model franchise. But three things pushed the club to the brink. The payroll had risen fourfold, largely due to WHA-induced inflation. The city imposed an onerous entertainment tax of some $4,500 per event. And there was a $5.4 million mortgage on the St. Louis Arena, which the team had to carry.

Costs had to be cut, and in mid-February general manager Emile Francis laid off ten employees. Senior vice-president Lynn Patrick, the first person hired by the Blues, was let go along with the team's publicity director, the assistant arena manager, the ticket sales director and the assistant trainer. Sid Salomon Jr., the sixty-six-year-old chairman who had given his players generous contracts and rewarded them with gold watches for scoring a hat trick, wasn't there to deliver the bad news. He was in a Florida hospital, recuperating from a major heart attack caused—some said—by stress related to the Blues' problems.

Then there was the crisis in Cleveland. It broke during the midseason all-star break. The game was held in Vancouver, and the governors gathered as usual to discuss league business. Barons owner Mel Swig informed the board that his team was headed for a multimillion-dollar loss. He needed a bailout or the Barons weren't going to finish the season. The board turned him down.

The club couldn't meet its February 1 payroll, and there was no money to pay the players on February 15, either. Defenceman Glenn Patrick quit and signed with the WHA's Edmonton Oilers. Five members of Cleveland's Central Hockey League farm team in Salt Lake City turned in their sweaters and declared themselves free agents. In late February, the entire Barons roster gave Swig an ultimatum: pay up or the team was dead. And they backed that up by threatening to sit out two weekend games.

The league was facing a public-relations disaster. Cancelling the team's remaining road games would cost other clubs tens of thousands of dollars in lost revenue. Ziegler and Alan Eagleson flew to Cleveland, met the players in their dressing room on the day of a game and persuaded them to play. Then they went to work on the governors. "It took us from nine in the morning till close to midnight to finally get the vote to support the team," Ziegler recalls.

Swig put up $350,000. The league matched it, and the players' association borrowed $600,000 from a Toronto bank and loaned it to Swig on the condition that it be used strictly to cover salaries. The *Hockey News*, in its issue of March 13, 1977, described the deal as "one of the most bizarre rescue missions seen in the realm of professional sport."

A perfectly apt description, perhaps, but the eighteen teams that started the season finished it. Campbell was there at the very end to present the Stanley Cup to the captain of the Montreal Canadiens. In early June, he attended the annual general meeting for the last time, and on June 22 the board named a successor and the long reign of Clarence Campbell was over.

No one could question or doubt his intelligence, his integrity, his dedication or his courage. But he had, without doubt, stayed too long, and even then Bill Wirtz and a number of other influential governors had had to convince him to retire. He remained bitterly opposed to peace with the WHA and regarded the rival operators as pirates who had stolen talent from the NHL. He had failed to build a head-office organization that was capable of handling the complexities of the day, and he had left some startling surprises for his successor.

PART III

AN AMERICAN AT THE HELM

(1977–1992)

10

"THIS LEAGUE IS INSOLVENT"
(1978–1979)

CLARENCE CAMPBELL REMAINED PRESIDENT for eighteen months after announcing he would retire, and curious minds naturally wondered: Who would succeed him? Press reports invariably cited several candidates: Emile Francis, general manager of the Blues and a former player, coach and manager of the Rangers; Robert Sedgewick, vice-president of the Maple Leafs; Ed Houston, a lawyer who served as arbitrator of disputes between players and teams; and James D. Cullen, a St. Louis lawyer and the Blues' general counsel. One name never surfaced in these periodic outbursts of speculation—that of John A. Ziegler Jr.

Ziegler was formally appointed to a five-year term at the board meeting of June 22, 1977—a decision that puzzled some media observers and more than a few fans. They simply had no idea why he had been chosen. "John Ziegler assumes the seat of power atop the National Hockey League as a mystery man," a *Montreal Star* reporter wrote. "Few people beyond the league's owners and governors, or the closely knit legal-financial community of Detroit can say, 'I know Ziegler.'"

The new president did little to enlighten the press or the sporting public. He did not sit for any in-depth interviews, nor did he say anything revealing in a brief encounter with the media immediately after he was appointed. But those who knew him spoke highly of his abilities. "He has a marvellous way of handling a meeting, telling people when to speak and when not to, letting people have their say without interrupting them," a league official told the *New*

York Times. "It's a real talent. I don't know where he picked it up, but it's great."

The *Times* report went on to say: "Ziegler projects a conservative style, and the solemnity of his quiet, well-cut suits and Gucci loafers is buoyed by a boyish face of rather straight and small features, including a dimpled chin. . . . One thing that needs little clarification is that the often-clannish owners like Ziegler. His opinions dovetail neatly with those of his employers."

Ziegler was the NHL's fourth president and the first American named to the post. He was forty-three and a father of four, though his marriage had dissolved. He had been raised in a middle-class family in St. Clair Shores, then a small town of five thousand just beyond the suburban fringes of Detroit, and he was a good all-round athlete, a high school quarterback, a shortstop who tried out for the University of Michigan baseball team and an intramural-calibre hockey player who competed in adult leagues twice a week till age thirty-six.

He graduated from law school in 1957 and was close enough to the top of his class to go straight from college to Dickinson Wright, one of Michigan's oldest and most prestigious law firms and, as it happened, the firm that handled the Red Wings' business. He had only been there a year when a senior partner in the litigation department asked him to assist with the Red Wings account, and so began his association with professional hockey.

By the time he became president of the NHL, he was the principal in his own firm, Ziegler, Dykhouse & Wise. He left one of his partners in charge, left his home in Detroit and took a suite at the Ritz-Carlton Hotel in downtown Montreal, a short walk from the league offices in the Sun Life Building overlooking Dorchester Square and opposite the Windsor Hotel. But he soon had reason to wonder whether these were wise moves.

The NHL was in bad shape. Attendance was down and would continue to slide for another season before recovering. Ten of the league's eighteen teams had lost money in 1976–77, and their combined losses totalled $18 million. The war with the WHA continued, and the board was badly divided over how to handle the conflict. One faction, led by Ed Snider and his supporters, wanted to negotiate an end and absorb some of the rival league's member clubs, while Bill Wirtz and his dwindling circle of holdouts said, "Let 'em die on the vine."

Guaranteed contracts, introduced to protect the league from a WHA antitrust suit, had become a big problem. "They came back to haunt us financially," recalls Ziegler. "Players knew their contracts were guaranteed. It was clear to general managers and coaches that in numerous instances the players weren't giving. They had to send some guys home and still they had to pay them. That created a big chunk of liability."

The owners wanted the problem solved, and Ziegler solved it. His term as president began formally on August 28, and one of his first moves was to call Alan Eagleson and ask for a meeting. He had known Eagleson—as an acquaintance rather than a friend—for almost ten years. They had negotiated contracts together, Ziegler acting for the Wings and Eagleson representing Red Wing players.

They met on September 8 in Toronto and sat for almost ten hours, exchanging proposals and counter-proposals, presenting arguments and counter-arguments, before settling on a package of changes to the collective bargaining agreement that had to be approved by their masters—the owners in Ziegler's case and the players in Eagleson's. The most significant was the end of the guaranteed contract. Henceforth, clubs could buy out a player at one-third his salary, but he became a free agent without compensation. In exchange for this concession and others, the league agreed to establish a dental plan to cover all players, coaches and general managers, and to pay off the $600,000 the NHLPA had borrowed to cover the Cleveland Barons' player salaries.

Having resolved one issue, Ziegler soon discovered another of eye-popping proportions. He was in the habit during his first few months of staying late and reviewing files to familiarize himself with all aspects of league business. But try as he might, Ziegler couldn't get hold of a monthly financial statement. One evening, he noticed a light in the office of Jim Ford, the chief financial officer, who had started as an outside auditor during Merv Dutton's tenure as president in the mid-1940s.

"It was about eight o'clock and I asked him if he had a moment and could he come to my office," recalls Ziegler. "And I said, 'Jim, I've looked all over and I've asked around and nobody can find the monthly financials.'

"And he laughed and said: 'I can give you the reason. We don't have them.'

"I said: 'You don't have them? We just passed an interim budget. How do you know how we're doing?'

"He said: 'Don't worry. We're always close.'

"That phrase—'we're always close'—has stuck with me ever since.

"Anyway, I said: 'Finance is not my strong suit, but I've been on two or three boards and I've come to be able to read financial statements. Let me bring in copies of those and you pick the one you like, and could you please set up the monthly financial statement.'

"He said, 'Sure, I can do that.'

"Two or three weeks went by, and again it's about eight o'clock at night and I see his light on. I ask him to come in and I ask him, 'Jim, how are you coming with those monthly financial statements?'

"He says, 'Oh, I just haven't had time.'

"I said: 'You haven't had time? Can you tell me what's taking up all your time?'

"And he said, 'Well, you know this league is insolvent?'

"And I said, 'What?'

"And he said, 'Don't you know this league is insolvent?'

"I said: 'Jim, I don't know this league is insolvent. The owners don't know this league is insolvent. And fortunately, the world doesn't know this league is insolvent.'

"And I said, 'How about at eight-thirty in the morning, you take me through the nature of this insolvency?'

"He said, 'Fine.'

"So I went back to the Ritz and I got my spot at the bar and ordered my martini, and my first thought as I'm taking a sip was, 'I wonder if my law firm has taken my name off the door.'"

THE FOLLOWING MORNING, they went through the accounts line by line and, sure enough, Jim Ford was right. The debts exceeded the assets and there were large and growing liabilities. The league was losing money on its U.S. TV contracts. Its licensing and merchandising agreements weren't generating sufficient revenues. And several financially shaky expansion teams weren't paying their annual dues or the promissory notes issued to the other clubs in lieu of franchise fees. That day, John Ziegler rearranged his priorities. Cleaning up the financial mess went to the top of the list. It took eighteen months, but he solved the problems one by one—and without alerting the owners to the true state of affairs. "I didn't tell them we were insolvent," he says, "because you tell one person and it's all over the world."

Ziegler tackled licensing first. NHL Properties, a New York–based subsidiary, was handling the business in-house. He went outside and negotiated a lucrative package with Licensing Corporation of America. "They paid a very large amount of money to get the licences and a guaranteed minimum as opposed to a percentage of sales, and they did all the work," he says. "I eliminated the licensing department except for one person. We cut our overhead substantially and we got a big chunk of money. We took a liability and made it into a major asset."

TV was a bigger challenge. The accounts were a shambles, and he spent several months untangling them. The league did not have a U.S. network deal. The teams held the rights to their local markets and the league owned the rest of the country, but had to sell packages of games to stations that would take them, sell most of the advertising and cover the costs of production. Ziegler hired veteran broadcast executive Eddie Einhorn. He founded the TVS Network in 1965, was a pioneer in sports programming, and lifted college basketball to national prominence with his 1968 telecast of the so-called "game of the century" between Houston and UCLA. Einhorn brought a more professional approach, improved the league's exposure and turned big losses into small profits.

While working out those problems, Ziegler was hitting the delinquent clubs with notices to pay up or else. He had the option of calling a board meeting and allowing them to explain themselves to their fellow owners. If worse came to worst, he reminded them, the league could take back the franchises. Several teams were under duress—the Cleveland Barons, Colorado Rockies, Atlanta Flames, Washington Capitals, Minnesota North Stars and New York Islanders, to name a few. Not all were in arrears, but the Islanders were, and this was an unpleasant surprise.

The Islanders were among the most successful of the league's twelve expansion franchises. They had built a powerful, young team by being patient, scouting the amateur ranks thoroughly and drafting wisely. In the space of five years, they had become one of the league's elite clubs, along with the Canadiens, Bruins, Flyers and Sabres.

In Ziegler's first season as president, 1977–78, they had another exhilarating newcomer in their lineup, the right winger Mike Bossy, who established a rookie scoring record with fifty-three goals. They won their division, finished third overall and went into the playoffs a Stanley Cup contender, though they absorbed a painful and unexpected seven-game upset at the hands of an inferior, but aroused Maple Leaf squad.

The Islanders were also a box-office success. They had averaged eight thousand season-ticket sales in each of their first three years. A surprising playoff run in the spring of 1975 enhanced their standing with local fans. They upset the Rangers, eliminated the Penguins after being down three games to none, and then lost to the Flyers in the semifinal. Every Islander home game after that was sold out.

Yet the Islanders were not only in arrears, they were one of the worst offenders, and Ziegler began pestering managing partner Roy Boe. "I kept serving notice on Boe because he hadn't been paying his dues to the league," he says. "He wasn't paying his expansion obligations. He wasn't paying his indemnification obligations to the Rangers. I started hitting him with notices of intent to take away the franchise, just to put pressure on him to do something."

Boe didn't pay up, and Ziegler didn't let up. He investigated further and discovered a looming financial disaster that might destroy one of the league's most exciting teams and damage the image of the NHL: the Islanders were $9.4 million in debt and bankrupt. Boe was on the verge of personal bankruptcy. He was being sued by a dozen creditors, including one of the club's limited partners. And he might face criminal charges if the wrong people learned of some of his financial shenanigans.

Boe was managing partner of both the Islanders and the NBA's New York Nets, and the Nets were the cause of most of his troubles. He had acquired the franchise in May 1969 and in the early 1970s moved from small, second-rate arenas to Long Island's brand new Nassau Coliseum. The NHL approached Boe when it was contemplating a second team in the New York area—largely to impede the WHA—and he put together a group of thirty limited partners to acquire the franchise.

The entry fee was $6 million. They covered it with promissory notes issued to the fourteen existing clubs, which were supposed to be paid off in annual instalments over twenty years. They also agreed to pay the Rangers $4 million in exchange for conceding their territorial rights.

The Islanders had paid a high price to get in; nevertheless, they broke even or made a small profit from the start, according to Bill Torrey, the general manager at the time. The Nets lost money year after year, and Boe began using Islander funds to prop up the basketball team. These loans, as he called them, eventually totalled $3.2 million. Meantime, interest was accumulating on the Islanders' unpaid promissory notes and Ranger indemnification, and the club's debts were growing.

When he became really desperate, Boe turned to the banks for help, and mismanagement began to resemble criminal misconduct. He went to one bank and borrowed money for the Nets, pledging hockey assets as collateral. He went to a second bank for a loan to keep the Islanders afloat and put up basketball assets as collateral. Had anyone blown the whistle, Boe might have been charged with fraud. But he was personable and popular and everyone agreed to sort things out internally.

"He was very likeable," recalls Ziegler. "He could talk you out of your watch and you wouldn't know it was gone. In fact, you'd probably be happy to know he had it. I don't think he thought he was doing anything wrong. He was just always in over his head."

The Islanders' financial debacle burst into public view during the league's annual general meeting in June 1978. "We were probably ten minutes away from going into bankruptcy," says Torrey. "The Rangers were applying a lot of pressure on us. They could see the team we were developing and thought if they could push us into bankruptcy, they could get their hands on some of our players."

Islander troubles were at the top of the agenda at the annual meeting. The board authorized Ziegler to review and, if necessary, veto any player transactions in case Boe tried to sell Denis Potvin, Bryan Trottier, Mike Bossy or any other valuable assets in order to alleviate his problems. The board gave the Islanders one month—until July 18—to come up with a financial restructuring plan that would bring the franchise up to date on its payments and ensure that it would continue as a viable business.

Two of the limited partners—John O. Pickett, a Long Island businessman, and Nelson Doubleday, head of a prestigious old New York publishing house—went to court and obtained an order from Justice Douglas F. Young that removed Boe as managing partner. Pickett took over and worked hand in hand with Torrey, whose tenacity and dedication, as much as anything, saved the franchise. They severed the Islanders from the Nets. They paid off a few of the creditors and provided working capital so the team could meet operating expenses. Some of the problems were too large and complex to be resolved in the space of a month. Nevertheless, Pickett and Torrey presented a credible restructuring plan. The board accepted it, Ranger governor Bill Jennings recommended it to the directors of the Madison Square Garden Corporation, and the league laid to rest one of its challenges.

ROY BOE AND THE ISLANDERS were merely the start of the league's franchise woes that off-season. The board had a restless, discontented owner in Denver. Jack Vickers had made his money in the oil and gas and mining industries. He had purchased the Kansas City Scouts in the summer of 1976, moved them, renamed them the Colorado Rockies and, in two seasons, lost $6 million. He showed up at the annual meeting in June 1978 and told the board he was either selling or relocating, possibly to Houston.

"Gentlemen," he said in a drawl that reflected his Colorado roots, "I learned a long time ago if you drill a dry hole, get out of the area. For the last two years, I've drilled nothing but dry holes. I don't know why I'm still here."

His fellow owners advised patience, to which he replied: "Gentlemen, you say there's light at the end of the tunnel. That may be, but it's a freight train coming at us."

The governors were convinced Denver was a viable market and vetoed a move. So Vickers found a buyer—Arthur Imperatore, a New Jersey businessman who had made his money in trucking. Imperatore had no keen desire to own a hockey club two time zones and hundreds of miles from his home base. He wanted to move it to East Rutherford, New Jersey, where a new arena—the Meadowlands—was under construction. The board approved Imperatore, but told him the team stayed put, and that problem was solved for the moment.

The board was compelled that summer to accept the demise of its most troubled franchise. The Cleveland Barons had begun life as the California Seals.

They had also been known as the Oakland Seals and the California Golden Seals. Owners, coaches, managers and dozens of players had come and gone. In eleven turbulent seasons that produced two playoff appearances, nobody had made money or put a winner on the ice.

The league had sunk $11 million into the franchise and run it for a season before selling to Mel Swig. He had given it a year in Oakland, and then moved the Seals to Cleveland, calling them the Barons—the nickname of a minor-league team based in the city from 1937 till 1972. That did nothing to inspire local fans, and the location of the Richfield Coliseum was actually a deterrent. It was some forty kilometres west of downtown Cleveland, halfway to Akron.

The Barons flopped as badly as the Seals, and Swig sold them at the end of 1976–77 to the Gund brothers—George III, then forty-two, and Gordon, thirty-eight. They were destined to play a prominent role in the affairs of the league for the next two decades. The Gunds were Cleveland-born and grew up with four siblings in a very wealthy family. Their father, George II, was worth an estimated $600 million at the time of his death in November 1966, and he bequeathed some of that vast fortune to the charitable foundation that bore his name, leaving the balance to his offspring. The brothers thus began their adult lives as wealthy men.

George, whose principal residence was in San Francisco, had little inherent interest in business, but was an avid art collector, a philanthropist and an importer and distributor of Eastern European films. Gordon, who lived in Princeton, New Jersey, was remarkably successful in business despite a significant disability: he began losing his sight at age twenty-five, when he was diagnosed with retinitis pigmentosa, a gradually narrowing of the retina that begins with the loss of peripheral vision. By age thirty, he was blind. However, his sense of hearing was extraordinary. He could listen to recorded versions of books and financial statements with the tape on fast-forward and understand perfectly what was gibberish to others.

The brothers had played hockey as boys in Cleveland, and for George, the sport became a lifelong passion. As an undergraduate at Case Western Reserve University in Cleveland, he organized the school's first hockey team. George invested in the Seals while they were located in Oakland and Swig was the owner, and he and Gordon purchased the team outright when the losses became too much for Swig.

The Gunds fared no better than anyone else who had owned the franchise. In 1977–78, their Barons lost twice as many games as they won. They finished fourteenth overall and missed the playoffs. The brothers lost $3.5 million, according to press reports, and saw no prospect of a turnaround. They hired a research firm to conduct a midseason market survey, and the results showed that there was very little interest locally in the Barons or the NHL.

The Gunds came up with a novel solution: merge the Barons with another of the NHL's money-losing underperformers. It had never been done in the league's six generally turbulent decades, but that didn't matter. Gordon Gund called John Ziegler one day in the spring of 1978 and suggested a union of the Barons and Capitals, since the Caps had never assembled a winning or even competitive team.

Ziegler thought it highly unlikely that the board would approve, but suggested the Minnesota North Stars might be a better candidate. The Stars had been a roaring success in the early years of expansion. They had winning teams. They made the playoffs year after year and their building was full night after night, and by March 1971 they had welcomed their two millionth fan.

Then two things went wrong: the team went downhill and management began rebuilding, and this happened just as the WHA came along, and a big, new civic arena was being erected in downtown St. Paul for the Minnesota Fighting Saints. Two pro teams playing in two rinks were chasing a limited pool of fans in one mid-sized market. Inevitably, both lost.

The Saints folded in February 1976 after failing to meet their payroll for two months. The Cleveland Crusaders were moved to Minnesota the following season and re-named the Fighting Saints, but the Saints were finished for good in January 1977. The Stars, meantime, produced a succession of weak teams. Season-ticket sales plummeted from twelve thousand to five thousand. The team lost an estimated $10 million over five years, and by the end of 1977–78 the owners wanted out.

"We were losing so much money, we had to make cash calls on the partners," recalls Walter Bush, the Stars' president at the time. "It got so bad that one of our guys said, 'Why don't we just get rid of the team, buy a jet and we'll get four tickets for every building in the NHL? Whoever wants to go watch a game can go. It would be cheaper than what we we're doing.' We just got tired of kicking a can down the road."

The Gund proposal was a godsend for the Stars' owners. By chance, Bush and George Gund both attended an international tournament in Prague that spring, and they worked out a tentative merger agreement. "We signed a deal on a napkin in the beer hall down in the basement of the Imperial Hotel," Bush recalls.

The Gunds brought a refined version of that rough draft to the annual meeting in June 1978, and their arrival left lasting impressions—Gordon finding his way into the room with the aid of a white cane and, with his free hand, pushing wheelchair-bound brother George, who was recuperating from a back problem.

Their proposal was equally startling. Nothing in the league bylaws provided for a merger of teams, and more than one participant inevitably thought, "Here we are, being led into uncharted waters by a blind man and his crippled brother." But they listened, deliberated, debated and, at one point, a wisecracking general manager even opined: "If you mix one bag of shit with another bag of shit, all you've got is a bigger bag of shit. But at least we'd solve a problem."

Whether that line of reasoning carried the day is not clear, but the measure passed. The Gunds folded the Barons and bought the North Stars for between $10 million and $12 million and the outstanding debts. The Minnesota group had paid $2 million for the franchise in 1966, but came out with what Bush describes as "a small profit, and I mean really small."

The new North Stars were allowed to keep ten players and a pair of goaltenders from the combined rosters of the two teams, and the rest were made available to the league's other weak clubs in a dispersal draft. "The amalgamation of the Minnesota North Stars and Cleveland Barons had one immediate effect," the *Hockey News* reported from Minneapolis in its issue of July 1978. "The switchboard was overloaded with calls from across the state. North Star executives were beaming. . . . Not in five years had the public shown as much interest."

In Cleveland, meanwhile, there were but a few cries of protest and disappointment. "When I heard the news, I just started crying and shaking for hours," Barons Booster Club president Kathy Rafferty told *Globe and Mail* columnist Allen Abel. "I couldn't believe it. They sent every season-ticket holder a letter last fall promising a three-year effort. They said they made their promise in good faith. What happened to their good faith?"

THE NHL HAD LAST LOST a franchise in the spring of 1942, in the grimmest days of World War II, when the league—as the rightful owner—had dissolved the New York Americans. And now, amid a dreary, no-win war with the WHA, the board had again expunged a franchise. The Islander mess had been cleaned up, the Rockies would stay where they were, and the league-owned assets were growing, liabilities were declining and solvency was just around the corner.

All of this had been achieved in twelve months—the first year of John Ziegler's tenure as president, as it happened—and now that he and the board had put their house in order, they could turn their attention to the problem that overshadowed all others: the debilitating war with the WHA.

11

A WALK IN CENTRAL PARK (1978-1979)

IN HIS HEYDAY, WHEN HE WAS HEAD of the players' association, hockey's busiest agent, the architect and promoter of international tournaments and perhaps the most plugged-in person in the game, Alan Eagleson could be blunt, bombastic and astonishingly forthright, and no subject was too slippery or too hot to handle. Bob Verdi of the *Chicago Tribune* discovered this one day in November 1978 when he caught up with this man of many hats and perpetual motion and asked, "How's the hockey business?"

"We're in trouble," Eagleson replied. "The Pittsburgh Penguins may not be around next year, or the Colorado Rockies, and a few like Minnesota, St. Louis and Washington can't keep drawing the way they are. Six sell out all the time— the two New Yorks, Montreal, Toronto, Buffalo and Philadelphia. Three others—Boston, Detroit and Vancouver—do very well but might not sell out except for the good clubs. Chicago, Atlanta, St. Louis and Los Angeles are struggling, but they aren't in the trouble that Colorado, Washington, Minnesota and Pittsburgh are. You won't see more than sixteen teams in the NHL next season. At most. . . . Too many teams in hockey are losing money. The league lost $20 million last year."

Eagleson delivered this whirlwind state-of-the-nation with characteristic haste. In a few briskly delivered statements, he had sized up the situation of all seventeen clubs in the 1978–79 NHL. His remarks appeared in a Verdi column in the *Hockey News* and prompted an aggrieved response from the president of the Pittsburgh Penguins.

No, the Pens were not on the brink, as they had been so many times before. The franchise had changed hands for the fifth time in twelve years. The new majority owner was Edward DeBartolo Sr., and he had the know-how and the financial wherewithal to keep the Penguins afloat. Otherwise, there was no argument with Eagleson's assessment, and how could there be?

The NHL was wobbling and tottering, and the WHA was in worse shape. The rival league had lurched and veered from crisis to calamity from the moment of inception to this, its seventh season. The WHA had hoisted its flag in cities across the continent, from Miami to San Diego, Quebec City to Vancouver, and in most cases had retreated as quickly as it arrived, leaving behind burnt investors and bad memories. A wild assortment of clubs had come and gone: Screaming Eagles, Fighting Saints and Golden Blades, Cowboys, Sharks and Roadrunners—and some never made it to an opening faceoff. The WHA had spawned twenty-seven teams and, according to one newspaper report, had generated losses of $55 million.

It had also created a deep fissure with the governing body of the NHL. On one side were the pragmatists who wanted to make peace and take in the best of the WHA franchises; they formed a growing majority as the seasons passed and the WHA defied all expectations and somehow survived. Opposing them were those who refused to consider an accommodation. They had legitimate concerns, but were also driven by pride and vindictiveness. Clarence Campbell had sided with the holdouts and never wavered. John Ziegler was a pragmatist who had worked long and hard to bring about an accord.

During his year as chairman, he had appointed a fact-finding committee co-chaired by Ed Snider, leader of the peaceable faction, and Bill Wirtz, a staunch holdout, who remained livid over the defection of Bobby Hull. Snider and Wirtz were authorized to hold exploratory talks with the WHA, and they reported back to the board in March 1977.

Three months later, at the league's annual meeting, Ziegler became president and the board gave the fact-finding committee a mandate to negotiate an expansion that would see six WHA teams join the NHL in time for the upcoming season. That led to nearly two months of frantic work and negotiation. Ziegler drafted an application for admission and a plan of expansion. Applications were circulated, and six WHA clubs completed and submitted them along with financial and other documents. A majority of governors actually voted in mid-August 1977 for the accommodation, but they fell short of the three-quarters majority required.

"The opponents had very good reasons," Ziegler says. "The WHA had so many problems that we were just going to take over a big mess. We were going to be litigated to death. We were going to be responsible for the WHA pension plan, which had not been fully funded. We were going to be sued for antitrust violations. All of these points had some validity. They weren't just picked from the air."

There was another problem: the NHL's divided board. "Bill Wirtz and Ed Snider had become estranged," recalls Ziegler. "You could feel the animosity in the boardroom. It was difficult to get things done because we had two camps, and there were loyal followers of Eddie Snider and loyal followers of Bill Wirtz. Sometimes it would take two meetings to accomplish what you could have done in one. I'd have to pick up the phone and talk to each of them individually to convince them to move on an issue."

The rupture in the board had to be healed, and Eagleson played the peace-maker. "He knew this clash was going on and that it wasn't good," says Ziegler. "He and I started talking about it, and we said we gotta get these guys together. We decided we would try to create a truce, and Alan came up with an idea."

Eagleson would invite Snider and Wirtz to lunch in New York without telling either that the other would be there. He was able to do this—not as head of the players' association, but because he was the biggest agent in the game. He had negotiated contracts for Black Hawks netminder Tony Esposito and Flyers captain Bobby Clarke, as well as lesser players on both sides, and he had become good friends with both owners.

"I phoned Eddie and said I'd meet him at the bar in the Waldorf-Astoria," Eagleson recalls. "I phoned Billy and told him I'd meet him there. John and I got there early. In comes Eddie. In comes Billy. They look at each other. They look at me like—'What's going on here?'"

The first reaction of the two adversaries was to head for the exit, but they didn't. Instead, they had drinks with Ziegler and Eagleson, they had lunch, and then they went for a walk in Central Park. Snider and Wirtz walked together with Ziegler and Eagleson a discreet distance behind them. "The two of them were talking and exchanging ideas," recalls Ziegler. "They were listening to each other instead of just shutting each other out."

OLD WOUNDS COULD NOT BE HEALED entirely over drinks, lunch and a walk in the park, but they had made a good start. This occurred in the spring of 1978, and, as it happened, several WHA clubs had again inquired about admission to the NHL. The governors took up the issue at their annual meeting in Montreal in mid-June—the same meeting at which they were dealing with the Islanders, the Rockies and the Barons–North Stars merger.

Despite the heavy agenda, the governors agreed to meet later that month with representatives of the WHA. On June 26, they reconvened, this time in Detroit. Don Conrad, chief financial officer of the Aetna Insurance Company of Hartford, Connecticut, the largest shareholder in the New England Whalers, presented a detailed proposal that would see four and possibly five of seven WHA teams admitted. The clubs in question were the Whalers, Quebec Nordiques, Winnipeg Jets, Edmonton Oilers and Cincinnati Stingers. The teams excluded were the Birmingham Bulls and Indianapolis Racers.

Ziegler polled the governors. He found that there was sufficient interest, appointed an expansion committee and negotiations began immediately. The two sides bargained around the clock because Birmingham and Indianapolis had imposed a forty-eight-hour deadline. That was too tight, given the complexity of the issues, and for the second time in two years an attempt at accommodation failed. The NHL and WHA went their separate ways. The war would continue and there would be more havoc and disruption.

John Bassett, the Toronto businessman and majority owner of the Birmingham Bulls, was furious at being excluded, according to newspaper reports. He would not be part of any future deal between the leagues. Therefore, he did not need the goodwill of the hockey establishment and felt no obligation to abide by the rules. That summer, he signed six underage juniors: Rob Ramage of the London Knights, Craig Hartsburg of the Sault Ste. Marie Greyhounds, Gaston Gingras of the Brantford Alexanders, Rick Vaive of the Sherbrooke Beavers, Michel Goulet of the Quebec Remparts and London Knights goaltender Pat Riggin.

The governing bodies of Canadian junior and amateur hockey protested, but a defiant Bassett told the *Hockey News:* "I will continue to sign good, under-age talent until the laws of junior hockey start conforming to the laws of Canada. I've said it over and over again, eighteen-year-olds are allowed to vote, drink and go to jail. . . . I don't understand why they can't play pro hockey."

There was one other young star Bassett coveted, but he was tapped out financially after awarding each of his six junior-age prospects one-year, $60,000 contracts. He recommended the youth to another WHA renegade—Vancouver-based real estate flipper Nelson Skalbania, the majority owner of the Indianapolis Racers.

The player was Wayne Gretzky—a slight, wispy-haired seventeen-year-old who looked more like a paper boy than a professional hockey player, but was in fact a prodigy of Mozartean dimensions. The kid who had scored 376 goals as a peewee a few years earlier had racked up 182 points the previous winter with the Soo Greyhounds of the Ontario Hockey Association and finished second in scoring.

Skalbania offered him a seven-year, $1.7 million contract, and the kid signed. He was off to Indianapolis when most teenagers were heading back to high school, but his stay was brief. He played eight games, scored three goals and assisted on three before the Racers hit the wall financially. Skalbania packaged him with goaltender Eddie Mio and forward Peter Driscoll and sold them to his pal Peter Pocklington, owner of the Edmonton Oilers. A few weeks later, the Racers folded.

Such wanton trafficking in teenage talent, the failed NHL-WHA negotiations and the generally chaotic state of pro hockey had by then drawn the attention of some senior members of the Canadian government, particularly as the Quebec Nordiques and Winnipeg Jets were looking for federal assistance for arena upgrades. "At this time, Canada had a minister of amateur sport named Iona Campagnolo," recalls Ziegler. "I used to get calls from her, on behalf of the WHA, saying, 'We've got these Canadian teams and why can't you bring them into the NHL?'

"I finally went up to Ottawa and had dinner with her, which was delightful because she was very attractive. She was going on and on about these teams, and I said, 'Everything you say is correct and I will work for this on one condition, and that is that the Canadian government will indemnify the NHL with respect to any and all legal problems.'

"She said, 'I can't do that.'

"And I said, 'Then I can't do what you want me to do.'"

THE BOARD OF GOVERNORS HELD its annual winter meeting in mid-December 1978 at a resort in Homosassa Springs, Florida, and received a highly encouraging report from the expansion committee, which had held further talks with representatives of the WHA. Five clubs were now prepared to pay $5 million each for admission to the NHL, which the *Hockey News* described as a "blockbuster offer" and concluded that it "may finally have broken the back of hard line resistance to the WHA."

But it wasn't that simple, even with a potential windfall of $25 million on the table. The negotiating teams for both sides began talking in earnest in the new year, and the outlines of an agreement began to emerge. "We're going back and forth and we finally get a format where we'll take in four teams," recalls Ziegler. "We had one meeting where we started at nine o'clock in the morning and went till two or three the next morning. There was one hurdle we couldn't get over. The naysayers on our committee kept saying we couldn't predict the future liabilities."

The WHA owners left on the sidelines might sue. Players who lost jobs might seek redress. Someone might file an antitrust or pension suit. There were plenty of possibilities, and the prospect of multimillion-dollar judgments sent shudders down the spines of owners who had been losing money for years. They weren't budging until someone agreed to indemnify the league.

And then, late into that marathon bargaining session, a solution appeared—out of the blue, as it were. "Don Conrad stepped forward and said the Aetna Insurance Company will indemnify the National Hockey League for any litigation that arises out doing this," says Ziegler. "I'll never forget it. That shut everybody down. We couldn't believe it. If we're sued, they cover it. The naysayers had no argument. That made it."

Or so he thought. The full board met on March 7 and 8, 1979, at a resort in Key Largo, Florida—this time to vote on admitting the Whalers, Nordiques,

Jets and Oilers. The terms were contained in a sixteen-page proposal, which was structured so as to meet the legal requirements of an expansion rather than a merger. This was done primarily to guard against an antitrust suit.

Thirteen of seventeen clubs—a three-quarters majority—had to vote in favour. Ziegler had consulted widely beforehand and was certain that the pro-accommodation side had the support required. But the vote went twelve for, five against. Toronto's Harold Ballard was the most vocal opponent, and afterward, he exuded triumph. "I feel so elated," he told the Canadian Press. "It's just like the North beating the South in the Civil War."

He was one of the few celebrants. A bitter Ed Snider snarled, "There is no reality in the NHL." And an equally sour Michael Gobuty, president of the Winnipeg Jets, declared, "We will never apply to the NHL again."

Those angry words were a mere prelude to the explosion of outrage that occurred in Quebec and across the West when it became known that the Canadiens, Leafs and Canucks had all voted no. The public immediately fingered Molson Breweries, which owned the Montreal Canadiens and was the lead sponsor of *Hockey Night in Canada*.

An anonymous caller phoned the Molson brewery in Quebec City and issued a bomb threat. In Winnipeg, someone fired a bullet through a window at a Molson facility. The *Winnipeg Tribune* printed coupons on its front page and urged readers to clip them, complete them and send them to their federal representatives in Ottawa to register their indignation. Members of Parliament hardly needed any prompting. They unanimously supported a motion urging the NHL to admit the Canadian clubs.

Meantime, the Jets immediately cancelled Molson's sponsorship of the postgame Three Stars award and removed the company's name from their VIP lounge. Sportswriters and broadcasters in various part of the West urged their audiences to boycott Molson products. "Don't get mad . . . get EVEN!" roared *Winnipeg Free Press* columnist John Robertson. "Repeat after me: I will NEVER watch another NHL telecast, or use their sponsors' products."

The blowtorch reaction could not be ignored. Canadiens president Jacques Courtois appeared on national television and attempted to explain his club's position. It was the expansion proposal itself, Courtois insisted, and not Molson's sponsorship that swayed his vote. In fact, as Ziegler recounts, Molson had wielded a big stick in order to protect its TV rights, especially since the Nordiques were owned by a rival brewer. "Molson did not want three more Canadian teams," he says. "They were afraid there would be competition for their rights. Those television contracts, for each of the existing teams, were probably greater, at least in Canadian dollars, than the rights for all but two of the teams in the U.S. The Canadian clubs were pawns of Molson Breweries on this issue. They were told they couldn't do this."

Vancouver Canucks owner Frank Griffiths had been prepared to defy Molson, but was unable to attend the Key Largo meeting and sent his alternate, William Hughes, who was president of the Canucks and a longtime business associate. Griffiths had instructed Hughes to cast a favourable vote. Instead, Hughes sided with the opposition. "He may have accepted the thinking of Toronto and Montreal that this was bad for business," says Ziegler. "I called Frank Griffiths immediately afterward and he was incensed. He fired the guy, and they had been friends for years."

In any event, Canadian public opinion carried the day. Molson executives—recognizing their blunder—backed off. The NHL governors met on March 22, a Thursday, at the O'Hare Hilton in Chicago to reconsider the matter. Representatives of the four incoming WHA clubs assembled at a Hyatt Regency, located a $12.50 cab ride away, to await the outcome of their deliberations.

The NHL meeting began, according to one newspaper report, at 12:36 p.m. and ended at 3:13 p.m. Fourteen clubs voted for the expansion and three against, those being Toronto, Boston and Los Angeles. Only the Bruins seemed to have substantive objections. They were opposed primarily because the Whalers were based in Hartford, a mere seventy-five miles south of Boston, and would cut into the radio and TV audiences for Bruins games.

At 5 p.m., Ziegler and the expansion committee met the WHA representatives to review a slightly revised twenty-page document that contained the terms of admission. They were non-negotiable, and this created a rift among the WHA clubs. The Winnipeg and Hartford delegations were prepared to make peace, but Edmonton and Quebec balked. The most contentious item stipulated that the WHA teams could protect two goalies and two skaters.

This seemed punitive even to some members of the NHL fraternity. Rangers executive Michael Keating disclosed in an interview that his club was prepared to admit the WHA teams intact in order to ensure that they were competitive. "But there are about five general managers who oppose that idea," he told the *Winnipeg Free Press*. "They say: 'We've had to suffer. They can too.' But that's the kind of argument that's hurting hockey."

Nevertheless, this was a take-it-or-leave-it proposition and Edmonton and Quebec eventually capitulated. At 4 a.m. on March 23, Ziegler emerged with Howard Baldwin, president of both the Whalers and the WHA, to announce that peace had finally been achieved. "For seven years, we have spent a good deal of time fighting between the leagues," Ziegler told the media. "Having one professional league in North America will permit us to devote the resources of time, of people and of money to further the development of hockey."

There was inevitably some grumbling, but not much. "It cost us $6 million to join the NHL and they take most of our players," sniped Oilers owner Peter Pocklington. Winnipeg general manager John Ferguson had hoped to keep up to five skaters, but wasn't prepared to risk everything over the issue. "I couldn't see myself jeopardizing the whole deal over one hockey player," he said. "All you had to do was think what it means to Winnipeg to have the NHL."

It meant a great deal indeed. "The Winnipeg Jets of the NHL," cooed Robertson, the previously furious columnist of the *Free Press*. "It has a sweet ring to it, doesn't it . . . it was worth the price, ANY price, to get into the NHL." Edmontonians were just as excited. That was evident when Oiler season tickets went on sale. The team had sold seven thousand for the team's final WHA campaign—less than half the 15,232 seats available at the Northlands Coliseum. In a matter of hours, fans snapped up 14,000 for the Oilers' inaugural NHL campaign and would have taken the rest, but Northlands withheld them to sell on game days. •

There was a final hurdle to clear before the marriage of the leagues was official: the NHL players had to approve it. This was a rare opportunity to demand better treatment from the owners, and they did that. They proposed, among other things, a substantial change to the compensation formula for free agents. Rather than surrender a current player of equal value, the team that signed a free agent would give up draft picks—a first-round selection for someone with a salary of $100,000 to $150,000, a second-rounder for someone with a salary of $75,000 to $100,000 and a third-rounder for someone in the $50,000-to-$75,000 range.

The owners, however, were in no mood for such ideas. Their accumulated losses during the war with the WHA had exceeded $100 million. Player compensation had quadrupled. By 1977, the NHL average salary was $96,000 compared with Major League Baseball's $76,000 and the NFL's $55,000. A more liberal approach to free agency would inevitably lead to continued escalation of salaries. Instead, the league offered an improved benefits package that included enriched pensions, a 100 per cent increase in disability insurance, life insurance and the dental plan and a larger pool of playoff bonus money.

The players could have opted for a strike vote or they could have filed an antitrust suit in order to press their demands. Instead, they heeded the advice of Alan Eagleson. He warned against disturbing the peace and argued that this was a moment for compromise, not confrontation. They player representatives heeded his word and voted thirty to one to accept the offer of the owners.

It was said then, and has been said many times since, that Eagleson failed his members. That he betrayed their interests. That he sold out. The only credible response to this line of reasoning is: Really? Would the owners have met the demand for more generous free agency? Not likely, given the catastrophic losses some had endured. Would the players have enjoyed any public support if they had torpedoed the deal? Hardly, given the roasting Molson took in the court of public opinion. Finally, was it the sole duty of the head of the players' association to fight for a measure that would have enriched his members? Eagleson thinks not.

"My job, as I saw it, was to keep the players working," says Eagleson. "There was no sense being confrontational when the bucket you wanted to share wasn't that big. NHL revenues were inhibited by the lack of a major TV contract. The WHA was as dead as a ghost. The three Canadian teams and Hartford were going to survive, but the others weren't worth fifteen cents. I had a lot of players in the WHA—they were my clients—and a lot of them weren't getting paid. My argument was, if we can bring in four more teams with twenty-five or thirty jobs each, it's not that bad a deal."

For all that has been said on this matter, some of the sagest words were written in the immediate aftermath. "If the players had called a strike, hockey would have been in chaos," the *Chicago Tribune*'s Bob Verdi wrote. "If the NHL owners had scrapped the merger, hockey would have been in chaos. And if there's anything hockey doesn't need now, it's more chaos."

12

BACK ON TRACK (1979–1990)

MIDWAY THROUGH THE FIRST PERIOD, Gordie Howe takes his second shift of the night. He carries the puck over the Pittsburgh blue line. Spots a Hartford Whaler teammate open in the corner. Fires a crisp, accurate pass. Then breaks for the net. The teammate returns the pass. Howe scores. The fans—hitherto quiet—erupt. They have witnessed a piece of hockey history— the fifty-one-year-old Howe's first NHL goal in nearly ten years, the 787th of his career, and "an absolutely gorgeous" one at that, according to a Canadian sportswriter in town to cover the World Series. Two dozen baseball writers have likewise dropped by the Pittsburgh Civic Arena on this Saturday evening to catch the return of the ageless wonder. Afterward, in the visitors' dressing room, they pepper him with questions about his durability and what makes him keep going, and he says, "I just wanted to be the first grandfather to score a goal in the NHL."

Youth was the story elsewhere that week—the first of the NHL's sixty-second season and showtime for the former WHA clubs. The rookie-laden Edmonton Oilers, dubbed the Clearasil Kids by one sportswriter, made their debut in Chicago against the Black Hawks. All eyes were on the teenage phenom Wayne Gretzky, who wasn't old enough to vote or buy liquor and would not be till he turned nineteen 107 days hence. "Hoo boy," he told a writer two hours before the opening faceoff. "I can't believe this is happening." A cluster of reporters gathered round him at the conclusion of the contest and he acknowledged, "I've never been that nervous before a game in my life." A few stalls away, teammate Mark Messier, an unheralded eighteen-year-old who had jumped straight from Tier II junior, added: "It really hit me in the afternoon. I sat in my hotel room and all I could think was, 'Hey, we're in the NHL.'"

Fans in the WHA cities were equally wide-eyed and elated. The Jets came home after two road losses to play Don Cherry's weak Colorado Rockies. The 12,648-seat Winnipeg Arena was packed to the rafters. Ben Hatskin, who founded the Jets and signed Bobby Hull, was introduced prior to the anthems and stood at centre ice, beaming and waving, and the entire crowd stood and, as columnist John Robertson wrote, greeted him with "a cacophonous tidal wave of appreciation for planting the seed from which an NHL franchise grew."

Lieutenant-Governor Bud Jobin bought a round of popcorn for the house. The Jets won, and as the players headed for the showers, the fans stood again, "screaming sweet superlatives," wrote Robertson. "It was wall to wall jubilation."

In Quebec City, celebrations began a full forty-eight hours before the Nordiques made their debut at home against the Atlanta Flames. Lieutenant-Governor Jean-Pierre Côté hosted a reception for the players and local dignitaries. There was a civic luncheon at a high-end hotel and a public corn roast where the beverage of choice was "Nordiques punch." Parti Québécois deputy Jean-François Bertrand introduced a motion in the National Assembly congratulating the team on its ascension to the NHL and wishing the players luck. All sides endorsed it.

The Nordiques lost their home opener, but it scarcely mattered. There was game two to think about—a Saturday night encounter at the Forum against the reigning Stanley Cup champions. "The National Hockey League returned to the ancient capital after an absence of sixty years," a *La Presse* journalist wrote, "but for fans of the Nordiques a victory over the glorious Canadiens of Montreal would constitute a truly historic event."

The game was sold out three weeks in advance. Hundreds of Quebec City residents had purchased tickets. Mayor Jean Pelletier and his Montreal counterpart, Jean Drapeau, both attended, and some two million Quebecers watched on TV. The teams went at it with playoff-level intensity, and after sixty minutes the scoreboard read: Canadiens 3; Nordiques 1. Afterward, left winger Yvon Lambert explained that the Canadiens hadn't played their best, the reason being, "We don't hate them enough."

John Ziegler attended the home openers in Quebec, Winnipeg and Edmonton. He participated in opening ceremonies. He granted interviews. And he expressed the hope that the NHL was on the cusp of a new and brighter era. "I'm rather excited and looking forward to this season," he said. "I'm going to be able to watch more hockey games and focus more attention on the game, I hope, than a lot of the business problems that have consumed so much of my time in the last couple of years."

It proved to be an exciting and memorable season. The Canadiens were chasing a fifth straight Stanley Cup without goaltender Ken Dryden, who had retired; without centre Jacques Lemaire, who had quit to play in Switzerland; and without coach Scotty Bowman, who had left for Buffalo after being passed over for the general manager's job. They struggled while others soared.

Pat Quinn's Philadelphia Flyers lost game two on October 13 and didn't lose again until January 7. In between, they won twenty-five and tied ten. It was the longest unbeaten streak in North American professional sport, surpassing the old record of thirty-three games established in 1971–72 by the NBA's Los Angeles Lakers.

Marcel Dionne, Charlie Simmer and Dave Taylor of the Los Angeles Kings formed the hottest forward line in the league. They scored twenty-nine goals in their first nine games and occupied the top three spots in the scoring race. A quarter of the way into the season, Dionne was on a pace to break Phil Esposito's all-time points total of 152. By mid-January, the three Kings had accumulated 92 goals and 118 assists.

The stop-and-go Canadiens were barely above .500. They had endured an eleven-game winless streak on the road, a club record. Their coach, Bernie Geoffrion, had quit because he couldn't handle the players or the public pressure, and Guy Lafleur was airing his grievances in the newspapers.

The Maple Leafs, meantime, were at war with their newly installed general manager, Punch Imlach. The players accused him of instituting a "reign of terror." Darryl Sittler—who had scored the 300th goal of his career and picked up his 750th point—refused to serve as captain. Imlach traded the stalwart Lanny McDonald to Colorado and shipped defenceman Dave Hutchison to Chicago. Before leaving, Hutchison told reporters, "I don't like the thought of leaving the guys, but, God, anything to get away from the situation."

Marcel Aubut, president of the Quebec Nordiques, issued an eyebrow-raising press release. Henceforth, he decreed, perhaps as a gesture of solidarity with Quebec separatists, "O Canada" would be sung in French only, unless the visitors were from a Canadian city and the anthem was performed in both languages at their home arena. Likewise, all announcements except goals and assists would be in French only. Ziegler promptly intervened. English, he said, was the official language of the NHL and had been for sixty years.

The Red Wings vacated the Detroit Olympia—their home for half a century—and moved into the brand new Joe Louis Arena. The once-illustrious Wings were a sad-sack team run by Ted Lindsay, a great left winger but an inept general manager, and the move did nothing to change their fortunes. The highlight of the season for many fans occurred on January 12, when Gordie Howe and the Hartford Whalers paid a visit and the adoring crowd gave Mr. Hockey a thunderous pre-game ovation.

Wayne Gretzky turned nineteen on January 26, and on February 24 became the youngest player in league history to score one hundred points. He blew by established stars such as Lafleur of the Canadiens and Bryan Trottier and Mike Bossy of the Islanders and closed in on the season-long scoring leader Marcel Dionne with one astonishing performance after another. "He's nineteen going on thirty-five," said goaltender Ron Low, who came to the Oilers in a mid-March trade.

On March 25, in a game televised nationally from Toronto, Gretzky scored two goals and assisted on four others and led the Oilers to an eight-six win over the Leafs. Afterward, a flabbergasted Sittler said, "For a nineteen-year-old to play on a new team and do as well as he has, well, it's unbelievable."

The 840-game schedule ended April 6 and Gretzky and Dionne were tied for top spot, but the Art Ross Trophy went to the great Kings centre on the strength of goals scored. Gretzky was denied rookie-of-the-year honours as well due to his WHA experience, but he had carried the Oilers to sixteenth place and the final playoff spot. They had earned the right to play the formidable Flyers, who had finished first, and Edmonton's season came to a quick end.

The Canadiens had put their problems behind them, and so had Lafleur. He hit the fifty-goal plateau for the sixth straight year and teammate Pierre Larouche scored fifty as well. The Habs made a late-season sprint to the playoffs and finished second overall. Fans and opponents alike held their breath and thought maybe the Montreal mystique would carry the Canadiens to another championship. It didn't happen. Their reign ended at home on a Sunday night with a seventh-game loss to the Minnesota North Stars.

The Flyers, meantime, rolled over the Rangers and the North Stars and advanced to the final against the Islanders, a very good team that was said to be haunted by memories of past playoff failures. This edition of the Isles was also coming off a troubled season. There had been injuries, discontent and a miserable first half in which they hovered around .500. But all that was history when the final opened May 13. It ended eleven days and six games later and they were champions.

Bob Nystrom scored the overtime goal that clinched it. Linemate John Tonelli assisted. The stars, role players and grinders had all done their jobs. Amid the postgame celebrations, jubilation rendered some of the Islanders incoherent. "All I want to do is cry," said centre Bob Bourne, a veteran who had endured all the bitter losses of past years. "Cry, cry, cry."

THE LEAGUE'S FIRST POST-WHA SEASON had been its best in nearly a decade. A teenaged superstar had emerged and was destined to become one of the greatest players of all time. A new champion had been crowned—one destined to become a dynasty. A five-year decline in attendance had been reversed. With the addition of the former WHA teams and with packed arenas in Quebec, Winnipeg and Edmonton, the NHL had drawn 11.5 million spectators, an all-time high and up from 8.5 million the previous year.

But the league still had several shaky franchises—a legacy of the long war with the WHA—and one of them expired on the very weekend that John Ziegler was presenting the Stanley Cup to the triumphant Islanders. The Atlanta Flames left Georgia after eight seasons and six playoff appearances and moved north to become the Calgary Flames.

Atlanta's demise had been rumoured for months, and the franchise had been financially precarious almost from day one. "The ownership group that bought the team based all their projections on information provided by the NHL when it was operating without a competing league," recalls Cliff Fletcher, who served as general manager.

Unfortunately, the WHA came along the same season the Flames entered the league. Costs quickly exceeded the projections and the club was hard pressed to boost revenues. The seating capacity in the Omni, the home of the Flames, could not be increased, and TV rights fetched less than the rights to radio broadcasts. Furthermore, hockey had to compete for attention with Major League Baseball, the NFL, the NBA, college football and one other sport. "You had over a quarter of a million people in the greater Atlanta area watching high school football on Friday and Saturday nights until early December," says Fletcher.

One by one, the original investors surrendered their shares rather than putting in more money to keep the Flames going. But Tom Cousins, the first chairman and owner of a large real estate company, stayed in. By 1979–80, Cousins held eighty-nine per cent and he, too, wanted out. A group of Calgary oilmen, led by brothers Daryl and Byron Seaman and Harley Hotchkiss, came south with a rich offer: $14 million cash, in U.S. currency.

Calgary did not have an NHL-calibre arena, but the Seamans and their partners had held discussions with the provincial government about erecting a new building. Meantime, the Flames were to play out of the 6,500-seat Calgary Corral, with the blessing of the league's board of governors. Before the Calgary group could close the deal, however, a competing offer appeared unsolicited.

The interloper was Vancouver real estate speculator Nelson Skalbania. He specialized in acquiring properties, usually with minimal money down, and reselling them as quickly as possible for a small profit. He sent his teenaged daughter Roxanne to Atlanta. She met with Fletcher and presented an offer jotted on the back of a cocktail napkin. Skalbania was prepared to pay $16 million, financed in part by selling TV rights to Molson Breweries for ten years for $6 million and by offering a minority interest to a small group of Calgary investors.

Cousins accepted the higher bid and Skalbania announced the deal on the Friday afternoon of the Victoria Day weekend. "We said we were going to have a season-ticket campaign starting on Tuesday morning," Fletcher says. "Then Nelson went on the radio and said, 'If you want to bring your money down to the Corral this weekend, we'll take it.' Next morning, there were about seven thousand people lined up.

"I flew in on Monday and checked into my hotel and then went up to Nelson's suite, and I nearly dropped. There was money all over the place. I picked up a cushion from a sofa and there was a $1,000 bill underneath it. They nearly sold the place out on the weekend. The corporate sector went into hysterics. By Tuesday morning, most of the tickets were gone."

Skalbania had no interest in operating an NHL team or building an arena. He had jumped in to make a quick buck. By the start of the 1980–81 season, he had sold forty-nine per cent to the Seamans and their group. He had sold another chunk by Christmas 1980 and the balance in the summer of 1981. By then, another NHL owner was headed for the exit.

FOR MONTHS, THERE HAD BEEN RUMBLINGS in Detroit and beyond that Bruce Norris was ready to sell the Red Wings. He was approaching sixty. His personal fortunes had fallen. He had been through four marriages. He had always been fond of drink—too fond, some said. He had health problems. Norris was a big man, but most of that bigness resided in his torso. He had slender legs and knees damaged by a few seasons playing football at Yale, and walking had become painful and difficult. On top of all that, he was having financial problems.

He owned a horse-breeding operation near Ocala, Florida—in the interior of the state, some eighty miles northeast of Tampa—and two very large cattle ranches, founded by his father. One was in Ocklawaha, a few miles from Ocala, the other in South Dakota. He owned a home in Chicago, a stunning ranch house in Ocklawaha, a condo in Miami and a large estate at Mattituck on Long Island. As well, he still controlled Norris Grain, which was by then a holding company and the largest shareholder in a publicly traded firm that had interests in banking, insurance and real estate.

"The Red Wings were losing money and eating up cash faster than he could make it elsewhere," recalls John Ziegler, then the league president and one of Norris's closest friends. "He had to divest."

The Norris family had owned the Wings for half a century, and Bruce Norris had taken over the team from his sister Marguerite in 1955. In those days, the Wings stood at the pinnacle of the sport. They had won seven straight league titles and as many Stanley Cups and hadn't missed the playoffs in nearly two decades. They remained competitive until the mid-1960s and the end of the six-team era, and then entered a period of prolonged and precipitous decline.

The Wings made the Stanley Cup final in 1966. In the next fifteen seasons, they compiled a winning record only three times. They made the playoffs twice, and on both occasions were eliminated quickly. They went through thirteen coaches and fifteen coaching changes because several men took two turns behind the bench. They were in twentieth place in the twenty-one-team league when Norris announced in March 1982 that the Wings were for sale. He issued a prepared statement, but other than that said nothing. There were no interviews and no press conference. "It was one of the most difficult things he ever had to do," says Ziegler. "It was extremely painful."

By early June, the papers were signed and the deal complete. The new owner was Mike Ilitch. He was fifty-three, a father of seven and a native of Detroit. He had grown up not far from the Olympia and had started going to Red Wing games in the mid-1930s, when he was seven or eight years old. He had been a lifelong fan of the team and the game. He and his wife and business partner, Marian, owned Little Caesars, a pizza chain that then had 288 locations in eleven states. He also owned eleven Wendy's restaurants and regional franchise rights for the restaurant-arcades known as Chuck E. Cheese.

Ilitch bought the Wings and two minor-league affiliates for the rock-bottom price of $3 million cash and three Chuck E. Cheese franchises. At the time, he described the Wings as "a sleeping giant waiting for someone to do something with it." In fact, they were more like a patient on life support. The team was terrible. The hockey operations department was mediocre. The fan base had eroded and season-ticket sales had sunk to around two thousand. In his first season as owner, Ilitch gave away a new car at all forty-one home games to create some promotional buzz, and he and his wife lost $2.1 million on revenues of $4.3 million, but he made one move that would prove itself over the long haul. He hired Jim Devellano to rebuild the Wings. Devellano was a high school dropout and former government worker who had started as an unpaid amateur scout for the St. Louis Blues, joined the Islanders in their first year and drafted most of the players that made them champions.

EVERY MONEY-LOSING OWNER has his pain threshold. Tom Cousins absorbed heavy losses in Atlanta for several seasons before calling it quits.

Bruce Norris did the same in Detroit. Once down that road was enough for Peter Gilbert. He had made his money in cable television in Buffalo, and he lost a chunk of it as owner of the Colorado Rockies in 1981–82.

Gilbert had bought the team from New Jersey businessman Arthur Imperatore, who had acquired the Rockies in the summer of 1978 under the assumption he could move them to a new nineteen-thousand-seat arena that was slated to open in July 1981 in East Rutherford, New Jersey. But the NHL board of governors made it clear that the club was staying in Colorado, so Imperatore sold.

Gilbert took over a dreadful team, and it remained dreadful under his brief, baleful stewardship. The franchise had begun life as the Kansas City Scouts in 1974–75. It was moved to Denver in 1976 and had never had a winning season in either locale. In seven years, the Scouts/Rockies had won 122 games, lost 342 and tied 96. Gilbert's one year as proprietor was typical: eighteen wins, forty-nine losses, thirteen ties and a loss estimated at $4.5 million.

As the financial shortfall grew, Gilbert began lobbying to move the franchise. His preferred destination was East Rutherford. But the league wanted to maintain its presence in the West. The Rockies—despite a woeful record—had averaged eight thousand fans a night and some governors were convinced that, with a good team, Denver would be a solid market. Besides, the league had a long-standing policy against relocating franchises, though exceptions were made.

"Gilbert bought the team with the expectation that he could move it," John Ziegler recalls, "even though he was told time and again that it would be very, very difficult. He was bleeding cash out there and he got very angry. He was a very disgruntled owner near the end."

The conflict with Gilbert escalated in the latter half of the 1981–82 season. The league began looking for a buyer, and Islander owner John Pickett recommended John McMullen, an acquaintance. McMullen was a naval architect and chairman of baseball's Houston Astros. He lived in New Jersey and had made his money in shipbuilding, mainly for the U.S. government. Pickett introduced Ziegler and McMullen at an Islander game at Nassau Coliseum, and they retreated to Pickett's office to discuss the Rockies.

"McMullen began by saying, 'I'm only interested if I can transfer the franchise,'" recalls Ziegler. "I said, 'Well, there's going to be a lot of problems with that.'

"He said, 'What problems?'

"I said: 'You're going to be within the broadcast territory of the Islanders and the Rangers. You're also in the franchise territory of the Rangers. You're only six miles away as the crow flies, and a franchise territory is fifty miles, so they're going to expect some indemnification.'

"He said, 'Oh well, we'll take care of that.'

"I said, 'It might not be as easy as you think.'"

It wasn't. Pickett later disclosed his price to Ziegler. Jack Krumpe of the Rangers made an astronomical demand, and Ziegler had to whittle him down. Then Ed Snider unexpectedly insisted on a payoff. He did not have a territorial claim, but maintained that a New Jersey team would infringe on the Flyers' radio and TV audiences—a position that some governors hotly disputed.

Meantime, Gilbert launched a last-ditch season-ticket sales campaign. He commissioned a TV commercial that opened with images of a team official removing sweaters from the dressing room and a voice-over question: "Are the Rockies leaving Denver?" Then the camera cut to veteran defenceman Mike Kitchen, who replied: "Not if I can help it. My teammates and I are buying season tickets for next year. We want to stay in Colorado." In the final scene, ten players were depicted writing cheques.

Matters came to a head at a meeting at the Waldorf-Astoria in New York on May 19, a Wednesday. It began at 10 a.m. and went till 3 a.m. Thursday. "They're dumping on Peter in there," one governor told a cluster of reporters during a break. Another disclosed: "They're trying to buy out Gilbert. Peter is going to be out of hockey and new group is taking over."

The board reconvened at 9 a.m. Thursday and by noon had concluded its business. Gilbert had agreed to sell. The franchise would be offered to McMullen and two partners: Brendan Byrne, a former governor of New Jersey, and John Whitehead, a senior executive with Goldman Sachs. A price had been set that included the cost of buying out Gilbert, a fee for transferring the team and indemnification for the Rangers, Islanders and Flyers.

A few days later, Ziegler met McMullen and Whitehead at McMullen's lavish suburban New Jersey home. They had drinks. McMullen showed Ziegler his art collection, which included several Picassos, a number of French Impressionists and other priceless works. Then they got down to business.

As Ziegler tells it, McMullen said: "C'mon, tell us. What's it going to cost us?"

"I said: 'Take a swallow of your drink. I only have an estimate. I've sounded out the board and it's $35 million.'

"McMullen said: 'Thirty-five million? Where in hell do you get that number?'

"I said, 'You've got to indemnify the Rangers, Islanders and Flyers.'

"He said: 'That's ridiculous. Absolutely ridiculous. They're not entitled to that.'"

But he didn't walk away. Negotiations went on for several weeks, and McMullen and his partners ended up paying close to the asking price. A year later, McMullen insisted on renegotiating, and he won some concessions. He was back the following year, demanding yet another adjustment, but got nowhere.

"He was a troublemaker," says Ziegler. "He was always complaining about how high salaries were in hockey and asking what I was going to do to get them down. I didn't know it at the time, but found out later that he decided the league needed a change at the top. He had a document drawn up and went around trying to get support, and he got some followers. Under the constitution, you could only remove the president with a two-thirds vote. He wasn't that well liked and couldn't get a majority, let alone two-thirds, but he was trying. From the point of view of the team, though, John was a good owner."

McMullen hired an out-of-work and down-on-his-luck hockey executive named Max McNab as general manager—partly on Ziegler's recommendation—and McNab remained with the organization for nearly a decade, first as GM and later as a vice-president. McMullen topped up McNab's paltry NHL pension and ensured that he and his wife lived comfortably in retirement, and he replaced McNab with Lou Lamoriello. It would prove to be one of the most astute hires of the expansion era. Lamoriello ran the Devils for more than a quarter of a century—leading them first to respectability, then contention, and finally, two Stanley Cup championships.

IF McMULLEN WAS AN IRKSOME PRESENCE on the board, the next new owner to join the fraternity was equally so. Harry Ornest was the Edmonton-born son of Eastern European immigrants, he was worth about $35 million—literally a small fortune compared to the wealth of some of the others at the table—and he had made it in a nickel-and-dime business, by selling pop and popcorn, chocolate bars, licorice and assorted confections from vending machines placed in movie theatres, rinks and other public venues.

Ornest had begun with a single machine in Edmonton. He acquired distribution rights for western Canada and wound up with hundreds in Alberta and British Columbia. He had invested some of his earnings in real estate and eventually moved to Los Angeles, where he was living when he acquired the St. Louis Blues in the summer of 1983. Ornest had risen, but had not forgotten his roots, and he ran his hockey team the way he ran his vending machine business. He was frugal, hands-on and kept close watch over revenues and expenses.

If others were paying their general managers $200,000, he was paying his $95,000. If they were paying coaches $200,000, he was paying $80,000. If their trainers got $50,000, his got $30,000. At board meetings, while the wealthier owners squirmed and fidgeted, he badgered John Ziegler about league budgets and what he perceived to be lavish spending. He frequently called Ziegler afterward to press his point.

"Thirty minutes was a short call for Harry," says Ziegler. "One time, we were in an old building at Fifth Avenue and 43rd Street. We were up on the thirty-third floor, and because this was an old building, we had fire drills every two weeks. I'm on the phone now half an hour with Harry and he's going on and on, and one of the people in the office comes to my door and says: 'John, it's a fire drill. We have to leave.'

"And I said, 'Harry, I may have to leave you.'

"He didn't even pay any attention. He just kept talking. Pretty soon, this fellow comes back and says: 'John, this is not a drill. There's a fire in the building.'

"I said, 'Harry . . . ahhh . . . there's a fire in our building and I'm going to have to leave.'

"And he says: 'John, that's the problem with you. You never want to listen to me.'

"I said: 'Harry, I'm looking at smoke outside my window. Whatever you think, this is goodbye. I'll call you later.'"

Ornest may have been a thorn in Ziegler's side, but he rescued the league from one of the messiest franchise fiascos of the expansion era. The Blues had been a very stable and successful operation in the early years. But a few poor seasons and WHA-driven inflation changed that. The original owners, Sid Salomon Jr. and son Sid III, were forced by mounting losses and their own financial difficulties to put the team on the market in 1977. Buyers were scarce, however, and the club's future in St. Louis was in doubt.

On that occasion, the team's pint-sized, high-energy coach and general manager, Emile Francis, convinced R. Hal Dean, chairman of pet food manufacturer Ralston Purina, that the company should buy the Blues as a civic responsibility. Dean retired at the end of 1981, and his successor, William Stintz, had no interest in owning a money-losing hockey club.

The company began shopping the Blues, and on January 12, 1983, announced that they had been sold to Batoni-Hunter Enterprises of Saskatoon. Company president Bill Hunter, one of the founders of the WHA, intended to move the club to Saskatoon and promised to build a $43 million, eighteen-thousand-seat arena in time for the 1983–84 season. He also embarked on a public-speaking tour of Saskatchewan to whip up support.

"During the last three months of 1982 and the first three of 1983, I had 196 speaking engagements," he later wrote in his autobiography. "Sometimes, I'd do three a day—breakfast, lunch and dinner. A friend donated his plane and hired a pilot to fly me around. . . . Everywhere I went, I pitched the dream of Saskatchewan joining the big leagues. I reminded the people about the long and passionate love they had for the game. People were hungry for this message. The Rotary luncheons and community halls were packed."

The reaction at NHL headquarters in New York was considerably cooler. "We knew Mr. Hunter from the WHA," recalls Ziegler. "Hunter doesn't have an arena. He doesn't have any money. The St. Louis people said he's going to do this and he's going to do that and I said: 'That's just talk. Show us the money.' Of course, they couldn't do it because there wasn't any."

Hunter's dream crashed on May 18 when the NHL board voted fifteen-three to reject the sale. Then things got ugly. Six days later, Ralston Purina filed a $60 million antitrust suit against the league, its governors and Ziegler. On June 3, the company announced that it "had no intention of remaining in the hockey business and no intention of operating the team next year" and it turned over the franchise to the NHL "to operate, sell or otherwise dispose of in whatever manner the league desires."

The NHL held its annual amateur draft June 8 in Montreal, but the Blues' table was empty. Ralston Purina had refused to send a delegation. The following day, the NHL filed a $78 million countersuit and accused the company of damaging the league by "wilfully, wantonly and maliciously collapsing its St. Louis Blues hockey operation." Ralston Purina responded with a statement to the effect that "the NHL has concocted an absurd series of charges and damage claims. Their lawsuit is utterly ridiculous."

Meantime, the league was desperate to maintain its presence in the Midwestern city. "Bill Wirtz and I went to St. Louis," says Ziegler. "We literally walked the streets from meeting to meeting with significant businessmen to try to persuade them to buy the team. We ran an ad in the *Wall Street Journal*. We were doing everything we could think of, and from California comes Harry Ornest. He was a character, and that's an understatement, but there was nobody else."

The board approved Ornest in late July 1983. He purchased the player contracts and other assets for $3 million cash and $9 million in notes. He acquired the Blues' arena—then known as the Checkerdome—for $5 million from Ralston Purina. The company had dismissed the front office staff and the hockey department, and Ornest had to rebuild the organization in a hurry.

He hired Jacques Demers from the Quebec Nordiques to coach the team and Ron Caron out of the Canadiens organization as general manager. He managed to fill all the other vacancies and, almost miraculously, had his departments staffed and a team ready to go when the season opened. The 1983–84 Blues compiled a record of thirty-two wins, forty-one losses and seven ties. They finished fourteenth in the twenty-one-team league, made the playoffs and won their first round against Detroit before losing in seven to the North Stars.

THE RESOLUTION OF THE CRISIS in St. Louis ended a turbulent era of change and instability. In the space of four years, eight new governors had joined the board. The newcomers represented the four former WHA clubs and the NHL franchises that had relocated, changed hands or both. The league was profoundly altered on the ice as well. The sixties had belonged to the Leafs and Canadiens, the seventies to the Big Bad Bruins, the Broad Street Bullies and the last great Montreal dynasty. The eighties belonged to the New York Islanders and the Edmonton Oilers.

The Islanders owned the first half of the decade, the Oilers the second. The Islanders had great players at every position: Billy Smith in goal, Denis Potvin on defence, and Bryan Trottier and Mike Bossy up front, and they had a superb supporting cast. They won four straight Stanley Cups and nineteen consecutive playoff series—a record that stood for the next three decades and may never be matched or broken.

The Oilers ended the reign of the Islanders in the spring of 1984, and their talent pool was even deeper. They had all the role players—the checkers, the agitators, the enforcers, the stay-at-home defencemen—and a core of great players that was as formidable as any ever assembled. Grant Fuhr was a nearly unbeatable goalie in big-money games. Paul Coffey was a fleet and riveting defenceman. Glenn Anderson was a chaotic and unnerving whirlwind on right wing. Jari Kurri was a creative and dynamic sniper on left wing. Mark Messier was all might and menace and a second-line centre only because he had to play behind the incomparable Wayne Gretzky.

Messier wasn't alone. Every other great player of the eighties performed in Gretzky's shadow—Pittsburgh's Mario Lemieux, Detroit's Steve Yzerman, Minnesota's Bobby Smith, Winnipeg's Dale Hawerchuk and Boston's Ray Bourque. But there was far more to the NHL of the 1980s than Gretzky, the Oilers and the Islanders.

It was also a decade of intense rivalries. In the first two seasons after the accommodation with the WHA, the league played a balanced schedule, in which each team met every opponent an equal number of times. In year three, the NHL adopted an unbalanced schedule in which there were more games against divisional rivals and teams had to win two rounds of divisional playoffs before advancing. Two points earned in December, or lost in February, might determine home-ice advantage in April. Midseason games between the Canadiens and Nordiques, the Oilers and Flames, the Rangers and Flyers or Black Hawks and North Stars were very often ferocious clashes with emotions running high on the ice and in the stands.

The rivalries raised the calibre of competition. A big influx of American and European talent had the same effect. Most NHL teams had scouted U.S.

colleges and European leagues on a sporadic, ad hoc basis in the 1970s. By the end of the decade they were paying much closer attention. In the fall of 1979, former Leafs general manager Jim Gregory took charge of the league's Central Scouting Service, which assessed draft-age North Americans and ranked them according to their presumed potential. He set up a parallel European service and hired two knowledgeable scouts to run it—Bjorn Stubb, an executive with the Swedish Ice Hockey Federation, and a former Finnish pro player named Esa Peltonen.

These initiatives quickly paid dividends. By 1983–84, Europeans accounted for 8.7 per cent of the players in the league, and that figure rose to 12 per cent by the end of the decade. Likewise, there were more and more Americans coming in. The number rose to 16 per cent in 1989–90 from 13 in 1983–84.

That meant fewer jobs for Canadians and caused a noisy backlash from displaced players, disgruntled parents and media commentators, most notably Don Cherry of the "Coach's Corner" segment on *Hockey Night in Canada*. But talent-hungry teams had no choice, as Harry Neale told the *Hockey News* while coaching the Vancouver Canucks in the early 1980s. "It's just a fact," Neale said, "that there are twenty-one teams and North America obviously can't produce enough new players every year to keep the teams that are trying to get better from looking elsewhere."

Almost all the Europeans came from Sweden or Finland because the best Russians and Czechs were prohibited from leaving their communist homelands. Nevertheless, a handful of Czechs ran great risks to defect. The Quebec Nordiques helped Peter Stastny, his brother Anton and Peter's pregnant wife escape in the summer of 1981—a daring escapade that generated headlines internationally. The following summer, their elder brother Marian fled as well.

The Czechs lost another top player when the slick young defenceman Petr Svoboda defected during the European championships in West Germany in the spring of 1984. Svoboda departed on his own and hid out with an aunt. His bold move went unnoticed by all except Montreal Canadiens general manager Serge Savard. He had Svoboda flown to Montreal and signed him to a five-year, $750,000 contract prior to the June 1984 amateur draft. The Canadiens selected him fifth overall, a few notches below number-one pick Mario Lemieux, and then stunned the entire crowd when Svoboda walked on stage to don a team jersey.

The Detroit Red Wings went to extraordinary lengths to get their hands on a promising young Czech named Petr Klima. General manager Jim Devellano and coach Nick Polano inherited a threadbare roster and a near-empty prospect pipeline when they joined the organization in the summer of 1982. In the amateur draft of June 1983, they chose Steve Yzerman first, Bob Probert third and Klima fifth. Neither man had seen Klima play, but they had received reports that he was a highly skilled offensive player.

Polano met Klima twice over the next two years, once in Buffalo and again in Vancouver while the young prospect was competing with the Czech national team. The clandestine meetings took place in hotel rooms, with an interpreter present since Klima spoke no English. At one meeting, Polano brought a copy of Steve Yzerman's first contract to illustrate the money available to top rookies.

By early 1985, Klima was ready to defect. He was scheduled to compete that summer in a tournament near the town of Nussdorf, in southeast Germany, and a rendezvous was arranged. Polano flew to Germany with a Czech defector from Vancouver (the interpreter) and Jim Lites, then the son-in-law of Mike Ilitch and the Red Wings' executive vice-president. Lites rented a big Mercedes-Benz and, as Polano recalls, brought "a bag of money to pay everybody off."

During a pre-game warmup, the interpreter approached Klima at rinkside on the pretext of asking for an autograph. He told the player to slip out of his hotel around eleven o'clock that evening and proceed to a thick woods behind the building. At the appointed hour, Polano was there with the interpreter. Klima arrived with nothing but a small bag that contained two sweaters. Then, as Polano recalls: "Petr threw a curve at us. He said the money wasn't enough. I went back to the car and said: 'Jim, we've got a problem. This guy doesn't want to leave unless we give him another $100,000.'

"Jim said: 'I can't do that, Nick. Tell him we'll buy him a Corvette when he gets there, but he's got to leave right now.'"

That did it. Moments later, they were on the Autobahn, driving two hundred kilometres an hour toward Stuttgart. Their destination was an American consulate, where a startled consular official told them it might take two years to get Klima into the U.S.—a hitch they hadn't anticipated. They contacted Ilitch, who promised to use his high-level political connections to resolve the problem. Meantime, Polano, Lites and the interpreter had to keep moving Klima from city to city because the Czech secret police were on their trail.

Klima threw them another curve while they were on the run. He announced that he was going home unless they could get his girlfriend out. They had to bring in reinforcements—namely a shady Czech defector from Toronto who went into Czechoslovakia, toting enough money to pay people to look the other way. He smuggled the girl out by hiding her in a false compartment in the trunk of a rented car.

Meantime, Ilitch had gone right to the top of the U.S. government. He appealed to Edwin Meese, attorney general in Ronald Reagan's cabinet, and they got Klima cleared to enter the country as a refugee, but the girlfriend had to stay with the Czech interpreter and his family in Vancouver until Christmas before she was admitted.

BY THE MID-1980S, THE NHL was healthier overall than at any time since the start of the expansion era. The ownership group was stable. There were no franchises in crisis or on the brink of collapse. Attendance had risen slowly but steadily each year since the accommodation with the WHA. Paid admissions in 1985–86—regular-season and playoffs—totalled 12,773,503, up from 11,510,322 in 1979–80. Above all, the competition had improved. Fewer teams were drawing from a wider pool of talent that included Canada, the United States, Sweden, Finland and, occasionally, Czechoslovakia. Divisional rivalries intensified as the decade progressed, and upsets, triumphs and disappointments multiplied. Fans could, after a time, expect the unexpected.

Few would have predicted in the spring of 1981 that the youthful Oilers would rout the remnants of the last Canadiens dynasty in three straight games or that a middle-of-the-pack Minnesota North Stars team would advance to the Stanley Cup final against a mighty Islanders squad.

The following year, the Oilers were an emerging power, but they were undone by a bad case of adolescent arrogance and fell to the unheralded Los Angeles Kings. In the east, a rising Quebec Nordiques team, led by the Stastny brothers, knocked off the resurgent Canadiens, who had finished third overall.

And the well-coached, disciplined, defensive-minded Vancouver Canucks took advantage of Oiler misfortunes to advance to the final.

The upset of the decade occurred in the spring of 1986. The Oilers were again victims. By then they were two-time Stanley Cup champions and a sure bet, most thought, to repeat. They had finished first overall. Wayne Gretzky had accumulated an astonishing 215 points. Paul Coffey had scored 48 goals and collected 138 points, both records for a defenceman. The Oilers breezed by the Canucks in the opening round and advanced to the divisional final against the Calgary Flames.

These two teams were more bitter antagonists than simple rivals. The animosity between them was enhanced and sharpened by the underlying civic tug-of-war between Edmonton and Calgary that predated the birth of the province in 1905. The Flames had won just two of twenty-four games against the Oilers since relocating, but the past counted for nothing. "We're going into this for one reason," Calgary forward Doug Risebrough said, "and that's to win, at whatever the cost."

And the Flames did it, though it took seven games, and no one could have foreseen how it would end. The whole series turned on a dreadful gaffe with the score tied early in the third period of the final contest. The fall guy was an Oiler rookie, Steve Smith. The young defenceman picked up a loose puck in the corner, skated behind his own net, spotted a teammate breaking for the blue line on the opposite side of the ice and fired a pass, but the puck hit the blade of Grant Fuhr's skate and ricocheted into the net.

The Calgary lead held and the Oilers were ex-champions. Edmontonians mourned. Calgarians celebrated. They placed twenty-seven thousand calls to friends and family in the provincial capital immediately afterward and jammed the phone circuits for half an hour. Some ten thousand fans headed for the airport to greet the team and created a traffic jam three miles long. A downtown street party lasted till two-thirty in the morning.

Upsets are an aberration, a disruption of the order of things, but an integral part of sports. They add drama and surprise, exhilaration and dejection and, for the losers, a long, painful off-season followed by a new season and an opportunity for redemption. In 1986–87, the Oilers waltzed through the eighty-game schedule with enough razzle-dazzle to finish first overall. They vanquished one opponent after another in the playoffs, won their division and the conference and advanced to the final for the fourth time in five years. There, they almost lost to Mike Keenan's Philadelphia Flyers—a team with less talent, but abundant character.

Headlines captured the ebb and flow of the series. Game one came down to this: GRETZKY IGNITES OILER BIG GUNS. In game two, it was JARI KURRI BREAKS FLYERS' BACKS. And game three in Philadelphia: FLYERS NOT ABOUT TO FOLD, OILERS BLOW 3–0 LEAD. The Oilers won game four. The teams returned to Edmonton, and a careless utterance by a member of the home side led to "WE WANT TO END IT TONIGHT."

So did the fans. They packed the Northland Coliseum as usual. Several thousand filled the Edmonton Convention Centre to watch on big screens and to celebrate the anticipated championship. A member of city council had announced a victory parade, but the Flyers spoiled the party. That produced the following headline: AND NOW IT'S BACK TO PHILADELPHIA. Where FLYERS SHOCK OILERS AGAIN.

The Oilers finally subdued their spirited opponent in game seven. They won their third Stanley Cup in four years, but after the jubilation and the celebrations—the hooting and hollering and the champagne sprayed around the dressing room and the spontaneous street party that erupted on Edmonton's Jasper Avenue immediately following the final buzzer—questions lingered about the temperament of this team.

NHL champions are made of equal parts talent and character. The Oilers had laid to rest all questions about the former earlier in the decade. They finally ended all debate about the latter in 1987–88—a tough season for them. Paul Coffey held out for a new contract for two months before being shipped to Pittsburgh. Backup netminder Andy Moog sat out till March before being dealt to Boston. Gretzky suffered two injuries, played only sixty-four games and surrendered the scoring title to Pittsburgh's Mario Lemieux. The Oilers finished second in their division, six points behind Calgary, and third overall and then went on a rampage. They beat the Jets in five, the Flames in four, the Red Wings in five and the Bruins in four. After sixteen wins and two losses, they were champions for the fourth time in five years, and they were still young. Gretzky, who piled up forty-three points in those eighteen contests, was twenty-seven.

So was Messier. Kurri and Anderson were twenty-eight. Fuhr was twenty-five. The best of the supporting cast, including Esa Tikkanen, Marty McSorley and Craig Simpson, were younger. It all raised a question: How many more could these guys win?

Yet, at the very moment of their ascendance, something unthinkable loomed. An idea had taken hold in the mind of the owner, Peter Pocklington—a notion so audacious that he felt compelled to sound out others. John Ziegler was one of them. The two men sat side by side at a playoff game one evening that spring, and, as Ziegler recalls: "Peter told me about it a few months before he did it.

"He said, 'What would you think if I sold Wayne Gretzky?'

"I said, 'To whom?'

"He said, 'To Bruce McNall.'

"I said: 'Peter, I can't stop you. If I could, I would. But I can't stop you. I wish you wouldn't do it because you're going to disrupt the league. It's going to change the economics. But if you do, you better be out of Edmonton and out of province because you're going to be hanged.'"

POCKLINGTON DID IT, OF COURSE. The deal was announced August 9, 1988. After nine NHL seasons in Edmonton, after 696 games, 583 goals, 1,086 assists, seven scoring titles and eight Hart Trophies, Gretzky was no longer an Oiler. He was a Los Angeles King. It was called a trade—Gretzky, Marty McSorley and Mike Krushelnyski to Los Angeles in exchange for Jimmy Carson, Martin Gélinas, first-round picks in 1989, 1991 and 1993, and $15 million (US). The other players and the draft choices were accessories. At the heart of the transaction, McNall got Gretzky; Pocklington got a bundle of money.

Fans everywhere were shocked. In Edmonton, they were outraged. They were hurt. They felt betrayed. Pocklington escaped the noose, though he was burned in effigy outside Northlands Coliseum, but what did it matter to him?

This one-time car salesman from London, Ontario, had arrived in Alberta when rising oil prices had set the province's economy on fire. He had made a fortune and built an empire. He was quintessentially nouveau riche—loud, brash, extravagant, flamboyant, always ready to pose for photographers or regale reporters with tales of his exploits. He was big. He was grand. A pillar of some purported new Canadian establishment.

The truth was somewhat different. His fortune was modest. His empire (two car dealerships, a trust company, several meat-packing plants and some real estate) was flimsy and could not withstand the cataclysmic recession that hit Alberta in the early 1980s. Some of his companies wound up in receivership. Lawsuits piled up from unpaid creditors, including skilled tradesmen and small service companies, each owed a few thousand dollars. In the spring of 1988, he needed money, and he responded almost reflexively.

In Peter's world, sometimes you bought and sometimes you sold. In his teens, he had sold a family car while Mom and Dad were away on a vacation. He boasted of having taken a ring off his wife's finger to complete one transaction and thrown in a work by a member of the Group of Seven to finish another deal. With his empire in tatters, he was a seller, and he peddled the most valuable asset in his depleted portfolio: that artist on ice who wore number ninety-nine and scored goals at the same prodigious pace as Picasso had produced paintings.

Pocklington found an equally desperate buyer in Bruce McNall, the third owner of the Los Angeles Kings. The original holder of the franchise—the expatriate Canadian Jack Kent Cooke—had sold the Kings, the NBA Lakers and the Fabulous Forum to Dr. Jerry Buss in 1979 for $67.5 million, in part to pay for his record divorce settlement of $41 million and the associated legal costs.

Buss was a native of Wyoming who had earned a doctorate in chemistry at the University of Southern California, hence the honorific. He was in his mid-forties, had made his money in real estate and was a sports fan. Basketball was his game. He wanted the Lakers and all the profile and prestige that came with owning them—not to mention the access to Hollywood stars and beautiful young women.

For him, the Kings were an afterthought. They lost money every year—about $700,000 on average—and he wasn't convinced they could ever be a major attraction in such a competitive market. He was, therefore, happy to sell an interest in the team to McNall in 1986 and the balance the following year. McNall was a hockey fan and an avid one. He loved the Kings. He was a regular at their games, and he and Buss had done other business together before—in the coin trade, where Buss was an occasional buyer and McNall was a prominent dealer.

McNall had begun collecting as a child growing up in the Los Angeles suburb of Arcadia and had never really stopped. It was an obscure and unusual business and an unlikely way to amass wealth, but McNall was clever, charming and convincing. He dealt in Greek, Roman and other ancient coins and sold his clients on the mystique, the cachet and the inherent value of these rare and precious objects. McNall's charm and powers of persuasion were equally effective with normally conservative bankers, and they financed many of his other business ventures, which included high-end sports memorabilia, racehorses and a movie production company.

McNall quickly realized, as Buss had, that the Kings were a tough sell in Los Angeles. They were always buried near the bottom of the depth chart in a cluttered market—behind the Lakers, the baseball Dodgers, the football Rams, the University of Southern California Trojans (in various sports) and probably half a dozen other pro, college and amateur teams. And this was in a megalopolis where sport competed with almighty Hollywood for attention.

Gretzky's arrival changed that. The—so-called—trade was announced first in Edmonton at a glum, terse, tearful press conference before a large, shaken media crowd. Immediately afterward, Gretzky and McNall boarded a private jet and flew south. They drove to a Sheraton hotel near Los Angeles International Airport. Gretzky tugged on a Kings sweater—not the gaudy purple and gold of seasons past, but the team's cool new black, silver and white—with his name and number stitched on the back. He stepped from behind a curtain and onto a stage and faced a crowd of men and women with cameras, microphones, tape recorders and notebooks, a crowd so large that even he was startled. Hockey was news in Los Angeles in the heat of the summer.

The next day, people lined up outside the Forum to buy tickets. Others called to place orders and kept the box-office phones ringing. The building was sold out on opening night—and most other nights during the 1988–89 season—and there were lots of celebrities in the seats. "It's hockey night in California," wrote Mike Downey of the *Los Angeles Times* in a column that captured the whole bewildering turn of events.

"Forget that stuff about the National Hockey League already having been in Los Angeles for more than 20 years. Hockey has never been here. Hockey has no more been here than the Ice Capades have been here. All hockey ever did was visit the Forum every year, same as the rodeo. Hockey was a ticket you bought to kill an evening every couple of years. Hockey was something your daughter played in school, with a stick.

"Not now, though. Now that The New Guy is here, ice hockey is hot. Ice hockey is cool. Ice hockey is hip. Hockey is right up there with October baseball. Hockey is right there on Page 1, with the other big guys. It's no longer stuck in the back with the mud-wrestling ads. We don't even care who the Kings are playing. We will pay attention even if they are playing . . . oh, heck, Winnipeg, even.

"All because of The New Guy. The Gretz. King of Kings. Lord of posts."

IN A SINGLE BOLD AND DARING TRANSACTION, the newcomer McNall had elevated hockey to unprecedented prominence in southern California. With a few strokes of the pen, he changed the economics of the game. Gretzky was making around $1 million a year in Edmonton. He would have been content if McNall had doubled his salary, but the image-conscious owner signed him for $3 million to put him on par with Earvin (Magic) Johnson, the Lakers star and the city's highest-paid athlete.

"Mario Lemieux had just renegotiated his contract to get up next to Gretzky," recalls John Ziegler. "Gretzky's salary goes way up and Lemieux's agent is knocking on the door saying, 'Hey, we agreed Mario would be just a little behind Gretzky. There's a big gap there now.' And they had to close it. As soon as Lemieux got what he wanted, Ray Bourque wanted to renegotiate. It went from player to player to player. The sale of Gretzky was almost as inflationary as the WHA. But in this case, we did it to ourselves."

McNall's financial adventurism coincided with two other significant developments. First, the NHL had recovered from the various WHA-inflicted miseries of the 1970s. In a speech to the Empire Club in Toronto in April 1989, Ziegler summarized the changes that had occurred since he had spoken to the same crowd in the spring of 1978.

"Eleven years ago," he said, ". . . the National Hockey League had accumulated a loss of $100 million. Today we have accumulated a $60 million profit over the last three years."

And warming to his theme, he said: "Eleven years ago, we had sold seventy-two per cent of all available seats. This year, for the season, we will have sold eighty-seven per cent of all those seats. . . . For the last five years in the playoffs, we have been running at ninety-six per cent of capacity.

"This year, thirteen million people in North America will have watched NHL games. . . . Eleven years ago, it was nine million. The players' average salary eleven years ago was $92,000 per year. This year it's over $200,000."

The changes in the league's fortunes aroused the ambitions of the owners. At their 1989 semi-annual meeting, held in early December at the Breakers Hotel in Palm Beach, Florida, they voted overwhelmingly in favour of expanding for the sixth time since 1967. They agreed to add up to three clubs by the start of the 1992–93 season and to become a thirty-team league by the year 2000. Finally, they set the fee for the first three new franchises at $50 million (us).

Many observers deemed that a staggering sum, given that the NHL had never charged more than $6 million for a new franchise and the NBA had sold four recently awarded franchises for $32 million apiece. Gil Stein, who was the league's general counsel at the time, later wrote: "No one talked about how an expansion franchise could earn enough to justify paying a huge fee. . . . No, they never talked about *how*, only *how much* . . . and all of it would have to be in U.S. dollars, no notes."

Ziegler contends that the price was based on a completely new model of arena design and construction. The template for the future was a building called the Palace of Auburn Hills, the suburban home of the NBA's Detroit Pistons. It opened in 1988, it had a seating capacity of 22,076 and it included 180 luxury suites in three tiers, the lowest being a mere fourteen rows from the playing surface.

"It revolutionized the arena business," says Ziegler. "It made the existing buildings obsolete. The long-term commitments you got from the sale of suites could be taken to the bank and used as collateral. If they were done correctly, they could finance the construction of the building."

The league wanted to add a second team on the west coast of the U.S. and asked Howard Baldwin to scout out the market. Baldwin was previously a part owner of the Hartford Whalers. He was interested in acquiring a franchise, and he had a wealthy partner in Morris Belzberg, a former Calgarian who was chairman and chief executive officer of Budget Rent-a-Car. They found San Jose, a rapidly expanding urban centre some fifty miles south of San Francisco, located in what was coming to be known as Silicon Valley.

"A young lawyer there read in the paper that I was looking at West Coast cities and invited me to San Jose," recalls Baldwin. "The moment I went there and met the mayor, I knew it was a great place for the NHL. The city had a plan for a building. You had the computer industry. You had a younger, educated workforce with high incomes. It was like Hartford or Calgary. You were the only show in town."

But after doing all the legwork, Baldwin and Belzberg were pushed aside by George and Gordon Gund in one of the most complex and unusual expansion transactions in league history. The Gund brothers had spent an increasingly frustrating decade as owners of the Minnesota North Stars. Things had started off well enough. The North Stars had advanced to the Stanley Cup final in 1981. However, between 1985–86 and 1988–89, they had missed the playoffs twice and been eliminated in the first round twice. The Gunds had lost millions of dollars. They had become embroiled in a dispute with civic authorities over improvements to the Metropolitan Sports Center in Bloomington, where the North Stars played. By 1989, they were fed up and wanted out.

They asked the league for permission to move the Stars to the San Francisco area for the 1990–91 season. That was too close to San Jose, and the board turned them down. The Gunds began making noises about an antitrust suit, and suddenly the league's well-laid expansion plans were in danger of becoming bogged down in a potentially nasty dispute. Then, a compromise emerged. Baldwin and Belzberg agreed to pay the $50 million franchise fee for San Jose and transfer the franchise to the Gunds for $19 million and the North Stars. The net result was that Baldwin and Belzberg got the Minnesota franchise for $31 million, the Gunds got out for $19 million and the league got its asking price for an expansion franchise.

The transaction was completed in early May 1990, and later that month the league began receiving inquiries from other parties interested in acquiring franchises. By early June, applications had been mailed to fifty different individuals or groups of investors across North America.

By the mid-August deadline, eleven applications had been submitted to the league offices, complete with $100,000 deposits. They arrived from Ottawa and

Hamilton in Ontario; Miami, Tampa and St. Petersburg in Florida; Houston, Texas; Anaheim and San Diego in California; and Seattle, Washington. Members of the franchise and market analysis committee visited each city that fall, met the applicants and toured the sites of their proposed arenas. Ziegler scheduled a full board meeting for December 4 to 8, 1990, at the Breakers in Palm Beach to interview the principals and award two new franchises.

The interviews were scheduled for December 5. Each applicant was granted forty-five minutes to make their pitch. According to Stein, they sat at a table at the front of a meeting room and faced the governors, Ziegler and a few senior leagues executives who were seated at small tables placed on three raised circular tiers. The setting was impressive, the presentations less so. One applicant after another flopped.

In some cases, their arena plans failed to meet league standards. Or they weren't certain they could be ready to start the 1992–93 season. Or they wanted to negotiate the franchise fee, or the terms of payment, or make a portion of the fee contingent upon future profits. Ron Joyce, president of the Tim Hortons donut chain and the money behind Hamilton's bid, presented a convincing case, and then killed the city's chances by proposing to pay half the fee by the fall of 1992 and the balance in five annual installments of $5 million.

At the end of the day, only two applicants were prepared to meet the league's terms: Phil Esposito's Tampa Bay group and Bruce Firestone's Ottawa delegation. There were serious doubts about both. Esposito was merely the promoter. Japanese investors were putting up the money—an unusual arrangement, to say the least. As for Ottawa, most of the skepticism originated north of the border.

"The Canadian teams were really anti-Ottawa," says Ziegler. "They all argued that Ottawa was a government town. They wouldn't support hockey. People really questioned Firestone. I had so many people call me privately before the meeting and say we were being fooled. It's never going to go. I liked Firestone. He was sincere. He wanted to do this project and I believed he could."

In the end, money talked. Ottawa and Tampa were in. At 1:30 p.m. on December 6, a Thursday, Ziegler walked into a ballroom at the Breakers flanked by Esposito and Firestone. A crowd of more than one hundred Ottawa residents, who had come south to support the city's bid, immediately erupted in joyous pandemonium. And the next day's *Ottawa Citizen* expressed the entire community's reaction in a large, bold, page-one headline:

JUBILATION! NHL RETURNS TO OTTAWA AFTER 57-YEAR ABSENCE

The reaction in Tampa and the neighbouring city of St. Petersburg was more modest, but it was still big news. THE PUCK STOPS HERE! proclaimed a banner headline on the front page of the *St. Petersburg Times*, and the paper went on to tell its readers that hockey was coming to "the land of heat, humidity, panthers and flamingos."

On the evening of December 8 and the morning of December 9, the owners and their delegations left the Breakers to catch their flights home—to Washington and Quebec City, to Los Angeles and Vancouver, and to nearly a dozen and a half cities in between. They could fly home contented. The league would collect $100 million in franchise fees, enriching each of its existing clubs by nearly $5 million when the big haul was split up.

Ziegler and his team of league officials flew back to New York, and they, too, were contented. The expansion project had been a gamble—as these things always were—but they had got the job done. And everyone—the owners and their management teams, Ziegler and his—could look forward to opening nights in two new cities in the fall of 1992.

Most of them would be around, but not Ziegler. No one knew it at the moment, of course, but the December 1990 meeting at the Breakers would be his last triumph as NHL president.

The league's long-docile players were in revolt against Alan Eagleson, their leader and representative for over two decades, and against an established economic order that, they believed, enriched the owners at their expense.

Ziegler was destined to become a casualty of the uprising.

13

THE SINS OF ALAN EAGLESON

THE BITTEREST FEUD IN NHL HISTORY occurred not on the ice or in the dressing room, but away from the rink altogether, and it pitted player against agent. The player was Bobby Orr. The agent was Alan Eagleson. The epic spat between these two titanic characters was prolonged and rancorous. It began with one man—the player—down and out, broken in body and spirit, while the other was enjoying his moment as a high and mighty personage.

The feud ended in a stark and stunning reversal of fortune—the agent ruined and vilified, the player elevated and sanctified. The player retreated from the battlefield under a halo, his fortunes restored, his spirit mended, his legend enhanced. The agent left a pariah, shunned and scorned by most in the hockey world, indicted, convicted and jailed, ousted from the Hockey Hall of Fame, stripped of the Order of Canada and booted from the National Hockey League Players' Association, which he had founded in 1967 and ruled for twenty-four years.

The relationship between the two began when Orr was a fifteen-year-old prodigy on the cusp of becoming a sensational professional unlike any the game had ever seen. Eagleson was thirty, an obscure backbencher in the Ontario legislature and a lean, tough, profane Toronto lawyer, by nature ultra-competitive and extraordinarily ambitious.

Eagleson negotiated Orr's landmark rookie contract with the Boston Bruins in 1966 and got Orr far more money than he could have got on his own. He negotiated the subsequent, ever-richer contracts that made the great defenceman wealthy at a very early age. He managed Orr's money, investments and business interests. And he benefited greatly from the relationship. Orr catapulted Eagleson to the forefront of the hockey business. With the young star as his client, Eagleson quickly became the sport's biggest and most prominent agent. With Orr behind him, Eagleson had the credibility and access he needed to form the players' association.

Orr and Eagleson had been more than mere business associates. They had been the closest of friends, almost brothers. They had risen together—the one to superstardom, the other to fame and power—and they had stuck together through Orr's slow, grim, painful decline due to a wonky, oft-injured left knee that the best surgeons could not completely repair. The end that nobody wanted to see began in the fall of 1975. Orr was in the final year of a lucrative contract with the Bruins. He was recovering from a fifth surgery. He played a mere ten games and could go no further. In the spring of 1976 he endured yet another operation and wrestled with all the existential anguish that comes with being a genius undone.

Eagleson, meanwhile, was attempting to negotiate a new contract with a new Bruins owner, Jeremy Jacobs, and it was not a straightforward or easy negotiation. Orr was the player who had, almost singlehandedly, resurrected a moribund franchise, led his teammates to two Stanley Cup championships and become one of Boston's most beloved athletes. It was equally clear that he could never be the player he once was, and in the worst-case scenario, he might be finished. However, Jacobs had given the league's board of governors assurances when he acquired the Bruins that he would re-sign Orr. In fact, Bill Wirtz, then the chairman, had made that a condition of approving Jacobs as an owner.

Eagleson slowly let it be known that the talks with Bruins management were not going well, and then reported they didn't want Orr. A hurt and dejected Orr became a free agent on June 1, 1976, and later that month reluctantly signed a five-year, $3 million contract with the Chicago Black Hawks. Many years down the road, this startling turn of events would become a central point of contention between the two men and would enflame their feud.

Meantime, Orr spent the summer of 1976 recuperating from his latest surgery. He played brilliantly for Team Canada in that fall's international Canada Cup tournament. He started the season for the Hawks, but had to quit after twenty games. He sat out the following season (1977–78) altogether, came back once more in the fall of 1978 and was finished for good after six games.

The rupture between player and agent occurred one evening in late August 1979, when Orr phoned Eagleson and informed him that he was severing their relationship. By April 1980, they had wound up their business affairs and Orr discovered the devastating truth about his financial position: his assets totalled $456,000, but he had tax, legal and accounting bills of $459,000. He was broke, and he blamed Eagleson, but what could he do?

His old friend and confidant was wealthy and powerful. He represented about 150 players, including many of the biggest names in the game. He was the unassailable executive director of the NHLPA. He was the promoter of the Canada Cup and other international competitions involving NHL players. And he was on cordial terms with John Ziegler and many of the league's most influential owners.

But slowly the ground shifted. Players challenged Eagleson. Journalists asked questions. Agents cried foul. A dogged reporter for a suburban Boston newspaper pried deeply and uncovered enough questionable conduct and possible wrongdoing to attract the attention of the FBI. The U.S. Attorney's Office in Boston got involved, and America's mighty, relentless and unforgiving criminal justice system began to move in on the man many regarded as the most powerful figure in hockey.

Orr intervened publicly only once, but to great effect, in August 1990, when he granted an interview to a journalist with the *Toronto Star* and made a sensational—though questionable—allegation about Eagleson's handling of the 1976 negotiations with the Bruins. And he was present along with some twenty other retired players for the denouement. It occurred on January 6, 1998, in a Boston courtroom. Eagleson entered, set to plead guilty to three counts of fraud, and Orr muttered to the person seated next to him, "There's the son of a bitch now."

MIKE MILBURY WAS THE FIRST PLAYER to openly challenge Alan Eagleson's one-man rule of the NHLPA. Milbury's initial act of brazen defiance occurred at an association meeting in the Bahamas in June 1979—while, purely by coincidence, a brooding, spiritually wounded Bobby Orr was contemplating his break with Eagleson. Milbury was twenty-seven, a university-educated defenceman from Brighton, Massachusetts, and the Bruins' player representative, and he wasn't afraid to ask questions or assert his position.

Others had raised pointed questions at NHLPA meetings, and Eagleson had usually responded like a quintessential street fighter. He told the players to sit down, shut up and not to be stupid. And since most team reps were Canadian—ferocious on the ice, but polite and deferential when they were out of uniform—they did what they were told. But deference was not part of Milbury's genetic code. He was upset that Eagleson had failed to push for more liberal free-agency provisions as a condition for approving the NHL-WHA merger. He pressed his point, provoked Eagleson, and a shouting match occurred. When the clamour subsided, Eagleson called for a vote on the merger, and every hand went up except Milbury's. That was the start of the Milbury revolt.

That fall, he collected $700 from his Boston teammates and hired Price Waterhouse to conduct a leaguewide survey of players. They drafted a resolution in two parts, which proposed that: (a) an independent committee be used to aid in the selection of a new executive director and (b) that a new executive director be hired on a full-time basis. Price Waterhouse distributed the resolution and asked for yes-or-no responses.

This was the first direct challenge Eagleson had faced in his thirteen years as head of the NHLPA, and as the *Hockey News* reported, "A large pro-Eagleson contingent comprised in part of clients handled privately by the attorney in his role as individual player representative is expected to support the status quo."

Price Waterhouse received responses from 154 players, about one-third of those eligible, and 101 favoured a new full-time director. Milbury presented the results at an NHLPA meeting held during the annual all-star break in early February 1980. Eagleson, surprisingly, agreed to set up a committee to find a successor. It comprised four players, a judge from Toronto, a law professor from Harvard and Eagleson. The committee met only once. The uprising fizzled and the status quo prevailed, just as the *Hockey News* had predicted.

MILBURY'S REVOLT WOULD PROVE to be the start of Eagleson's troubles, and most of his problems would originate south of the border among players, journalists and agents who were less enthralled than their Canadian counterparts with the man known as the Eagle. In early 1984, two journalists working for *Sports Illustrated*, John Papanek and Bill Brubaker, began investigating Eagleson's business practices, and they published a long, unflattering profile in the edition of July 2.

Eagleson was unlike anyone else in North American professional team sports. He was, at once, labour leader, player agent, wealthy lawyer, backroom political operative and promoter of international hockey tournaments. The writers concluded that conflicts of interest were inevitable, that Eagleson used his influence to extract benefits for himself and his business associates, who were usually close friends, and that he was indifferent, if not downright dismissive, toward those who questioned him.

They quoted Robert Bradshaw, a Toronto insurance broker whose firm had handled NHLPA medical, dental and disability policies until December 1979. The business was lucrative, but came with strings attached, according to Bradshaw. "As time went on, his demands became unbusinesslike," he told the *Sports Illustrated* writers. "We kept a car and driver in Toronto. He'd phone up and tell us when he was using them. Then he would advise me when he was staying in my flat in New York and when his wife was."

Former players complained that Eagleson refused to help them collect disability insurance when their careers ended. Murray Wilson, who started with the Canadiens and finished with the Kings, claimed he had to spend $70,000 pursuing the Kings for $210,000 owed and an insurance company for $83,000 due to him under his NHLPA policy. "In his team meetings with players, Eagleson would always say, 'Don't worry about anything. The players' association will take care of it,'" Wilson said. "Alan didn't help me a bit. He never gave me a reason other than that I was a client of [New York agent] Art Kaminsky. He said, 'Let Kaminsky handle it. I've got no goddam use for Art Kaminsky.'"

Glen Sharpley played six seasons with the North Stars and Black Hawks before suffering a career-ending eye injury. An Eagleson client, he related how he had paid $60,000 in agent and management fees and then had to cough up another $14,250 to collect $325,000 in disability insurance. "Mr. Eagleson told me that he wouldn't handle this if I didn't sign," Sharpley said, and by that he meant a contract guaranteeing Eagleson a share of his claim.

Sports Illustrated also raised questions about Eagleson's handling of international tournaments on behalf of Hockey Canada and what happened to all the money. He always boasted that the profits went to the players' pension fund, but nobody outside of Eagleson himself seemed to know how much actually went there. As Wayne Gretzky told the magazine, "A lot of players don't have a clue what's going on."

Eagleson maintained he charged Hockey Canada for his expenses, but did not collect a salary or fees. However, *Sports Illustrated* pointed out that he put his employees to work on the tournaments, charged exorbitant rates for their services and then paid them their regular salaries. As he explained it: "The guy works for me and if I can put him to work and make a million dollars, it's my million, not his. If I pay my guy thirty and rent him out for fifty, that makes me smart."

There was one other startling allegation, and it came from an unnamed general manager who was quoted as saying, "He delivers the players and we give him international hockey." In other words, Eagleson had made a sort of deal with the devil. He would keep the players and their demands—for things such as free agency—under control and the league gave him a free hand to run the international tournaments.

The *Sports Illustrated* piece provided readers with their first extensive look at how things worked inside the Eagleson empire and how he seemed to collect coming and going on every transaction, often at the expense of the players he represented in one way or another. But the writers were under no illusions about the impact of their work. They concluded, "Most of the people in and around hockey agree that until proven otherwise, Eagleson, skilled politician that he is, is all but invulnerable."

ONE OF ALAN EAGLESON'S LAST triumphal moments as executive director of the NHLPA and all-purpose, almighty hockey czar occurred late in the evening on July 24, 1986. He and a contingent of player reps had spent the better part of four days cooped up in a meeting room at a downtown Toronto hotel, seated across a table from John Ziegler and a delegation of owners. After a final thirteen-and-a-half-hour negotiating session, the sides emerged to announce that they had reached a new, five-year collective bargaining agreement, and much of the credit for the successful outcome went to Eagleson.

The players had begun by demanding total free agency at age twenty-six, and they had threatened to strike on September 15, the day the agreement expired, if they didn't get what they wanted. The owners were steadfastly opposed, but John Ziegler and Ken Sawyer, the league's chief financial officer, had come up with a compromise designed to satisfy both sides. It was called the senior player benefit. Those who had appeared in four hundred games or more would be entitled to a lump-sum payment of $250,000 at age fifty-five.

Sawyer had calculated that the league would need to create an investment fund of about $12 million to finance the benefit, and as it happened, the league had a pool of capital available. It had come from the players' pension fund. According to Ziegler, Sawyer had done an analysis of owner contributions to the plan over a period of years and determined that Manufacturers Life Insurance, which managed the fund, had overcharged the owners. The excess contributions amounted to almost $26 million.

It was not entirely clear, however, who the money belonged to: the owners or the retired players. The league consulted its outside pension expert, Marcus Grayck, a lawyer with Baker & McKenzie, a large, multinational, Chicago-based firm. "We determined that some of it was rightfully the players' and a major portion was the owners'," recalls Ziegler. "We had a legal opinion that said we were entitled—carte blanche—to the surplus that arose from contributions by the owners. I'd never seen a legal opinion use that term 'carte blanche,' meaning without restrictions or limitations."

Ziegler then sounded out Bill Wirtz on the notion of using some of the surplus to fund the senior player benefit, and Wirtz's approval was essential. He was the owner of the Chicago Blackhawks, he was chairman of the board and he was widely respected and enormously influential. Ziegler also floated the idea with Eagleson in advance of the negotiation. "He was intrigued because this would go to the journeymen who had made a contribution, but were never going to make a million dollars," says Ziegler. "Everybody was going to get the same amount."

But all the advance work could not prevent some fireworks at the bargaining table. Eagleson attempted to lay claim to the entire $26 million. "Wirtz got incensed," says Ziegler. "He said: 'That's not the players' money. That's money we paid in and we overpaid. It's a refund.' This went on for a couple of days."

At one point, Wirtz walked out in a huff and Ziegler immediately adjourned the session. "I went upstairs to his room and he had his bags packed," Ziegler says. "He was headed back to Chicago. I had Eddie Snider with me and we each cut him off at the door. I said, 'Somebody go get Al.'

"I said: 'Bill, you're chairman of the board. You can't do this.'

"And he said: 'I'm not going back in there if Alan keeps insisting it's his money. It's not.'"

Ziegler managed to lower the temperature, restore reason and get everyone back to the table. The owners stuck to their original position of funding the senior player benefit to the tune of nearly $12 million, but Eagleson wrangled concessions on free agency. Under the old regime, the team that lost a free agent was entitled to compensation in the form of a player of equal value or players and draft choices. The price was so steep that few general managers risked signing high-profile talent. For all intents and purposes, free agency in the NHL existed in theory only.

Under the 1986 CBA, active players would no longer be part of any compensation package, and at every salary level the compensation requirements were lowered. For instance, a team that signed a free agent at a salary of $135,000 to $160,000 per season would forfeit a second- and a third-round pick. Previously, signing a free agent in the $125,000-to-$149,000 range would cost a team a first-round pick and/or a player.

At the higher end of the salary scale, the price for signing a player paid $210,000 to $260,000 would be a first- and a second-round pick. Previously, the price for any player over $200,000 was two first-rounders and/or a first-rounder and a player. The owners made other significant concessions. A team about to lose a free agent would be allowed to match the offer from a competing team. This would allow a free agent to test the market, determine his value and capitalize on it.

The reaction to the agreement in the days and weeks that followed was overwhelmingly positive. "The old Eagle did a reasonably good job this time," declared player agent Bill Watters, a former employee who had left to form his own agency. Philadelphia-based hockey writer Jay Greenberg added: "There's only so much money in hockey's pot, and the players got a fair increase in the amount to which they are entitled. The owners realized they had to give something and they did." Longtime Toronto-based writer Al Strachan added, "It's a collective bargaining agreement that seems to exemplify the best kind of compromise—one that is good for the sport and one that accommodates both sides."

The players gave their blessing through a mail-in vote. Eagleson sent out 480 ballots. Over 300 were returned and there were only 4 dissenting voices. Despite that resounding endorsement, *Hockey News* editor Bob McKenzie added words of caution: "It may take the cold and snowy days of this coming winter before the hockey community fully digests the details and ramifications of the collective bargaining agreement."

In fact, perceptions among the players would shift with the passage of time, and for a variety of reasons, the July 1986 negotiations would become one of the turning points in the deteriorating relationship between Eagleson and the membership of the NHLPA.

THE UPRISING THAT EVENTUALLY UNSEATED Alan Eagleson began through a chance meeting of two young agents at Pepperdine University in Malibu, California, far from the centre of the hockey world. The agents were Ron Salcer of Los Angeles and Ritch Winter of Edmonton, and they had come to Pepperdine to attend a seminar on protecting the athlete from the unscrupulous agent. This was in the mid-1980s. Salcer had been in the business for about five years. He had come to know the landscape of pro hockey and the NHL, and he had formed a very unfavourable opinion of Eagleson.

"My first client was Dave Taylor of the Kings," Salcer says. "I was in my mid-twenties and enthusiastic and I wanted to do a great job for Dave, but I couldn't get much information about the CBA or what we could and couldn't do. When I phoned the players' association, they'd always say, 'Alan's tied up. He'll get back to you.' But I wouldn't hear from him for months."

In his early days as an agent, Salcer decided to attend the annual June meeting of player reps, which that year was held in Las Vegas. He sat in on a session until his presence was noticed. "Sam Simpson, who was Alan's right-hand man, walked over to me and said, 'Who are you?'

"And I said: 'I'm Ron Salcer. One of the agents. I'm representing Dave Taylor. I want to know what's happening here because his contract is very important to me.'

"He says, 'Okay.' He walks away. Then he comes back, maybe half an hour later, and he says, 'You've got to leave.'

"I said: 'What do you mean? Why would I have to leave?'

"He said, 'Because you're an agent and no agents are allowed here.'

"I pointed to Eagleson, who was standing at the podium, and said: 'How about that guy over there? Isn't he an agent?'

"He said, 'That's different.'"

Winter followed a slightly different path, but reached the same conclusion about Eagleson. "He was operating this thing as his own private fiefdom," says Winter. "I talked to Ian Turnbull and a whole pile of other players and I heard story after story about this guy Alan Eagleson who wasn't taking care of any of their issues and seemed to be dipping into the NHLPA coffers for his own benefit. It was unbelievable."

But where to turn? And what to do? Eagleson's influence in the hockey world was pervasive. He could quickly and easily discredit newcomers like Salcer and Winter. So they went outside. In the summer of 1988, they contacted Ed Garvey, a labour lawyer from Madison, Wisconsin, and a former executive director of the National Football League Players' Association. "We needed someone who understood player rights, the inner workings of a union and what a union actually does," recalls Salcer. "Garvey knew what the obligations were and he started looking under the stones."

Garvey investigated while Salcer and Winter talked to the players and enlisted their support. Salcer met with a number of teams when they came through Los Angeles, and he travelled to several NHL cities and held player meetings. Eagleson learned of their efforts and attempted to cast doubt. Management was wary of them in some places as well. "In Boston, the word was out that I was trying to stir things up," says Salcer. "Harry Sinden found out I was at the Garden and wanted to have the police arrest me for trespassing."

Instead, Sinden sent coach Terry O'Reilly, a former player and a very intimidating one, to escort him from the building. "I'm sitting in the dressing room, addressing the entire team, and out of the corner of my eye I see

O'Reilly walking toward me and he says, 'Harry told me to throw you out of here, but I didn't see you.' That was a real affirmation that we were doing the right thing."

The two agents asked the players for cheques of $100 each as a demonstration of their support and to pay Garvey a retainer. A total of 225 contributed. Meantime, Garvey compiled a fifty-three-page report on the Eagleson regime. It was a scorching critique, loaded with sensational allegations.

He described the NHLPA as the least democratic labour organization in pro sport. He maintained that, among other things, Eagleson had denied the players basic financial information about the operation of the association, had failed to gain any significant benefits through collective bargaining in the 1980s and refused to advise or assist other agents who were negotiating contracts. In short, Garvey concluded, "What we found can only be described as a scandal."

That was just the start. Garvey accused Eagleson of shocking conflicts of interest due to his multiple roles as labour leader, player agent and promoter of international tournaments. He had allegedly never prepared properly for collective bargaining, nor had he advised the players of their goals and objectives. He was incapable of driving a hard bargain with the league, Garvey charged, because he was close friends with John Ziegler and Bill Wirtz.

Garvey went so far as to suggest that CBA negotiations were a charade and that Eagleson, Ziegler and Wirtz actually agreed upon the terms before they ever got to the bargaining table. Furthermore, Garvey accused Eagleson of costing his members millions of dollars in potential salary gains when he urged them to approve the 1979 merger with the WHA rather than holding out for improved free-agency provisions.

His report also contained a startling revelation about the 1986 CBA negotiations. Garvey told the players that, shortly before the talks were to begin, Eagleson had announced to a roomful of stunned player reps that he wanted a new six-year, guaranteed contract, with salary paid in U.S. dollars, and a $50,000 pension for life, also paid in U.S. dollars, or he was resigning. And he allegedly gave them five minutes to make a decision. "His actions were confrontational, but effective," Garvey wrote. "His demands were outrageous, but he got what he wanted. He is a different person when he negotiates for you against his friends Wirtz and Ziegler. Our tiger becomes a pussycat. No research, no preparations, no surprise attacks, no strike threats, no goals."

GARVEY COMPLETED HIS INFLAMMATORY SCREED just in time for the June 1989 annual meeting of the NHLPA, which was being held in Palm Beach, Florida, and a contingent of some seventy angry players turned up at the gathering, spoiling for a fight and determined to sack Eagleson.

The NHLPA delegation—Eagleson, his assistants, the twenty-one elected team reps and the appointed members of the executive council—stayed at the Breakers, an early-twentieth-century oceanside resort of world-class opulence, and frequently the venue for the semi-annual winter meetings of the owners. Ed Garvey, Ron Salcer, Ritch Winter and the dissident players had booked rooms in a more modest beachfront property a few miles away that was managed by former NHL netminder Denis Herron. "A union that holds its meeting at the Breakers," sniffed Garvey. "That tells you something."

The first confrontation occurred early Saturday morning just as the opening session began. Los Angeles Kings defenceman Marty McSorley demanded that Garvey and the agents be allowed to speak. As Salcer recalls: "Alan said: 'Fine. We'll put you on the agenda for the last day. After we've played golf.'

"Marty said: 'No, no. We want to hear what they've got to say right now.'

"Al said, 'No, I'm sorry.'

"Marty said, 'Why don't we put it to a vote?'

"We went to a vote and the players said, 'We want to hear them now.'"

That was the start of a thirteen-hour dustup, and an excruciating one even for a combative and truculent personality like Eagleson. He and Garvey addressed the gathering and engaged in some sharp tit-for-tat sparring. Garvey insisted that NHL gross revenues had to be at least $400 million; Eagleson said $350 million. Garvey put the players' share of revenue at twenty-four per cent; Eagleson at forty-five. Garvey estimated that player payrolls totalled about $84 million; Eagleson said it was $130 million.

Garvey finished with a jab: "Since the union doesn't have a research department, Alan doesn't have a clue as to what gross revenues are. Since the union doesn't have copies of player contracts, it really has no idea of the money spent on wages. It's almost like a time warp, like someone has come across a players' association that's still in the 1950s."

The players grilled both men, and that produced startling revelations of questionable conduct. The players learned that Eagleson had loaned more than $2 million in NHLPA funds to friends and associates, including his law partner Howard Ungerman, and that he had charged the association transaction fees on some of the loans. They learned that the association was paying Eagleson rent for the use of a portion of his Maitland Street headquarters in downtown Toronto, even though he owned the building. They heard that he had charged the association $463,839 over a two-year period for expenses related to meetings and $43,269 for car rentals and leases.

The fractious weekend meeting culminated with a vote on Eagleson's leadership. He survived, but it was a tenuous victory. The twenty-one elected player reps voted twelve-nine to remove him. He survived on the strength of support from the president and six vice-presidents, all of whom he had appointed. However, his opponents imposed terms that redefined his position.

Eagleson was instructed to cease representing individual players; to devote himself full time to the association; to hire a labour lawyer as an assistant and potential successor; to allow an audit of his tax returns for the previous three years and in future years; and to disclose fully all financial statements. Finally, the players scheduled a second meeting for later that summer to deal with unfinished business. They intended to form a search committee to hire the assistant and to draft a new constitution that would, among other things, abolish the seven unelected executive positions.

It was all a humbling experience, but Eagleson declared that he was ready to make peace and get on with the job. "I told the players I don't have an ounce of malice toward anyone," he said in an interview after the meeting, "and when something is over, it's over. I've had a lot of scraps in my life, and that's been the philosophy."

Eagleson's fight for survival wasn't over, though. It was really only beginning.

BOBBY ORR ADMINISTERED THE NEXT BLOW. He had remained silent for a decade about his split with Alan Eagleson. He had played no discernible role in the Mike Milbury–led uprising, the *Sports Illustrated* investigation or the attempted coup at the Breakers. But he had grievances against his former agent, friend and mentor. He had regrets about the role he had played in Eagleson's rise to prominence and, equally, the blind, childlike faith he had placed in him.

Orr broke his silence in early August 1990. He was vacationing at a cottage near the Quebec-Ontario border with wife Peggy and their two teenaged sons. He was still on the mend from his thirteenth knee operation, and he granted a long interview to Ellie Tesher of the *Toronto Star*. Her stories ran in the Sunday edition of August 5 under a bold, all-caps, front-page headline that read:

BOBBY ORR
SPEAKS OUT
AT LAST

Orr confirmed that he was broke when he retired at thirty and that this had come as a profound shock. He had, after all, made a lot of money as a very young man and was assured he would never have any financial concerns. "Al promised me that, with my income, I'd be a millionaire by the time I was thirty," he told Tesher. "He had total control. He said we were brothers. And I trusted him like a brother."

Even all those years after the implosive end to his brilliant career, he seemed uncertain where the money had gone. As he explained it: "Al was looking after everything and I believed him. When he said we were investing in something, I just said 'great.' I didn't check anything. I just signed the papers and that's my fault."

He began his post-hockey life with one modest source of income: a contract to make public appearances on behalf of the food company Standard Brands, the last deal Eagleson had negotiated for him. By the end of the 1980s, promotional work for major brands such as General Motors and sound investments had made him wealthy. He told Tesher that he was making $1 million a year, owned a $1 million home in Weston, Massachusetts, and a three-bedroom townhouse at a golf and residential complex in Florida, and his boys attended private schools.

But his name remained his most valuable asset, and recent newspaper articles had impugned the Orr brand. Eagleson had accused him of reneging on a

$90,000 contribution to York University's sports injury clinic that was to bear Orr's name. Orr maintained that Eagleson had pledged the money in November 1978 without his knowledge and at a time when his career was ending and he was broke. Orr charged that he had first heard about it when a sportswriter called to congratulate him on his generosity.

The former Bruins great made one other sensational allegation, one that would do lasting damage to Eagleson's reputation. As Tesher put it: "Orr recently learned from insiders that, during the unsuccessful 1976 contract negotiations with the Bruins, he had been offered a share—more than ten per cent of the team. But Eagleson did not tell him of that during negotiations or after, Orr said."

Tesher asked Eagleson to respond, but he declined. "Bobby can say whatever he likes," he said. "It was like a divorce. And I haven't talked about him in twelve years. I have no intention of discussing it."

Orr's revelations were so startling that friends told Eagleson he had to answer them and he sat for an interview with the *Toronto Sun*. But it was merely his word against that of a hockey legend and a Canadian icon, and his carried no weight. And Orr's allegation that Eagleson had failed to inform him of Boston's offer—however questionable—would stick and become fresh ammunition for those determined to bring him down.

A LITTLE OVER FOUR MONTHS LATER, in mid-December 1990, Eagleson found himself under attack again, and this time not from active players but retired ones. The instigator was Carl Brewer. The bald, intense, heavy-set Brewer had been one of four pillars of the stalwart defence corps that had made the Leafs Stanley Cup champions three years in a row in the early sixties. He was a natural on the ice, but in life he was a brooding, restless, temperamental individual who never found a line of work or a place of employment where he was a good fit. His on-again, off-again career had lasted until the late seventies. He had left the game angry and aggrieved and certain that the players of his generation had been wronged by the league and badly represented by Eagleson.

He and Eagleson had once been close friends. Eagleson had represented Brewer early in his career, and Brewer had been the godfather of one of Eagleson's children. But he had spent most of the previous decade looking for evidence of wrongdoing on the part of the league and his former friend, and his sleuthing eventually led him to the players' pension fund.

The fund had been started in 1947 at the behest of Clarence Campbell, and the players had initially contributed $900 annually, which represented a significant portion of their salaries. The owners added the net proceeds from the annual all-star game and twenty-five cents from every playoff ticket sold. The league created a separate organization known as the NHL Pension Society to administer the fund, and the players were granted two seats on the board.

In 1969, the owners and the players negotiated a new arrangement. The players, then represented by Eagleson, asked the owners to take over the contributions. The owners agreed, but insisted that the players give up their seats on the board of the pension society. There were further changes in the 1970s. Eagleson brokered a deal under which the players would be allowed to compete in periodic international tournaments, which he organized and promoted, provided all profits went to the pension fund.

Pensions also figured into successive rounds of collective bargaining in the seventies and eighties. The players invariably demanded more liberal free-agency provisions, the owners steadfastly refused, and the two sides settled on enhanced pension benefits as a compromise. Likewise, the owners offered to enrich the plan in 1979 to convince the players to approve the merger with the WHA. At every turn, the owners assured the players that sacrificing present gains for future benefits was a wise move because they had the best pension plan in pro sport.

This proposition was put to the test when former players began to collect. Many were stunned by what appeared to paltry, even pathetically small benefits. Gordie Howe's twenty-six seasons yielded a pension of under $13,000 (Canadian) annually. Jean Béliveau played twenty seasons and got $12,000. Bobby Orr's twelve-year career netted him $8,400. (Brewer was receiving a little over $6,200 per year for competing in 604 games over twelve seasons.) A few inquisitive alumni made inquiries of the league office or the pension society, but they invariably received unsatisfactory answers or none at all. Brewer was more persistent and pursued the issue with greater vigour than the others.

The turning point occurred in November 1988, according to his partner Susan Foster, who assisted Brewer and later wrote a book about their solitary crusade. Brewer received a letter, signed jointly by Eagleson and John Ziegler, declaring that the retired players would be receiving an increase in their benefits thank to an unspecified agreement reached in August 1986 and recently approved by regulatory authorities in Canada and the U.S. "We hope this makes your Christmas even merrier," they concluded.

In fact, it made Brewer and Foster suspicious and more determined than ever to get to the bottom of things, but they needed expert assistance. In 1989, they retained Mark Zigler, a pension expert and partner in the Toronto law firm Koskie Minsky. Zigler had represented several employee groups who sued corporate employers over pension disputes, and he usually won. He produced a short and startling legal opinion for Brewer and Foster.

The plan had been reorganized in 1982. Manufacturers Life Insurance (Manulife), the company that administered it, had declared that the value of the investments exceeded by some $25.9 million the benefits owed to the participating players. The league had used nearly half the money to fund the senior player benefit introduced during the 1986 CBA negotiations. Another $9.2 million had been assigned to the NHL's twenty-one clubs to give them a "pension contributions holiday." Finally, $6.2 million, which had accrued from pre-1969 player contributions, was left in the plan to enhance the benefits of retirees. Zigler concluded that the entire surplus should have been used for that purpose.

Brewer and Foster were shocked, angry and appalled and decided something had to be done. But rousing the ire of the hockey fraternity proved a challenge. They spent over a year meeting with small groups of retired players—mostly ex-Leafs. They gradually reached out to other alumni, and their crusade slowly gathered momentum.

Their efforts culminated in a mass meeting of nearly seventy former players, including Gordie Howe, Bobby Hull, Bobby Orr, Frank Mahovlich, Eddie Shack and Johnny Bower. About half had brought their wives. They gathered at a suburban Ramada Inn on a wintry Toronto evening in December, 1990. The atmosphere in the room ranged from frosty to red-hot as the assembled alumni listened attentively to presentations from Brewer, Zigler and player agent Ritch Winter, who flew in from Edmonton and reported on the campaign to topple Eagleson. At the conclusion of the proceedings, they took a momentous step. They agreed to sue the league to recover, in full, the millions of dollars they believed to be theirs.

THE RETIRED PLAYERS FILED THEIR SUIT against the league in a Toronto court in the spring of 1991. Mr. Justice George Adams reviewed hundreds of pages of NHL Pension Society documents dating back to the formation of the plan. He issued his decision eighteen months later, in October 1992, and he ruled for the players. The surplus in the fund and the accumulated interest, approximately $43 million, belonged to them. The league appealed and lost and then applied for leave to appeal to the Supreme Court. The application was denied, and that ended the dispute. The league did win on one point: it sued Baker & McKenzie and Marcus Grayck for having rendered poor advice and reached a significant out-of-court settlement.

The pension dispute was a public-relations disaster for the NHL. It tarnished the image of the league and left a smudge on the reputations of those involved. And it coincided with a seismic shift in attitudes among the players. The long-standing culture of deference, in which players of previous generations had reflexively deferred to the authority and perceived wisdom of the owners, was replaced by a new culture of defiance. It had taken hold among the active players first and the retired players second. The latter had taken on the league and won. The younger players had risen against Alan Eagleson and they, too, had prevailed. Eagleson had survived the Palm Beach coup, but was unwilling to accept the newly imposed and restrictive terms of employment and resigned effective December 31, 1991.

EAGLESON LEFT THE PLAYERS' ASSOCIATION full of his customary bravado, and he presented his side of the story in a hardcover volume entitled *Power Play: The Memoirs of Hockey Czar Alan Eagleson*. It was published in the fall of 1991 and included an account of the attempted coup of June 1989 and the follow-up meeting of the players' association in August that year. He did not answer the substance of the allegations, but attacked the motives of the ringleaders—Ed Garvey, Ron Salcer and Ritch Winter. "To put it simply," he wrote, "I saw the whole operation then, and still do, as an attempted U.S. take-over of a Canadian union."

He devoted a good part of the memoir to Bobby Orr and the end of their partnership, which was more akin to a nasty divorce than the dissolution of a business arrangement. Orr, in his *Toronto Star* interview, had hurled as much mud as he could at Eagleson, and now Eagleson responded in kind. He portrayed Orr as a petulant young man who lived lavishly, spent freely, would not adhere to a budget and was a disinterested business partner. He answered the allegations Orr made about financial mismanagement, the fight over the York University sports injury clinic and the 1976 contract negotiations with the Bruins.

But just as he published his defence, he faced a whole slew of fresh allegations. They came from an unlikely source: an obscure, mid-sized daily newspaper that served the suburban Boston community of Lawrence, Massachusetts. In September 1991, the *Lawrence Eagle-Tribune* published a series of investigative articles over a period of five days. It was called "Cracking the Ice: Intrigue and Conflict in the World of Big-time Hockey," and it was a departure for such a publication, as editor David J. Warren explained in an introductory note.

"The *Eagle-Tribune* is a 58,000-circulation, community newspaper," Warren wrote. "Its mission is to cover local news. But sometimes duty causes us to go beyond local boundaries. Veteran hockey writer Russ Conway saw such a duty when he detected, over years of covering his beat, something was seriously wrong inside the National Hockey League."

Conway spent fifteen months investigating Eagleson and his relationship with those who ran the league. He interviewed more than 200 people, logged more than 1,600 phone calls, examined more than 150 documents and extended his inquiries to England, Switzerland and Bermuda. Conway covered some familiar ground—matters such as the Orr-Eagleson fight, the pension dispute and player complaints about restrictions on free agency—but he also produced startling new revelations.

He was able to compare the rent that Eagleson charged the NHLPA for the use of a portion of his building at 37 Maitland Street with the rent the association had previously paid elsewhere. He found that Eagleson had charged nearly double. He disclosed that Eagleson had loaned well over $3 million in player funds to friends and associates—usually on terms favourable to the borrowers—without informing the NHLPA executive or the membership.

Conway examined the files of forty players who had tried to collect disability insurance after sustaining career-ending injuries and found numerous irregularities. Some had had to hire lawyers and pay thousands of dollars in legal bills to collect on policies that either the NHLPA or the league had purchased on their behalf. In some cases, players whom Eagleson had represented got paid without difficulty while those who were simply members of the association had to fight for their money.

Conway's revelations about the Canada Cup tournaments and other international competitions of the 1970s and 1980s infuriated many players. Eagleson had conceived these events, organized them and promoted them. He had persuaded the NHL's best to compete for their countries by promising that the profits would be used to enrich the pensions of all the players. Conway examined financial statements from the 1981, 1984 and 1987 tournaments and discovered that expenses had consumed seventy-five cents out of every dollar of revenue.

Revenues from ticket sales, TV rights, advertising and other sources totalled some $24 million. Expenses consumed $18 million. The combined profit from the three events amounted to about $6 million and was split equally between the NHL, NHLPA and Hockey Canada, the organization that ran the tournaments as part of its broader, decades-old mandate to promote the growth and development of the sport at all levels. The players netted $1.9 million—or, as Conway pointed out, about eight cents on the dollar. Unspecified management services had cost $1.5 million, and there were questions about other expense items as well.

Conway's series—the first of five such investigative reports he would produce over the next several years—caught the attention of FBI agents in Boston, and they began to investigate. There was a second reason why the Bureau took up the case, according to Paul Kelly, who ultimately prosecuted Eagleson on behalf of the U.S. Attorney's Office. "A number of current and former players living in the Boston area, one of whom was Bobby Orr, made a direct complaint about Eagleson to the FBI," says Kelly, who was assigned the case largely because he was a hockey enthusiast who had played the game all his life, had coached kids for many years and at the time was coaching a high school team in Needham, Massachusetts.

The FBI investigation lasted two years. The Bureau found evidence of fraud and embezzlement in Eagleson's handling of disability claims and Canada Cup funds, all of which had to be presented to a grand jury, the twelve-member body that would ultimately decide whether charges could be laid. Kelly also had to keep the U.S. Department of Justice in Washington informed due to Eagleson's prominence in the world of professional sport.

"About three or four months before we asked the grand jury to issue the indictments, I went to Washington with the agents and we spent the better part of the day discussing the charges," says Kelly. "The Justice Department made it very clear that no charges would be issued until they had been reviewed at the very highest levels—one step shy of the attorney general."

The department also took the rare step of granting Eagleson's lawyers an opportunity to review and respond to the charges before they went to the grand jury. "It was a private session in a big conference room and lasted for several hours," Kelly recalls. "Mr. Eagleson had two or three lawyers. There were four or five high-ranking officials of the U.S. Justice Department, myself and a couple of FBI agents. None of their explanations convinced us."

On March 4, 1994, the grand jury issued a thirty-two-count indictment that included charges of fraud, embezzlement, obstruction of justice and racketeering. That was the start of a four-year battle. Eagleson's lawyers had assured the Department of Justice that he would surrender, but he refused and the American authorities were forced to launch extradition proceedings. Meantime, the RCMP belatedly began an investigation and eventually laid their own charges.

Eagleson spent, by his own admission, $3 million defending himself before he capitulated and authorized his lead lawyer, Brian Greenspan, to negotiate the deal that brought the matter to a close. On January 6, 1998, Eagleson appeared before Judge Nathaniel Gorton in the U.S. District Court in Boston. He stood charged with three counts of fraud and embezzlement. The public galleries were packed with journalists and former players who had flown in from far and wide to witness the humiliation of the once-powerful figure who had humiliated them. Statements of fact, agreed upon by prosecution and defence, were read into the record. Judge Gorton asked the accused how he pleaded to the first charge.

Guilty, Eagleson replied.

And to the second: Guilty.

And the third: Guilty.

Judge Gorton ordered him to pay $1 million in restitution, and the next day, in a filled-to-capacity Toronto courtroom, he faced another judge. The facts were read. Three times he was asked to enter a plea, and three times he replied, "Guilty." The Canadian court sentenced him to eighteen months in jail. On January 7, Eagleson spent his first night behind bars at the medium-security Mimico Correctional Centre. Six months later, on July 7, 1998, he was released.

Eagleson departed an unrepentant felon. He expressed no remorse at the time and has not done so since. He has earned no forgiveness from the players he wronged, and therefore receives no credit for the good he did. In the aftermath of all this, many have said—and some have written—that the Eagleson years were lost years for the players, a quarter-century in which they achieved little or nothing through collective bargaining and fell behind their counterparts in the other major North American team sports.

These assertions are the equivalent of piling on or running up the score. Such things happen in the world of sport when passions are inflamed and judgment impaired. They should not happen in the realm of historical writing. Those who write history should not be swayed by the din of the crowd or the passions of the moment. They should be clear-eyed and dispassionate and recognize that in any conflict there are always two sides, and that telling only one never leads the reader to the truth. It is worth remembering that the average NHL salary when Eagleson founded the players' association was just over $18,000 a year. The average was $276,000 when he left. The presence of the WHA between 1972 and 1979 was the single biggest factor, but Eagleson the agent represented more players during those years than any other agent, negotiated more contracts, and arguably did more than any other individual to drive up salaries.

The terms of employment evolved and improved throughout the Eagleson era. At the outset, clubs refused to give players copies of their contracts. He got that changed. The league routinely scheduled games on Christmas Day, something most players hated. It took five years, but he got that changed. A vindictive or capricious general manager could send a player to the minors for getting married in midseason, for making a bad pass or sneezing during a pep talk. He negotiated a waiver rule that forced GMs to offer a player to every other team in the league before sending him down.

He won the right to salary arbitration, and the league appointed three arbitrators, though initially the players rarely took advantage. Per-diem and training-camp allowances were increased several times, and so were playoff awards and bonuses. From the perspective of hindsight, such changes may appear trivial. However, the combined effect of many amendments and additions to the collective bargaining agreement meant that the players of the late 1980s enjoyed much better working conditions than their counterparts of the late 1960s.

The international tournaments he organized changed hockey forever, and for the better. The NHL was a closed system until 1972. For all intents and purposes, Canada was the only source of talent, and there was only one style of play: Canadian. The Canada Cups and other events opened our eyes and extended our horizons. We saw the players of other nations play our game as well as or better than our best. This was the revelation that led to the influx of Europeans and the internationalization of the NHL.

Finally, Eagleson made decisions that served the long-term interests of the sport. He supported—even facilitated—the 1979 merger with the WHA. Many have portrayed this as a betrayal of the players. The WHA had created a competitive market. Unrestrained competition drove salaries to hitherto-unimaginable levels. This was good for the players, but bad for hockey. It was inflationary. Inflation will destroy a family budget, a national economy or a league, and the salary escalation unleashed by the WHA was destroying the NHL. The talent was spread too thin, it was priced too high, and the league endured more franchise crises, failures and crashes than at any time since the Great Depression.

None of this should be seen as an attempt to rehabilitate a fallen man, but to see him for what he was. Alan Eagleson was one of those rare men who had greatness in his grasp and threw it away. He was capable of great things and did great things, but was undone by pride, which manifested itself in arrogance and greed, which led to criminal conduct.

14

GOODENOW'S WORD (1990-1992)

FIVE THOUSAND VISITORS, GIVE OR TAKE, descended on the city of Pittsburgh one weekend in late January 1990 for the NHL's forty-first annual all-star game. The influx pumped a million dollars into the local economy, tourism officials estimated. A capacity crowd filled the Civic Arena, home of the Penguins, for a Saturday alumni game and skills competition, and another packed the building on Sunday for the main event. NBC televised the game nationally—the first time in a decade that one of the three big U.S. networks had carried an NHL contest of any kind. Mario Lemieux scored four goals, outshone Wayne Gretzky, dazzled the hometown fans and was declared the MVP, for which he won a brand new car. It was a fine show and good fun and nothing more. However, two things did occur that weekend that would prove profoundly transformative in the decade ahead.

John Ziegler announced that the league would begin disclosing player salaries and that the information would be released early in February. Salary disclosure was late in coming to the NHL. Major League Baseball players had begun voluntarily disclosing their compensation, through their association, in 1985, while the NFL Players Association had appealed to the National Labor Relations Board, which ordered the league to release salary information. The NHL had agreed to turn over contract data in a belated attempt to quell the player unrest that had led to the uprising against Alan Eagleson in the spring of 1989. Disclosure had proved to be a powerful tool to drive up salaries in the other sports, and it would have the same impact on hockey.

The NHLPA made an announcement that weekend as well. The association's search committee had selected Bob Goodenow to fill the newly created role of deputy executive director. He was not a big name in the hockey world, and his appointment was not big news. The next day's papers ran brief stories, noting that Goodenow was thirty-seven and from Detroit, had been captain of the Harvard Crimson varsity hockey team in 1974, had played briefly in the minors, had earned a law degree and had become a player agent. He represented about twenty NHLers, the most prominent being Brett Hull, the St. Louis Blues sniper and son of Bobby Hull, and Goodenow had recently negotiated a multi-year, multimillion-dollar contract for him.

Goodenow would serve for two years as Eagleson's deputy before taking over. He would be responsible for negotiating a new collective bargaining agreement. Eagleson, meantime, would busy himself with international hockey and another Canada Cup, which was scheduled for the fall of 1991. In his first perfunctory interviews, Goodenow revealed little of himself or his intentions.

"No two people are the same," he told Steve Dryden of the *Hockey News*. "I'm going to be a different type of quarterback."

More adversarial than Eagleson? Dryden wondered.

"It's a fine line," he replied. "I think you've got to be friends. I'm friends with some of the general managers, but they know I'll tell them to hit the road and walk out. . . . One thing I've learned in the last ten years doing labour negotiations is that I try as best I can to separate the issues from personalities."

Was he working for Eagleson or vice-versa?

"I work for the association," Goodenow replied. "So does he."

But who's in charge? Dryden asked.

"The executive committee," he said. "We both work for the executive committee."

THE LEAGUE GOT ITS FIRST REAL TASTE of Goodenow in 1991. The CBA was set to expire on September 15 that year. The termination clause stipulated that the party serving notice had to do so 120 days in advance of expiry and had to submit its demands in order to start the negotiation. Otherwise, the CBA automatically rolled over for another year. The players' association served notice, but there were no demands attached.

"I waited and I waited and I finally sent him a letter," Ziegler recalls. "I said we can start talking when you're ready, but it'll be for an agreement that starts a year from September because we didn't receive your demands. The only conclusion I could come to was that he hadn't read the agreement."

Goodenow disputed the automatic extension. The league held fast, but proposed arbitration to settle the matter. Meantime, the two sides met in early June in Toronto. Ziegler led the NHL delegation, which included a select group of owners and league counsel Gil Stein, and they came well prepared. Ziegler opened the session by presenting Goodenow with a seventy-two-page document entitled "Collective Bargaining Handbook."

The handbook included a concise history of negotiations between the league and the PA, a section on player benefits, another on player compensation and league financial data, and twenty-six pages of proposed revisions to the CBA. The historical piece noted that confrontation and conflict were the norm in baseball, basketball and football. Repeated strikes and lockouts had been the inevitable outcome. The NHL, on the other hand, had enjoyed a quarter-century of labour peace.

"What are the factors that have created this unbroken track record of harmony?" the handbook asked. "First of all, players and owners meet with each other. That sounds simple, but it is unique in major league sports and is the cornerstone of the player-owner relationship. . . . Hockey players are envied by football, baseball and basketball players who have never had the opportunity to meet with owners face to face."

The sides met twice a year as the owner-player council to discuss issues and resolve problems, and they frequently reached consensus on midstream amendments to the CBA. "The approach to collective bargaining is also unique," the handbook stated. "Unlike the other sports, neither hockey players nor owners have ever delivered public ultimatums or practised confrontational negotiations. Those tactics are designed to result in one side 'winning' and the other 'losing.' . . . Hockey players and owners have always practised 'win-win' negotiations. Problems have been solved quietly through responsible give and take."

According to the data presented in the compensation section, the players had fared pretty well under this approach. Average salaries over the previous five years had jumped to $276,000 from $159,000—a seventy-four per cent increase. Player compensation as a share of revenues rose from forty-nine per cent in 1985–86 to fifty-three per cent in 1990–91. Furthermore, given the annual rate of increase of the previous three seasons, the average salary would exceed $1 million by the year 2000.

The league's barrage of information caught Goodenow and the player reps by surprise. According to Stein's account of the meeting, which appears in his 1997 book *Power Plays: An Inside Look at the Big Business of the National Hockey League*, they had arrived more or less empty-handed. They hadn't put together a set of demands, and they weren't prepared when reminded that the CBA automatically renewed for a year since the PA had not served proper notice of termination. "Goodenow was shaken," Stein wrote. "He was red-faced, figuratively and literally."

It was far from a promising start, but the parties agreed to meet again the following month. The players again showed up without a set of proposals. Nor did they offer a response to the demands of the owners. Goodenow announced that they weren't prepared to begin negotiations until the league waived its right to extend the contract. Then they walked out. By that point, Ziegler had begun to understand Goodenow's approach.

"General managers who had dealt with him told me that they would make an offer, but he wouldn't respond," said Ziegler. "He wouldn't return their calls. A couple of managers who were negotiating with key players said their owners called them and asked, 'Have you got an answer yet?' Each said: 'No. He's had the deal for a week or so and I've got no word from him.' The owner would say, 'Call him up and raise the offer.'

"This happened on numerous occasions. By doing nothing, he kept getting the offers raised. It carried over into collective bargaining. There was negotiation, but it always stalled."

The players finally presented their demands on August 14. The proposed revisions ran to fifty-four pages and represented a nearly complete rewrite of the CBA. Furthermore, they continued to insist that the extension of the agreement had to be rescinded. The owners relented and the parties met in Chicago for four days during the last week of August. According to Stein, Goodenow set the tone early when he told the owners: "We are not interested in give and take. We are only interested in take."

The talks lasted four days but went nowhere. They reconvened in Montreal in mid-September, and three days later the parties remained as divided as ever. They met for two days at the end of the month and again adjourned without reaching an accord. By then, the CBA had expired, but owners and players agreed to start the season and to continue negotiations.

A short time later, Ziegler flew to Toronto for a one-on-one meeting with Goodenow. "Bob always said he didn't understand the economics," says Ziegler. "He heard what we were saying, but didn't know if he could trust us.

"So I said: 'We've got a year. We'll pick three or four teams and we'll get you their financial statements, and that way you'll have the whole picture.'

"He said, 'That seems like a good idea.'

"So I put my hand out and I said: 'I'll make you this deal: no strike; no lockout.'

"He stuck his hand across the table. We shook.

"I said, 'Call me when you want to start picking the teams and start your investigation.'

"He said he would, and we said our goodbyes."

Ziegler waited several weeks. Goodenow didn't call. Ziegler called him on several occasions. Goodenow put him off. He was busy. He had other problems. He would get to it. The two finally met for dinner in Montreal in mid-January.

"I said: 'Bob, time is running out. When are you going to start looking at the books of some of these clubs so you understand what we're dealing with?'

"He says, 'Well, John, I think I've got a bigger problem.'

"Right then, I thought, 'The guy is going to renege.'

"And he says: 'I don't think I can control the players. If we don't get a collective bargaining agreement before the playoffs, they're going to have to strike.'"

NEGOTIATIONS RESUMED ON FEBRUARY 24 in New York. There was another session on March 9 and a third on March 13. The talks were stalled on a number of big issues: free agency, the amateur draft (the players wanted fewer rounds), pensions, insurance, waiver rules for veterans, playoff compensation and revenues from hockey cards, which that season were expected to bring in $11 million. On March 20, the players brought down the hammer. They set a strike deadline for noon on Monday, March 30—nine days before the Stanley Cup playoffs were scheduled to begin.

Owner and player committees spent many hours at the bargaining table as the deadline approached—nine hours one day, nine the next, even more the third—and then ground their way through a marathon session that began late Saturday morning, March 28, and went well past midnight. The players made a last counterproposal at 2:30 a.m. Sunday. The owners studied it till 5 a.m., then held a press conference to announce that they had turned it down.

A few hours later, the owners caught a flight to Chicago for a prearranged board of governors meeting. The board stood with its bargaining committee and rejected the players' final proposal. Goodenow had a mandate to take the players out twenty-four hours later. Instead, he rolled the deadline back to 3 p.m. Wednesday to allow time to consult the players and to hold a strike vote. It went 560 in favour, 4 opposed.

This was a stunning break with the past. For the first time in seventy-five seasons, the players had shut down the NHL. "We decided we'd learn the issues, develop the issues, argue the issues among ourselves," declared Washington Capitals goaltender Mike Liut, a key member of the bargaining committee. ". . . We decided we weren't going to be an apathetic group anymore."

The players were through with the collaborative and co-operative approach of the departed and discredited Alan Eagleson. Henceforth, collective bargaining would be adversarial.

HOURS AFTER THE STRIKE BEGAN, John Ziegler and Bob Goodenow were talking again. And almost as quickly, the unity of the owners crumbled. They argued among themselves, factions formed and their differences immediately became public. Norm Green, owner of the Minnesota North Stars, was the first to speak out. "I feel we should lock Mr. Ziegler and Mr. Goodenow in a room until they come up with a solution," Green told an interviewer. "I feel the issues are not serious enough to warrant a strike."

Globe and Mail hockey writer Al Strachan reported that nine of the league's twenty-two owners were prepared to accept the players' last offer. But they were up against a small majority of hard-liners led by Philadelphia's Ed Snider, Boston's Jeremy Jacobs and Chicago's Bill Wirtz, who was chairman and generally regarded as the most powerful member of the board of governors. "There are governors who are saying they want this strike settled quickly," Strachan reported. "If it means a showdown with Mr. Wirtz, so be it."

Five days into the work stoppage, Sunday, April 5, the players presented new proposals. The following day, the owners met for seven and a half hours. They put together a counterproposal and sent it to the other side with an ultimatum: a deal had to be reached by 3 p.m. Thursday, or the season was over. The deadline passed, and a few minutes before 6 p.m. that day Ziegler addressed the media in New York and he was sombre. "The players' bargaining committee unanimously rejected our offer," he said. "We are at an impasse. It's a sad day, my friends, a sad day."

The next morning's headlines declared NHL SEASON OVER. But it wasn't. On Thursday evening, Goodenow had sent new proposals to the league by fax. The board was badly divided. A significant number of owners wanted to cancel the playoffs and lock out the players in the fall. But the moderates prevailed and authorized one last bargaining session.

It began at 9 a.m. on Friday, April 10. It was held at the NHL's New York headquarters. Ziegler and Goodenow were to negotiate one on one, though each had an outside lawyer at his side and two key members of the players' association were on hand: president Bryan Trottier and vice-president Mike Gartner. There was no room for posturing or mistakes. "This was truly a drop-dead date," recalls Ziegler. "If we didn't have an agreement by midnight, we would lose three or four buildings to other events and we would have to cancel the playoffs."

The session took place in Ziegler's spacious midtown Manhattan office. It had a sitting area with a round table, chairs and a couch and overlooked the intersection of Fifth Avenue and 52nd Street and St. Patrick's Cathedral. The two sides went back and forth all morning, through the afternoon and into the evening. Ziegler left frequently to consult with Wirtz and a small group of owners by conference call or to give Goodenow and his advisors time to discuss a point.

"Bob is sitting with all these papers on the round table, going through files and other stuff, and I would come in and say, 'Let's try this.'"

"Gartner would respond and Bob would say, 'I don't think we can do that.'"

"Gartner would say, 'What about this, Bob?' And Bob would say, 'No, I don't think we can do that, either.'"

"Obviously, this was getting very frustrating."

Nevertheless, after hours of going back and forth, between his conference calls and their caucuses, they managed by late evening to reach agreement on most of the major issues.

"It's about ten-fifteen," Ziegler recalls, "and I walk in, and instead of talking to Goodenow, who's over to my left, I say to Mike, who's to my right, 'What about this, Mike?'"

"Mike says: 'John, that may work. What about this issue?'"

"And I said: 'Oh, my gosh. I forgot about that. Give me ten minutes and I'll be back.' I'm about to leave and Goodenow says: 'Wait a minute. Wait a minute. We haven't dealt with the meal money.'"

"I couldn't believe what I'd just heard. It was totally irresponsible. By this time, I'm no longer cool. I turned and I was going to go over and hit him, and Mike Gartner says, 'You know, Bob, I think that could go to the small items committee.' And Bryan Trottier says, 'Yes, that's where that goes.'"

"With that, I walk out. Steam is coming out of both ears."

Ziegler cooled off, held another brief conference call and then returned.

"Basically, I made the agreement with Mike Gartner, Bryan Trottier and their outside lawyer and Bob just sat there growling. He was totally out of it as far as I was concerned."

REGARDLESS OF HIS PERFORMANCE in those final, crucial hours, Bob Goodenow emerged with his stature enhanced. He had not flinched or buckled through the entire ten months of meetings and negotiations. He had led the first general strike of the players in the league's seventy-five years and he had kept them united through ten pressure-packed days.

They had given up almost nothing and they had made gains. They had kept the revenues generated by the sale of trading cards bearing their images. The qualifying age for total free agency had dropped to thirty from thirty-one. Restrictions for those aged twenty-four or younger were loosened. The playoff bonus pool in 1992 was set at $7.5 million, more than double the $3.2 million of the previous year, and it would grow to $9.2 million in 1993. They did concede one major point to the owners: they agreed to an eighty-four-game schedule, up from eighty.

The players voted 409–61 in favour of the agreement. They rushed back to rinks across the continent and completed the schedule. The playoffs began on April 18. The defending champion Pittsburgh Penguins romped through the east while the Chicago Blackhawks rolled over their opponents in the west. But the final was no contest. The Penguins swept the Hawks in four and John Ziegler presented the Stanley Cup to Mario Lemieux at centre ice in Chicago Stadium on June 1.

This was Ziegler's last hurrah as NHL president. In the wake of the strike, a small group of owners, led by Jeremy Jacobs of Boston, Richard Gordon in Hartford and John McMullen in New Jersey, had urged a review of Ziegler's performance. Their expressions of discontent quickly led to a full-blown revolt against the president and a movement to unseat him. League chairman Bill Wirtz responded by appointing a five-member committee to examine the matter of succession and report to the board during the annual meeting in late June.

The bylaws stipulated that a two-thirds majority was required to remove an officer of the league, and Ziegler contends that the malcontents didn't have the necessary support. "McMullen was going around with a petition, but he wasn't getting many signatures," he says. "Bruce McNall did the poll out west. He reported to Bill that everybody out there thought they ought to make a change. I'd just talked to Frank Griffiths in Vancouver and Harley Hotchkiss in Calgary. McNall hadn't talked to either of them."

Ziegler might have survived, but he would have faced a divided board, and there were other issues. He couldn't trust Goodenow to keep his word, and he had grave doubts about the character of McNall, who appeared the likely successor to Wirtz, who was relinquishing the chairman's post after twelve years.

Ziegler's skepticism about McNall arose out of private conversations between them.

"One time, he came to see me," recalls Ziegler. "He said: 'John, you do a fine job, but there's one thing you gotta learn. In this life, perception is more important than reality.'

"That knocked me out. I wondered how I was going to deal with a chairman who thought like that."

Rather than become embroiled in a boardroom brawl, he decided to leave quietly. He negotiated a settlement that ensured he would be financially secure for life. He performed his last duties as president at the annual meeting, and then departed after fifteen trying and often tumultuous years.

Ziegler was more damned than praised as he exited. Hartford's Gordon contended that the league had fallen way behind the other major team sports in the 1980s. The NHL had had no network television presence in the U.S. throughout Ziegler's tenure, and in his final season the league had sold its national rights to a secondary, all-sports cable channel for $5.5 million. By comparison, the NBA's TV deals were worth $231 million a year, Major League Baseball's were estimated at $400 million and the NFL's a stratospheric $905 million.

The harshest criticism came from *Globe and Mail* columnist Al Strachan, who declared it "a great day for hockey" when Ziegler announced his departure. "Ziegler has presided over the worst fifteen years in the NHL's corporate history," Strachan wrote. "In that time, the players improved, the coaches improved and the general managers improved. But the league lost fans, lost stature and, in the case of many teams, lost money."

In fact, Ziegler took over in one of the darkest periods in NHL history. The league was insolvent. A majority of the clubs were losing money and at least a third of them were in a state of financial crisis. There was an enormous competitive gap between the best teams and the weakest, and there was no prospect of closing it. Furthermore, after fourteen seasons of growing fan support—1960–61 through 1974–75—attendance had fallen for four straight years. By the time Ziegler left, the league had enjoyed thirteen consecutive seasons of rising attendance. The competitive balance had improved. Player compensation had risen dramatically. The NHL had grown from eighteen to twenty-four teams and enjoyed a return to prosperity and modest profitability. The league clearly had not done as well as the NBA, MLB or the NFL. But, by any other measure, it had done well.

15

STEIN'S SEVEN MONTHS
(JUNE 1992–FEBRUARY 1993)

GIL STEIN HOLDS THE DISTINCTION of being the NHL's shortest-serving president. The board appointed him on June 22, 1992, largely to fill in while a committee of governors searched for a permanent replacement for John Ziegler. Stein stepped aside on February 1, 1993, to make way for Gary Bettman, the league's first commissioner. His seven months represent little more than a blip in the long, tumultuous history of the NHL, but cannot be reduced to a footnote or overlooked altogether.

Stein aspired to be more than an interim appointment. He coveted the top job and moved like a whirlwind to impress his masters. He pushed through several significant changes to the rules of the game. He set up an owners' committee to negotiate a new U.S. television deal. He had a hand in awarding two new franchises. In the end, though, he was passed over, and he departed in disgrace after he was caught rigging his own election to the Hockey Hall of Fame.

Stein was sixty-four when he became president. He was a Philadelphia lawyer. He had served as Flyers legal counsel and chief executive officer in the mid-1970s, then moved to the league as vice-president and general counsel under Ziegler. His first move as president was to embark on a tour of NHL cities. He met the owners and their general managers and made himself available to the local media. Ostensibly, he was taking stock of the state of affairs in each market, but his underlying objective was to lobby for support to make his appointment permanent.

Stein returned from his travels and promptly eliminated four of the league's seven vice-presidents. Among those affected were Scotty Morrison of the Toronto office, a former on-ice official who had served as referee-in-chief for a number of years, and Montreal-based Brian O'Neill, who had been hired by Clarence Campbell in April 1966 and had served in a variety of roles, including vice-president in charge of hockey operations.

Stein stripped Morrison of his title while allowing him to keep his position and salary. He was not so kind to O'Neill. He made him a consultant without specific duties and told him he would be finished on June 30, 1993, the day his contract with the league expired. He was also prepared to allow O'Neill to announce that he had resigned and could issue a press release to that effect. O'Neill wasn't interested.

"I was fired by Gil Stein," he said in an interview many years later. "He gave me my notice in New York on August 20, 1992. It was my wedding anniversary. I didn't understand it. I didn't accept it and I wouldn't sign the papers he gave me to sign."

Next on Stein's agenda was a board meeting set for August 25 in St. Petersburg, Florida. The president and a committee of general managers had drafted several rule changes, including a minor penalty for holding an opponent's stick and a game misconduct for instigating a fight, and the governors approved. Prior to the meeting, Stein had also worked with an advisory committee of owners on a plan to allow NHL players to compete for their countries in the 1994 Winter Olympics at Lillehammer, Norway.

Stein saw the Olympics as an opportunity to promote the game on the world stage and build the audience for hockey in the U.S. However, a number of governors objected, in part because it would mean shutting down the league for two weeks in February. The board instructed Stein to study the issue and report back at the semi-annual December meeting, but the opponents could not be swayed and the idea fizzled.

Everyone agreed with Stein on one point. The NHL needed better exposure on U.S. television, and an opportunity was at hand. The league's contract with SportsChannel of America had expired at the end of the 1991–92 season. Meantime, ESPN, the premier sports cable network, was launching a second service, ESPN2, and needed programming. Stein appointed a four-member committee of governors to negotiate a deal.

The owners had three objectives: they wanted a game of the week on the main ESPN network; they wanted ESPN to arrange for the broadcast of at least five Stanley Cup games per season on one of the big three over-the-air networks, either ABC, NBC or CBS; and they were demanding $30 million a year. ESPN agreed to the league's terms, but was only prepared to pay $125 million over five years. That was a big improvement over the measly $5 million per annum that SportsChannel had paid for the rights, as Stein later noted. "After years of virtually no national exposure," he wrote, "we were back in the big time with ESPN and ABC showing NHL games."

Stein's crowning moment occurred at the semi-annual meeting. It was held at the Breakers in Palm Beach in mid-December 1992. Following a closed session with the board, he and league chairman Bruce McNall met the assembled media and announced that the league had awarded two new franchises. One went to the Walt Disney Company of Anaheim, California, the other to Wayne Huizenga, the Miami-based founder of the Blockbuster Video empire. The announcement, though rumoured, still came as a surprise. The board hadn't declared months in advance its intent to expand. It hadn't put out a call for applications. This round of expansion had occurred suddenly and more through chance and circumstance than careful planning and deliberation.

It happened because McNall had bumped into Disney chairman Michael Eisner at a Los Angeles gala several months earlier. The two men were well acquainted. Eisner sometimes attended Kings games with his three sons, who happened to play minor hockey, and McNall had once allowed the two older boys to accompany the Kings on a road trip. In the course of their conversation, Eisner asked who would be playing in the lavish new arena that the City of Anaheim was erecting less than two miles from Disneyland. "Not a hockey team," McNall replied. "I own the NHL rights to this area."

McNall soon had second thoughts. Disney would be a remarkable addition to the NHL, and he—McNall—would reap a cash windfall by giving up territorial rights. McNall approached Eisner and, as it happened, he was receptive. Disney had released—on September 20, 1992—a kids' movie called *The Mighty Ducks* with a storyline about a hard-luck minor hockey team that achieves great success while coached by a down-and-out lawyer. The movie was a hit, and

Eisner could see endless possibilities to market *Mighty Ducks* merchandise if Disney owned an NHL team.

But he was put off by the NHL's asking price of $50 million. He argued that the league should award the franchise for free just to have Disney as a partner. That wasn't going to happen, McNall assured him. Negotiations ensued. Disney agreed to pay the price of entry and McNall got half the franchise fee in indemnification.

While all this was happening, McNall was also in discussions with Huizenga. The two had met purely by chance while Huizenga was in Los Angeles on business. He had flown from Miami on a private aircraft and left his pilot, David Linnemeier, at the airport. While he was waiting, Linnemeier took a look at a Boeing 727 that was parked on the tarmac and was for sale at a good price.

Huizenga arranged a meeting with the plane's owner—Bruce McNall—and they met in the conference room of Clay Lacy Aviation at Van Nuys Airport. They began by discussing the Boeing, but ended up talking hockey. Both men later provided accounts of what happened next. In his 2003 autobiography, *Fun While It Lasted*, McNall wrote: "I said: 'Wayne, this league is going places. Disney is getting involved. If you put a team in South Florida, you'll never regret it.'"

For his part, Huizenga told *Sports Illustrated:* "He said if I were serious about wanting a team in South Florida, something would probably be happening at the next owners' meeting. He said Disney was in. It all happened so quickly—five weeks—there wasn't time to put a partnership together. I was afraid if I didn't move, Miami would be sitting here in five years waiting for a hockey team. It was grab your ass and go."

Stein handled the paperwork and McNall persuaded Eisner and Huizenga to attend the board meeting at the Breakers to support their applications for franchises. The meeting opened on the morning of December 10, 1992. "We arranged to have Eisner and Huizenga hide out in my suite until after lunch when we would present them to the board," Stein later wrote. "The board was flabbergasted when McNall and I produced Eisner and Huizenga in person. The approval was a mere formality." And with that, the league grew from twenty-four to twenty-six teams.

Stein had one other piece of business in mind before he took his leave of the league. He wanted to be inducted into the Hockey Hall of Fame. And he almost made it. In late March 1993, the Hall announced that he had been nominated. The twelve-member board approved unanimously. Stein was to be formally inducted in the fall. People throughout the hockey world gasped. Gil Stein in the Hall of Fame as a builder? Alongside Frank Calder, Merv Dutton, Clarence Campbell and John Ziegler? How could this be?

"Maybe," Senator Hartland Molson told the *Toronto Star*'s Milt Dunnell, "we have overlooked the guys who drive the Zambonis.

"I don't consider myself a spokesman for the Hockey Hall of Fame," continued Senator Molson, who was a member himself. "It's just that I find it terribly disappointing when something is done to downgrade the thing."

It quickly emerged that there had been irregularities in the selection process. Stein had appointed five new board members a week before the vote, including Jim Gregory, an NHL vice-president who worked directly under him, and John Turner, former leader of the Liberal Party of Canada. Rules had been changed as well. The vote was taken by a show of hands rather than secret ballot and the threshold for admission had been reduced from seventy-five per cent to a simple majority.

Murray Costello, a board member and president of the Canadian Amateur Hockey Association, resigned in protest a short time after the vote. Several owners, quoted anonymously, questioned Stein's selection, and Chicago's Bill Wirtz sent each of his counterparts a package of highly critical newspaper clips in advance of a May 10 board meeting. Freshly appointed commissioner Gary Bettman adroitly defused the controversy by retaining two highly regarded outside lawyers to investigate. They were Yves Fortier, a Canadian, and Arnold Burns, an American.

They submitted their report in mid-August, and it confirmed all the worst suspicions and speculation. They concluded that Stein had manipulated the process and, in effect, orchestrated his election to the Hall. Among other things, they found that Stein had asked McNall in December 1992 to nominate him and had drafted the letter McNall submitted. He had compiled and distributed a press kit that celebrated his achievements as a league executive and as president. He had made it clear to those NHL employees who were on the board that he expected them to support him. Furthermore, Bettman had advised him on three occasions that allowing his name to stand could be perceived as a conflict of interest and urged him to withdraw.

Stein did withdraw—a few hours before Fortier and Burns released their findings. By then, the damage was done. Whatever his accomplishments, Stein would be remembered as the guy who tried to weasel his way into the Hockey Hall of Fame.

PART IV

THE BETTMAN ERA

(1993–)

16

GOING SOUTH (1993-2005)

ON HIS FIRST DAY ON THE JOB—February 1, 1993—Gary Bettman held a news conference at the NHL's midtown Manhattan offices. He took questions directly from those in attendance and by conference call from curious journalists scattered across the continent. Many addressed him as Mr. Bettman, to which he replied, "Call me Gary." He had wisely decided to connect with the hockey-writing fraternity and the fan base because neither constituency knew the freshly appointed commissioner. He was an outsider. He had had no previous contact with the sport or the league, other than as a spectator, yet here he was, suddenly catapulted into the loftiest position in professional hockey.

The forty-year-old New Yorker had been hired away from the NBA—the league that had advanced furthest and fastest in the 1980s in terms of fan support, television exposure, revenue growth and public prestige. Bettman, a Cornell-educated, New York–trained lawyer, had been vice-president and general counsel and worked directly under commissioner David Stern, the brilliant executive credited with lifting the NBA out of the muck and mire of ownership squabbles, player drug scandals and poisoned labour relations.

The NHL board was looking for a similar transformation after the troubles of John Ziegler's final year. Chairman Bruce McNall personally recruited Bettman after failing to entice Stern. He introduced Bettman to the search committee of Ed Snider, Mike Ilitch, Ronald Corey and Peter Pocklington, and the smart, energetic, ambitious young executive easily outshone several competing candidates. Gil Stein withdrew his name from consideration in order to avoid a split at the board level, and Bettman became the unanimous choice. "From what we've been told," an unnamed governor told the *Toronto Star*, "this guy knows the problems of our business better than we do. He's going to hit the ground with both feet running."

Bettman said little of consequence in his New York news conference, but did speak openly and candidly later in his first week, when he travelled to Montreal for the NHL All-Star Game. He sat for an hour-long, one-on-one interview with Réjean Tremblay of *La Presse*, and Tremblay posed a question that hockey fans across Canada were wondering at that precise moment.

"I ask myself," Tremblay told Bettman, "how someone who knows practically nothing about hockey, has never been part of the small hockey fraternity and who knows nothing of its profound traditions can find himself commissioner of the National Hockey League?"

And Bettman said: "First, I reject your premises. I know enough about hockey to follow a game live, or on television or on the radio. But above all, the owners of the National Hockey League didn't hire me to be a coach or general manager. They didn't hire me because I knew hockey but because I knew how to run a professional sports league. My training as a lawyer and my dozen years spent as an assistant to David Stern . . . prepared me for the position I occupy now.

"David Stern has been a great commissioner. And it should be said in passing that he was not a basketball man when he arrived at the NBA. He became one. It's like me. Do you think that at five-foot-six, I was a basketball guy?"

But Bettman had become one, and he would become a hockey guy, and he would bring to the top job at the NHL the template created by his mentor at the NBA. The secret to Stern's success was to identify the sport's problems and to solve them so that the fans could devote their attention to the sport rather than its problems.

"The fans don't want to hear us talking to them about strikes or drug problems," Bettman said. "They want to hear about their favourite teams and players. If I can make the public forget my existence while the sport and the players thrive, then you can say I've done my job."

Tremblay was a tough journalist. He was not easily impressed, but he was impressed by the new commissioner of the National Hockey League. "Gary Bettman has arrived in hockey like E.T. arrived on earth," he concluded. "This is an enormous advantage. He has not been tainted by ten, twenty, thirty, forty, fifty years of reactionary decisions. This young man has ideas. In the NHL, this is a rare commodity."

GARY BETTMAN MAY HAVE GENUINELY HOPED to play the part of *éminence grise*—the powerful figure who exerts influence and shapes events from the behind the scenes. But that proved impossible. In the opening act of the Bettman era, four teams relocated, and all moved from north to south (greatly extending the NHL's continental footprint), four new franchises were granted at $80 million apiece, four clubs filed for bankruptcy and had to be rescued from financial ruin, several shady owners had to be flushed out of the sport, three U.S. television contracts were negotiated (bringing nearly $1 billion into league coffers), player salaries exploded, the gap between the rich teams and their poor cousins grew perilously wide, labour relations went from bad to deplorable, and the owners twice locked out the hired hands, for half a season on the first occasion and a full season the next time around.

Bettman's first priority as commissioner was to negotiate a new collective bargaining agreement with the players. The deal hastily concluded under great duress in April 1992 was set to expire September 15, 1993, and Bettman immediately reached out to Bob Goodenow, executive director of the NHLPA. Two months after taking over, Bettman told the *Toronto Star* that he and Goodenow had already met half a dozen times and they were talking by phone two or three times a week.

"It's important for us to spend time with each other," the commissioner said. "If we can work on the little problems that crop up day by day, we can build up a level of mutual trust and respect that will enable us to solve bigger problems. I would say we're off to a good start. . . . I am looking forward to tackling the problems in our game with Bob Goodenow. I have no interest in tackling him."

Bettman hoped to conclude a new agreement with the players by the time the 1993–94 season opened. Coincidentally, the league also had to strike a new deal with its referees and linesmen, and he planned to begin reorganizing and expanding the NHL's head office in New York and its satellite operations in

Montreal and Toronto. "If I can do all that," he said, "it'll be a pretty good run for my first eight months."

But Bettman underestimated the complexities and challenges of running the NHL. He would discover that Goodenow was better at acting nice than being nice. He also discovered in very short order that the owners could be nearly as troublesome as the hard, unmovable union leader he would face at the bargaining table.

ON MARCH 11, 1993, NORM GREEN announced that the Minnesota North Stars were moving to Dallas at the end of the season. Green was the owner. He was fifty-eight, a Calgary-based businessman who had made his money in real estate, and he was a former minority owner of the Flames. He had acquired the North Stars in the summer of 1990 and had made a big first impression on the fans. "He immediately established himself as a civic whirlwind, shaking hands, making demands, showing up at the Met Center in a black Rolls Royce with his wife and two dogs, leading cheers during the good times," Leigh Montville reported in *Sports Illustrated* in April 1993.

And there had been good times, however brief. In the spring of 1991, the North Stars and their rookie coach, Bob Gainey, had squeaked into the playoffs, upset several stronger rivals and made an improbable dash to the Stanley Cup final, where they lost in six games to the Pittsburgh Penguins and the magnificent Mario Lemieux. That brush with glory did nothing to resolve the organization's underlying financial problems.

The North Stars had rarely been able to sell enough season tickets, and in 1992–93 they sold only 6,400. Attendance that season hovered around thirteen thousand per game, but the Stars had the lowest average ticket price in the league—$21 and change. As well, there weren't enough high-revenue corporate boxes in the Met Center. Costs, meantime, were rising, due largely to the explosive growth in player salaries, and Green complained that he was covering losses of $6 million to $7 million a season.

He made legitimate efforts to solve the revenue problem, according to Lou Nanne, a former North Star who was team president at the time. Nanne says the City of Bloomington turned down Green's proposal to develop a shopping centre adjacent to the Met Center. Green spent $7 million renovating and refurbishing the building while the Metropolitan Sports Authority, which owned it, refused to contribute. Nanne attempted to negotiate a deal with the owners of a new downtown arena being erected for the Minnesota Timberwolves of the NBA. It fell through in a dispute over rinkboard advertising. As Nanne tells it: "Norm said: 'Screw it. They won't put money into the building. They won't let me build a mall so I can generate revenue. I'm out of here.'"

The NHL board gave Green permission in December 1992 to relocate, and he announced in mid-March, with fifteen games remaining, that he was moving the North Stars to Dallas when the season ended. That was bad enough, from a public-relations perspective, but there was more. A former female employee filed a civil suit against Green for sexual harassment, and when the story broke in the local papers, several other women accused him of inappropriate behaviour.

North Star fans were outraged. They chanted "Norm Green sucks" throughout the final home games. They had the slogan printed on buttons and T-shirts and wore them to the rink. One diehard fan, Wendi Rodewald, told *Sports Illustrated*: "Norm Green is a money-hungry, egotistical, country-club-seeking lizard. Wait a minute? Did I say greedy? He's a greedy, money-hungry, egotistical, country-club-seeking lizard. And he looks like Satan."

The *SI* writer Montville expressed a bewilderment widely held. "The idea that this guy, that anyone, for that matter, could move major league hockey from Minnesota, the American home of hockey, is hard to believe," he wrote. "How could that happen? How could anyone *let* it happen?"

THE DAMAGE TO THE NHL'S IMAGE was limited largely to one small, northern market, albeit an important one. The fallout from the next ownership fiasco cast a shadow over the entire league. In late 1993 and early 1994, the truth about Bruce McNall began to ooze from the ruins of his disintegrating business interests. For years, the short, rotund, round-faced McNall had presented himself as an easygoing, perpetually smiling charmer who had, through acute business acumen, turned a childhood fascination with rare and ancient coins into a substantial fortune—no less than $433 million, he once boasted to a Canadian journalist.

In fact, McNall had borrowed hundreds of millions of dollars from at least a dozen financial institutions, including Bank of America and the Rotterdam-based Crédit Lyonnais Bank Nederland, to finance his coin business, his movie production company and his sporting interests, which included racehorses, a vast and supposedly invaluable collection of sports memorabilia, the Toronto Argonauts of the Canadian Football League and, of course, the Los Angeles Kings.

McNall had wrought a miracle with his daring and dramatic acquisition of Wayne Gretzky. He had made hockey hot in Los Angeles—something hitherto unimaginable—and he had transformed the previously uninspiring Kings into one of the hottest attractions in the game. In so doing, McNall dazzled his fellow owners as thoroughly as he had charmed his bankers, and he was their unanimous choice to succeed Bill Wirtz as chairman in June 1992.

He promptly rewarded their good judgment. He brought Disney and the king of Blockbuster Video—Wayne Huizenga—into the fold, and the profile and prestige of the NHL soared to unprecedented heights. McNall's remarkable run of good fortune crested in the spring of 1993, when his Kings advanced to the Stanley Cup final against hockey's most hallowed franchise, the Montreal Canadiens.

For that brief moment, most of Los Angeles and much of Hollywood fell into a swoon over hockey. The games immediately sold out. Scalpers commanded $500 apiece for tickets. Celebrities rolled up to the Fabulous Forum in long, black stretch limos, stepped into a blitz of spotlights and walked a red carpet to the entrance. Mick Jagger was in the stands one night, and McNall was photographed sitting at rinkside with Disney's Michael Eisner to his left and Ronald and Nancy Reagan to his right.

In the fall of 1993, Disney's Mighty Ducks of Anaheim, Huizenga's Florida Panthers and Norm Green's Dallas Stars made their NHL debuts, and rumours began to circulate that McNall was trying to sell the Kings. He informed his fellow owners that a sale was imminent when they held their semi-annual meeting in early December, but he assured them that he would retain a minority interest and would remain president.

To all who asked, McNall coolly maintained that the sale was part of a grand plan to move the Kings out of the Forum and into a big new building and had nothing to do with financial troubles. In fact, he was in desperate straits. For months, his companies hadn't been able to make interest payments, let alone retire any principal, and their debts were growing at a rate of $100,000 a day. Bank of America, which had loaned McNall around $100 million, moved his accounts into a workout program, a final step before putting a lender into bankruptcy, and gave him permission to unload the Kings as part of the salvage operation.

McNall's fortune took a dire turn in early 1994. One of his accountants, a recent hire, complained of irregularities in the books. These included duplicate tax returns, multiple sets of financial statements, altered contracts and shell companies used to acquire bank loans. If he protested too loudly, or talked to the wrong people, the accountant might kibosh the sale of the Kings. So McNall fired him, and two months later, in mid-March 1994, the ex-employee was talking—to the FBI. The bureau promptly launched an investigation, and by late April agents were visiting employees at their homes and asking questions.

McNall had always hoped for a miraculous big score that would solve all his problems, but knew then there was no escaping his myriad misdeeds. He managed to complete the sale of the team on May 16, 1994, a Monday, literally minutes before a judge in a Los Angeles court began hearing a bankruptcy petition filed by the European American Bank of Long Island. McNall's fall was far from complete. He would be charged with four criminal offences, and several former employees would face similar charges. He would plead guilty and receive a prison term of seventy months.

McNall had brought shame upon himself and embarrassment upon the NHL. He had duped his fellow owners as thoroughly as he had conned his bankers. The owners caught a break, though. The whole ugly mess broke during the playoffs. Mark Messier and the New York Rangers captivated the hockey world that spring with one of the most compelling runs to the final in the modern era. When they got there, they beat Vancouver in a thrilling seven-game series and won the club's first Stanley Cup in fifty-four years. New York was suddenly as mad about hockey as Los Angeles had been a year earlier. It was a triumphant moment for the franchise and the league, but the NHL's second labour war was about to remove most of the shine.

———

THE LEAGUE NEEDED A NEW collective bargaining agreement with the players. The previous agreement had expired on September 15, 1993, but its terms had been extended for the 1993–94 season. The sides did not begin serious negotiations until mid-August 1994, and they were deeply divided from the outset. At the board's annual meeting on August 16, Gary Bettman told the media that the league had three objectives: the next agreement must enhance the competitive balance; it must be fair to players and owners; and it must establish a relationship between salaries and overall revenues.

Players saw the third goal as code for "salary cap," a concept that was radio-active. "We have let them know we are not interested in any type of salary cap," NHLPA president Mike Gartner said. "Meaningful negotiations will not include that and they have continued to keep it on the table."

Player costs were going through the roof. The average salary had jumped to $520,000 in 1993–94, up from $276,000 at the end of the Alan Eagleson era. The number of players earning $1 million or more per season had skyrocketed from three in 1990 to seventy-five in 1993–94. In the previous year alone, several elite players had signed king-sized contracts of three to five years' duration. Wayne Gretzky led the way with a $25.5 million deal, followed by Brett Hull at $20.7 million, Pittsburgh's Jaromir Jagr at $19.2 million and two Russians, Detroit's Sergei Fedorov and Buffalo's Alexander Mogilny, at $12 million each.

Several forces were at work. Salary disclosure allowed players to compare their compensation with that of their peers and demand the same or more. Salary arbitration, which came with some restrictions and limitations, provided the players with another lever with which to extract more money from reluctant owners. Expansion was also a factor. The league had added five franchises in the space of three years, increasing the number of teams by nearly twenty-five per cent. The demand for players spiked accordingly, but the supply rose only marginally. Owners and general managers were desperate to keep their top talent, and the inevitable happened. Prices went up.

NHLPA executive director Bob Goodenow was making an impact. He was transforming the players' association into a coherent and formidable force. He created a marketing department to generate revenue through licensing deals. He used these funds to finance an expanded operation and to help support his members during a work stoppage. He created a legal department that, among other things, prepared agents for arbitration hearings and in some cases argued them. He monitored every contract negotiation and chastised agents if he believed they could have got their clients more money—even $20,000 or $30,000 more.

Goodenow was determined to drive salaries up, and he shocked a group of general managers shortly after he was hired when he disclosed how far he intended to go. "He told them that the players should earn enough to be financially secure for life when they retired," recalls former goaltender Mike Liut, who was very active in the players' association at the time. "That was an unbelievable statement. People couldn't fathom it. Bob set out to make it happen."

Given his thinking, Goodenow would not consider any proposals to curb the growth of salaries, and he had the membership behind him. Bettman and the owners were equally determined to check the rise in team payrolls, which was killing the small-market teams, most of them Canadian, and jeopardizing the viability of the newly created franchises. The sides met half a dozen times or more in late August and all through the month of September, but made no progress.

Meantime, the league had allowed training camps to open and had gone ahead with a full slate of exhibition games—114 in all—but Bettman stipulated that the regular season would not start October 1, as scheduled, unless a new CBA was in place. Goodenow made a last-minute offer of labour peace. His members would play the season. They would not strike provided there was no threat of a lockout. But the owners remembered 1991–92 and Goodenow's betrayal of John Ziegler and the strike on the eve of the playoffs.

On October 1, Bettman appeared at a New York news conference, flanked by ten owners and seventeen general managers, and announced that the start of the season was being postponed two weeks. The commissioner chose his words carefully. He did not use the term "lockout," but nobody—least of all Goodenow—was fooled.

"This is a lockout, pure and simple," he snapped. "The league has clearly rejected our offer to play a full uninterrupted season and imposed a lockout instead."

The war was on, and it quickly got nasty. Several players took turns sniping at Bettman, none more provocatively than Chicago's Chris Chelios, who told reporters: "If I was Gary Bettman, I would be worried about my family, my well-being. Some crazed fan or even a player, who knows, might take it in his hands and figure if they got him out of the way this thing might get settled."

Public opinion supported the owners by a margin of two to one, according to an Angus Reid survey, but media criticism tended to focus on Bettman, and some of it became personal. Will Exton, a columnist with the New York weekly *Village Voice*, chided *Toronto Sun* writers for what he viewed as anti-Semitic digs at the commissioner. One had referred to him as a "nebbish," a term for a small Jewish man, and another consistently referred to him as a "New York lawyer."

"What is most dangerous about this narrow-mindedness is that it strikes at the heart of what is so great about today's NHL," Exton wrote. "More than the continent's other major pro sports, the NHL embraces many nationalities, with players of incredible skills from both hemispheres and a wide variety of backgrounds and who together have raised the level of play to unprecedented creativity and popularity. To allow anti-Semitic codes to creep in at this critical moment can only poison the atmosphere far worse than any economic impasse."

THE LOCKOUT LASTED 104 DAYS. The arenas opened and the players resumed practice on Wednesday, January 11, after Bettman and Goodenow reached a tentative deal. The players quickly ratified it. The governors approved, and on January 15 the commissioner announced at a news conference, "We have a signed document."

Both sides had given considerable ground to get there. The owners had proposed a payroll tax as a method of slowing the growth of salaries. Teams that spent above a specified ceiling—$18 million (US) at the outset—would be taxed at a rate of twenty-five per cent. This was a less restrictive approach than a hard salary cap, but it remained anathema to the players, and the owners dropped it.

The union bargaining team agreed to a cap on rookie salaries starting at $850,000 and rising to $1.075 million in 2000, the sixth and final year of the agreement. Players under the age of twenty-four, or with less than five years' professional experience, would no longer be eligible for salary arbitration. Veterans could become unrestricted free agents at age thirty-two during the first three years of the agreement and thirty-one in the last three, whereas the association had begun by demanding free agency at twenty-eight.

The players accepted an agreement laden with concessions only because the alternative would have been worse: the owners would have cancelled the season. "Are we happy about the scars that have been created for the game of hockey?" Mike Gartner asked. "Are we happy about losing millions of dollars? Are we happy that the relations between owners and players have been severely hindered? No, we're not happy about all that. But we're happy that hockey is going to be played very soon."

The owners were more circumspect. Few said anything for the record, and Bettman dismissed reports of factionalism and infighting on the board. Yet it was evident that a chasm was emerging between the proprietors of big-market teams and their small-market counterparts. Hockey had entered the big-money era, and franchises in Quebec, Ottawa, Winnipeg, Calgary, Edmonton and Hartford were finding it increasingly difficult to keep pace. This agreement would do little to solve their problems.

Salaries would continue to rise faster than anyone anticipated. Small-market finances would become ever more precarious. Talent would migrate from smaller centres to the larger ones. Ultimately, the underlying structural problems would produce competitive imbalances, and the game itself would suffer. In other words, the seeds of another labour war were sown with the CBA of 1994–95.

THE QUEBEC NORDIQUES BECAME THE first casualty of the big-money era. They played their final game on May 16, 1995, against the Rangers in the opening round of the Stanley Cup playoffs. They lost the game and the series, and nine days later, team president Marcel Aubut faced TV cameras and microphones and said, "I regret to announce that the owners have at last resigned themselves to accepting the purchase offer of Comsat Video Enterprises of Denver, Colorado."

Comsat had paid $75 million (US) for the Nordiques, a sum that nobody in the province or Canada was willing to pay. Quebec City was the smallest market in the NHL. The Nordiques' arena—the 15,750-seat Quebec Colisée— opened in 1949. It had no corporate boxes or suites—a big source of revenue in the new-generation arenas then being built around North America—and the small, isolated, unilingual French-speaking capital didn't have much of a corporate sector anyway. TV rights generated very little revenue, and the payroll was going up.

To make matters worse, the Nordiques, like the other Canadian teams, paid player salaries in U.S. dollars while earning revenues in Canadian currency. The weakness of that currency against its U.S. counterpart—trading in the sixty-to-sixty-five-cent range—inflated the payroll by thirty to thirty-five per cent.

Aubut claimed that the team had lost $10 million in the forty-eight-game, lockout-shortened season, and he could only foresee bigger losses ahead. He and his partners had attempted for two years to negotiate a salvation package with the provincial government. They wanted the province to build a twenty-thousand-seat arena, with a casino attached, and profits used to support the team. They were also asking the government to cover their losses till the new arena complex opened.

Premier Jacques Parizeau and his Parti Québécois administration offered $21 million over three years to prop up the Nordiques and said they would study the arena proposal. That was as much as they were prepared to commit at a time when the government was wrestling with fiscal deficits and closing nine hospitals in the Montreal area.

THE WINNIPEG JETS WERE THE NEXT TO GO. They were undone by the same forces as the Nordiques, but their departure was prolonged and painful. Jets owner Barry Shenkarow and his partners were prepared to sell for $32 million to a local group called Manitoba Entertainment Complex (MEC). Shenkarow had set a deadline of May 1, 1995, to complete the deal; otherwise, the Jets would go to the Minneapolis businessmen Richard Burke and Steven Gluckstern, who were prepared to pay $65 million (US) or about $100 million (CDN).

On April 27, Bettman and the league imposed several conditions that made it considerably more difficult to complete the local deal. The principals of MEC cried foul. They saw this as a sly attempt to pry the Jets from Winnipeg and move them south to enhance the NHL's presence in the U.S.

SHAFTED BY THE NHL, declared a large, stark, front-page headline in the April 28 edition of the *Winnipeg Free Press*. At noon that day, nearly fifteen hundred placard-bearing, slogan-shouting protesters staged a noon-hour demonstration at the intersection of Portage and Main, and then marched on the provincial legislature.

The following day, Bettman arrived to attempt damage control. He held a conference at the airport with Shenkarow and the principles of the MEC group and then went downtown, under a police escort, to meet the local media. His mood, demeanour and comments did nothing to ease the hostility Winnipeggers felt for him. "It's easy to pick on me because I'm American," he said. "If you want to do it, go ahead. But it's not accurate. I'm not the one who created the situation. I'm trying to deal with it."

The May 1 deadline passed. The sale to MEC had not closed. Shenkarow, Mayor Susan Thompson, Premier Gary Filmon and several others held a press conference at the Westin Hotel to announce that the Jets were leaving, and nearly everyone, except Filmon, shed tears when it was their turn to speak. Next, the Jets announced a commemorative event at the Winnipeg Arena for May 6. It was dubbed "The Funeral." More than fifteen thousand Winnipeggers packed the old building to pay their respects. Don Cherry made a surprise appearance and told the crowd, "They made a big mistake here."

But it wasn't over for the Jets. A new group of investors, calling themselves Spirit of Manitoba, formed around Izzy Asper, the chain-smoking, straight-talking newspaper and TV mogul who was no fan of hockey and rarely, if ever, attended a Jets game. He was stirred by a sense of civic pride and duty. His group faced two steep challenges: they had to raise $32 million to acquire the team and another $50 million to $100 million to cover future losses. Meantime, Premier Filmon would try to line up municipal, provincial and federal support to fund a new $111 million arena. All this had to be accomplished by a self-imposed deadline of noon on May 18.

Ordinary Winnipeggers threw themselves into the frantic effort to save the team. Over thirty thousand attended a Save the Jets rally held on May 16 at the Forks, the municipal park at the confluence of the Red and Assiniboine Rivers. The event generated pledges of $100,000. Another at the Winnipeg Convention Centre raised $200,000. On May 18, a second Save the Jets rally was held at

Portage and Main. Radio personality Peter Warren and several others arrived on a float and people threw money at them.

"I saw kids crying while they were emptying their piggy banks and jars of pennies," Randy Gilhen, a Jets left winger and Winnipeg native, later recalled. "You can't imagine how that touches you, how it hurts."

The deadline passed. Spirit of Manitoba hadn't come up with the money, nor had the premier lined up support for an arena, but negotiations with Shenkarow's group continued until mid-August, when he at last announced that the Jets would be moved at the end of the 1995–96 season. The team was losing too much money, even with a payroll of $13 million, which was below the league average of $16 million and not even in the same neighbourhood as the Los Angeles Kings, one of the league's big spenders at $24.3 million.

The 1995–96 Jets won thirty-six, lost forty and tied six. They made the play-offs, but lost in six to the Detroit Red Wings. They played their last game on April 28, 1996. The Winnipeg Arena was packed and the fans bid their Jets a sorrowful farewell as the final seconds ticked away. Jordy Douglas, a former player and then the colour man on the CJOB radio broadcasts, later told the *Free Press*'s Randy Turner that he had never heard anything like it.

"We didn't say anything on air," Douglas said. "I remember the deafening noise in the old barn. It was dripping with emotion. To me—and this is going to sound a little crazy—it was almost like an animal in pain. That was my interpretation. It wasn't like a 'thank you for a great season' cheer. It was like a wounded animal crying out 'save me.' We weren't talking. There was nothing to say. That sound spoke volumes."

IN THE FALL OF 1995, the Quebec Nordiques had become the Colorado Avalanche. One year later, the Winnipeg Jets became the Phoenix Coyotes. And the Hartford Whalers were destined to become the third small-market team in three seasons to die in the north and be resurrected in the southern U.S.

The Whalers had struggled throughout the 1990s. Their payroll rose five-fold in the space of eight seasons—from $4.5 million in 1988 to $22 million in 1996–97, their last in Hartford. They played in the aging Hartford Civic Center, which had a capacity of 15,635. Their season-ticket base was small, typically around five thousand, and the best seats went for $42. The Civic Center boasted forty-five corporate boxes, but they were rarely fully leased and the Whalers' TV rights fetched as little as $1 million a season. Peter Karmanos, founder of the Michigan-based software developer Compuware Corporation, acquired the Whalers on June 1, 1994, along with two partners. They paid $47.4 million, although only $22 million was cash, and their Civic Center lease stipulated that they had to keep the team in Hartford at least until the end of the 1997–98 season. But after losses of $11 million the first year and nearly double that the next, Karmanos wanted out. "All I want," he told the *Hartford Courant*, "is a situation where we can just stop the bleeding."

Connecticut governor John G. Rowland launched a "Save the Whale" campaign on April 2, 1996. The objective was to sell 11,000 season tickets by May 1. Forty-five days later, fans had purchased 8,300 and Karmanos agreed to stay put for another season, but he insisted that the Whalers needed a new arena with more seats, more corporate boxes, bigger and brighter concessions and all the other amenities that went into a state-of-the-art building.

Karmanos negotiated on and off with state and civic officials for nine months, but they eventually balked at his demands. He wanted the state to pay for the arena. He wanted the use of it rent-free and he wanted the state to put up $45 million to cover the team's losses until the new facility opened. The talks collapsed on March 27, 1997, and Karmanos immediately announced that the Whalers would not be back the following season. A *Courant* reporter asked Hartford mayor Michael P. Peters how he would respond if he met Karmanos. "I'd be in jail," the mayor replied. "I'd probably hit him in the back of the head."

The Whalers played their last game on April 13, 1997, before a sellout crowd, and it was an unhappy occasion. At the sound of the final buzzer, the players raised their sticks and circled the ice to acknowledge the fans, and then tossed sticks, gloves and pucks into the stands as keepsakes. "I saw a lot of familiar faces out there in the crowd and they were breaking down," goaltender Sean Burke said afterward. "I feel bad that so many of those good people have had a big part of their life taken away from them. It was sad. I choked back the tears because I didn't want to cry in front of fifteen thousand people, but it was tough."

Less than a month later, on May 6, 1997, a beaming, exuberant and optimistic Karmanos held centre stage at a reception and news conference in Raleigh,

North Carolina. Some two hundred politicians, dignitaries and journalists turned up to hear Karmanos announce that the Hartford Whalers would become the Carolina Hurricanes that fall. The team would be based in Raleigh, the state capital, a city of under 250,000, but would draw from a market of around 800,000 that included the nearby cities of Chapel Hill and Durham. Governor Jim Hunt foresaw big things ahead. "The team will be a great economic boon for our state and this area," he told his receptive audience. "We'll see all about wins by the Carolina Hurricanes on CNN. . . . They'll help bring new business and instill new life."

But hockey was no surefire bet in this secondary, out-of-the-way corner of the southern U.S. The Hurricanes would have to play home games more than sixty miles away in Greensboro, North Carolina, for two seasons until a new, 18,680-seat arena was built on the outskirts of Raleigh. They were taking up residence in an area that was home to three powerful college basketball teams— one in Raleigh, one in Chapel Hill and one in Durham—and each had its own loyal and ardent fan base. Furthermore, the populace was unschooled in hockey basics, and the Raleigh-based *News and Observer* newspaper took up the task of educating its readership on the day that Karmanos made his announcement.

The paper ran a hockey primer that began: "Five skaters and one goalie make up a team on the ice, and teams play three 20-minute periods with 15-minute breaks in between. The skaters try to shoot a frozen rubber puck into a goal at the end of the rink. Watch the puck and you'll be following the game of hockey. The red light behind the net signals a goal, and the green light marks the end of a period."

The primer included illustrations and captions to explain how the players lined up for an opening faceoff, the dimensions and layout of the ice surface, and the equipment worn by skaters and goaltenders. Such was the starting point in the NHL's newest southern market, and the southern U.S. was the league's new frontier.

THE LOSS OF THEIR TEAM may have caused rage against the owner in Minnesota, communal grief in Winnipeg or a quiet lament in Hartford, but so be it. Those running the league viewed things differently. If they examined a map of the NHL from 1990, they saw a regional entity with seven Canadian teams—three in the East and four in the West—and fourteen American clubs, ten of them clustered in the Northeast, three in the Midwest and the Los Angeles Kings out on the West Coast by themselves.

Seven years later, a new geography had emerged. Thanks to expansion and relocations, the NHL now had a presence in nine cities that could be defined as southern or western, or both, and they were San Jose, Los Angeles, Anaheim, Phoenix, Denver, Dallas, Tampa, Miami and Raleigh. Still, the league had room to grow and to expand its continental footprint and, in so doing, to make itself more appealing to the major television networks and the national sponsors who were only willing to align their brands with a sport that could deliver national audiences.

By late 1996, the board of governors was contemplating another round of expansion. For a good number of owners, especially those in small or newly established markets, expanding the footprint was a secondary consideration. They were preoccupied with their bottom lines and the pools of red ink accumulating there. Expansion fees would ease their pain and suffering. So they enthusiastically endorsed a plan to add four new franchises and bring the league to thirty teams by the turn of the century. The league put out a call for applications and, in short order, received eleven from nine cities, complete with $100,000 deposits. Gary Bettman and a small committee of owners met the best prospects, examined their finances and inspected their arenas—or the blueprints and architectural drawings for arenas yet to be built—and took their findings back to the board.

On June 25, 1997, amid a governors meeting in New York, Bettman announced, with little or no fanfare, that a team based in Nashville, Tennessee, would join the league in 1998–99. An Atlanta club—the second the NHL had awarded to that city—would make its debut the following season. Two more teams—one based in Minnesota, the other in Columbus, Ohio—would begin play in the fall of 2000. The owners had paid $80 million apiece for their franchises, or $320 million in total, producing a windfall of some $12 million for each of the existing twenty-six teams.

The board stipulated that their new partners must sell twelve thousand season tickets each before opening night, or risk having their franchises revoked, and all four succeeded with time to spare. The Nashville Predators, who drew their nickname from the skeletal remains of a prehistoric sabre-toothed cat discovered at the site of their arena, ran a multi-faceted sales campaign. It included billboards featuring beaming country music stars with their front teeth blacked out and a "Bring It Home" party at the arena on March 28, 1998, two days before the deadline for meeting the season-ticket goal. They sold 543 at that event, pushing their total to 12,139.

Atlanta's Thrashers, named for the state bird of Georgia, ran ads in local movie theatres in conjunction with a $1 million print, radio, TV and billboard campaign. They sold out their ninety corporate suites and surpassed the twelve-thousand-ticket threshold in March 1999, while their arena was still under construction, and a writer in the *Journal-Constitution* noted, "If the team didn't sell another ticket it would still average more than the Flames did in their last three seasons in Atlanta, 1977–80."

The NHL proved an instant hit in Columbus, a state capital with a famous college football team, the Ohio State Buckeyes, but no major-league franchises. The Blue Jackets, a name chosen to reflect Ohio's rich Civil War history, sold over thirteen thousand season tickets and sold out fifty-eight consecutive home games from January 27, 2001, to October 14, 2002. The Minnesota Wild did even better. They started with a season ticket base of over fifteen thousand, enjoyed forty-three straight sellouts in their inaugural season and set a record for an expansion franchise by drawing more than 750,000 fans.

EXPANSION WAS ALWAYS A RISKY VENTURE, but the latest round had gone well, at least in the short term, and this was a good thing. The NHL began the new century with myriad problems. More than half a dozen U.S.-based teams, including the Islanders, Penguins, Lightning, Panthers, Hurricanes, Coyotes and Mighty Ducks—were experiencing ownership problems or falling attendance.

The devalued dollar and rapidly rising salaries were crippling burdens for every Canadian franchise, with the exception of Toronto's invincible Maple Leafs. "We went through a really bad time," recalled Calgary Flames co-owner Harley Hotchkiss in an interview granted a few weeks before his death in June 2011. "It was doubtful if we could stay in Calgary.

"We missed the playoffs seven straight seasons. We lost a lot of our fan base. Two of our partners—Ron Joyce and Grant Bartlett—said it was never going to work in Calgary. We bought them out. It got to the point where we were losing $6 million a year. The money had to come out of our pockets, and we were just a group of individuals. That wears thin pretty fast. Two things let us survive: our determination not to give up and our relationship with the community."

Even the venerable Montreal Canadiens were in peril. "The first four years I was here, we never participated in the free-agent derby that occurs every July," recalls former president Pierre Boivin, who started in September 1999. "We didn't even pick up the phone. There was no point when you've got $3 million to spend and players go for $6 million."

The NHL was fast becoming a two-tier league. There were big markets and small ones—haves and have-nots. Big-market teams spent freely. They snapped up free agents. Their payrolls soared to levels that small-market rivals couldn't hope to match. Talent migrated to the bigger, richer teams, and mostly from north to south, from the secondary Canadian cities to their wealthier American competitors.

Hockey's distorted economics ultimately affected the game itself, as Bettman observed in an interview granted for the present volume. "Some people refer to it as the 'Dead Puck Era,'" he said. "The game had a lot of clutching and grabbing and hooking, Skill and speed were being stifled. Some teams couldn't afford to compete. You had some with $20 million payrolls and others with $80 million payrolls. I would talk to the coaches with the $20 million payrolls and they would say: 'Of course we're hooking and holding. . . . We can't win if we get into a foot race with these clubs.'"

Something had to be done. Players and owners had to be reined in. Salaries and payrolls had to be capped, and as early as 1999, Bettman reached out to NHLPA executive director Bob Goodenow. They had made an accommodation in June 1997. The league had asked for a four-year extension of the collective bargaining agreement, pushing the expiry date back to September 15, 2004, to ensure labour peace while the four newly awarded franchises established themselves.

The players had agreed then, but would yield nothing for the duration of the CBA. "I sent Bob a letter back in 1999 telling him exactly what the problem was and the fact that it was only going to get worse and we needed to address it," Bettman says. "But that wasn't something the union was prepared to do. The union wanted the status quo and insisted on it through 2004."

A SHOWDOWN WITH THE PLAYERS and their leader, Bob Goodenow, was inevitable, and Bettman began to prepare for it more than four years in advance. He held weekly meetings on Tuesday mornings, and these increased in duration and intensity as time passed. He convinced the board to amend the bylaws to strengthen his hand during collective bargaining. Henceforth, a simple majority, rather than two-thirds, could approve a deal on his recommendation; on the other hand, if he were to argue against an agreement, he needed only eight votes to kill it. He insisted that each team arrange a $10 million line of credit to see them through the conflict. He persuaded the owners to accept a gag rule, enforceable by fines of up to $1 million, which he could levy at his discretion if an owner or any member of his management group broke ranks and spoke out during the negotiations.

From the commissioner's perspective, the only solution to the league's economic woes and competitive imbalance was a hard salary cap that tied payrolls to revenues. In the latter half of 2002, Bettman toured the league and met with each owner to ensure that he had their support. The commissioner was preparing for Armageddon. He was certain that the league would have to lock out the players, possibly for an entire season. Few, if any, on the ownership side harboured illusions about Goodenow. He was a formidable, unmovable, destructive adversary.

"I always felt that somewhere, somehow, common sense and caring for the game would help us reach an accommodation that made sense for everyone," recalled Harley Hotchkiss, who was chairman of the board of governors at the time. "I'm not sure Bob thought that way. He was of the view that if Calgary couldn't make it, that's too bad. We'll get a team in Houston or San Diego."

"He was impossible," recalls Jim Devellano, former general manager of the Detroit Red Wings. "The commissioner would say: 'Bob, you're creating problems for the league. We've got teams that are hurting because of what you're doing with salaries.' He would say: 'It's your job to look after that. I work for the players.'

"Gary would say: 'Edmonton will fold. Ottawa will fold.' Bob would say: 'Let them fold. That's not my problem.'

"Gary would say: 'Bob, you're making me very nervous. Our owners are going to close down and we're going to close for a year.' Bob would say: 'Close down for two years. There's no cap.'

"That's how he would talk. The owners got so fed up, they decided to have a lockout just to get rid of him."

FIRST, THOUGH, THERE WERE NEGOTIATIONS. They started in early January 2003. Gary Bettman and Bob Goodenow sat across the table from each other, aides and assistants at their sides. Amid the talks, the Ottawa Senators and Buffalo Sabres declared bankruptcy within a few days of each other— seemingly validating all Bettman's warnings about the dreadful economics. Nevertheless, these sessions went nowhere. The principals removed themselves and let their deputies search for common ground, and they met off and on in New York over the next four months. In June, Bettman and Goodenow returned to the table, but again could make no progress.

The NHLPA offered a package of concessions in early October, including additional restrictions on rookie salaries, a luxury tax and a five per cent rollback on salaries. The league wanted a lot more in light of the astronomical growth in compensation over the past decade and countered with a proposal to limit team payrolls to $31 million per year. (At that point, the New York Rangers and Detroit Red Wings had the top payrolls, both approaching or slightly exceeding $70 million.)

Given the colossal chasm between the sides, there was no basis for negotiation. Instead, both attempted to sway public opinion. The league disclosed that the combined losses of its thirty teams in 2002–03 had hit $300 million. The players' association argued that it had examined the books of four clubs and found $52 million in hidden revenues. *Forbes* magazine waded into the dispute with a report that estimated leaguewide losses at $96 million. The magazine also accused two clubs—the New York Islanders and Chicago Blackhawks—of hiding significant sources of revenue.

The league had one more card to play, and it settled the debate. The Levitt Report, released on February 4, 2004, painted a devastating picture of the

NHL's finances. The author, Arthur Levitt Jr., a former chairman of the Securities and Exchange Commission, was retained by the NHL in April 2003 and asked to examine the books of all thirty clubs for the 2002–03 season.

Levitt found that league revenues had totalled $1.996 billion, but $1.494 billion—or seventy-five per cent—had gone to the players, well in excess of the percentage their counterparts in the NBA or NFL were getting. Nineteen teams wound up in the red. Eleven had made a profit. The profits averaged $6.4 million, the losses $18.6 million, and four clubs had lost more than $30 million. Levitt concluded that the combined operating shortfall totalled $273 million and would have been $101 million higher had he included interest payments on money borrowed to acquire franchises or build arenas.

The NHLPA dismissed the report as "simply another league public-relations initiative," but Levitt's blunt remarks at a press conference suggested otherwise. "I would not underwrite any of these ventures as a banker," Levitt said. "Nor would I invest a dollar of my own personal money in a business that, to me, appears to be heading south."

There were further abortive, unproductive talks in June, July, August and early September of 2004. The league insisted upon a hard salary cap. The players said let the market prevail. The CBA expired at midnight on September 15, 2004, and training camps were supposed to open the next day. Instead, the players were locked out for the second time in ten years, and some were talking tough.

"The owners are being so hard-nosed about a salary cap, but they have to realize it's not going to happen," insisted Jeremy Roenick, the outspoken member of the Philadelphia Flyers. "We'll be down to ten teams before that happens."

Bettman took an equally hard line: "They are apparently convinced that sometime this season the owners' resolve will waver and I tell you that is wrong, wrong, wrong."

THE LOCKOUT WAS A RAW and primal test of wills. The two men at the top—Bettman and Goodenow—had no intention of bending. The big question was: Could they keep their constituents united? Bettman had a decisive advantage. He had to maintain unity among a group of thirty owners—the majority of whom were losing millions of dollars annually and some of whom were said to be better off if their teams weren't playing. Goodenow had to keep seven hundred players in line. Most were making more money than they had ever dreamed possible, though most would earn a lot less or nothing during the lockout and most wouldn't be making big money for long, given that the average career was under five years.

Nonetheless, Goodenow had two things going for him. No North American pro sports league had ever cancelled an entire season, and it seemed inconceivable that the NHL would be the first. Second, Goodenow's track record put him in a position of strength. As the Edmonton-based agent Ritch Winter puts it: "The players had benefitted so much under Goodenow that they said: 'Bob must be right. He got us this far. We've got to let him coach another season.' They followed him blindly."

For a time. In early November, Pierre Dagenais, a fringe player with the Canadiens, broke ranks. Dagenais was one of those athletes who faced the prospect of a short career and was seeing a significant chunk of it wiped out by a labour dispute. "Guys have started to talk in the last three weeks," he told a Montreal radio interviewer. "It could open Bob Goodenow's eyes. I'd be curious to see if they took a poll of the players on a salary cap. They may be surprised to see how many players in my situation would vote for a cap."

Goodenow responded with that tried-and-tested labour tactic, the show of solidarity. He summoned the player reps to Toronto for a meeting and a pep talk. He held a press conference and brought out Dagenais to recant while wearing an NHLPA ball cap. "There is absolutely no crack, no divisiveness," Goodenow told the assembled media. "We have seven hundred players, and you'll never get seven hundred people to agree on everything."

The players undoubtedly listened when Goodenow spoke. They also listened to their agents, and a number of these influential advisors had come to harbour deep misgivings about the union leader even before the lockout. They had begun to see him as arrogant, unreasonable and out of touch. "I used to call him for advice when I was negotiating a contract," recalls the Los Angeles–based agent Ron Salcer. "I would describe a situation with a GM.

"I'd say: 'Listen Bob, here's my situation. Here's what they're saying. Here's where I'm at.' He'd say: 'Fuck them. Tell them that. Tell them to go fuck themselves.'

"I'd hang up and I'd say, 'Why did I just make that call?'"

Salcer had stopped calling about routine contract negotiations, but picked up the phone again as the lockout approached. "I said: 'This thing is not going to be good. Let's work things out.'

"He said: 'Nope. Tell your players to be ready to sit out one year. Maybe two.'

"If you brought up the salary cap, he'd drop the F-bomb and tell you, 'Don't even think about it.'"

Rick Curran, a longtime agent, had staunchly supported Goodenow for years until he witnessed his intransigence during the negotiations with Bettman. "I trusted him and encouraged others to trust him," says Curran. "At some point, everybody said: 'Wait a minute. Where's he going? Is he really implying he'll hit the red button and blow up the season?'"

Curran and another agent paid an impromptu visit to the NHLPA offices in Toronto as the lockout dragged on, and both were stunned by the conversation. "We popped in to say hello," recalls Curran. "I said, 'We all know what's happening, but what is the Plan B?'

"He looked at us like, 'What do you mean Plan B?'

"I said: 'We know what you want to achieve. But what is Plan B?'

"He was like, 'There is no Plan B.'

"We were like, 'Do you really believe the players are going to stay out two years in a row?'"

Goodenow made a dramatic move in early December to test the resolve of the owners. The players had been willing to take a five per cent pay cut. He raised it to twenty-four per cent. Bettman's response shocked the membership and their leader. The league would accept the twenty-four per cent rollback, but would settle for nothing less than an entirely new regimen that included a salary cap and other constraints on compensation.

Goodenow had miscalculated. He had made a major concession and got nothing in return, and his attitude hardened further. The union would make no further offers. The New Year arrived without the slightest prospect of a settlement or even a hint of goodwill on either side. This lockout was going to last longer than the 104-day stoppage of 1994–95. With each passing day it became more likely that there would be no season. Goodenow informed the members that he did not expect any further negotiations till the summer and that the dispute could drag on till Christmas. That caused the first rift between him and the players.

In mid-January, NHLPA president Trevor Linden requested a face-to-face meeting with league chairman Harley Hotchkiss. Goodenow and Bettman were not invited, though each sent two representatives. The meeting took place at a hotel adjacent to Chicago's O'Hare Airport. It lasted five hours. There were no new offers and no negotiations, but Hotchkiss was convinced that his one-on-one, heart-to-heart with Linden was a turning point.

"We had a chance to look each other in the eye and talk openly," Hotchkiss recalled in an interview. "I remember saying: 'Trevor, you don't have to believe me, but unless we get this solved there's no future for the Flames in Calgary. I know that. I've been an owner from the start. I know the numbers.' I said, 'Trevor, we're not a bunch of liars and thieves.'

"He said, 'Harley, I know you're not, but I think some of that is going on.'

"I said: 'Well, I don't think it's a significant issue. We've got to find a way. We can't be enemies like this going forward. The game is more important.'

"As we moved through January and into February, the tone of the meetings changed," Hotchkiss recalled later. "I could sense that. There seemed to be an element of common sense that hadn't been there before."

The breakthrough occurred on February 13, a Sunday. The league and the players' association met with a U.S. federal mediator in Washington, and the players capitulated. They agreed to accept a salary cap. It was, by then, too late to save the season. Nevertheless, the parties exchanged offers over the next forty-eight hours. The players started by proposing a cap of $52 million and came down to $49 million. The league moved from $40 million to $42 million.

That's where they stood on Wednesday, February 16. Shortly before 1 p.m., Bettman stepped up to a microphone in a hotel meeting room in New York, faced a crowd of journalists and television cameramen and announced the cancellation of the 2004–05 season. "This is a sad, regrettable day and all of us wish it could have been avoided," he said. "If you want to know how I feel, I'll summarize it in one word: terrible."

BOB GOODENOW HAD LED THE PLAYERS over a cliff, as the agent Ritch Winter later put it. All that remained to be seen was how far they would fall and how hard they would land. Those questions would be answered in the impending negotiations. They began in early May and consumed both parties for nearly ten weeks. Most of these sessions were held at the offices of a New York law firm located near the NHL headquarters. Rumours that a settlement was close at hand began to circulate early in July, and the league and its players finally announced on July 14 that they had reached an agreement in principle.

The longest lockout in pro sport was over. It had lasted 301 days, and the end brought more relief than jubilation. The dispute had caused immense and, at that moment, incalculable damage. The league and its thirty clubs had lost some $2 billion in revenue. The image of the NHL had been tarnished. No one could predict how the fans would respond and whether they would return to the rinks.

The players had taken a mighty fall, though the magnitude of their defeat could not be measured by the details of the agreement. They had taken a firm stand. They had vowed never to accept a salary cap and they had been compelled to capitulate. They lived by the proposition that nothing mattered more than winning, and they had lost. Their salaries were going to be cut by twenty-four per cent. Team payrolls would be capped at $39 million in year one of the seven-year deal, though there was a sweetener: the cap would rise in step with league revenues.

The owners had achieved their avowed objective: cost certainty in the guise of firm limits on team payrolls. They had also beaten Goodenow and would soon be rid of the man they had come to regard as a scourge. Goodenow's position had become untenable. His uncompromising approach to collective bargaining had been a catastrophe. He had been compelled to reverse himself after years of refusing even to consider a salary cap. Furthermore, he had lost the trust and confidence of the leaders among the players.

"The two people most instrumental in turning the tide were Trevor Linden and Brendan Shanahan," says Rick Curran. "They weren't militant. They were intelligent guys who wanted to make the best deal possible. They had been there from the beginning and knew what was being said in the meetings.

"They were coming out and listening to what Bob was saying about the tenor of the meetings. They said: 'Wait a minute, Bob. You're not characterizing what was said in there.' It reached a point where they said, 'That's not what happened.' That's where the mistrust started. There was a falling out."

Goodenow had been marginalized by the time the negotiations gained momentum and the sides began moving toward a resolution. Linden and Ted Saskin, a lawyer and the NHLPA's senior director of business affairs and licensing, were doing the hard work at the bargaining table. "I remember toward the very end," says Curran, "there was a group of fifteen or sixteen agents who had been around a long time and we were all talking about what was going to happen. The new deal was being put together, and the question in everybody's mind was, 'Whose deal is it?' We knew it wasn't Bob's. Then, all of a sudden, he resigned."

Goodenow announced on July 28 that he was quitting. He collected a multimillion-dollar settlement from the players' association and, for all intents and purposes, disappeared. He has had no visible role in the game since his departure, nor has he been spoken about his role as executive director of the NHLPA or what drove him.

However, it can be said that he was a transformative figure. He remade the players' association, turning it into a credible organization with a professional staff that was capable of advancing the interests of its members. He drove salaries up with the single-mindedness of an obsessive-compulsive, and, in so doing, he changed the economics of the NHL as profoundly as Gary Bettman had rearranged the geography.

17

THE KNOCK AGAINST GARY (2005–)

IT IS JUNE 15, 2011. Another marathon season—with its 1,230 games and two months of playoffs—has reached its endpoint, and those of us who have given up a June evening to watch a game played on ice are awaiting the presentation of the Stanley Cup after a long, punishing final. The members of the opposing teams—the Boston Bruins and Vancouver Canucks—shake hands. Then the vanquished Canucks retreat slowly and stoop-shouldered and dejected to their dressing room, leaving the playing surface (their home ice) to the victors—the bearded, beaming, sweat-drenched, ecstatic Bruins and their street-clothed entourage of coaches, managers and team officials. And while they celebrate, the capacity crowd at the Rogers Arena stays put.

These fans, among the most loyal and long-suffering in hockey, and surely deserving of a championship, display a rare and remarkable generosity. They congratulate the Bruins, applauding warmly and sincerely, until a red carpet is laid on the ice, a table is placed at the end of it, the Conn Smythe Trophy is deposited on the table and a short, slight man in a suit raises a microphone and begins to speak in his distinct, slightly nasal, New York–accented voice. Gary Bettman, commissioner of the National Hockey League since February 1993, summons Boston goalie Tim Thomas and the fans begin to boo—so loudly that they render the commissioner's words inaudible.

They keep on booing as the two white-gloved guardians of the Stanley Cup—Phil Pritchard and Craig Campbell of the Hockey Hall of Fame—bring out the sport's luminous, thirty-five-pound, silver grail and Bettman calls forward the Bruins' six-foot, nine-inch, Bunyanesque captain, Zdeno Chara, to receive the trophy. And you wonder: Heckling the commissioner? Does this happen often?

YouTube provides the answer. Typing the phrase "Booing Gary Bettman" into the search bar yields a raft of results. "Bettman Booed At Draft Ottawa 2008." "Bettman Booed At Draft Montreal 2009." "Detroit Boos Gary Bettman During 2009 Stanley Cup Presentation." "Fans Boo Gary Bettman . . . Again." Compilation videos reveal that crowds in New Jersey, Florida, Buffalo and Columbus have jeered Bettman since the mid-1990s.

Scroll through these entries, and things go rapidly downhill. Someone identified as Captain Jack has posted a piece entitled "If You Dislike Gary Bettman, You'll Like This Video." Another fan, posing as Protectorian, has posted "Fire Bettman—Fight for Hockey." And a third, self-identified as tytsports, has put up "Why I Hate Gary Bettman."

The animus toward the commissioner extends well beyond YouTube cranks. It colours the views of older, more mature and otherwise reasonable people. Mention Gary Bettman at a backyard barbecue, at your local pub or while suiting up for an oldtimers' game, and you will get an earful of vitriol and invective—almost none of it fit to print. They say he has ruined hockey. They don't like games decided by shootouts. They don't like all those southern teams. They say he doesn't care about the small-market Canadian teams. They blame him for the league's labour troubles and the lockouts of 1994–95, 2004–05 and, most recently, 2012–13.

Many simply dislike the man himself, though they catch only glimpses of him. Occasionally, a camera zooms in on Bettman, seated a few rows up from the ice and looking very corporate in impeccably tailored suits and perfectly knotted ties. Now and then, they hear him speak and perhaps put off by the body language, the slight twitch of head and shoulders, the words enunciated with remarkable clarity and his habit of referring to hockey as "our game." That phrase—"our game," with its overtones of kinship and communality— may be the nub of the problem. The ordinary fan feels little or no kinship with the commissioner. He is way too corporate, too "head office" for them.

Bettman insists he is not bothered by the abuse. "If I go out there and it's silent, then I know I have a problem," he says. "That means nobody cares. If you ask people why they're booing, they don't know why. People will come up to me when I'm walking around the concourse and they'll apologize. They'll say, 'Pittsburgh's not like that,' or 'Philadelphia's not like that.' You don't do a job like this if you're thin-skinned."

The commissioner is wise enough to know that crowds are fickle and that he whom they hail on Sunday, they will crucify on Friday. Besides, his position is safe as long as he keeps the owners happy, and he is a master at that. In two decades on the job, he has made their league bigger, brighter, flashier and more prosperous than it has ever been, and they have rewarded him with contract extensions and a salary in the neighbourhood of $7 million per annum.

THE NHL'S HEAD OFFICE, as of this writing, is located at 1185 Avenue of the Americas in midtown Manhattan. The league occupies floors eleven through fifteen of the forty-two-storey building—or about 120,000 square feet, which is equivalent to a Costco warehouse or a Loblaws Superstore. The reception area is dominated by the NHL shield—a gleaming, silver-plated, four-foot-high version of it—that stands on a two-foot pedestal.

The commissioner's corner office is on the fifteenth floor, and to get there, an assistant guides the visitor past meeting rooms with floor-to-ceiling windows that open onto the corridor and past a small, semicircular alcove that resembles a chapel where the devout kneel to pray or to pay homage to a saint. There are no flickering votive candles or sacred imagery, though there is a replica of the Stanley Cup, a little smaller than the real thing. It rests serenely on a waist-high pedestal. It is illuminated by overhead lights, and the walls are lined with bands of silver that replicate the rings of the trophy.

Bettman's sanctum is warm, spacious, tastefully decorated and well lit, owing to six-foot-high windows along the wall that faces the street. There is a round table in one corner. There is a leather couch along one wall, a coffee table and three armchairs for small, informal meetings. There is a bookcase filled with volumes devoted to hockey, and a credenza, its surface cluttered with family photos.

The commissioner's desk overlooks the broad, six-lane Avenue of the Americas and its relentless, one-way, northbound traffic. Radio City Music

Hall is a couple of blocks north, on the opposite side of the street, and Central Park is visible beyond that as a splash of green. When he is not travelling—and he tries to get to a game in each of the league's thirty cities at least once per season—Bettman spends his days here, arriving very early and usually working late into the evening, presiding over a league that has grown steadily on his watch.

Over 23 million people attend NHL games each season. That's up from 13.8 million in 1990–91. Per-game attendance has risen to 18,000, versus 14,000 in 1990. And here's what really puts a smile on owners' faces: leaguewide revenues have grown nearly eightfold during the Bettman era, from $430 million a year when he took over to $3.3 billion in 2011–12.

The organization has grown accordingly. The NHL employed about forty to fifty people in its New York, Toronto and Montreal offices at the start of his tenure. Today, the payroll exceeds four hundred. The legal, finance, IT, marketing and public relations departments have all grown substantially. So has the special-events department, which handles all-star weekend, the annual Winter Classic, the amateur draft and the postseason awards show. The NHL's website (NHL.com), satellite radio channel (NHL Radio), cable television channel (NHL Network) and other digital services have all been created since Bettman's arrival. NHL.com attracts some seventeen million unique visits per month, and a whole new analytics department has sprung up to monitor and assess the use of the site.

Running a league used to be a simple business. Not anymore. "If you go back forty years," Bettman says, "sports leagues were in charge of scheduling and the officials. Now they're doing lots of business on a worldwide basis, and when I say business, it's the way leagues connect with their fans. It's more sophisticated and complex than it's ever been."

THE GAME IS AT THE HEART of the enterprise. It must be good if a league is to succeed, and there was a consensus going into the 2004–05 lockout that the quality of the NHL game had deteriorated. The speed, flair, finesse and creativity that make hockey so riveting and captivating were being undone by various forms of obstruction—hooking, holding, interference and the notorious neutral-zone trap in which one team's five skaters clogged up centre ice to prevent the other side from mounting an attack.

Hockey had to change. Obstruction had to go. The game had to be transformed, and it was. Gary Bettman, the architect of its ruin in the minds of many, handed the job to one of his most loyal and trusted lieutenants: Colin Campbell, the league's director of hockey operations. Campbell formed and chaired the league's new competition committee. He recruited four general managers (Bob Gainey, Kevin Lowe, David Poile and Don Waddell) and four players (Brendan Shanahan, Trevor Linden, Rob Blake and Jarome Iginla). Ed Snider represented the owners, and Martin Brodeur the players' association. They met throughout the lockout, but most frequently from March through May of 2005.

"We had some time," recalls Campbell. "We had a non-competitive atmosphere. Everybody was thinking, 'What's best for the game?' Not 'What's best for my team? Because I need to win.' We talked about a ton of issues. Getting rid of icing. Not being allowed to ice the puck on a penalty kill. Going to four-on-four in overtime in the playoffs. Bob Gainey came up with the phrase that captured up what we were trying to do: reward offence."

The committee agreed on a package of rule changes designed to open the game and generate more scoring chances and goals. For example, two-line passes from a player in his own end to a teammate about to hit the opposition blue line would be legal. But throwing the puck over the glass while being pressured by a forechecker would be penalized—a measure that sparked considerable debate.

"You don't always know whether it's intentional or not," concedes Campbell. "Bob said: 'This is simple. The defensive team is putting the puck into the stands and stopping an offensive play. Even if they do it accidentally, too bad. They're not good enough to get the puck out of their own end any other way.'"

By and large, the rule changes have worked as intended. Rampant obstruction has been eliminated. The game has become faster. It is more wide-open. "We had a real tough learning period where we would have eighteen or twenty minors a game," says Campbell. "Gary warned the referees: 'You better stick with the process. Don't back off.' Refs felt they had to make calls to get noticed or they would get canned. Essentially, we changed hockey for the better, not just in the NHL, but around the world."

The new rules dealt with obstruction. The salary cap addressed the league's competitive-balance problem. It imposed both a ceiling and a floor and fixed the gap at $16 million. It gave the small-market teams a chance to keep their best players rather than losing them to free agency. It allowed them to bid on free agents alongside their wealthier, big-market rivals. It meant that brains, rather than bucks, would produce a competitive team.

In an ideal world, each team would start each season with a reasonable chance of winning. That hasn't happened in the NHL, but consider what *has* transpired. In the seven seasons commencing in 2005–06, all but one of thirty teams qualified for the playoffs at least once. Only the ultra-wealthy, big-market Toronto Maple Leafs failed to get a sniff of the postseason. Twenty-three different clubs won divisional titles. Half advanced to the Stanley Cup semifinal, and seven seasons produced seven different champions—those being the Carolina Hurricanes, Anaheim Ducks, Detroit Red Wings, Pittsburgh Penguins, Chicago Blackhawks, Boston Bruins and Los Angeles Kings.

"Cost certainty [i.e., the salary cap] brought back parity," says Pierre Boivin, former president and chief executive of the Canadiens. "There's always a couple of markets where the fans begin the season saying, 'What hope have we got?' There used to be fifteen or twenty. We sell hope—the hope that our team will win. We're in the business of putting smiles on people's faces. If you take that away, you may as well shut the doors."

THE NHL BEGAN ALLOWING VIDEO REVIEWS of goals in 1991–92—John Ziegler's last season as president. Each club set aside an enclosed booth high above the ice, usually as part of the press gallery. Two judges watched the games from such a vantage point and relied on a small bank of television monitors to review controversial or questionable goals. For the next eleven years, they made the calls—goal or no goal. The league's thinking changed one night during the 2002–03 campaign.

"I remember it to this day," says Colin Campbell. "Calgary was playing Detroit. Mike Murphy and I were watching the game here on our own screens. Murph said, 'Oh boy, that goal's in for Detroit.'

"I said, 'I hope they make the right call.'

"Murph said, 'I hope so too.'

"All of a sudden, we hear, 'No goal.'"

Campbell promptly received a call from an exasperated Ken Holland, Detroit's general manager. He suggested that the league's hockey-operations department make the calls. The results would be more consistent if the same small group reviewed contentious goals rather than individuals based in arenas across the continent. As well, decisions would be made in an atmosphere of calm as opposed to rinks full of impassioned fans. Campbell saw merit and challenges in the idea. "I said: 'Geez, Kenny, we'd need a few more people. We'd have to watch every game every night. We'd have to be able to call the video review judges. They'd have to call us.'"

Despite the logistical hurdles, the league set up its own video review room in Toronto, and since the start of the 2003–04 season, Campbell's department has made the call on all disputed goals, with input from the video goal judges in each arena. The "situation room," as it is now called, has been upgraded several times to incorporate improved technology, and the latest iteration was up and running for opening night of the 2011–12 season. It is on the eleventh floor of the Bay Street office tower that houses the league's hockey-operations department and overlooks the roof of the Air Canada Centre, which bears the airline's enormous, illuminated corporate logo.

Mike Murphy, senior vice-president of hockey operations, is in charge most nights. He supervises from a workstation on a raised platform that runs the length of the rectangular room and can keep an eye on nine games simultaneously via the bank of television screens that lines one wall. The centrepiece is a ninety-two-inch flat-screen television, the largest available at the time of purchase, and it is flanked by eight forty-two-inchers. He manages a crew of eight to ten nightly, and each member watches a different game from an individual workstation.

Over the course of a season, they are called upon to rule on about four hundred goals. Each time, Murphy and several members of his team watch replays from multiple angles, in slow motion and super-slow motion. They can freeze the action or reverse it, and all the while they are in direct contact by phone with the referee and the video goal judge. However, their mandate goes well beyond video reviews. "Quality control is done, as much as possible, out of this room," says Murphy. "Our job is to make sure all things are done to NHL standards, which are the highest in the sport."

These days, an NHL game is a precisely timed event. Among other things, Murphy's crew ensures that games start on time, that commercial breaks occur at set points in the period, that they do not run beyond the prescribed two minutes and that intermissions last seventeen minutes. They pay close attention to pre-game ceremonies, which are allotted fifteen minutes, with a three-minute skate for the players before the opening faceoff. They also monitor the work of the referees and the ice conditions.

But for all the rules, regulations and precautions, there are periodic moments of crisis that require good judgment and quick decisions. "One night," recalls Campbell, "a Zamboni broke a line and spilled all its hydraulic oil in the middle of the ice. It was the last flood after warmup. We might not be able to play the game. I call Gary because Gary's the only guy who can call it off.

"The power goes out in New Jersey one night. It's a new arena. One team's up two-nothing. We have to decide how long we wait before calling the game. A player almost dies in Detroit. Nashville is up by one goal. The other players are all shocked. They saw him almost die and brought back to life. I'm talking to Gary and the general managers to decide if we call the game off."

Campbell and his wife were in Buffalo the night an errant skate blade sliced open Richard Zednik's neck, severing an artery. "I see this happen," says Campbell. "I see the blood spurting. I tell my wife, 'I've got to go down. This isn't good.' I'm standing in the Zamboni entrance. I'm two feet away when they put him in the ambulance. I ask the doctor, 'Is he going to make it?' He shrugs and I say, 'Uh-oh.'

"I went to talk to Billy McCreary, who was refereeing. I talked to Jacques Martin, Zednik's coach, and Darcy Regier, Buffalo's manager. 'How are your players? Should we go on?' I'm talking to Gary. Talking to the guys in Toronto. It's all part of managing our game and maintaining our status as one of the top four sports on the continent."

THE AVERAGE FAN SCARCELY NOTICED in November 2006 when John Collins became chief marketing officer (CMO) of the NHL. Collins—since elevated to chief operating officer—was in his late forties, a native of the New York area and a graduate of Long Island University. He was a former CMO of the NFL and worked for the league for fifteen years. He had been president of the NFL's Cleveland Browns for two years, but was between jobs when Gary Bettman recruited him. It would prove an astute appointment.

The 2005 collective bargaining agreement had levelled the playing field between big markets and small. The rule changes had improved the game. Bettman wanted someone to sell the product and grow the business, and Collins delivered. He put money and resources into the league's website and other digital platforms. He developed new events—the Winter Classic being the most important—and put more sizzle into established ones like the all-star weekend. The investments in these projects paid off in lucrative sponsorship agreements and the best television deal in the league's history—a ten-year, $2 billion contract with NBC.

Leaguewide revenues were $1.8 billion per year when Collins started. By the end of 2011–12, they had nearly doubled, to $3.3 billion. "I saw a lot of opportunity to grow," he says. "The game was ripe for some innovation and the introduction of new programming. There was a real opportunity to bring a lot of the things we had done at the NFL to the NHL."

The league likes to boast that its fans are better educated, more affluent and more technologically savvy than those of the other major team sports. Collins commissioned research that revealed another significant difference: they are far more tribal. They form deep attachments to one team, and if that teams fails to qualify for the postseason, or gets eliminated early, they tend to change the channel. Hockey's over for them for another year.

NFL fans are different. They pay attention to other teams and the league as a whole, and they will stay tuned even when their side has been eliminated. As Collins likes to say, "Nobody ever cancelled their Super Bowl party because they didn't like the two teams in the game."

His goal was to get hockey fans more engaged with the league and to create a bigger national audience. "This was a strategy we shared with the teams and our business partners," he recalls. "We said, 'We're not trying to transfer fan loyalties from clubs to the league, nor are we shifting advertising dollars from a club to the league.' It's a strategy that's supposed to create a halo over everybody's business, make it bigger and more relevant and drive more money to the sport. I can't honestly say that there was a 100 per cent buy-in."

Collins believed that enhanced use of digital media was one way to create the "halo." NHL.com became the point of entry, and under his watch the site has become the most comprehensive source of news and information about the league. It is also the most current. The scores in every game are posted as they change. League, conference and divisional standings are updated daily. So are individual stats. Fans can watch a selection of each night's highlights. They can peruse boxscores and summaries immediately after the final buzzer—the type of information formerly available only to accredited media working in press boxes. They can keep pace with player moves and other developments through a selection of news stories that are refreshed daily. They can access the sites of all thirty teams, other leagues and individual players, and all this is merely the tip of iceberg.

NHL.com is the gateway to the league's subscription services, which include NHL Centre Ice and NHL GameCentre Live. Fans who purchase Centre Ice can watch as many as forty games a week on TV from the comfort of their living rooms. GameCentre delivers the same number of weekly games, but on computers, smart phones, tablets and other Internet-connected devices, and fans can take advantage of a multitude of services. Among other things, they can listen to the home or visiting team's broadcast, choose the goals, hits and saves they want to replay, and engage in live chat with other fans.

In short, the league has created its own multifaceted media operation that offers an alternative to the mainstream coverage available through TV, radio and newspapers, and fans have responded. According to Collins, NHL.com has been the most popular sports site in Canada for six straight years. The site has also allowed the league to circumvent traditional media in the U.S., which have for decades buried the news about hockey, if they covered the sport at all.

"Your local news outlet in the U.S. was covering the local team, but wasn't giving the fans all the great stories and highlights from around the league," says Collins. "Digital media gave us a unique opportunity to fill that void."

The league has also rolled out foreign-language editions of the website in French, Russian, Swedish, Finnish, German, Czech and Slovak. "Our fan and brand research shows that hockey is either the number one or number two sport in a lot of European countries," he says. "The fan relationship in Europe is centred on the individual players they followed until the player reached the NHL, and that's where the relationship was severed. We wanted to create a direct path so European fans could connect through players from their own country to the entire league."

Collins saw a second way to create the national halo that would attract sponsors, advertisers and perhaps a lucrative network television contract. The league would create big events, or add some sparkle to existing ones, and the Winter Classic has become the cornerstone of this piece of the strategy. As Collins explains, NBC came to the league shortly after he signed on and presented an opportunity. The network was dropping its coverage of the Orange Bowl college football game on New Year's Day and needed a replacement. The league had just the thing: an outdoor game.

The concept had already been tested. The Oilers and Canadiens held an alumni game—and a real NHL contest—at Commonwealth Stadium in Edmonton on November 22, 2003. The temperature dropped to about minus-twenty Celsius. The players had to wear toques and headbands under helmets to avoid frozen ears, but the stands were packed with bundled and shivering fans who nonetheless revelled in an experience that seemed to take big-league hockey back to a now mythical and vanished past.

The first Winter Classic had the same transformative effect. It was played on New Year's Day 2008 at Ralph Wilson Stadium in Orchard Park, New York, home of the NFL's Buffalo Bills. The Sabres faced the Penguins. The game ended in a one-one tie. Sidney Crosby scored the winning goal in a shootout. Snow flurries and squalls rolled in off Lake Erie most of the afternoon. The game had to be stopped several times to repair the ice or scrape the surface, but 71,217 fans packed the place. They seemed more enchanted than troubled by the less-than-ideal conditions, and the spectacle proved equally captivating to the TV audience, which hit a remarkable 3.8 million.

Winter Classics have since been held at Wrigley Field in Chicago, Fenway Park in Boston, Heinz Field in Pittsburgh and Citizens Bank Park in Philadelphia, and players and fans have had to endure rain, wind, cold and glaring sun. But none of that seems to matter. The stadiums have been full and the event has attracted some of the biggest TV audiences ever for regular-season NHL games, earning the league uniformly glowing media coverage. "Hockey owns New Year's Day the way baseball owns the Fourth of July and football owns Thanksgiving," *Sports Illustrated*'s Dan Shaughnessy wrote in December 2009. Two years later, on January 2, 2011, a *New York Post* headline read, "How about Central Park for the next Winter Classic?"

The success of the Winter Classic has spawned other special events: a season-opening festival called Face Off that has landed in selected cities; opening games in European capitals; Thanksgiving Friday games in the U.S.; Hockey Day in America in February; a dressed up All-Star Weekend; and a glitzy year-end awards ceremony broadcast live from Las Vegas. The objective, of course, was to grow the national audience and attract major national sponsors who would pay big dollars to align their brands with the NHL.

The strategy has paid dividends. League-generated revenue exceeded $300 million for the first time in 2010–11. Sponsorship revenues grew 350 per cent between 2007–08 and 2010–11. The league's roster of blue-chip corporate sponsors includes Honda, McDonald's, Geico (the automobile insurer) and Enterprise Rent-a-Car. In February 2011, the league announced a seven-year, $400 million agreement that made Molson Coors the official beer of the NHL in Canada and MillerCoors the official beer in the U.S.

"The Molson Coors buy-in was a validation of our business plan and sent an important signal to the rest of corporate North America," says Collins. "It validated the league's potential and its growth possibilities. It created a lot of momentum for us at a very important period as we went into another round of negotiations for the next U.S. TV contract."

Indeed, two months later, on April 19, 2011, the league announced that it had signed a landmark ten-year, $2 billion television rights agreement with NBC and cable provider Versus. The deal was bigger in dollar terms than any previous broadcast arrangement and provided for more comprehensive coverage. NBC and Versus had committed to carry more than one hundred regular-season games and all Stanley Cup games up to and including the finals.

THE NHL HAS MADE REMARKABLE STRIDES in recent years—and they have been remarkable by almost any metric—but no matter how many major national sponsors board the bandwagon, no matter how good the ratings, no matter how many fans visit NHL.com each month, hockey is still the number-four team sport in the U.S. and will remain so for the foreseeable future. And no matter how big or bright or prosperous the league has become, Gary Bettman and the board of governors have been dogged by some of the same problems as their predecessors—namely, franchise troubles and on-ice mayhem and injuries. They have also faced challenges unique to their day—namely, labour troubles.

Since the 2005 collective bargaining agreement went into effect and a new economic era commenced, there have been ownership changes in Toronto, Montreal, Buffalo, Tampa, Nashville and Dallas, and ownership troubles in New Jersey, Atlanta and Phoenix. The latter two proved most troublesome.

The Atlanta Thrashers officially became a failed franchise in the spring of 2011, when the owners sold the team to a Manitoba group and the Thrashers resurfaced as the Winnipeg Jets and received a joyous welcome in their new home. The Phoenix Coyotes, as of this writing, were still alive and property of the other twenty-nine owners, who bought the franchise out of bankruptcy proceedings in the fall of 2009 and, nearly four years later, hadn't been able to find anyone to take the team off their hands.

The league put franchises in those cities because both are major regional markets, Atlanta in the southeast and Phoenix in the southwest. Hockey is a tough sell in such non-traditional venues, and to make matters more difficult, both the Thrashers and Coyotes had to build fan bases in cities with established NFL, MLB and NBA franchises. The competition didn't end there, at least in Atlanta, according to Don Waddell, who served as general manager of the Thrashers for their first eleven seasons and president in their final year.

"We talk about a city with four major sports, but in Atlanta it's really five, and nobody recognizes it," Waddell told this writer in an interview in February 2011. "The fifth is college football. It's the biggest thing in this city, bigger than pro sports. It's not even close. The worst thing we could do was go head to head against a college game. We didn't stand a chance."

Friday night games in October and November were also a washout for the Thrashers, Waddell added. High school football was the big attraction. There were numerous games in the region, attended by a total of 100,000 people or more. In such a congested market, the window of opportunity for the Thrashers to earn the attention of the public extended from January to March. A team that was a perennial playoff contender might have succeeded. The Thrashers made the postseason once in twelve tries.

Add to that dismal record a fractious group of owners who bought the team from Turner Broadcasting System following the 2005 lockout. Some were from Atlanta, some from Boston and Washington, and some only met each other for the first time moments before attending a press conference to announce the purchase. Disputes inevitably arose among them. Partners sued partners and the franchise floundered. There was one other problem: the home of the Thrashers was the Philips Arena, located downtown, and getting there from the suburbs was a challenge, especially on weeknights, because traffic is so bad virtually everywhere in Atlanta.

The Coyotes have become an enduring headache akin to the league's protracted difficulties with the Oakland Seals in the 1970s. There were three changes of ownership between 1996 and 2009, when the league took possession, and one of the groups included a minor shareholder named Wayne Gretzky, who also doubled as head coach for several seasons. The team initially played in a downtown arena that had been built for the NBA's Phoenix Suns, but the sight lines and seating configuration didn't work for hockey. A plan to build a suitable rink in the affluent suburb of Scottsdale fell through, and the team moved in December 2003 to a newly constructed, municipally owned arena in the more distant and less desirable suburb of Glendale, a half-hour drive by expressway from central Phoenix.

The Coyotes racked up catastrophic losses after the move to Glendale. Steve Ellman, a local real estate developer and the majority partner at the time, sold his interest in the fall of 2006 to Jerry Moyes, founder of Swift Transportation, one of the largest trucking companies in the U.S. Moyes had contributed $5 million when Ellman purchased the team, but had increased his stake by repeatedly covering the team's losses. He ran into financial trouble in the latter half of 2008 after buying back the public shares of Swift, and he could no longer afford to bankroll the Coyotes. The league was forced to keep the team afloat for the 2008–09 season at a cost of nearly $32 million.

Moyes claimed to have put $380 million into the franchise during his seven years of ownership and was desperate to get out. As it happened, he found a would-be buyer in Jim Balsillie, who was desperate to get his hands on an NHL franchise. Balsillie had the money; he was worth an estimated $1.4 billion, having made his fortune by transforming Research In Motion, creator of the BlackBerry wireless device, from a high-tech startup in Waterloo, Ontario, into a multinational company with worldwide sales. He dreamt of acquiring an NHL franchise and moving it to southern Ontario.

Hamilton was his preferred location. In 2007, he had tried to buy the Pittsburgh Penguins. A year later, he had set his sights on the Nashville Predators. Both times, he had played by the rules as set out by the league, and both times he had been rebuffed.

Bettman and some members of the board, it was said, simply didn't like Hamilton and its image as a blue-collar, industrial city. Furthermore, the southern Ontario market was too valuable to give away through a relocation. If there *were* to be a second team, the league would award a new franchise and sell the territory.

Balsillie was not easily deterred. In early May 2009, Moyes put the Coyotes into Chapter 11 bankruptcy, which meant that a court would review offers to purchase the team. The RIM billionaire offered $215.5 million and made it clear he intended to move the team to southern Ontario. He also appealed to the Canadian public to put pressure on the league. He granted a series of interviews in which he portrayed himself as a patriotic Canadian attempting to repatriate a piece of the country's national sport. He created a website—www.makeitseven. ca—where people could register their support for what would have been a seventh Canadian franchise. By the end of June, over 200,000 had put their names behind the cause. Balsillie's antics infuriated Bettman and the governors. They categorically rejected his offer in late July, and then the league purchased the franchise to ensure that it did not fall into his hands through a court order.

For many Canadians, the fiasco in Phoenix was further proof of Bettman's disregard for their country. It was an affront to deny the people of Hamilton and, more broadly, hundreds of thousands of other hockey-loving southern Ontarians. It defied logic to support a failed and money-losing experiment—hockey in the Arizona desert. It reaffirmed what many Canadians have long felt: that their game didn't belong in the U.S. Sun Belt. The sport that they held sacred had been commoditized and treated as just another entertainment product to be packaged, branded, marketed and sold to people who had no authentic connection to it or inherent interest in it.

While researching the present volume, I frequently encountered such attitudes in casual conversations with fellow Canadians. I encountered entirely different perspectives while talking to fans outside the RBC Center in Raleigh, the home of the Carolina Hurricanes, on a Sunday afternoon in January 2011 prior to the NHL All-Star Game. "I didn't grow up a hockey fan, but I love the sport as much as anybody in Ottawa or Toronto," Greg Batts, a wildlife biologist from Zebulon, North Carolina, told me. "If Canadians are looking for a team for Hamilton or Quebec City, they'll have to look elsewhere. The Hurricanes aren't going anywhere."

The evidence was all around us as he spoke. It was warm and sunny—perfect weather for a tailgate party. The parking lot was packed with vehicles and people. Everywhere I looked, I could see Hurricane red. There were people in team sweaters, T-shirts, hoodies and ball caps. They tossed Frisbees and footballs, barbecued burgers and hot dogs, played music and, in short, had a blast. "I know people up in Canada want to keep hockey there, but it's already big there," Batts continued. "Why not grow the game?"

"WHY NOT GROW THE GAME?" Gary Bettman's mandate, when he became commissioner, was to do just that. And he *has* done it—and been damned and criticized for it. There are many in Canada who would just as soon the league rid itself of "all those southern teams," as they put it. They have written off the whole ambitious enterprise, and in so doing, have passed judgment on the Bettman era. But they have done so prematurely. The best that can be said at the moment is that the game has taken hold in some places and failed in others.

Hockey must be sold in most U.S. markets, especially the new southern ones. The game must compete against other sports for fans, advertisers and broadcast audiences. Hockey is the only game in town all winter in Montreal, Ottawa, Winnipeg, Edmonton, Calgary and Vancouver, and it is the only one that counts in Toronto. Fans in most Canadian cities—Toronto, in particular—will support the home team night after night and season after season, even if the side rarely rises above mediocrity or makes the playoffs.

In most U.S. cities, especially the South, hockey succeeds when the team succeeds. The banners hanging from the rafters of the RBC Center in Raleigh and the Philips Arena in Atlanta in the winter of 2010–11 explained loud and clear—to this northern visitor—why the Canes were solid and the Thrashers were sinking. One lonely banner proclaimed that the Thrashers had been Southeast Division champs in 2006–07. By comparison, the Hurricanes could remind fans that they had been divisional champions in 1998–99, divisional and conference champs in 2001–02, and divisional, conference and Stanley Cup winners in 2005–06. As well, the club had retired the jerseys of defenceman Glen Wesley and centre Ron Francis and hung banners to commemorate both.

The southern expansion will stand as one piece of Bettman's legacy. The salary cap is another. The new economic regime has undoubtedly achieved its principal objective: it has made the league as competitive as it has ever been. That's good for the fans, but there have been unintended consequences. Managing in the NHL has become more complex than playing chess. Even the best hockey executives make mistakes—sometimes big ones. Managers of average—or less than average—ability commit blunders that can hurt a franchise for years, or even jeopardize its viability. They do this by signing players to enormous, multi-year, multimillion-dollar deals. When those players fail to perform as expected due to age, injury or declining skills, the team is stuck with them.

One of the game's wise old men feels for today's GMs. Cliff Fletcher started out in the Canadiens' front office in the late 1950s and managed for twenty-five years in Atlanta (the Flames), Calgary and Toronto. "During my whole tenure, the job was a lot easier than it is today," he says. "These guys are really hand-cuffed. If your team is struggling, your ability to get things done is severely limited. There are only a fraction of the trades that there were in the pre-cap days. When you trade today, you usually have to trade dollar for dollar. If you're taking on a $5 million contract, you're going to have to get rid of $5 million in some form. That makes it extremely difficult."

Most insiders expected there would be a good pool of free agents available each year on July 1, says Fletcher, but that hasn't happened. "Teams aren't getting the big shot in the arm through free agency," he says. "There are fewer trades, so you have to draft well and develop your own players. That's a slow process. It's a challenge, and the margin for error is much smaller."

Bettman's tenure as commissioner has coincided with hockey's big-money era, but the money has brought neither bliss nor contentment. On the contrary, it has caused big fights. The disputes have been prolonged, rancorous and, for the fans, exasperating. Owners locked players out for 104 days in 1994–95, for the entire 2004–05 season and for four months in 2012–13, reducing an eighty-game schedule to forty-eight and forcing cancellation of the Winter Classic and the all-star weekend.

Donald Fehr, executive director of the NHLPA in round three, was an experienced labour leader and not one to bend. Fehr, who turned sixty-five in July 2013, came to hockey from baseball—a sport that experienced five player strikes and three lockouts between 1972 and 1994. A native of the Kansas City area, and a labour lawyer by training, he became general counsel of the Major League Baseball Players' Association in 1977, acting director in 1983 and executive director two years later.

Fehr led his members through a brief strike in 1985 and a long, disastrous one—for the sport—that began in August 1994. It resulted in the cancellation of the World Series and wasn't settled till the following April. He stepped down as executive director of the MLBPA at the end of 2009, financially comfortable and prepared to slow down, if not retire—until some NHL players came calling. They were looking for a new leader, having dumped Ted Saskin, successor to Bob Goodenow, and Saskin's successor, Paul Kelly.

Fehr consented to help them reorganize the association, and then agreed to become executive director, largely because he liked the players. "They're first-class individuals," he says. "They're great guys, good role models, everything you'd want in a pro athlete."

There is nothing sweet or subtle about labour negotiations in North American pro sport, says Fehr, be it baseball, football, basketball or hockey. As he puts it: "The owners come in and they say: 'We have a monopoly and we're not concerned that our customers are going to go anywhere else. You guys [players] can't go anywhere because there's no other league. So we're going to lock you out until you give us what we want. That's what we're going to do.'

"It's happened in hockey three times. It happens in football. It happens in basketball. It's straight economics. It's a power struggle. The owners may love the players or hate the players, and vice-versa. The relationship is irrelevant.

The owners are going to say, 'We want to keep a lot more money and we're going to lock you out until you agree we can keep it.' They may dress it up, but that's all there is to it. It's basic, gut-level, elementary stuff."

The players were getting fifty-seven per cent of hockey-related revenues when the 2005 CBA expired. The owners opened negotiations by demanding that the proportions be reversed. *Their* take would increase to fifty-seven per cent; the players would get forty-three. This appeared—to outside observers—to be clever posturing aimed at shocking and irritating the players, and to judge from their public statements, it worked.

The owners' real objective also appeared evident from the outset: they were determined to get the same deal as their counterparts in the NFL and NBA, who had recently locked the doors until the players agreed to a fifty-fifty split. Early on in the negotiations, the NHLPA conceded the point, at an estimated cost of $230 million a year to the members. They held out to preserve most of their existing rights and privileges. They negotiated several significant improvements in working conditions and won a defined-benefit pension plan. "It will be extraordinarily beneficial to a whole lot of players," says Fehr. "It will allow them to have a lot of money sheltered for retirement."

There was considerable speculation during the latest lockout about how the fans would respond when it was over. In fact, they behaved the way economists tell us people behave—that is, if you reduce the supply, you will increase the demand. The NHL opened for business again on January 19, 2013, a Saturday, with thirteen sellouts and record TV ratings in Canada and the U.S. The vast majority of fans could hardly care less about the nitty-gritty of a CBA. What mattered most to them was this: the latest agreement is for ten years, though either side can opt out after eight. That means there will peace in the NHL until at least 2021, and ideally 2023.

Donald Fehr will surely depart long before either date, though he was coy about his plans in the aftermath of the lockout. "I'm happy with what I'm doing," he said. "After watching this game for a couple of years, I have come to appreciate it in a way I never could have before. You develop enormous respect for anybody who can play this game at this level. Your physical abilities, your intelligence and your situational awareness are off the charts."

Gary Bettman will surely stick around for a while. He turns sixty-five in

June 2017—just as the league completes its 100th season. There will be a centennial to celebrate.

As the foregoing pages attest, a league that began its life with four teams clustered in three cities—Montreal, Ottawa and Toronto—has survived two world wars, a great depression and multiple recessions, the advent of radio, television and the Internet, not to mention the shysters and charlatans who have occasionally gotten hold of franchises. The NHL has endured nothing less than ten decades of turmoil, crises, setbacks and occasional triumphs, all of which surely makes it one of the most remarkable stories in all of professional sport.

ACKNOWLEDGEMENTS

The list of sources on the following page includes the names of many people who consented to be interviewed, and all are deserving of my gratitude. I would like to extend special thanks to Gary Bettman, John Ziegler, Jim Devellano and Bob Gainey, as well as to Colin Campbell and Mike Murphy in NHL Hockey Operations. Nicole Buckley, Julie Young and Frank Brown in the NHL's communications office assisted in many ways large and small, and I thank each of them.

The resources of the Hockey Hall of Fame are indispensible to the researcher and writer, and they are accessible thanks to the generosity and helpfulness of Craig Campbell, Phil Pritchard and Miragh Bitove. I owe a special debt of gratitude to Ken Leger, the New Hampshire schoolteacher who retrieved the verbatim transcripts of the board of governors meetings from a garbage bin, preserved them at considerable personal expense and donated them to the Hall of Fame. Those transcripts are an extraordinarily rich source of information and will prove valuable to others for years to come.

Leonard Kotylo of the Society for International Hockey Research steered me in the right direction at moments when I was perplexed. Publisher Kristin Cochrane and my editors, Tim Rostron and Zoë Maslow, of Doubleday Canada, have supported this project from start to finish. Lloyd Davis has done a deft job copyediting, and my publicist, Ruta Liormonas has been energetic and creative. As always, my wife, Hélène, offered encouragement when I had doubts, and my daughter, Isabel, provided timely help with the endnotes.

SOURCES

Unpublished NHL Archival Documents

Verbatim Minute Books, Board of Governors Meetings
  Special Meeting, February 15, 1941, Royal York Hotel, Toronto.
  Annual Meeting, June 27, 1941, Royal York Hotel, Toronto.
  Semi-Annual Meeting October 24, 1941, Royal York Hotel, Toronto.
  Annual Meeting, May 15, 1942, Royal York Hotel, Toronto.
  Semi-Annual Meeting, November 23, 1942, Copley Plaza Hotel, Boston.
  Special Meeting, March 5, 1943, Royal York Hotel, Toronto.
  Annual General Meeting, May 8, 1943, Sun Life Building, Montreal.
  Special Meeting, December 8, 1944, Roosevelt Hotel, New York.
  Special Meeting, February 2, 1945, Sun Life Building, Montreal.
  Special Meeting, December 14, 1945, Royal York Hotel, Toronto.
  Special Meeting, February 14–15, 1946, Commodore Hotel, New York.
  Annual General Meeting, June 18–19, 1946, Commodore Hotel, New York.
  Semi-Annual Meeting, September 4, 1946, Windsor Hotel, Montreal.
  Special Meeting, March 4, 1947, Biltmore Hotel, New York.
  Special Meeting, March 17, 1947, Biltmore Hotel, New York.
  Annual General Meeting, June 2, 1947, Windsor Hotel, Montreal.
  Semi-Annual Meeting, September 4, 1947, Windsor Hotel, Montreal.
  Semi-Annual Meeting, October 14, 1947, Royal York Hotel, Toronto.
  Special Meeting, March 16, 1948, Commodore Hotel, New York.
  Annual General Meeting, June 2, 1948, Windsor Hotel, Montreal.
  Special Meeting, March 11, 1949, Royal York Hotel, Toronto.
  Annual General Meeting, June 1, 1949, Windsor Hotel, Montreal.
  Semi-Annual Meeting, September 7, 1949, Windsor Hotel, Montreal.
  Special Meeting, January 30 and 31, 1950, The Breakers, West Palm Beach, Florida.
  Special Meeting, March 20, 1950, Commodore Hotel, New York City.

Annual General Meeting, June 10, 1953, Windsor Hotel, Montreal.

Semi-Annual Meeting, September 10, 1953, Windsor Hotel, Montreal.

Special Meeting, March 10, 1954, Biltmore Hotel, New York.

Semi-Annual Meeting, September 15, 1954, Park Lane Hotel, New York.

Special Meeting, March 14, 1955, Commodore Hotel, New York.

Annual General Meeting, June 1, 1955, Windsor Hotel, Montreal.

Semi-Annual Meeting, September 20, 1955, Commodore Hotel, New York.

Reports of the President to the Board of Governors of the National Hockey League for the seasons 1961-62 through 1965–66.

Molson, David J., Expansion Proposal, Presented to the Board of Governors of the National Hockey League, February 26, 1963.

National Hockey League, Outline of Expansion Program, June 1965.

Provisional Agenda for Meeting of Owners-Governors of the National Hockey League, St. Regis Hotel, New York, February 7, 1966.

Minutes of the Forty-Eighth Annual Meeting of the Governors of the National Hockey League, Montreal, Thursday, June 10, 1965.

Garvey, Ed, Ron Salcer, Ritch Winter, John Agro, Bill Dermody and David Dempster, *Players Voice:* Confidential Report to NHLPA Members, June 3, 1989.

Meagher, Gary, Memorandum to John A. Ziegler Jr., Background Information re: Expansion, November 27, 1990.

National Hockey League, Collective Bargaining Handbook [created to assist in collective bargaining negotiations with the NHLPA], June 13, 1991.

BOOKS

Albert, Marv, with Stan Fischler. *Ranger Fever.* New York: Dell, 1973.

Batten, Jack. *The Leafs: An Anecdotal History of the Toronto Maple Leafs.* Toronto: Key Porter, 1994.

Blair, Wren, with Ron Brown and Jill Blair. *The Bird: The Life and Times of Hockey Legend Wren Blair.* Kingston, Ont.: Quarry Heritage Books, 2002.

Boucher, Frank, with Trent Frayne. *When the Rangers Were Young*. New York: Dodd, Mead, 1973.

Bruneau, Pierre, and Léandre Normand. *La glorieuse histoire des Canadiens*. Montreal: Les Éditions de l'Homme, 2003.

Brunt, Stephen. *Searching for Bobby Orr*. Toronto: Vintage, 2007.

Clayton, Deirdra. *Eagle: The Life and Times of R. Alan Eagleson*. Toronto: Lester & Orpen Dennys, 1982.

Coleman, Charles L. *The Trail of the Stanley Cup: Volumes I, II, III*. Montreal: National Hockey League, 1964–1976.

Conway, Russ. *Game Misconduct: Alan Eagleson and the Corruption of Hockey*. Toronto: Macfarlane, Walter & Ross, 1995.

Cruise, David, and Alison Griffiths. *Net Worth: Exploding the Myths of Pro Hockey*. Toronto: Penguin, 1991.

Devellano, Jimmy, and Roger Lajoie. *The Road To Hockeytown: Jimmy Devellano's Forty Years In The NHL*. Mississauga, Ont.: Wiley, 2008.

Dowbiggin, Bruce. *Money Players: The Amazing Rise and Fall of Bob Goodenow and the NHL Players' Association*. Toronto: Key Porter, 2006.

Eagleson, Alan, and Scott Young. *Power Play: The Memoirs of a Hockey Czar*. Toronto: McClelland & Stewart, 1991.

Fischler, Stan, and Shirley Walton Fischler. *The Hockey Encyclopedia: The Complete Record of Professional Ice Hockey*. New York: Macmillan, 1983.

Foster, Susan, with Carl Brewer. *The Power of Two: Carl Brewer's Battle With Hockey's Power Brokers*. Bolton, Ont.: Fenn, 2006.

Frayne, Trent. *The Mad Men of Hockey*. Toronto: McClelland & Stewart Limited, 1974.

Gatehouse, Jonathon. *The Instigator: How Gary Bettman Remade the League and Changed the Game Forever*. Toronto: Penguin, 2012.

Greenberg, Jay. *Full Spectrum: The Complete History of the Philadelphia Flyers*. Chicago: Triumph, 1997.

Grove, Bob. *Pittsburgh Penguins: The Official History of the First 30 Years*. Dallas, Tex.: Taylor Publishing, 1997.

Holzman, Morey, and Joseph Nieforth. *Deceptions and Doublecross: How the NHL Conquered Hockey*. Toronto: Dundurn, 2002.

Hunter, Bill, and Bob Weber. *Wild Bill: Bill Hunter's Legendary 65 Years in Canadian Sport*. Calgary: Johnson Gorman, 2000.

Jenish, D'Arcy. *The Montreal Canadiens: 100 Years of Glory*. Toronto: Doubleday Canada, 2008.

Kitchen, Paul. *Win, Tie or Wrangle: The Inside Story of the Old Ottawa Senators: 1883–1935*. Manotick, Ont.: Penumbra, 2008.

Kurtzberg, Brad. *Shorthanded: The Untold Story of the Seals, Hockey's Most Colorful Team*. Bloomington, Ind.: AuthorHouse, 2006.

McFarlane, Brian. *The Blackhawks: Brian McFarlane's Original Six*. Toronto: Stoddart, 2000.

———. *The Bruins: Brian McFarlane's Original Six*. Toronto: Stoddart, 1999.

McNall, Bruce, and Michael D'Antonio. *Fun While It Lasted: My Rise and Fall in the Land of Fame and Fortune*. New York: Hyperion, 2003.

Samuels, Charles. *The Magnificent Rube: The Life and Gaudy Times of Tex Rickard*. New York: McGraw-Hill, 1957.

Smythe, Conn, with Scott Young. *If You Can't Beat 'Em in the Alley: The Memoirs of the Late Conn Smythe*. Toronto: McClelland & Stewart, 1981.

Stein, Gil. *Power Plays: An Inside Look at the Big Business of the National Hockey League*. Secaucus, N.J.: Birch Lane Press, 1997.

Turner, Randy. *Back in the Bigs: How Winnipeg Won, Lost and Regained Its Place in the NHL*. Winnipeg: Winnipeg Free Press, 2011.

Wesley, Sam, with David Wesley. *Hamilton's Hockey Tigers: The Forgotten Tale of Hamilton's Short-lived NHL Franchise*. Toronto: Lorimer, 2005.

Willes, Ed. *The Rebel League: The Short and Unruly Life of the World Hockey Association*. Toronto: McClelland & Stewart, 2004.

Wong, John Chi-Kit. *Lords of the Rinks: The Emergence of the National Hockey League, 1875–1936*. Toronto: University of Toronto Press, 2005.

NEWSPAPERS AND MAGAZINES

Atlanta Journal-Constitution

Boston Daily Globe

Boston Herald

Chicago Tribune

Hamilton Herald

Hartford Courant

Hockey News

Los Angeles Times

Mail and Empire, Toronto

Montreal Herald and Daily Telegraph

New York Sun

New York Times

Sources

New York World   St. Louis Post-Dispatch

News and Observer, Raleigh, N.C.   Sports Illustrated

Ottawa Citizen   Toronto Daily News

Ottawa Journal   Toronto Star

Philadelphia Inquirer   Toronto Sun

Pittsburgh Press

AUTHOR INTERVIEWS

Bettman, Gary	Kelly, Paul
Blair, Wren	Kelly, Red
Boivin, Pierre	Leiweke, Tod
Bowman, Scotty	Lindsay, Ted
Bush, Walter L.	Liut, Mike
Campbell, Colin	Murphy, Mike
Collins, John	O'Neill, Brian
Conway, Russ	Polano, Nick
Curran, Rick	Renzulli, Don
Devellano, Jimmy	Riley, Jack
Eagleson, Alan	Salcer, Ron
Firestone, Bruce	Savard, Serge
Fletcher, Cliff	Selke, Frank
Gainey, Bob	Stroud, Steve
Gartner, Mike	Torrey, Bill
Gregory, Jim	Vinik, Jeff
Hotchkiss, Harley	Waddell, Don
Hull, Bobby	Winter, Ritch
Ilitch, Mike	Yormark, Michael
Irvin, Dick	Zeigler, John
Jennings, Brian	Zigler, Mark

ENDNOTES

CHAPTER 1

p. 23   *. . . had never been compensated* Livingstone brought several suits against the NHA, the NHL and the Toronto Arena Company and won several favourable judgments. In October 1923, a justice of the Supreme Court of Ontario declared that the defendants "have left nothing undone that could be done to the injury of the plaintiffs by long, drawn-out, cold-blooded conspiracy to ruin the plaintiffs" and awarded damages of $100,000. In another action initiated by Livingstone, the presiding judge described the conduct of the defendants as "utterly dishonest and despicable."

p. 26   *The directors of the Abso-Pure Ice Company* The Abso-Pure Ice Company harvested blocks of ice from Hamilton Harbour and other local bodies of water and sold them to residential buyers as well as businesses that used them to refrigerate food.

CHAPTER 2

p. 36   *Eddie Livingstone was back* Livingstone played a central role in the development of professional hockey in Toronto. But his inability to get along with fellow promoters overshadowed his contributions to the game. In 1926–27, Livingstone managed the Chicago Cardinals of the American Hockey Association and shared the Chicago Coliseum with Major Frederic McLaughlin's Black Hawks. McLaughlin raided the Cardinals lineup, and Livingstone responded with a $700,000 lawsuit. The Cardinals were Livingstone's last pro team. He spent his final years in Toronto and died there on September 11, 1945, of arterial sclerosis at age sixty-one. He was buried in the family plot in Toronto's Mount Pleasant Cemetery.

p. 39   *Nothing was overlooked* The menu, printed on a brochure distributed to every guest, included Crab Meat Cocktail à la Calder, Chicken Gumbo à la Canadiens,

Tenderloin of Beef Pique Perigueux à la NHL, Frozen Pear Cardinal à la Stanley
Cup and Demi Tasse à la Madison Square Garden.

p. 42   *New York and their home opener* Dwyer was unable to attend the Americans'
home opener. He had been arrested along with nearly two dozen other kingpins
in the illicit liquor trade earlier in December 1925. He was convicted on conspiracy charges in the summer of 1926, fined $10,000 and sentenced to two years,
though he served only a year at a federal penitentiary in Atlanta. He was released
in August 1928 and scaled back his bootlegging activities to concentrate on his
sporting interests.

p. 45   *the Canadiens' Leo Dandurand* Canadiens owner George Kennedy died in
October 1921 at age thirty-eight. His widow promptly sold the team to the triumvirate of Leo Dandurand, Joseph Cattarinich and Louis Letourneau, who
were partners in a business that owned or managed horse racetracks in Canada
and the U.S. Dandurand was the managing partner and handled the day-to-day
affairs of the team.

p. 49   *instructed Calder to devote his full attention to hockey* Tex Rickard's association
with the NHL was brief. He was promoting a prizefight in Miami when he died
of infected peritonitis following an appendectomy on January 6, 1929, age
fifty-eight. Newspapers celebrated Rickard's career and accomplishments, and
Americans mourned his passing. The body was placed in a bronze casket (it cost
$15,000). The casket was placed on a bier in a private rail car and the car was
hitched to the Havana Special, the fastest train between Miami and New York.
Crowds gathered at every stop along the way for a glimpse of the casket. New
Yorkers poured into the streets to pay tribute to Rickard.

CHAPTER 3

p. 62   *suspend operations for one year* The Quakers never did return to the NHL, nor
did the Pirates. Ottawa was back in 1932–33 and again the following season.
The franchise was moved to St. Louis in 1934–35 and rechristened the Eagles,
but folded for good after one dismal season.

p. 63   *teams with big, up-to-date facilities* The construction of new arenas in Detroit,
Boston and Chicago had a major impact on attendance and gate receipts.
Detroit's revenues in 1926–27 totalled $81,494 when the Cougars played the

entire season in the Border Cities Arena in Windsor, Ontario. The following year, with the Olympia open, they jumped to $210,568. Bruins revenues rose to $477,130 in 1928–29, the team's first in Boston Garden, up from $249,106 the previous winter. Likewise, Black Hawk gate receipts jumped from $97,848 in 1928–29 to $282,350 in 1929–30 after relocating to Chicago Stadium. These figures appeared in a prospectus issued by Maple Leaf Gardens, Ltd.

p. 68   *The only alternative was to cut costs* According to a report in the Toronto *Globe*, attendance in 1931–32, by team, was as follows: Boston, 295,548; Toronto, 249,400; Canadiens, 229,328; Rangers, 213,241; Maroons, 201,485; Chicago, 168,192; Americans, 139,804; Detroit, 130,207.

p. 72   *joined the American Hockey Association in 1930–31* Other teams in the AHA included the Minneapolis Millers, Kansas City Pla-Mors, Duluth Hornets, Tulsa Oilers, St. Paul Saints, Buffalo Majors and St. Louis Flyers.

p. 93   *John R. Kilpatrick was also reluctant* John Reed Kilpatrick was born in 1889 to a Canadian mother and an American father and raised in New York City. He attended Yale, where he was a top football player and track athlete, and he later served in the U.S. Army during World War I. Upon his return, he embarked on a successful business career and in 1933 became president of Madison Square Garden Corporation. He remained president until his death in 1960, except for the year 1949, when he served in the U.S. Army and attained the rank of brigadier general.

p. 95   *gone to the Canadian Navy* Only one league executive enlisted: the Leafs' managing director, Conn Smythe. A decorated veteran of the first war, Smythe was in his mid-forties, a father of four and itching to join the fight, despite wife Irene's frantic and vigorous opposition. In September 1941, Smythe took command of the 30th Battalion, a militia unit that became known as the sportsmen's unit because it attracted a large number of athletes. The unit went active as part of the 6th Light Anti-Aircraft Regiment of the Royal Canadian Artillery. He took a leave of absence from Maple Leaf Gardens and in October 1942 went overseas. His unit was sent to France in July 1944, and three weeks later Smythe was seriously wounded.

p. 96   *production while they are on the job* Some government ministers continued to argue that professional hockey should be suspended for the duration of the war. They changed their tune in 1943. The government placed advertisements in newspapers across the country over several weeks asking Canadians to send in spare binoculars that could be used in the war effort. The ads produced thirteen sets. The government then decided to make an appeal during a Saturday night hockey broadcast from Toronto. Within a week, Canadians had sent in so many pairs—3,500—that the government had to ask them to stop.

CHAPTER 5

p. 115   *L-shaped shingle-board home*   The Campbell family home is still standing and occupied at the time of writing. When it was built, in the first decade of the twentieth century, it would have been a substantial and impressive dwelling in a typically windswept, hurled-together prairie village like Fleming, where tarpaper shacks and flimsy clapboard houses were the norm and some nearby farm families lived in sod shanties.

p. 118   *We are opposed until such time as there are more teams in the league*   Northey stated later in the meeting that the Canadiens had consulted their fans and found that they were not interested in more games. But there may have been another factor that he chose not to disclose: the Canadiens were still on shaky ground financially, even though the team had won the Stanley Cup in 1944 and again in 1946 and the brightest star in the game, Maurice Richard, was then in his prime. The problem, according to Frank Selke Jr., son of the club's general manager, was that the Forum only sat 9,300 and barely generated enough revenue to cover expenses. Ten extra games likely would have put the team back in the red. However, the Forum was renovated in time for the 1949–50 season and the capacity boosted to about 14,000.

p. 125   *James Norris joined the melee*   Norris was then in his early seventies and known in Detroit as the "mystery owner" because he was rarely seen at Red Wing games. This was because he had a heart condition and his doctors advised him to avoid becoming overexcited—which meant not attending games or listening to them on the radio. Nevertheless, he expected a phone call from Adams after every game, whether he was at one of his three estates—which were located in Lake Forest, Illinois; Ocala, Florida; and Mattituck on Long Island— or on his 107-foot yacht, which was equipped with ship-to-shore communication. When the Wings were in Chicago, his chauffeur drove him to the Stadium and he would give the players a pre-game pep talk and then head for his car.

p. 128 *all he'd need ... to get crowds* The Hawks shifted a Sunday game from the evening to the afternoon on January 20, 1952, and drew 13,500, the largest crowd of the season. Tobin rescheduled five more games that season and began admitting kids under sixteen free of charge.

p. 129 *became the governor of the Hawks* The elder Norris, known as Pops, ran a vast business empire from Chicago. He served as Red Wing governor on the NHL board until his death. Jack Adams replaced him there, while Marguerite Norris, the youngest of Norris's four children, served as president until the estate was settled. Then her brother Bruce, who was sixteen years younger than James D., became president and governor.

CHAPTER 6

p. 146 *threatening to fold the team* In an interview with the author, Frank Selke Jr. maintained that at one point during the early 1950s, the Hawks were losing so much money that James D. Norris offered the team to his father for $1, provided he keep it in Chicago.

p. 150 *That became apparent when the CBC ... Stanley Cup champion* Regular television broadcasts of NHL action began in the U.S., according to Toronto hockey historian Paul Patskou. A New York station televised Ranger home games during the 1946–47 season and paid $45,000 for the rights. In September 1952, the CBC went to air with Canada's first TV stations, and from the start, hockey was a programming staple. René Lecavalier called the play-by-play for the first televised hockey broadcast in Canada—a game between the Canadiens and Red Wings on October 11, 1952. Foster Hewitt called the first English-language broadcast from Maple Leaf Gardens on November 1 that year.

At the behest of Hewitt, the CBC broadcasts began one hour after the opening faceoff. In the late 1940s, Conn Smythe had asked Hewitt for a report on whether hockey should be televised. Hewitt was strongly in favour, with one caveat: "[T]hey should follow the same pattern as our radio broadcasts—in other words, miss the first period and cover the last two. In this way, you will eliminate any chance of the gate being affected and the hour and a half on radio or television makes it an ideal length of time. Doing the whole game makes it long and tiresome and detracts from its promotional value."

p. 153 *all but one player onside* The one holdout was Toronto's Ted Kennedy, who had retired in the spring of 1955. He sat out one full season, but returned to the Leafs midway through the 1956–57 campaign. He played thirty games and then quit for good.

p. 165 *long after Adams was dead* Adams died of a heart attack in May 1968 at age seventy-three. Upon hearing the news, Gordie Howe told a reporter: "Mr. Adams was like a father to me. [He] had more love and dedication for hockey than any man I ever knew. He helped me tremendously in every phase of my career."

p. 167 *Madison Square Garden Corporation* Arthur Wirtz and James Norris were the largest shareholders. They owned 219,350 shares, or about forty per cent of the common stock. Wirtz and Norris also controlled the International Boxing Club, which had branches in Chicago and New York. Through these two organizations, they completely dominated professional boxing. They arranged and promoted almost every major prizefight held in the U.S. in the 1950s. Federal authorities eventually charged them with violating the antitrust laws, and on March 8, 1957, New York–based Judge Sylvester J. Ryan ordered them to dissolve the IBC and to sell their stock in MSG—a major venue for fight cards.

CHAPTER 7

p. 170 *amounted to $10.7 million* These figures are taken from the Report of the President to the National Hockey League Board of Governors, Season 1965–66, found in the Molson Fonds, National Archive and Library, Ottawa.

p. 175 *It also didn't hurt . . . knew him personally* Bush recalled in an interview with the author that the Yale alumni wanted blue and white for their team, the colours of the Yale Bulldogs. He argued that the combination would encroach on the colours of some of the established teams and persuaded them to go for green and white, like that of his alma mater, Dartmouth College.

p. 180 *I think we should clear it with the [composer W.C.] Handy estate first* Musician and bandleader W.C. Handy (1873–1958) was born in Florence, Alabama, the son of a preacher. He popularized the music of poor, rural, southern blacks and became known as the Father of the Blues. "St. Louis Blues," composed by Handy himself, was one of his most successful recordings.

CHAPTER 8

p. 192 *Pittsburgh Penguins* Jack McGregor's wife came up with the nickname, according to Bob Grove, author of *Pittsburgh Penguins: The Official History of the First Thirty Years*. She wanted something alliterative and asked her husband what they called the Civic Arena. He said "the Big Igloo," and she thought, "Penguins."

p. 193 *one of the classiest rinks in the NHL* The Salomons financed the improvements to the Arena by signing a long-term deal that awarded the rights to arena concessions to Sportservice, a Buffalo-based company owned by the Jacobs family. The deal would come back to haunt the Salomons in the mid-1970s when the war with the World Hockey Association drove salaries up astronomically. Without concessions revenue, the Blues went broke and the St. Louis–based Ralston Purina Company had to rescue the team.

p. 206 *all in their mid to late thirties* The Penguins' new ownership group consisted of Peter Block, a lawyer and an original investor; Elmore Keener, a partner in a brokerage firm; A.H. Burchfield III, vice-president of a renowned Pittsburgh department store; and T.R. (Tad) Potter, a marketing executive with a natural gas company and the managing partner. "We bought the Penguins as a matter of civic pride," Potter said when the deal was announced.

CHAPTER 9

p. 216 *They lost eleven, including five of their top six scorers from the previous season* This was no accident, according to former NHL president John Ziegler. In an interview with the author, Ziegler maintained that the Seals' obstreperous owner, Charles O. Finley, simply let the players go. He refused to make counteroffers if they received offers from WHA teams.

p. 236 *In 1972 . . . and had to step aside* Jennings was chairman of the expansion committee that reviewed the Kansas City and Washington applications. One of his sons was a minor investor in the Kansas City group, but Jennings did not recuse himself, and his fellow governors viewed this as an unacceptable conflict of interest.

p. 236 *He called a board meeting . . . in Toronto* The subsequent account is drawn from Stein's 1997 book *Power Plays: An Inside Look at the Big Business of the National Hockey League*, as well as author interviews with Ziegler.

p. 239 *the Black Hawks signed him for . . . $3 million* Orr's 1976 contract negotiations with the Bruins and his trade to Chicago are dealt with in greater detail in chapter 13.

CHAPTER 10

p. 252 *Boe . . . most of his troubles* Roy Boe grew up in Brooklyn, the son of Norwegian immigrants, attended Yale and then went into the food business. His first wife was a fashion designer who created brightly coloured wraparound skirts that became very popular in the late 1950s and early 1960s. The couple formed their own clothing company, Boe Jests, and later added swimsuits and other sports-wear. They sold the company in 1966 for several million, and Boe began investing in sports franchises. After the Islanders fiasco, he resumed his business career, and in the early 1990s he got back into pro sport as owner of the Springfield Indians of the American Hockey League. He died of heart failure in 2009.

p. 253 *Islander troubles . . . at the annual meeting* Rinkboard advertising was a minor item on the agenda in 1978. The governors agreed to allow it for the upcoming season on a one-year trial. They tapped a lucrative source of revenue and never gave it up.

p. 254 *The board approved Imperatore . . . for the moment* The Rockies lasted in Denver till the end of the 1981–82 season, then relocated to the Meadowlands in East Rutherford and became the New Jersey Devils. The short-lived Rockies made one lasting contribution to the sport: they helped popularize recorded music as a substitute for the live organist. Rockies marketing manager Kevin O'Brien began playing Gary Glitter's "Rock and Roll, Part II" as the team skated onto the ice and crowds loved it. The NFL's Denver Broncos and the NBA's Denver Nuggets followed suit, and soon the practice was inescapable.

CHAPTER 11

p. 260 *The new majority owner was Edward DeBartolo Sr., . . . keep the Penguins afloat* Edward DeBartolo Sr. of Youngstown, Ohio, was one of the wealthiest men in America in the late 1970s. He had studied civil engineering at Notre Dame

University and after World War II pioneered the development of suburban strip malls. DeBartolo later became one of the leading developers and builders of enclosed shopping centres, and his company also built hotels, office parks and condominiums. He and his son Edward Jr. acquired the San Francisco 49ers of the NFL at about the same time they bought the Penguins. They remained owners of the Penguins until the end of the 1991 season, when the team won its first Stanley Cup.

p. 268 *My argument was . . . it's not that bad a deal* Eagleson tells this story to illustrate his point: "In 1977, when I negotiated Bob Pulford's contract to become general manager of the Chicago Black Hawks, the team's total revenue for forty home games was $3.2 million. He would get a bonus if they got more than $3.5 million in gate receipts. It was an asses-in-the-seats business. Ancillary revenues scarcely existed."

CHAPTER 12

p. 282 *Their lawsuit is utterly ridiculous* The Ralston Purina lawsuit went to trial in St. Louis before a jury on June 10, 1985. In his opening statement, NHL lawyer Herb Dym uttered the following memorable line: "The National Hockey League does not wish to be known as the league that took the noon balloon to Saskatoon." On June 27, the day he was to testify, Ralston Purina CEO William Stiritz decided to avoid a grilling in the witness stand and accepted a settlement offered earlier by the NHL.

CHAPTER 13

p. 303 *Chicago Blackhawks* They became the Blackhawks in 1985.

p. 307 *Furthermore, Garvey accused . . . free-agency provisions* Time and again in his fifty-three-page report, Garvey accused Eagleson of withholding information and failing to keep the players fully informed. Garvey was guilty of the same sin here. He failed to inform the players about the perilous state of NHL finances after the seven-year war with the WHA. He did not tell them of all the franchises that had gone bankrupt or had to be relocated. He also neglected to mention that the NHLPA and its members would have caused a godawful uproar in Canada if they had rejected the merger and denied Quebec City, Winnipeg and Edmonton entry to the NHL.

p. 311 *But Eagleson did not . . . Orr said* Frank Orr of the *Toronto Star* wrote on June 7, 1976, that the Bruins had offered Orr either of a five-year deal at $295,000 a year or 18.6 per cent of the team, but Eagleson had turned them down because he thought it unwise for a player to be a part owner. The *Globe and Mail* reported the same information two days later. Orr was either negligent in the extreme in 1976, or he was less than forthright in 1990.

p. 317 *On March 4, 1994, the grand jury . . . and racketeering* Racketeering is a charge laid under the Racket Influenced Corrupt Organization (RICO) statutes, which are commonly used against members of the Mafia and other criminal entities. It implies that a series of offences are part of pattern of illegal activity, and a RICO conviction can lead to very stiff penalties. The U.S. Department of Justice dropped the racketeering charge because Canada, which does not have a similar statute, likely would not have extradited Eagleson.

CHAPTER 14

p. 320 *The NHL had agreed to turn over . . . spring of 1989* Contrary to the assertions of Ed Garvey, disclosure came late to the NHL because the players resisted it. Alan Eagleson recognized the advantages and frequently recommended disclosure during NHLPA annual meetings. The star players were always the most reluctant, and others tended to follow their lead. According to former goaltender Mike Liut, who served for several years as a player rep and a member of the executive, the issue was put to a vote on one occasion and it went 39–3 against.

p. 324 *He said he would, and we said our goodbyes* Goodenow visited Mike and Marion Ilitch, owners of the Red Wings, at their summer home in upper Michigan prior to the start of the 1991–92 season and offered similar assurances of labour peace. "He was as sweet and nice as you could be and charmed the heck out of us," Ilitch said in an interview with the author. "He said there wouldn't be any problems, no strike or anything. He turned out to be a different person. We lost a lot of faith and confidence in him."

p. 329 *He negotiated a settlement . . . financially secure for life* The terms of Ziegler's package were not disclosed, though various figures were reported. Let it suffice to say that he has enjoyed a comfortable retirement, mostly in a small community in south Florida. He has served on the boards of a Miami-based bank and a local hospital and returned to the board of the NHL as alternate governor of the Chicago Blackhawks, a capacity in which he is said to have been a constructive presence.

CHAPTER 15

p. 331 *I didn't understand it . . . he gave me to sign* Stein had told Brian O'Neill he was finished as of June 30, 1993. By then, Stein was gone, owing to the Hall of Fame fiasco. Meantime, Brian Burke, one of Bettman's lieutenants, asked O'Neill to stay on. As of this writing, O'Neill was in his late seventies and still working in the league's Montreal office.

CHAPTER 16

p. 346 *The demand for players spiked accordingly, but the supply rose only marginally* The collapse of the Soviet Union in 1991 gave the NHL access to Russian talent, while the growth of U.S. programs, at both the minor hockey and college levels, increased the supply of American players.

p. 359 *The league wanted . . . over the past decade* Amid the stalled negotiations with its players, the league successfully concluded two major deals. It signed a five-year, $155 million contract with News Corporation's Fox network that was to begin with the broadcast of the all-star game in San Jose on January 21, 1995. This marked the first time in twenty years that a U.S. broadcast network would carry NHL games. The league also reached an agreement with the International Ice Hockey Federation that would allow NHL players to compete with their national teams in the Winter Olympics, starting with the games in Nagano, Japan, in 1998.

p. 359 *The league wanted . . . over the past decade* Average annual salaries, based on the value of contracts filed with the league:

1992–93	$463,200	1998–99	$1,288,975
1993–94	$558,000	1999–00	$1,365,380
1994–95	$732,400	2000–01	$1,434,885
1995–96	$892,200	2001–02	$1,642,590
1996–97	$984,500	2002–03	$1,790,209
1997–98	$1,167,713	2003–04	$1,830,126

IMAGE CREDITS

INDEX